For Andy Goodpaster —

With warmest personal
regards and best wishes for
a great admirer of General
Marshall's and with deep
appreciation for his strong support
of the Marshall Foundation,

Friends [signature]

GEORGE C. MARSHALL

✳

EDUCATION OF A GENERAL

1880-1939

SECOND LIEUTENANT GEORGE C. MARSHALL

STAFF COLLEGE, FORT LEAVENWORTH

1908

GEORGE C. MARSHALL:

EDUCATION OF

A GENERAL

☆

☆ 1880 ☆
—
1939

☆ ☆

By FORREST C. POGUE

DIRECTOR OF THE RESEARCH CENTER
GEORGE C. MARSHALL RESEARCH FOUNDATION

WITH THE EDITORIAL ASSISTANCE OF
GORDON HARRISON

Foreword by General Omar N. Bradley

NEW YORK: THE VIKING PRESS

FIRST PUBLISHED IN 1963 BY THE VIKING PRESS, INC.
625 MADISON AVENUE, NEW YORK, N.Y. 10022

DISTRIBUTED IN CANADA BY
PENGUIN BOOKS CANADA LIMITED
ISBN 0-670-33685-8
LIBRARY OF CONGRESS CATALOG CARD NUMBER: 63-18373

SET IN BASKERVILLE, WEISS AND TRAJANUS TYPES

PRINTED IN THE U.S.A. BY THE BOOK PRESS

A portion of this book first appeared in *Look*.

Second printing January 1978

Contents

Illustrations

(Based on a map in the *West Point Atlas of American Wars;*
New York: Frederick A. Praeger, Inc., 1959; by permission of
the publishers)

Foreword

BY GENERAL OF THE ARMY OMAR N. BRADLEY

W E are always in need of leaders—in government, in military service, in business, and, in fact, in all walks of life. The question is often asked, Are leaders born as leaders or are they developed? I believe it is a little of both, but certainly development and training have great influence on the final product. Usually there is one great influencing factor, or maybe more, that makes a great leader.

In the case of General Marshall, I believe his mother played a determining part in developing in her son his ideals of integrity, fair play, ambition, and a desire to succeed. Later, the influence of his training at the Virginia Military Institute brought out and helped develop his qualities of leadership.

The author has forcefully described these influences in this volume, *Education of a General.*

I first worked under General Marshall as a member of the faculty of the Infantry School, Fort Benning, Georgia, when he was Assistant Commandant in charge of training. When he became Chief of Staff I served for about a year and a half in his office as an assistant secretary of the General Staff before being appointed Commandant of the Infantry School. My last close collaboration with General Marshall came in the 1950-1951 period when he was Secretary of Defense and I was chairman of the Joint Chiefs of Staff.

As a result of my association with General Marshall during the period of preparation for World War II and my knowledge of his accomplishments during the war, and afterward, I consider him the man who contributed more to our efforts from 1939 to 1951 than any other individual. He was my ideal of the best type of officer.

Because of my esteem for the General's great contributions to

the Army and to his country, I accepted in 1959 the presidency
of the George C. Marshall Research Foundation, which had been
organized six years earlier for the purpose of building and en-
dowing a Marshall Research Library in which to house his papers
and memorabilia.

One aim of the George C. Marshall Research Foundation
was the writing of a biography based on the General's personal
and official papers and on interviews with him and his associates.
The project was made possible through the backing and support
of three presidents, Harry S. Truman, Dwight D. Eisenhower,
and John F. Kennedy, and of many friends and admirers of the
wartime Chief of Staff.

After refusing many lucrative offers for his memoirs, General
Marshall, in 1953, at the suggestion of President Truman, decided to give his papers to a research library at Lexington, Virginia. President Truman directed the General Services Administrator, the Secretary of State, and the Secretary of Defense to
cooperate in this project by making available to the biographer
records pertaining to General Marshall. President Eisenhower
and President Kennedy in turn have given this project their full
support. The initial research was made possible by a personal
gift from John D. Rockefeller, Jr., who early expressed his interest in the program of the Marshall Foundation.

Among the stipulations laid down by General Marshall as a
basis for his cooperation were: (1) that the selection of the project
director be made by the board of directors of the Foundation
without reference to him for comment or concurrence and (2)
that any funds accruing from sale of publications based on his
statements or his personal papers should remain with the Foundation. The author was selected to conduct the interviews on the
basis of his experience as a combat historian in World War II
and later as a member of the Office of the Chief of Military History, Department of the Army. The interviews with General
Marshall were made in 1956 and 1957. These recollections, while
incomplete, have supplied invaluable material on his childhood
and on his early life as a soldier. Fresh in his mind after fifty
years were the impressions he gained from visiting the sites of
the French and Indian War battles fought within a few miles

of his birthplace in Pennsylvania, and the impact made by the examples of Robert E. Lee and Stonewall Jackson. His vivid stories re-creating his experiences as a young lieutenant in the Philippines in 1902, on a mapping expedition in Texas in 1904, as a staff officer in World War I, and as a regimental officer during civil war in China help us understand the history of his times as well as his own development as a soldier.

The author has also drawn heavily on the files of the National Archives, the Library of Congress, and the memories and private papers of General Marshall's associates, for the expansion of the General's personal narrative. Reports, sketch maps, maneuver outlines, battle plans, and correspondence furnished a rich store of material for this biography. As a result, we get new light on such leaders as former Secretary of War Baker, General Pershing, General Dawes, General Craig, Secretary of War Woodring, Harry Hopkins, and President Roosevelt. Especially interesting is the new material on the Army's role in the development of the Civilian Conservation Corps, the facts concerning the so-called Marshall–MacArthur feud, the background of General Marshall's selection as Chief of Staff, and the early relationship between General Marshall and President Roosevelt.

In graphic language drawn from General Marshall's written and spoken comments we learn of our lack of preparations for World War I and the prodigious task the Army faced in getting units ready for battle in France. His first-hand analyses give new perspective to the battles of Saint-Mihiel and the Meuse-Argonne and to the controversial race for Sedan. Through the pages of this book we follow the ups and downs of the Army in the period between wars and sense the frustrations and disappointments faced by many officers in that era. General Marshall, we find, was one of those who continued to build the best units he could for the day when they might be needed. The book should be an inspiration not only for young soldiers but for men in any field who may at times believe that their work is unappreciated and that there is no purpose in continuing to do their best.

As a soldier during part of the period here discussed, and as a long-time associate of General Marshall, I have been forcibly impressed by the significant information on the Army in the years 1900-1939 and the perceptive insight into the training and character of General Marshall shown in this book. It will be a revelation for every soldier and every student of the period. For all who admire General Marshall, it is this book which best tells his story.

Education of a General catches the true spirit of General Marshall. His soldierly firmness, his intelligence, and his humanity show through the pages. The author makes clear that the General, far from being a cold, impersonal individual, showed friendliness and great consideration for others. Numerous anecdotes illustrate his paternal feeling for those who served under him and the great devotion which he gave to members of his family. Far from confining itself to a recital of soldierly activities, the book is concerned with the personal life of the man. As a result, the reader can glimpse a picture of General Marshall previously known to only a few intimate friends.

As a result of General Marshall's reluctance to write his memoirs, and scarcity of material for a biography, we have lacked up to now an adequate study of him. This comprehensive and authoritative account admirably fills that gap for his formative years. It is expected that the forthcoming volumes on the war years and the postwar years will do the same for the later periods of his life.

Preface

F R O M sad experience, General Marshall concluded that soldiers should not write memoirs. As aide and associate of General Pershing, he had seen the flames of controversy fanned by books of World War I commanders and resolved to avoid anything which would provoke similar discord after World War II. His remark, prompted by this resolution, that he could not write a book without telling everything and that such a volume would hurt too many people has been misinterpreted to mean that he was deliberately withholding damaging information pertaining to some of his former associates. Such was not the case. He believed that it was unfair to air military and political controversies without careful investigation of all the background. And he believed that the publication of such a book by one of the principals created bad feelings among former associates which could do great harm to the causes for which they had served. He was not opposed to a careful examination of the facts by a trained historian.

His refusal to write his memoirs threatened to leave a serious gap in our knowledge of one of the great leaders of World War II. Pressed repeatedly during the war by friends to keep some record, he declined, saying that a diarist ran the risk of doing only those things which would look good in the journal or of putting down only those actions which would make him look good. A journal which he kept in World War I was later destroyed on the grounds that he may have been unfair to some of the men discussed therein.

Despite pressure from publishers and friends to write his autobiography, he refused to listen to lavish offers of money and declined all inducements to write articles or sketches or to use the services of a ghost writer. Only when the George C. Marshall Research Foundation was organized did he finally agree to co-

operate with a trained historian in a series of interviews. Even
here, he drew back from pronouncing harsh judgments on his
contemporaries, constantly reminding his biographer that he
didn't want readers turning through the book to see who had
been insulted on page nine.

The dictated portions of the book were incomplete but they
reflect the spirit of the great soldier-statesman and help flesh out
the records of the archives. It is thus possible to gain a glimpse
of his past and put together something of the story of how he
rose to the top of his profession. Fortunately, the official record
has made it possible to confirm many of the points at which he
merely hinted. In addition, a number of his former associates are
still living and their recollections and personal papers add
greatly to the account. The coverage of his early years is thus
far more extensive than is the case with many public figures.

I have used all the interviews with care, inasmuch as most
of the former associates who recorded their recollections were
reluctant to criticize, and some individuals who had disagreed
with the General declined to talk to me. I have also been aware
of the fact that when one works closely with an individual's own
statements and papers, there is the likelihood of exaggerating
his role in activities with which he was associated. For that
reason, I have tried to strike a proper balance, but I know that
in some cases it will seem that Marshall's activities are permitted
to dominate situations in which he was a minor participant.
Fortunately, the contemporary record makes clear that, from the
time he was a first lieutenant, Marshall filled a role normally
reserved for one much senior to him in rank.

From the beginning of my research on General Marshall seven
years ago, I have been especially interested in his preparation
for the Chief of Staff position. I was interested less in the schools he
attended and the courses he took than in the experiences he had
as a staff officer and troop leader, his service in different parts of
the world, and the development of his views on military subjects.
For the officers of his generation, who went into military service
at the turn of the century, when the Spanish-American War was
opening up a new era in American history, the story is also one
of their growing up with a new Army. Confronted by the re-

sponsibilities of the new colonial possessions, by involvement in
the First World War, and by the growth of antagonistic world
forces in the 1930s, the American Army found itself caught between demands for more adequate defense and the traditional
American opposition to maintaining large military forces in
peacetime. Frustration was the lot of many officers, eroding their
will to achieve and creating an unfortunate gulf between them
and the civilian authority. General Marshall managed to survive, to grow, and to retain his confidence in the processes of
democracy.

Born of Virginia and Kentucky stock in western Pennsylvania,
he grew up with an understanding of both northern and southern
viewpoints. Reared in a small city, he retained through all his
life a love for the country. Conservative in habits and thoughts,
he was able to adapt to the demands of a changing world. Born
in an era which spoke often of responsibility, duty, character,
integrity, he was marked by these so-called "Victorian" virtues.
A natural reserve, simplicity of living, aloofness of manner were
strengthened by the austerity of Army life. Taken together, these
various elements helped prepare him for the leadership of the
greatest army of the free world in the final phases of the war
against the combined forces of Germany, Italy, and Japan.

To find the record of this man, and the family, the environment, and the forces which made him, has taken the efforts of
several people besides myself. Outlining the nature of the project, interviewing General Marshall, interviewing more than three
hundred of his former associates in the United States and abroad,
corresponding with more than five hundred of his former associates, directing the main research project, and writing the original draft of the manuscript were my primary responsibilities. I
visited Uniontown; Augusta, Kentucky; Lexington, Virginia;
Fort Leavenworth; the Presidio of San Francisco; Fort Benning;
Fort Screven; Fort Moultrie; Monterey; Vancouver Barracks;
Gondrecourt; Chaumont; Neufchâteau; and the battle area near
Metz, to study places and posts he had once known.

As the first customer of the Marshall Research Library, I have
received invaluable aid at every turn from Miss Eugenia Lejeune,
librarian and administrative assistant to the Foundation, and

from her staff. I had as research assistant for the year 1960-61 Dr. Edward M. Coffman, now of the University of Wisconsin, who searched the files of the National Archives for pertinent material for me. His special knowledge of the Army in the 1898-1920 period, drawn from his research on the career of General Peyton C. March, and a special study he did on the reorganization of the Army in 1920, were of tremendous help to me in writing this volume. The assistance of a number of others is acknowledged at p. 351.

General Marshall's dictated material on his career prior to 1939 was completed only to 1924 and had to be supplemented by letters, interviews, and official records. Inasmuch as his taped interviews ran to 125,000 words, the maximum limit set by contract between the publishers and the Foundation for the first volume, it was not surprising that the first draft of the manuscript more than doubled the agreed-on length. When this draft was completed, Dr. Gordon Harrison, an old friend and colleague in the Army's Office of the Chief of Military History, where he wrote *Cross-Channel Attack,* was brought in at my recommendation to review, condense, and rewrite. His assumption of this task brought a fresh perspective to bear on the book and, as a bonus, enabled me to push on with the research and writing of volumes II and III. In Dr. Harrison's revision the bulk of the original has been reduced roughly by half, while some new background and reflective passages have been added on the times and the Army. During the nearly year-long process of reweighing, readjusting, and rewriting, he and I worked closely together to assure a text as accurate and readable as we could jointly make it. We were fortunate in our association with Denver Lindley of The Viking Press, whose editorial judgment eased the collaborative task and improved the final product.

Among the people who granted me interviews or responded to my letters with information, and whose contribution I have acknowledged elsewhere, are included a number who went much farther in their assistance. Some checked or copied documents, answered numerous inquiries, trusted me with cherished albums and diaries, shared with me their research notes, sometimes ran a taxi service for me, entertained me during my visits to various parts of the country or wrote narrative accounts of Marshall's activities. In most cases, I believe that their contributions will be apparent from the footnotes or from other references. Here, I have space only to express my profound thanks for their generous aid.

For patience, understanding, and sound counsel during many difficult hours of research and writing, a special word of appreciation to my wife, Christine.

FORREST C. POGUE

Arlington, Virginia
April, 1963

GEORGE C. MARSHALL

✳

EDUCATION OF A GENERAL

1880-1939

The Marshalls of Uniontown

"I thought that the continual harping on the name of John Marshall was rather poor business. It was about time for someone else to swim for the family."

AT three o'clock in the morning of September 1, 1939, General George C. Marshall, acting Chief of Staff of the United States Army, was wakened by the telephone. He needed no more special knowledge to anticipate the news he was about to receive from the War Department than millions of his fellow citizens who had been living by their radios for days as their world moved toward war. Now it had happened and the word was official. From Paris, Ambassador William Bullitt had just phoned President Roosevelt that Hitler's legions had crossed the frontiers of Poland, an aggression that France and Britain were pledged to resist. From Warsaw, Ambassador Anthony J. Drexel Biddle reported that German troops had seized Danzig, and German planes, even as he talked, were overhead.

By coincidence September 1 was the day that ended the terminal leave of the retiring Chief of Staff, General Malin Craig; the day that George Marshall was to be sworn in as his successor, dropping the "acting" from his title and succeeding to Craig's permanent and temporary ranks. In swift reaction to the news, Marshall hastened the formalities. Within a few hours of his waking, he took the oath as permanent major general, without ceremony, in the presence of the Adjutant General. That done, he raised his hand again and swore, as Chief of Staff (and temporary four-star general), "to support and defend the Constitution of the United States against all enemies, both foreign and domestic." [1]

At about the same time President Roosevelt was meeting the press. In shirt sleeves on this warm September day (the thermometer in Washington touched 86) he was grave and looked tired. There was a barrage of questions, but the big one for all America was: Could we stay out? The President dropped his head a moment and then replied that he hoped and believed we could.

When the newspapermen had departed, a little group of men in lightweight suits and straw hats entered the White House offices and was brought at once to the President. In appearance they might have been businessmen or politicians on a routine call. In fact, they were America's high military command, summoned to an urgent special meeting: Secretary of War Harry Woodring, Acting Secretary of Navy Charles Edison, Assistant Secretary of War Louis Johnson, Admiral Harold R. Stark, Chief of Naval Operations, and General Marshall. With these military advisers and later with his whole cabinet, the President arranged to put into effect measures already approved to preserve neutrality and protect the United States against possible attack.

All day news of the developing war came in over the wires in a series of hard, sharp reports. Prime Minister Neville Chamberlain, who had spoken so recently of "peace in our time," summoned Parliament to meet in an extraordinary session that evening, inevitably to declare a state of war. The government was already taking preliminary steps to move three million children out of cities in the British Isles that lay open to air attack. In Paris, Premier Edouard Daladier called the French cabinet together to consider a declaration of war. Stalin's governing machinery in Moscow hastily stamped approval on the Soviet-German Pact whose signing four days before had cleared the way for the invasion of Poland. In Berlin, Hitler announced that he would solve the Polish question even if it meant matching bomb against bomb with all comers.

So it began. And the new Chief of Staff was at once plunged into the immense technical and political difficulties of preparing the United States Army to play its role in the world of war, whatever that role might turn out to be. For him personally, September 1, 1939, was the first day of almost twelve years of continuous concern with the top-level military and political problems of the war and the aftermath of war. With the single exception of Major General Henry H. Arnold, then Chief of the Air Corps,[2] Marshall was the only member of the combined American-British directorate of the war to serve in the same post from the first to the last day. Roosevelt died four months before the end. Winston Churchill took cabinet post as First Lord of the Admiralty three days after the war began in Europe, but did not become Prime Minister until eight months later and relinquished that position to Clement Attlee a few days before the final victory over Japan. Admiral Ernest J. King succeeded Admiral Stark as Chief of Naval Operations after Pearl Harbor. Admiral William D. Leahy, Chief of Staff to the President as Commander-in-Chief, and member of the Joint Chiefs of Staff, did not emerge until 1942. Not one of the three British Chiefs of Staff who was in office at the beginning remained to the end.

Within a few weeks of leaving the post of Chief of Staff, Marshall at the end of 1945 was to undertake a fourteen months' mission to China in a futile effort to save our wartime ally from anarchy and Communist conquest. He returned to become Secretary of State. Forced by a serious operation to resign two years later, he enjoyed only a brief rest before becoming president of the American Red Cross, and then Secretary of Defense for a year. Not until September 1951, when he was in his seventieth year, was he permitted at last to step aside.

George Marshall arrived in the places of power almost unknown to the average American. When he left, his name, his rather homely face, some part of his wartime achievement, his plan for reconstructing Europe, the fact at least that he had been to China, were familiar to millions. He had his devoted admirers, here and in Europe, and—on the far political right—his bitter detractors. Yet in a real sense he remained unknown. His selection as Chief of Staff was widely considered a kind of fluke, and it was said then and repeated since that Roosevelt, inspired or sinister, depending on one's point of view, had reached deep down into the list of generals to raise up a man who had no obvious claim on the job. It was not so. To a remarkable degree, with a consistency rare in the careers even of the great, Marshall's abilities were marked clearly in everything he had done. He was not only outstanding but in the Army he was known all along to be outstanding. Moreover he himself worked at it with extraordinary energy and singleness and intensity of purpose. He was able and he was ambitious. When his chance came, only four generals senior to him were eligible for the post. Those in position to weigh the choice had no serious doubt that on the record of his ability and professional achievement he deserved to be chosen first.

From the beginning, almost as soon as he was conscious of self at all, Marshall had wanted to be first in everything. The intensity of that drive owed much to his father. When George Catlett Marshall, Jr., was born on that last day of 1880, George Catlett Marshall, Sr., was already at thirty-five a citizen of some note in Uniontown, Pennsylvania. He was prospering as an independent businessman, a prominent Mason, a regular churchgoer,[3] and an active member of the Democratic party. He was gregarious and easy to like, though inclined to be pompous—a solid and sufficiently lively specimen of the middle-class doers who in the last quarter of the nineteenth century were rushing to make their fortunes and complete America's extraordinary industrial revolution. He was all that—and he was also a Marshall.

Throughout his boyhood years young George* heard over and over the tales of his distinguished Virginia and Kentucky ancestry. He was not very old when inevitably he had a look for himself at the family genealogy, *The Marshall Family*, a compendium of fact and legend, misspelled names, pious recollections, epitaphs, and bad verse assembled by W. M. Paxton. The book had been published before he was five, and he was chagrined to find that it did not mention him.[4] What good after all was a book that purported to tell about your family and did not include you?

---

* To avoid confusion, the father of General George Marshall will arbitrarily be referred to as George Catlett, his son as George.

Nevertheless he explored the dull pages and hit upon one fascinating item (which happened also to be quite spurious). According to Paxton, one Marshall daughter of the eighteenth century married the famous pirate Blackbeard. The boy carried the book to school and lorded it over his classmates because he was descended from "a pirate who had a very bloody and cruel history and a long beard to help out." Soon the tale reached one of the fathers, who used it one day to poke fun at George Catlett and his blue blood. "Father," the General recalled, "was perfectly furious that out of all the book I had chosen Blackbeard as the only one who interested me and publicized him in town as being descended from a pirate."

Perhaps the boy enjoyed a little innocent revenge, or perhaps he was only innocent. His insistence, however, that no other part of his heritage interested him is not credible. He was a boy who loved history, and some of the liveliest tales of history concerned his own forebears. He was a boy with a strong, sensitive ego, which could hardly have been totally indifferent to its derivations. Born a Pennsylvanian, he became in maturity, by residence, by taste, and even by manner, a species of Virginian. Among the influences molding his Southern inclination it is impossible to believe that his family origins, so constantly impressed upon him from the beginning, were insignificant.

Marshall said later that genealogy "rather bored me." More obviously it embarrassed him. "My father was so keen in family interests that I was rather sensitive about it and I was embarrassed by his keenness. I thought that the continual harping on the name of John Marshall was kind of poor business. It was about time for somebody else to swim for the family." That revulsion was understandable and the response characteristic. He himself would always be reticent about his qualities but energetic in demonstrating them.[5]

In any case, John Marshall, the great Chief Justice, was only a collateral ancestor. He and Martin Marshall, George's great-grandfather, were first cousins.[6] Both were grandsons of John Marshall "of the forest," born about 1700 in Westmoreland County, Virginia. William Marshall, Martin's father, lived riotously until past the age of thirty, when he married and (in the late seventeen-sixties) joined the Baptist Church. Focusing all his great vitality and passion on the saving of souls he became an evangelist of such vehemence that he was once confined for fear he was mad. In 1780, William and his brother, Colonel Thomas, father of the Chief Justice, a surveyor for part of that area of Virginia known as Kentucky, moved from Virginia into the new lands. William settled eventually at Eminence, in Henry County, where he continued to preach. Even in old age, after a crippling fall from his horse, he had himself propped up in the pulpit of the Fox Run church to carry on his vigorous struggle with the devil.[7]

Colonel Thomas Marshall had settled in Washington, Kentucky, and there Martin Marshall, William's son born in 1777, came as a young man to study law. He developed an affection for his uncle which he apparently never felt for his own father, and that filial attachment for the family of the Chief Justice was cherished by Martin's descendants. The Marshall house in Washington came to be regarded as the ancestral home, and young George was taken to visit it on his first trip to Kentucky.

In his early twenties, Martin moved to Augusta, a town on the Ohio River some twenty miles from Washington. The young lawyer prospered, as did Augusta, and he became one of its first landowners and one of the town's earliest trustees. He married Matilda Taliaferro, whose family too had come from Virginia, and in time built a substantial brick house which still stands near the river.[8] His son William Champe Marshall, George's grandfather, studied law with his father, and at twenty-seven launched his career by winning a seat in the Kentucky legislature and the hand of Susan Myers, daughter of the town's leading merchant. He bought a three-story brick house with sixteen large rooms, big halls and a copious cellar—a place that impressed young George, when he saw it some sixty years later, as designed for bountiful living and continuous entertaining. An ambitious man quick to use his money and his family connections for his own preferment, William Champe was six times a member of the state legislature, a member of the state constitutional convention of 1849,[9] once commonwealth's attorney for his district, mayor of Augusta and reputedly the Whig boss of Bracken County.[10] Before the Civil War broke out, he turned Democrat, and as such was elected to the Augusta City Council the day after the firing on Fort Sumter. The Council voted to form and equip a home guard to enforce neutrality in the town, divided in its sympathies between North and South, and to defend it from outside attack.

In fact, Augusta was attacked in September 1862, as part of the duel for possession of Kentucky. Confederate General Edmund Kirby Smith detailed Colonel Basil Duke, a distant relative of the Marshalls, with a detachment of 450 cavalry and a light artillery company, to break up a reported concentration of Federal troops at Augusta and then ford the river to threaten Cincinnati.[11]

The two oldest of William Champe Marshall's three grown sons were by then away serving with the Confederate Army. The youngest, George Catlett, was sixteen and along with his father was enrolled in the Augusta Home Guard, a force of about one hundred men commanded by Dr. Joshua Bradford, a distinguished surgeon of the town who had served with the Union Army during the battle of Shiloh.[12]

When Colonel Duke and his men reached a little hill south of Augusta early in the morning of September 27, they observed two small Federal gunboats tied up at the wharf, each with a twelve-pounder aboard. Duke emplaced his howitzers on the high ground and dispatched some men into the town with orders to fire on the boats. Dr. Bradford came down to the wharf with the word that the "rebels are coming" and urged the captain of one of the gunboats to open fire. But neither he nor William Champe Marshall, who joined him by the river, was able to prevail on the "Navy" to take any action until a Confederate shell struck one of the boats. Then both boats cast off and moved across the river, firing three random shots in the direction of the attackers as they departed.

Duke, who had feared the naval cannon as much as Bradford depended on them, decided to move in as soon as he saw the gunboats withdraw. Without artillery to oppose the enemy's superior force, Bradford had no choice but surrender. He raised a white flag from an upstairs window as soon as Duke's men came down the Main Street, but the Home Guard, scattered in various houses, did not see it and began shooting at the invaders at close range. The Confederate commander then turned his cannon on houses from which the shots came and set fire to several. In the brief but wild melee which followed, twenty-one of Duke's men lost their lives and eighteen were wounded, as against seven of the defenders killed and fifteen wounded. In less than twenty minutes it was over and Bradford's surrender was accepted, though Duke had difficulty in persuading his angry men not to kill them all. The little battle had proved so costly that Duke abandoned his plans to cross the river and pulled back, calling his day in Augusta "the gloomiest and saddest that any among us had ever had."

Among the hundred prisoners that Duke took from Augusta was George Catlett Marshall. He was paroled shortly, possibly because, as legend has it, Duke had taken him only as surety for the lives of several of his wounded whom he left for Mrs. William Marshall to nurse back to health. It was George Catlett's first and last taste of war. Prohibited by the terms of his parole from fighting again, he entered Augusta College shortly before the end of the war. Yet his short service in the Union cause may not have been altogether insignificant from his own point of view. His commanding officer in that engagement, Dr. Joshua Bradford, was not only the first citizen of Augusta but the uncle of the girl George Catlett was to marry. In Augusta at that time Bradfords and Marshalls did not ordinarily mix, perhaps for personal but more obviously for political reasons: both Dr. Joshua and his physician brother, Jonathan, were vigorous advocates of abolition,[13] whereas William Marshall had no record of devotion to the Union except his possibly reluctant participation in the battle of Augusta. The day of the battle, according to family lore, was one of the very few occasions on which the Bradford brothers and William Marshall spoke to each other, and the estrangement of the two families continued after the war. Still, despite Marshall's impression of a kind of Montague-Capulet feud, George Catlett did succeed in marrying Laura Emily, the daughter of Dr. Jonathan Bradford, and his sister, Margaret, married Laura's brother, Thomas.

Augusta had been good to William Champe Marshall but by the sixties steamboat travel was losing out to the railroads and the once-flourishing river port's decline was clearly marked. George Catlett apparently tried his hand at business there, but by 1869 he was discouraged by his prospects. While visiting his sister Elizabeth, who had married a Union colonel, John Ewing, and was living near Pittsburgh, he heard of an opening as a clerk in an iron works in Dunbar, a little town on the Youghiogheny River at the western edge of the Alleghenies. He applied and was hired.

The year George Catlett Marshall got his first job was the year the golden spike was driven near Ogden, Utah, completing the first trans-continental railroad. It was also the year that the Knights of Labor were organized, though that fact and its portent of industrial wars to come were concealed from most contemporary eyes. It was the year that General Ulysses S. Grant was first inaugurated President, and his administration embarked on a course of boodle and bathos that ushered in a generation of stagnancy in political leadership and political imagination. Stimulated by the war, and now faced with huge pent-up consumer demand, Northern industry was already in the midst of reckless expansion. Inflation made the wheels spin faster, and would also contribute to the severity of the collapse just ahead in 1873. The application of corporate organization first to railroads and then to industry showed the way to pyramid capital and created a whole new kind of business. The 1860s and the 1870s were the watershed years between the traditional economy of individually owned enterprises and the modern society of huge, impersonal economic organizations. Fresh tides of immigration, in which the Irish and Germans continued dominant until the 1880s, assured an abundant, cheap, and—for a while—docile supply of labor. Nature yielded whatever else was needed: coal, iron, oil, from Pennsylvania; iron from Michigan; lead, silver, copper, gold, from the West (the great Comstock lode had been tapped just before the war).

It was a time to become rich. Four famous fortunes were even then being founded on the natural wealth of Pennsylvania alone. In 1870 John D. Rockefeller incorporated the Standard Oil Company of Ohio, fed initially by the wells of Pennsylvania. In 1871 Henry Clay Frick, a clerk in a distillery, borrowed ten thousand dollars to buy fifty coke ovens and three hundred acres of land in the area of the great Connellsville vein of bituminous coal. This, it turned out, was the down payment on a vast coal and steel empire. His future associate, Andrew Carnegie, already a millionaire, established the J. Edgar Thomson Steel Works in Pittsburgh in 1875. The fourth of the tycoons, Andrew Mellon, was born to fortune, the son of the Pittsburgh banker who lent Frick his stake.

George Catlett Marshall took the crest of this breaking wave of industrialism with similar assurance, at least at the start. In partnership with the young bookkeeper at the Dunbar Iron Company, Arthur Weir Bliss from Alabama, he began manufacturing brick for coking ovens, the beehives in which the coal was roasted; forty such ovens had been built in Dunbar in 1869. By August of 1872 Bliss, Marshall and Company was producing seven thousand brick a day—the beginning of a solid business with wealth perhaps ahead.[14]

Marshall, well pleased, went back to Augusta in the spring of 1873 to marry Laura Bradford, to whom he had been engaged for four years. At the wedding on April 30 at Dr. Jonathan Bradford's house supper and dancing followed the ceremony; the correspondent for the Cincinnati *Times and Chronicle* found that "the 'poetry of motion' was exemplified as dainty feet tripped lightly on the linened floor. . . ." The bride played some tunes on the piano and "about two o'clock, May-day morning, the crowd began to disperse, well-pleased with the night's entertainment." [15]

For Laura the move to Western Pennsylvania was a return to familiar country. Her mother's father, James Peyton Stuart, had moved from Alexandria, Virginia, to Pittsburgh in the 1830s and had become president of the old Liberty Bank of Pittsburgh, and she had aunts living in Pittsburgh whom she visited often.[16] In February 1874 her first son was born at Augusta, Kentucky, where she had gone to be with her parents. Named William Champe for his grandfather, the child lived only six months and in the summer of 1874 was buried in Augusta. A second son, Stuart Bradford, was born near Washington, Pennsylvania, in February 1875, and a daughter, Marie, in December 1876.

Shortly after the birth of their first child the Marshalls moved from Dunbar eight miles south to Uniontown, the county seat of Fayette County, which was to be the family home so long as George Catlett lived. They spent part of their first year there as guests, or boarders, with the Gilmores, one of the old Uniontown families. In 1875 they rented from A. W. Boyd a solid, two-story brick house at 130 West Main Street next to the Gilmores'. In this house the last of the family, George Catlett Marshall, Jr., was born on December 31, 1880.[17]

George Catlett's business fortunes had fluctuated during his first five years of marriage. In 1873, Marshall and Bliss had leased the coal works of Thomas Frost and announced plans to sell lump coal and to build additional coking ovens. But 1873 was the first year of the first of the great depressions,[18] caused largely by the overbuilding of the railroads with an accompanying inflation of credit, and the Connellsville region was hit hard by the precipitate fall-off in the demand for iron and for coke to make it.

It is likely that the young partners had difficulties in holding on through the first year, but by 1874 they were able to acquire additional property in Dunbar. By 1875, the large backlog of pig iron began to disappear and demands for new production began to mount so that the year saw a slightly larger output by the iron furnaces than had the boom year 1871. Affected favorably by this upsurge in the iron business, Bliss, Marshall and Company built eighty-nine ovens in 1876 and was reported to be "running full force." When full prosperity returned to the country in 1879, Fayette County coke prices leaped from under a dollar a ton to five dollars. Three-fifths of the latter price represented clear profit.[19] Marshall and Bliss now took in other partners and incorporated as the Percy Mining Company, of which Marshall eventually became president. While they continued to make brick, their main business became the manufacture of coke. In 1880 they organized the Fayette Coke and Furnace Company which purchased the Oliphant furnace and eventually built there 150 ovens. They also bought coal lands.[20]

Marshall and his partners were among the larger coke manufacturers in the region, in the eighteen-eighties, but they were a long way from being the biggest. Henry Clay Frick, having greater resources of capital, had not only survived but had used the depression to buy out competitors, and by 1882 H. C. Frick and Company owned 1000 ovens and 3000 acres of coal—about one-eighth of the region's production at that time. In that year Frick joined with Carnegie, incorporated with two million dollars' capitalization and began the inexorable march to monopoly.[21]

In history the last decades of the nineteenth century were a time of tremendous, immoderate innovation, economic, social, political, artistic. But to the boy born on that last day of 1880 it seemed when he looked back that he had come rather at the end of an era, that his boyhood in fact was lived in an antiquity more remote, less easily recoverable, than most boyhoods. In some sense that impression, too, was just.

Not only are conclusions in the historical flow distinguished from the beginnings only by a point of view, but a child is born into the lap of the past—at least as much of the past as is represented by the life span of his parents. He is also set down in a community that inhabits buildings as well as traditions normally a generation or more old. George Catlett and Laura were of the vintage of the Civil War. While they themselves were making their way as rapidly as they could into the new industrial world of postwar America, they carried into that world the manners and morals of their prewar youth. General Marshall, remembering his own youth from the vantage point of the mid-twentieth century, was contrasting in part the attitudes and ways of life of generations one hundred years apart. And what a hundred years! From Appomattox to Hiroshima, from the transcontinental railroad to satellites in orbit, from a nation of fifty million provincials, mostly farmers, to an industrial superpower of a hundred and eighty million whose every move sends tremors of consequence into what used to be called the far corners of the earth.

It was, broadly speaking, the Civil War itself that ended one era and began another. But the break was not made cleanly. Out of the war the nation emerged triumphant over the smaller and divisive jealousies of its parts. Northern finance capitalism won the American future from Southern agrarian feudalism; manu-

facturing replaced farming as the nation's primary economic
concern; cities were fated to grow, villages to decline; a free society, having turned its back on slavery, was to struggle to create
an egalitarian democracy that would recall the Southern experiment in landed aristocracy only as literary romance. But this
whole accounting due the victors was not rendered at Appomattox and would not be settled for generations. The defeated South
resisted the attitudes of surrender, as well as a good part of the
reality. The West, for many years after the war, was still absorbed
essentially in the problems of settling the wilderness and even
more acutely than ever in the problem of the Indian. The same
year (1876) that saw the invention of the telephone and brought
thousands of Americans to the Philadelphia centennial to admire
the modern city and the triumph of the machine also witnessed
the slaughter of General Custer's army at the Little Big Horn.

To talk of the urbanizing and industrializing of the United
States after the war is to describe a tide rising in the East as though
it were already national because in fact it became so. Before that
tide was full, however, the old dry land of rural America behind
dikes of tradition put up a sturdy defense of old ways and old
values. In 1880 rural America still flourished outwardly even
though, like those green fields around Uniontown which were
underlain by coal, it had already a mortal vulnerability to progress.

For George Marshall the old ways were embodied in Augusta,
Kentucky. The boy's visits to his parents' birthplace were infrequent, but in a literal sense Augusta and Uniontown were
poles of his young world. Already a place grown old and nostalgic
when he first saw it, Augusta—unlike Uniontown—has not
changed much since. The town, less than ten streets wide,
stretches along the Ohio River at the foot of a high hill.[22] A ferry
still plies between the sparsely settled, wooded river banks, rem-
iniscent of stretches of the Rhine. For the boy the chief differences between Uniontown and Augusta may have been between
native haunts and a museum of cousins in which it was forbidden
to roughhouse or stick out your tongue; but there would come a
time when he recognized Augusta as the representative of something enduring, Uniontown as the symbol of change.

Uniontown was actually a few years older. Its first town lots were laid out in July 1776, making it by the standards of the American West an ancient settlement. A waystop on the old National Road across the Alleghenies, it had been cut off when the railroads drove out stagecoaches, just as Augusta had been when steamboat travel on the Ohio declined. But Uniontown was not destroyed because under it lay that great vein of coal for which the railroad age developed an enormous demand. If Augusta was a window on the past, Uniontown was a door to the twentieth century. The western counties of Pennsylvania lay squarely and imminently in the path of change.

Yet even while coal miners tore up the farmlands; even while immigrants (first the Irish and then the Hungarians) came in thousands to work the mines, bake the coke, and disrupt the more or less comfortable homogeneous pattern of native-born, Anglo-Saxon, Protestant communities; even while the cities grew and the countryside shrank and blackened—still the old inhabitants were not at once jarred out of their rural isolation, still less out of their rural habits of mind. Uniontown's citizens were still largely of the English and Scotch-Irish stock which had populated most of the area. This was Whisky Rebellion country, strongly Jeffersonian and Jacksonian in politics until the Civil War, and it continued to poll a large Democratic vote until the McKinley-Bryan campaign.[23] The pioneer, individualist tradition remained strong and was echoed throughout Marshall's youth in the impassioned editorials in the local Democratic paper, *The Genius of Liberty,* to which the Marshalls subscribed. It was a culture that had a strong bias for the frontier virtues of hard work and self-reliance.

As though to mark his position at the cusp of an age, the house on West Main Street in which George Marshall lived all his boyhood was at the very edge of Uniontown, the last house on the west before Main Street crossed an ornamental stone bridge over one of the Monongahela's lesser tributaries, then called locally Coal Lick Run. Coal Lick Run curled around the Marshall back yard, dividing in one place around an island orchard consisting of four large apple trees. Then it flowed north into fertile fields, which in the boy's concentric geography were known as first, sec-

ond, and third hollows as they receded from his home. To the east
the city clustered, counting thirty-five hundred inhabitants in the
year of Marshall's birth. Although expanding rapidly, it remained small enough for a few years to be encompassed as a kind
of family domain by a small boy who "knew about everybody in
town" and walked everywhere. Only after he went away to school
did the town spill westward across Coal Lick Run and "buried
my childhood under twenty feet of fill."

Visiting Uniontown today one may feel something of the
General's sense of loss. Of the happy, green years of the 1880s
there is not a trace remaining. Where 130 West Main Street stood,
big, comfortable, ugly, and serene, now stands a glaring white,
oblong, concrete building with neon signs in front proclaiming it
the home of the VFW. Next door is a Texaco filling station built
on the twenty-foot fill that covers the old slope down to the
stream. Asphalt and grime pave the Marshalls' back yard. The
orchard can no longer even be imagined. Coal Lick Run flows
thin and milky under a railroad trestle, along a station yard,
through urban wastelands that have expropriated the green hollows of youth. West on the hill that was the Gilmore place rise
a multi-level yellow brick motel and rows of ordinary houses,
neither new nor old.

Across Main Street (which is the old National Road) there is
now another filling station. It uses a piece of a red brick house
which in George Marshall's time was the home of his closest
friend, Andrew (Andy) Thompson. Andy's father was J. V.
Thompson, banker, who in time became wealthy. But as long as
the Thompsons lived in that house across the road it was known
as "Miss Minnie Redburn's place." For George and Andy their
two houses and yards, separated by the Pike but joined by the
same stream, were one realm. Stretched by a boy's imagination, it
was big enough and wild enough to grow in.

There is a special irony in the fact that the west end in which
George and Andy played has now been pre-empted by no less
than three gas stations. Of all the destroyers of nineteenth-
century rural life, the most ruthlessly effective has been the automobile. The General remembered with particular wonderment
the very small size of his childhood realm. He thought it hardly

extended in any direction more than five miles from his home. It is true that often in the summers the family boarded up in the mountains, usually on Chestnut Ridge, the closest of the Alleghenies. Once he recalled having gone with his mother to Pittsburgh to shop. There were besides, of course, the trips to Augusta and a visit to Virginia when he was ten. Yet despite these excursions, the country he knew well and considered home was only as much of the environs of Uniontown as he could visit on foot.

The United States in the history books appears always on the move, and our national story can almost be told in terms of migrations, large and small. Yet while the nation was thus grandly mobile, the individual for the most part was not. He might pick up his home and move it many hundreds of miles, but when he set it down again he stayed close by. In George's boyhood the streetcar came to Uniontown. But the biggest event here, and indeed throughout most of rural America, was the coming of the bicycle —the kind introduced in 1884 with two equal-sized wheels that could be mounted without ladders and ridden without acrobatic training. The bicycle—a million of them in use by 1893—effected on a small scale the sort of social revolution that the automobile was to carry out on such a colossal scale in succeeding generations.

To return to George Marshall's youth, this double revolution in mobility must in imagination be unmade. One must burrow under the filling station by Coal Lick Run and find not just a rural idyl of carefree lads at play but a representative corner of an America that once seemed perfectly secure and has now vanished, leaving hardly a trace.

II

End of an Era

"In this life of Uniontown, I saw what you might call the end of an era because it was a very simple life and a very charming life and it had a long history behind it."

W H A T sort of boy was he? What promise did he show? These are questions no biographer can answer with any assurance. The records are always scant and the temptation all but irresistible to find the lineaments of greatness already prefigured in the child. For Marshall, the records—that is, contemporary testimony—are almost wholly missing. Almost all that can be reported of the boy is what the man at the age of seventy-six recalled and chose to reveal.

This then is a chapter of memories.

He remembered summer, a whole boyhood of summers with only an occasional winter to accommodate Christmas, some sliding down snowy hills, and of course school when its impress was too painful to be forgotten. It seemed to him that it was in summer that he first saw the world. He was very small. Following behind Stuart, who was six years older, he ran one day into the stable east of the house where for a few years his father kept a horse and cow. Stuart clambered up a ladder into the haymow. George followed, but slowly and frightened, until he came abreast of an opening in the wall and looked out through the rungs of the ladder. For the first time he was tall enough to look down on his world and see it whole. He saw the winding stream and at some distance some brightly colored ducks, a dog along the bank and some chickens strutting about. That was all, but seventy years later he recalled the scene as revelation. "It seemed a whole world exposed in an instant to my eye." [1]

And the stream that bounded and washed it was the center of the boy's interest, "the jewel of the production" he called it later. That summer or one near it, he and his chum Andy excavated a canal along the creek, some two inches wide, and built a fleet of naval vessels with matchstick masts which they called "the Great White Fleet," in honor of that other fleet with which America in the 1880s was beginning its rise to first rank among naval powers. The Coal Lick Run navy drew "most of the other boys of the town" to watch and play.

Another later exploit on the stream drew mostly the girls. It was some time later, for Mr. Marshall had got rid of the horse and cow; the stable was torn down and the lumber from it neatly stacked. George and Andy tried to use some of it to make a raft but the timbers were heavy, their carpentry clumsy. (Marshall, though he would never confess himself mechanically helpless, had no facility with his hands.) A friend came to their rescue. The brother of the man who owned the town's toy store built a flat-bottomed boat for them that would float, and the boys pressed it at once into service as a ferry. Since the stream was hardly wider than the boat, the ferry was scarcely more than a steppingstone, but it was more or less mobile (Andy as engineer poled it), and it was fitted out with imagination. George was its conductor, partly because he had recently received a toy typewriter for Christmas and printed up some tickets and partly because he evidently liked the position of authority. With his cap turned backward, he solemnly sold the tickets for pennies and pins and punched them for fares with his mother's Five Hundred punch. The passengers were mostly girls from school who traveled back and forth as long as pennies and pins lasted. Then one day the girls rebelled. They boarded the ferry but refused to surrender their tickets.

"I was terribly humiliated," the General recalled, "and what made it worse, my chum Andy began laughing at me. And there I was—the girls in the flatboat all jeering at me and my engineer and boon companion laughing at me and I was stuck. Just then my eye fastened on a cork in the floor of the boat which was utilized in draining it. With the inspiration of the moment, I pulled the cork and under the pressure of the weight of the passengers, a stream of water shot up in the air. All the girls screamed and I sank the boat in the middle of the stream. They all had to wade ashore. I never forgot that because I had to do something and I had to think quickly. What I did set me up again as the temporary master of the situation."

He always hated to be laughed at. It was one of the things that made school hard for him. A poor student for many years, he shrank from recitations in which his inadequacies were publicly exposed. He had a bad start. When he was a baby, his mother's aunt, Eliza Stuart, then in her eighties, came to live with the Marshalls. A woman of keen intelligence and insatiable hunger for learning, who could read the New Testament in French and the Old Testament in Hebrew, Eliza Stuart began educating George when he was five. With more zeal than understanding, she kept him by her chair repeating his lessons on Saturday mornings when outside he could see his friends at play. "She so soured me on study and teaching that I liked never to have recovered from it."

From Eliza Stuart's tutelage, he passed at six to Miss Alcinda Thompson's school on Church Street—one of those genteel private schools by which gentlewomen in the nineteenth century strove for a respectable livelihood and a sense of being useful. Having learned from his great aunt to hate studying, George was pleased to find at Miss Thompson's that it was apparently unnecessary. So he drifted until at nine or ten he was transferred to public school and found to his chagrin so many better prepared than he. He had, he recalled, "a very painful time," not only because in some things (mathematics in particular) he found himself comparatively ignorant, but because he was ashamed to admit that ignorance in front of those who could feel superior and might laugh.

He remembered being particularly awkward at the age he went first to public school. He was rather tall and slender, snub-nosed, with a mop of sandy hair parted, as the fashion was, squarely in the middle.[2] He remembered having big feet, though in fact his feet were not large. He was quiet, shy, and perhaps unusually serious. He remembered that people "made fun of me a great deal." Though he knew everybody and ran happily with the gang, he was apparently even then learning the reserve for which he was afterward noted.

Throughout his boyhood, Andy Thompson, handsome, self-possessed, imaginative, remained his fast and special friend. But there were others, who gathered for games or for that endless talking and hanging around which is part of every boy's growing up. They had a number of clubs. One was Kramer's store just up the street near the White Swan Inn, where there was the usual "open barrel of oyster crackers and tight barrel of dill pickles." They were "allowed to loaf in there, I guess to Mr. Kramer's irritation, though he suppressed it. His clerk was very nice to us." In the course of loafing they might spend a penny, no more. The local men's club was the barbershop, run by a Negro man "who was quite a friend of mine." On the whole they were not welcome there where the men came in regularly to be shaved in the era before safety razors. Yet George lingered on occasion, fascinated by the row of shaving mugs painted "in very fanciful letters, so you could see the names of the patrons." The third and perhaps favorite hangout was Gadd's blacksmith shop. "If one of us would pull the bellows, the rest of us could sit there and talk and listen to the others talk."

They were pretty much a cross-section of Uniontown, these companions of Marshall's boyhood: Andy Thompson and his brother John; Jim Conrad, whose father worked at the railroad ticket office; Billy Ewing, who owned a dogcart and was the son of a judge; Herbert Bowman, later to become a noted athlete at Yale; Bill Wood, whose father ran the harness shop; J. T. ("Jap") Shepler and Alex Mead, cousins of the Thompsons; Ed McCullough, O'Neil Kennedy, and Ed Hustead. Among the girls, not club members, of course, but schoolmates and occasional after-school companions, were the daughters of Marshall's partner,

Adele and Florence Bliss; Helen Houston, a close neighbor; Lida Nichols, another cousin of the Thompsons, who later became the Princess of Thurn and Taxis; Mary Kate O'Bryon, who, though younger than the others, was distinguished by having a father who ran a locomotive; and the Lindsays, Catherine and Nannie, daughters of a judge. Catherine was, in later recollection, "the pretty girl I was devoted to though she didn't pay any attention to me." Because of her he even tried to learn to spell in order to stand beside her where she normally stood, at the head of the spelling-bee line. One day he got there briefly, then missed a word and went disconsolately to the bottom. Love had its limits. He recalled that he "never tried again." Of his many young acquaintances the General would speak with special warmth of Bill Wood, a boy of a "philosophic frame of mind" who, when he grew up, stayed on in Uniontown and opened a shop where he made and sold stogies.

George Marshall's need for that sort of companionship and his ability to respond to it were to lead him in his early teens into a close and adult friendship with the young pastor of the Episcopal church which the Marshall family attended,[3] John R. Wightman. Wightman is a hazy figure in the records, and the General, while recalling him as an important influence, said little about him. Apparently the young minister was not readily accepted by the conservative parish of St. Peter's Church and "had a very difficult time." He was lonely because all the men in town worked all day and there was no men's club and little entertaining at night. "So, particularly during the vacations, Mr. Wightman and I used to take long walks, and he seemed glad of the association with me because I was literally the only person that he had to go around with at that hour of the day. I came to know him intimately and was very much impressed by him." But just how and why, the General never made clear. One can only speculate that the boy found in the minister one of the rare adults to whom he could freely talk and that he was perhaps enabled in this way to reach out intellectually along paths not opened by his father or by his schoolteachers.

One subject he liked in school—and liked still better out of school—was history. In reporting that he was consistently a poor student, Marshall always added, "except in something like history. If it was history, that was all right; I could star in history."

History in Uniontown lay all around him—the liveliest sort to stir a boy's imagination. He was deeply conscious of living directly on the National Road over which the commerce and the great men of the new West had passed. Lafayette, whose wooden statue might still be seen in the courthouse,[4] and Andrew Jackson, had come this way. So, according to tradition, had Henry Clay, whose carriage was reported once to have hit a pile of limestone and spilled him in Uniontown, causing him to remark that the "clay of Kentucky mixes with the limestone of Pennsylvania." Two or three houses from Andy's was the White Swan, built in 1805, twelve years before the National Road was completed. The inn flourished as a stopping place for travelers who made the long journey over the mountains between Cumberland and Brownsville on the Monongahela River.[5]

More exciting were the sites and reminders of war. For much of the way the Pike follows roughly the course of Braddock's trail—the path through the wilderness that General Braddock hacked out and fought for in an overland expedition to attack Fort Duquesne, where Pittsburgh now stands. Just east of Chestnut Ridge is General Braddock's grave. He died there of wounds in July 1755, while retreating after his defeat at the hands of the French and their Indian allies. In Marshall's day the grave was on a knoll by the road in a grove of trees surrounded by a white board fence. On an occasional picnic here (nine miles from Uniontown) young Marshall and his friends would sit on this fence in the moonlight and talk to their girls.

East of Braddock's grave, scarcely a mile away (Marshall got there on hunting or fishing trips with his father), is Fort Necessity, where Colonel George Washington on July 14, 1754, fought the first real battle of the French and Indian War. George Marshall heard the story of the battle in detail from his father, saw again the Indians fighting from behind trees ringing the bowl of the meadow, and traced the remains of the earth entrenchments from which Washington's men had fought.[6]

Marshall senior evidently took pleasure in telling his son the tales of local history and also, during the evenings, in reading aloud, particularly from historical romances. The General recalled that his father read very well "and we all liked to listen." To the family assembled several nights a week, he read *Sant' Ilario* and *Don Orsino* by F. Marion Crawford, many of the books of James Fenimore Cooper, Conan Doyle's *The Refugees,* Eugène Sue's *The Wandering Jew,* Prescott's *Conquest of Mexico.* In old age the General remembered some of the tales, particularly those that concerned Indians, so vividly he could hardly forbear to retell them and recapture the excitement of those evenings long ago.

Some part of the boy's pleasure certainly was a feeling of closeness to his father—a feeling as rare as it evidently was precious. His father found it difficult to unbend except on occasions which were obviously special and so permitted a comradeship clearly exceptional and not to be traded on. Such occasions were hunting trips into the mountains to shoot grouse. Marshall, who owned an especially fine shotgun, was an excellent shot and no doubt enjoyed teaching his son and showing off a bit himself. It was on these trips that young Marshall became familiar with sections of Braddock's trail, because these were grass-covered clearings in the woods where the grouse liked to come to earth. In such casual ways did history make contact with the excitement of the moment and become fixed in memory as something personal.

There were also fishing trips along the Youghiogheny River, where they caught salmon pike. One day young George went along with his father and two of his father's friends. It was hard going for the boy, clambering over the large rocks lining the banks of the river. All of the morning passed without a strike. The men then wanted to go on two or three miles upstream to a place of reputation among fishermen called "Rattlesnake Hole." But the boy could not have made the climb and Marshall senior "very generously and wistfully" said he would stay behind.

"We went up to a rock which had halved off, leaving a flat surface on one side about a foot above the water." Here was a pool in which they decided to try their luck. Young George fished with one of his father's poles. He had no reel because his father thought he was too small to manage one. "When he baited my hook with minnows, I threw it in and he started to bait his own. I got a strike, the first strike of the day for any of us. When I began to pull the fish in, I had two bass, one on each hook. My father had to help me land them and lift them out of the water. Then he had to get them off the hook and rebait it." Scarcely had the boy dropped the hooks into the pool again than he had another bite. Between them that afternoon father and son pulled in thirty bass, and with creels filled and a string of fish besides they returned to the mountain cabin in which they were staying, to bathe and eat. When, after dark, the other two fishermen came in empty-handed, the Marshalls side by side, father and son, displayed their catch and were men together, full of a good warm pride.

These were moments to be cherished. For the most part, Mr. Marshall had his own sense of rather prickly importance. He had by this time acquired a little paunch, though he carried it trimly. He wore the pince-nez then in vogue and a full mustache. Sensitive to criticism and quick to anger, he did not enjoy jokes on himself. Yet he was well liked in town, especially by the newer families, "because he was convivial and liked people and they liked him." Perhaps he was inclined to be stiffer within the family because families are notoriously less considerate of the slight ego-stuffing that he seemed to feel was necessary to keep him properly poised. Or perhaps it was only that in an age when father was still taken seriously as the head of the household he took seriously his obligations to command.

The boy often felt that his father did not like him and that Stuart was favored. At least the elder Marshall had a lively concern for his younger son's advancement. The General remembered only one incident connecting his father with early schooling, but it was revealing. When young Marshall transferred from Miss Thompson's to public school he was taken by his father to an interview with Professor Lee Smith, head of the public schools.[7] Professor Smith asked a number of "simple questions" to which the boy could give no answers. His own pain over his inadequacy was keen enough and lasted long in memory. In recounting it, the General significantly added that his father "suffered very severely."

Father and son were alike in the tenderness of their egos, but the goals of their ambition were significantly different. The father seems always to have craved the recognition of the local society in which he found himself. The son sought personally to excel and to be without visible flaw in whatever he tried to do. When frustrated, as in his schoolwork, the boy wished above all to avoid the appearance of failure even if he could do so only by seeming not to try. His fears made him diffident, yet he seems to have been happiest when he could conquer them and command. While the father found sustenance in being a Marshall, the boy wanted to strike out on his own.

In some of his more enterprising extracurricular activities his father strongly encouraged him. He and Andy got a notion one summer, when they were both very small, of going into business. They decided to grow plants and, supposing that the first necessity was a "green" house, they borrowed remnants of green paint from their friend Frank Llewellyn, who ran the carriage shop. Thinning it with turpentine, they painted as much as they could of the shed in the back yard. Plants were more difficult to come by, so they began with weeds potted in tin cans. In soil dug out of the old stable, the weeds flourished even more luxuriantly than weeds commonly do, and Mr. Marshall, visiting the greenhouse one day, was impressed. He suggested that they ought to buy some seeds. "He gave me seventy-five cents and Andy's mother gave him the same thing." With their money the boys went to the town greenhouse, whose owner proved a man of generous good humor. "We picked around so long that he asked us what we had in mind. We were looking at the smallest pots he had because we thought we could get more for the money. When he found that we were getting them for our greenhouse and were going to be his competitors in business, he gave us quite a large collection of these small pots"—far more than they could have bought for a dollar fifty.

The enterprise began to flourish. Shortly the boys read in the Peter Henderson seed catalogue of a contest to name a new tomato, the winner to receive fifty dollars. "Well, that was the largest sum I think we had ever heard of at that time. So we sent for the seed and proceeded to grow the plants." In the rich soil that had once been the floor of the stable the plants put forth very

large tomatoes. "My father showed me how to prune the plants."
When they were ripe the boys rushed out to sell them to the
grocer downtown for a few pennies. "My father was rather con-
temptuous of us for selling them so cheaply." Presently the
groceryman was asking for more for "one of his richest clients.
We came back and reported with great glee that our stock was
in great demand and particularly by this well-to-do family. Then
my father told us, 'Now you set the price,' and suggested it. Well,
the grocer blew up because he thought he would get them for
almost nothing."

The largest tomato the boys saved to photograph with a
Brownie camera, using a silver dollar to show the scale, and sent
the picture to Henderson's with a suggested name. Henderson
& Co. did not like the name but were so impressed with the tomato, which they said was the largest they had ever seen, that
they asked "our parents to write and tell how the tomato had been
raised. I told my father and he was intensely interested and wrote
to Peter Henderson. He finished by saying, however, that you
couldn't tear down a stable every time you wanted to raise a tomato. That was the Ponderosa tomato and the man who proposed
'Ponderosa' was the winner of the contest." [8]

Despite this triumph the greenhouse came to a sudden, un-
deserved end. Its principal steady customers were the girls who
would come down after school to buy "green things," and the
young entrepreneurs, eager to please, were out one day in a pony
cart in which they roamed the countryside looking for old
bones and other salable items when they came upon a patch of
forget-me-nots in the third hollow. They spaded up a number
of plants, brought them home, and boxed them in strawberry
boxes which they cleaned and painted green with a black stripe
around each. During a recess period they rushed home, got the
boxes, and sold them to the girls.

But, alas, a little later "we were having a May Day picnic with
these same girls in this hollow as we called it, where the little
waterfall was." And there, of course, were the rest of the forget-
me-nots. The girls turned on the florists, saying they had been
cheated into buying flowers that were grown free by nature in
the fields. It was in vain that they spoke of the labor of digging
and carrying, the service of personal delivery, the art of painting

the boxes with a neat black stripe. From then on the girls would not buy and the greenhouse had to close.

George and Andy tried the restaurant business at the old spring house, where in the winter they sold apples and sweet potatoes made attractive by lots of sugar. One day, however, Andy ran out of sugar and sprinkled on sand instead—and again the customers balked. Then there was the bar set up in the cellar for the sale of root beer and corn-silk cigars. Unfortunately the root beer belonged to George's father, who had put it down to age. This was one enterprise he discouraged firmly by confiscating the stock. Yet his son recalled no display of anger. Probably Mr. Marshall continued to be pleased by the boy's show of business enterprise, if not always of business acumen.

George always struggled for his father's approval but was also a little afraid of him. He shared triumphs with his father; the scrapes—and he got into them often enough—he concealed when he could. In this his mother abetted him. It was his recollection that he told her everything. "She never corrected me, because, if I told her, I realized it was wrong and there was no use telling me again it was wrong." She had a special tenderness for her youngest and in various small ways made a world for him in which he stood happily at the center. There were miniature pies for him at baking time, and at Christmas his most important toy was featured under the tree. He remembered during the winters sitting by the fireplace with an iron upside down between his knees, cracking hickory nuts with a hammer "for Mother's very famous hickory nut cakes. . . . I always liked our fires, because we . . . had what we called cannel coal and it made a soft, delightful, homelike flame. . . . Later on when natural gas was piped in, the fireplace lost a great part of its charm."

From manhood looking back he thought probably he was spoiled. He had wanted nearly all the things his brother and sister got, and "too often, I think, I was allowed to have them." Yet he spoke then as a man who had developed an abhorrence of anything that smacked of favoritism toward others or of indulgence toward self. What he remembered as spoiling sounds only like the expression of natural, relaxed affection in a home where affection often was not easily expressed.

Mrs. Marshall was not gregarious like her husband. She enjoyed the society of a few close friends—the Blisses, the Gilmores—but did not share her husband's love for constant community activity, and of course it was not usual in those times for a wife to do so. She liked to play the piano, which she had learned as a girl in Philadelphia when she had stayed with her aunt in Rittenhouse Square. Her son recalled that she played almost every night.[9] Sometimes there was singing. The family liked to sing, and Stuart played "two or three instruments" besides. Only George lacked a voice. Although he could strum a little on the banjo and guitar, he did not enjoy the singing much, particularly when his mother and father sang together and he "had to sit around on a hassock and listen and keep quiet." But he loved to hear his mother play, semi-classical music that included most of his favorite tunes.

She was a quiet woman, tall and stately. One who remembered her after more than half a century said that her image tended to merge with that of Queen Mary of England.[10] But she was easy with children, and her younger son remembered her patience, her unfailing sympathy, edged with a sense of humor that permitted her to laugh at her son's exploits without wounding him. The truth is that she seems to have rejoiced in him as he was and did not seek out and reprove his faults as his father so often did. He depended on her for that. Already his sense of self and his wish to excel were strong in him. He needed the release which he found in her love and laughter.

There was the episode of banditry, for instance, when George was eight. In the early spring of 1889 a gang of robbers broke into several houses in Uniontown and then fled to the mountains where eventually they were rounded up. Fired by tales of the outlaws, George and Andy armed themselves with air rifles and took to the hills to play highwayman. They would hide beside the road until a farmer's buggy passed, then pretend to hold it up and fire when it had gone by. It happened that on one of these buggies the little isinglass window behind the farmer's head was broken and one of the BB pellets "went through and hit the farmer on the back of the neck." There followed what the General remembered as "one of the most thrilling escapes we ever went through." Since little boys can notoriously run faster or scurry more nimbly than irate farmers, they got away. But afterward they were afraid to go home.

"Finally we turned our coats inside out and set our hats on backwards thinking that we were disguising ourselves and returned home. My mother thought that was the funniest thing she ever saw when we turned up in this 'disguise.'" She laughed at them but she took their fears seriously, shielding them from embarrassing questions during the three subsequent days in which they lived in dread of being captured and would not leave the premises. No other punishment was needed. That was George's last holdup.

It was not his last experiment in lawlessness. Perhaps four or five years later he and Andy became interested in raising fighting chickens. They started with bantams, then got some eggs from Georgia and raised Georgia Reds. Inevitably they reached the point where they wanted to pit their cocks against outside competition. Since cockfighting was illegal, boys would not have been allowed into the clandestine pits, so they persuaded their older friend, George Gadd, the blacksmith's son, to enter their cocks. One day they slipped off to watch them fight. Having left their horse and cart some distance away, they arrived late. Moments later, the gathering was raided by the sheriff. The two boys "squirted out into the forest and got separated and hid out." George, with visions of arrest, jail, and his father's wrath, hid out most of the afternoon before he dared begin to creep "Indian fashion" out of the woods, pausing at every sound. Presently, to his horror, he became aware of someone else prowling furtively through the trees. Becoming an Indian in earnest, "I scouted him and he scouted me." This double-stalking went on for about an hour before he discovered his shadow was Andy. "We were the only people left up there."

Close to one in the morning he reached home and crept upstairs without waking his father. His mother, however, was up and came into his room. He told her the whole story. "Parts of it she thought were very funny, and I remember she laughed until she cried." No word of reprimand came. To mother and son it was equally clear that he "was not going back to any other chicken fight and go through that again."

Although not, in the ordinary sense, spoiled, in some ways George Marshall does appear to have grown up as an only child. His brother Stuart was six years older. There was little contact

between them and still less affection. In later years their estrangement was complete. Marie, four years older, in the period before
George went away to school regarded him largely as a pest, and
whether by instinct or in retaliation he gave her cause. The memories in which Marie figured were the classic big-sister tales. She
discovered him one day playing hookey at Gadd's blacksmith
shop and reported him, so that he got a licking. Once at church,
when she was home from private school on vacation, he imitated
her affected tremolo until she had him sent outside. From an upstairs window on another day she watched and jeered while poor
George, on his father's orders, hosed down the street in front of
their house. This was a chore imposed on George after the street-
cars arrived and Main Street was paved; it was a chore he resented
with peculiar intensity, for while he worked the boys and girls
going by on their way to school stopped for such rude and gig-
gling comments as they calculated might make him angry. He
decided on this particular morning to get even with Marie. Hearing her come out of the house as he finished his work, he whirled
and turned the hose on her. He caught her square, but when he
looked it was not Marie but his mother. Laura Marshall's understanding and sense of humor proved equal even to this. She recovered her glasses, which had been knocked askew, the General
recalled, and was "rather shocked but much amused because
she knew the terrible plight I was in." The terrible plight was Mr.
Marshall, who, not at all amused, gave the boy the last licking he
remembered ever to have had.

Marie escaped that time but suffered on another occasion. She
was having a party one summer day for a schoolfriend who had
come to visit from Philadelphia, and decreed that her barbarian
brother should be kept out of the house for the duration. He
wandered over to Andy's place, where some of the fellows had
gathered. Being in that sort of mood, they decided to fight bees.
The sport consisted in whittling a bat out of a shingle and cutting
a few air holes in it. Then you stirred up a bees' nest, and as the
bees came out you swung at them with the paddle; the object was
simply not to get stung. Among the bee fighters that day was
Herbert Bowman. He and George and an angry bee tangled in a
wild melee of swatting, ducking, splintering shingles, shouts,

and buzzing. Before long Bowman's athletic talents proved too much for George, who found that the bee was giving him almost undivided attention. "In a desperate effort to get free of the bee, I broke loose. With the bee chasing me, I came from the back yard of my chum's house and passed his house in a flash and crossed the street. My front door was open and I went straight down the long hall. Then I remembered I was forbidden the house. The party was going on on the side porch, peaceful and delightful. So at the last moment I turned to the right and went off into the dining room. But the bee went straight ahead and stung the guest of honor. I didn't dare come home until late that night."

Marie was to wonder later how she ever managed to get married, for George, in the manner of younger brothers everywhere, was impossible to the young men who called on her. She recalled that he used to drop water bombs on their heads from the second-story windows.

Probably he did—once anyway. But that he did is less revealing than that the act stuck in the older girl's memory as the way things were at home. Long afterward, when she had grown to admire her younger brother, it was the sort of anecdote she liked to tell—the classic humorous touch to the portrait of an ordinary middle-class family, so normal that it could be remembered by Marie as well as by George in terms of something like folklore. The General himself liked to tell of how he was fired from his Sunday job of pumping the organ in St. Peter's Church because one morning he became so immersed in the adventures of Nick Carter during the sermon that he missed his cue at the end to start pumping.[11] He was fond, too, of a farcical adventure in playing soldier. Stuart and some of his friends, inspired by a summer encampment of the Pennsylvania National Guard regiment at the Uniontown fairgrounds, set up a tent in which to spend the night on a nearby creek. George, who was then very young, wheedled permission (with his mother's help) to join them. In the middle of the night a cow stumbled over the tent ropes. The older boys, imagining an enemy attack, rushed out, tumbled into the creek, and ran home. They arrived to discover that George was not with them. George was still in the tent, sound asleep through both invasion and retreat.

These are the tales of a small-town boy—one who grew up in intimate association with the lovely land of western Pennsylvania before it was blighted by coal mining. Associating the country with play and not work, as a farm boy does, George Marshall developed a lifelong attachment to simple rural pleasures. His only experiences on a farm were in the summers he spent as a youngster at Andy's grandfather's place west of Uniontown. Jasper M. Thompson was the town's leading banker, but he and his wife remained simple in their habits. Andy's grandmother helped the maids in the kitchen and waited on the table where she fed "masses of food" to the harvest hands. "You all washed out in the yard near the horse trough and you had a tin basin and one little broken mirror and an old comb. You would slick your hair down and make a sort of curl around on your forehead. That was the way you got ready for lunch." The boys "were allowed to sit at the table with the harvest hands and listen." George was fascinated, though perhaps a little dismayed with what he heard. "The conversation at the table . . . smacked very much of the conversations in the Westerns . . . always making fun of each other and dressing down one of their members if he in any way seemed to brag of any achievement of his. They were always tearing down a fellow and making little of him to the immense amusement of all the others."

Various chores were found for George; he helped in the barn —"a beautiful barn"—and in the field, "hauling in the hay shocks" and "distributing manure." He enjoyed it all and "learned a great deal about it, without being really conscious of the fact that I was learning." In other summers later on he went back for brief visits with Andy, and "we were always rewarded with whole pies and that was a wonderful thing." In these later summers, beginning in his teens, he had jobs, usually in the icehouse in town. The Marshalls by then were in straitened circumstances, but in any case it was the thing to do, for Uniontown, like most American small towns, admired work and thought idleness in young or old a temptation to the devil. So strict was this article of faith that when a bright young blade of means spent his leisure driving his buggy and fine horse around the countryside while others worked, he was virtually ostracized until he got a job and walked back and forth to work, carrying his lunch pail.

It is part of the picture of a normal happy boyhood that the General's memories reflected no sense of the passage of time. He could add to a reminiscence that he was quite small on that occasion or that on another he was older. Aging, however, was largely an external fact to be reckoned in various practical ways but not in the way he felt. He himself divided his youth into only two acts: the first was domestic, and he called it the period when he was "running a greenhouse and things of that sort." The second he thought might be called the "bicycle age," when in a day he might travel ten or twelve miles from home to discover, for instance, the town of Brownsville on the Monongahela, which had produced James G. Blaine, Speaker of the House and Secretary of State, and Philander C. Knox, soon to be Attorney General and then Secretary of State. At Brownsville, once, he and his friends loaded their bicycles on a boat and traveled a few miles away to New Geneva, Albert Gallatin's town, where artisans from Switzerland and Germany had developed glassworks. He watched the glassware being loaded on river boats and was reminded of the fact, which to him seemed rather like a miracle, that artisans from Europe so many years before had brought to this country not just themselves but skills they had learned in alien lands. The bicycle age was literally a time of liberation from the immediate confines of Uniontown; in a larger sense it was a time of release, of expanding imagination, a time when in retrospect he had begun to step out of the comfortable world of childhood and, indeed, out of an era.

There were many other ways in which from the outside his growing up could have been related to history. The year 1890 might be taken as a watershed, for it was then that the family fortunes drastically changed. In the previous year George Catlett Marshall and his partners, needing money for some of their operations, offered to sell Frick their Oliphant holdings. Frick, whose company was on the way to getting a monopoly on coke operations in the Connellsville area, insisted the sale include also the Kyle Coke Company, which Marshall and Bliss had formed in 1888 with a capital stock of a hundred thousand dollars.[12] The partners and their associates ended by selling all of their holdings south of Uniontown for a good profit, realizing at least four hundred and fifty thousand dollars on the transactions.[13] Marshall, who probably got as much as a third of this sum, chose against the strong advice of Mrs. Marshall to put the money into land speculation. He had apparently been attracted for some time by schemes to develop industrial centers and resort towns in the Shenandoah Valley of Virginia. Unfortunately the boom, in progress for nearly ten years, had reached its peak when Marshall plunged heavily in the Valley Land and Improvement Company of Luray. The company, capitalized at two million dollars, acquired the Luray Inn, controlling interests in Luray Caverns, and more than ten thousand acres of land which were to be subdivided and sold. Marshall became vice-president and general manager, took his family to Virginia for the summer, and for a moment seemed to have crowned business success with affluence and power. He brought up a riding horse from Kentucky which was said to move "like a king." [14]

Mercifully, perhaps, the reckoning was swift. Luray lots were widely advertised for sale and in September potential buyers were brought down from New York, Philadelphia, and Baltimore. But of one thousand parcels of land offered, only three hundred were sold. For a month or so afterward the boom talk, to which the local newspaper contributed its utmost, continued in Luray, but Marshall probably had few illusions left. With the approach of winter he sent the family back to Uniontown. In December he resigned as manager of the land company and went back home himself on the plea that business matters there required his attention.[15] A sign of approaching disaster came a few days later when his draft on the Luray bank, drawn to pay Stuart's tuition at Virginia Military Institute, was not honored. Early in the new year the bank, headed by the president of the Valley Land and Improvement Company, closed its doors. So presently did banks nearby in New Market, Waynesboro, and Warrenton. In November 1891, the Luray Inn burned to the ground at a loss of one hundred thousand dollars.[16]

Besides losing his direct investment, Marshall made himself liable for thousands of more dollars by signing personal notes to back up company credit. During the eighteen months following the first indications of failure he was sued by three of his chief creditors and at least one judgment was entered against him.[17]

Out of the crumpling of his fortune Marshall managed to save his one-third interest in the Percy Mining Company near Dunbar and some coal lands in West Virginia. Mrs. Marshall retained some property in Pittsburgh and Augusta, which in the years to come would furnish a large proportion of the family's modest income. There was also some cash put aside to pay for Stuart's and Marie's education.[18]

The General recalled that after 1890 "we had to economize very bitterly," and that the burden fell, he thought, most heavily on his mother. She, accustomed throughout her life to servants, now did all of her own housework and attempted to make her personal income meet current expenses. Mr. Marshall kept up a front—sometimes bringing home expensive gifts to his wife which she felt they could ill afford, and talking more and more about the Marshall family tree. He had more time for local politics, for Masonic activities, and for hunting and fishing, and indulged them all. He became secretary of the Sportsman's Club, helped pick slates of candidates for local offices, and took a hand in organizing political parades and barbecues.

As for George, he had to learn an unaccustomed and unwelcome respect for money and he developed a passion for solvency which he never lost. In comparative poverty he found new sources of humiliation. Since the family could no longer afford a cook and the two older children were away at school, the Marshalls began to take some of their meals at one of the local hotels. To feed their dogs and—local tradition has it—to furnish meat for an occasional stew, Mrs. Marshall asked for scraps from the hotel's kitchen. George had to carry them home. Later he thought the experience contributed to his education, but he remembered it as "painful and humiliating" and called it "a black spot on my boyhood."

Yet in larger matters the financial pinch does not seem to have altered his daily life in any essential way. Even in relative affluence that life had been rural and remote from sophisticated (and expensive) urban pleasures. So it continued happily enough for him in harder times. The fishing with Andy, attendance at county fairs (where he learned the tricks of the concessionaire's wheel), watching the local baseball team, playing football (at which he was not very good), courting a pretty girl (at which he was apparently never particularly assiduous), and, of course, attending school—these things went on without interruption or change. It is not even clear that his transfer to public school at about the time his father's financial troubles began was enforced by poverty. In any case the General remembered the experience gratefully and thought that "every boy in a democracy should attend, for at least a period of time, a public school." Money was somehow found after he entered high school to send him back to private school. His last two years were spent at the University School under Professor Albert H. Hopkins, a "handsome, popular, beautifully educated" man who regrettably had no financial talent and stayed in business only just long enough to graduate George Marshall.[19]

If family difficulties did not seriously impinge on the boyhood idyl, still less did the larger difficulties of the nation, which during Marshall's years in Uniontown was passing through one of the great upheavals in American history. The fabulous wealth extracted and created in the postwar decades flowed into very few pockets. Under the impact of inflation, coupled with high tariffs, the real wages of the average worker were actually declining. In the depression of 1873-78 America had its first experience with mass unemployment, and in the railroad strikes of 1877 its first flare-up of industrial war. Recovery put most of the unemployed back to work but did not materially improve wages or working conditions. So long as immigration kept the labor market full, employers saw no reason to reduce hours or raise wages. The result was labor organization and endemic strikes throughout the period. Between 1881 and 1900 the United States Bureau of Labor estimated that the country endured at least twenty-four thousand strikes and lockouts. The harsh reality summarized in these statistics could be seen close up in Uniontown and as grimly as from any other vantage point in the nation. Marie Marshall recalled that her father seemed always to be coming home with word that the miners were out on strike again.[20] During Marshall's boyhood three region-wide strikes, all attended by violence, erupted in the Fayette and Westmoreland coal fields and coke plants, in 1887, 1891, and 1894. In all three cases the large operators employed private police forces and strikebreakers who were chiefly Negroes imported by contract labor agents at fifty cents a head from West Virginia and farther south.[21] In all three, miners were killed, and in all three the operators were victorious, often with the help of the militia called out to keep order. Although the implications of class, or even economic, warfare were scarcely recognized, on one occasion Uniontown's Company C was discovered to have a disturbing sympathy with the strikers and was sent home.[22]

The bitterness of these conflicts endured and made a strong impression on Marshall. Twenty years later, as an instructor with the Pennsylvania National Guard, he observed that few miners signed up for service with the organization and considered the military in general as anti-labor.

There is no record of what Mr. Marshall senior felt about the strikes—when the last two (and worst) came along he was no longer a major employer—or what was said about them in the Marshall home. Marshall recalled only one personal experience when (possibly in 1894) he went to a coke plant at Percy during a strike and sat in an empty freight car watching the picket lines. Someone threw a lump of coal which hit the tipple under which the car was halted. Hurtling down the chute, it struck him on the forehead. He was knocked out for a moment and for the rest of his life was to carry a small blue scar as a memento. But that was all.

So far as local opinion can be deduced from the *Genius of Liberty*, it reflected chiefly a rural distrust both of big business and of union interference with the right of any man to do as he liked with his own. There was not at this time a class-conscious cleavage in the county. The *Genius of Liberty* stood firmly on the virtue of self-reliance and deplored all seductions to dependency either by organization or by such alien philosophy as was supposed to have been imported by the Hungarian immigrants.[23]

So the larger significance of what was happening was missed. The revolution swirled around and through Uniontown but it did not breach the sturdy defenses set up by rural, traditional America. When George Marshall left Uniontown in 1897 he left the town he had always known, not outwardly changed nor, so far as he was aware, inwardly disturbed. He stepped out, he thought, of an era. In fact the world he entered, in which he was to carve so brilliant a career, had already at least one foot in the next age— the era in which America would spend a good part of its energies on two great problems bequeathed to it by the nineteenth-century coming-of-age: how to reconcile industrial concentration with democracy and how to harness democracy with world power.

III

First Captain

"This institution gave me not only a standard for my daily conduct among men, but it endowed me with a military heritage of honor and self-sacrifice."

S O M E W H E R E in the course of growing up the idea of becoming a soldier occurred to George Marshall. At some point he considered the idea more or less seriously, though it is impossible to guess—and he himself did not remember—when or how deeply he thought about it. In any case he got no encouragement. His father and mother were opposed.[1] Certainly the chances could not have seemed bright to achieve distinction in a professional army of twenty-five thousand, which was no longer needed to fight Indians and seemed to face only a penurious future as a dubious sort of constabulary.

The elder Marshall could see other objections. He thought it would be politically difficult, if not impossible, to get an appointment to West Point, the only sure road to an Army commission. He was a Democrat, locally prominent as a Democrat. Uniontown's representative, Ernest Acheson, was a Republican[2] and so were Pennsylvania's two senators, Boies Penrose and Matthew Quay. Even though the competitive examination system used by Mr. Acheson in selecting his nominees for the Military Academy seemed fair to so partisan an observer as the Democratic editor

39

of the *Genius of Liberty*,[3] Marshall was unwilling to risk a political rebuff. His reluctance was possibly reinforced by doubts that
George would do well in the competitive examinations. The boy
remained a poor or, at best, erratic student, and it was made clear
that the applicant, on the basis of tests administered by the
county superintendents of the congressional district (two of whom
were Democrats and two Republicans), would be selected with
special care.[4] For whatever reason, George Marshall never applied for West Point.[5]

The idea of attending the Virginia Military Institute was an
early one and does not seem to have been connected with
thoughts of a military career. In 1897 the Institute offered courses
in civil engineering, chemistry, and electrical engineering. Although students lived in barracks and followed a strict military
routine, the purpose was the inculcation of discipline and not
preparation for a military life. Indeed, graduation from VMI at
this time not only offered no assurance of a commission; it offered
little reasonable hope. In 1890 not more than ten VMI graduates
were on duty with the regular Army.[6]

The Institute's military traditions were more intimately linked
with the Confederate past. It seemed to many Southerners (and
even to some Northerners) to be the guardian of some of the
nobler traditions of the lost cause, and particularly the ideal of
pure, brave, and self-sacrificing manhood. So it seemed to Colonel Charles Marshall, a distant cousin, who had been Lee's aide.
George later believed that the colonel was mainly responsible for
persuading his father of the virtues of VMI. In Uniontown, VMI
had an enthusiastic supporter in James Hustead, whose son Ed
was one of George's companions. Hustead, commanding a detachment of Northern troops at the Battle of New Market, had
been so impressed with the gallantry of the contingent of cadets
who fought there that he pressed his own two sons to go to
VMI.[7] The older one, Albert, yielded but stuck it out for only
three years. Ed would not go at all. It was some solace to Captain
Hustead when Stuart Marshall decided to enroll and still more
when George came along later.[8] Stuart did well in the Institute's
chemistry course and on his graduation in 1894 took a job as
chemist in the main iron works at Dunbar.

The VMI road was thus prepared and there was apparently no pull in any other direction. But George Marshall believed that his own resolution was only hardened at last by an incident which affected him so strongly that sixty years later he recalled it with unique intensity of feeling. "When I was begging to go to VMI," he said, "I overheard Stuart talking to my mother; he was trying to persuade her not to let me go because he thought I would disgrace the family name. Well, that made more impression on me than all instructors, parental pressure, or anything else. I decided right then that I was going to wipe his eye." And, the general concluded with satisfaction, "I did finally get ahead of what my brother had done. That was the first time I had ever done that, and it was where I really learned my lesson. The urgency to succeed came from hearing that conversation; it had a psychological effect on my career."

His mind was made up but the means were still to be found. It is clear that sending George to college at all put a great strain on the family resources. To get him started, Mrs. Marshall at the last minute sold some land in Augusta.[9] The next year she sold a lot in Uniontown next to the Gilmores' on which she had hoped someday to build a house of her own.[10] Even so they had to scrape for the tuition. Mr. Marshall in the middle of the first year wrote the superintendent, General Scott Shipp, apologizing for "the grace taken" in sending his check; his own collections, he explained wryly, were "very slow under McKinley prosperity." [11]

On the other hand, there were no academic bars even high enough to bother an applicant with young George's poor scholastic record. The chief hurdle was an examination given personally by Superintendent Shipp, who cared more about an applicant's background than his academic achievement. One of Marshall's contemporaries, the son of a Confederate veteran, missed every question General Shipp asked but was nevertheless admitted after his father pledged to remove him at Christmastime if by that time he was not doing well. There is no record that George took any examination at all. He bore a great Virginia name (there were seven other Marshalls at VMI during the time he was there); his father had a solid local standing (the superintendent was always careful to address him as "Colonel"), and Stuart had made a satisfactory record. George's principal difficulty—once the tuition money was found—was a bout with typhoid fever that made him miss the opening of school by several days. On September 11 Mr. Marshall at last wrote Superintendent Shipp: "I send you my youngest and last. He is bright, full of life, and I believe will get along well." [12]

In the round, and omitting a number of uncomfortable details of four years in a school dedicated to the Spartan thesis of building men, it was a fair prognosis and, in fact, from a father, a considerable understatement. There was no doubt that George Marshall was bright, eager to get along well, and perhaps for the first time in his life placed in an environment that gave him confidence. When he arrived and made the long walk down along the parade ground toward the towered and crenelated yellow stucco barracks of VMI he was stopped by the notes of a bugle sounding assembly. Out onto the tree-lined ground strutted the adjutant and sergeant major and set the line on which the cadet battalion, already then in residence more than a week, would form for dress parade. The boy watching—he was still only sixteen, tall, gangling, shy—felt excited and happy. "They were very wonderful-looking figures to me." The next day he wrote his father that he was not homesick and thought he would like it.

Perhaps Superintendent Shipp found him with the excitement of that moment still bracing his shoulders for he wrote Mr. Marshall, who had worried lest the effects of the fever and "this intense weather with the little *et ceteras* at barracks may go hard with him on the drill grounds," that he had "just seen the cadet son and he already looks the soldier." [13]

General Shipp set a high value on the look of a soldier. A small brusque man with a goatee and a stern and rigid manner that had won him the nickname of "Old Billy," he was then fifty-eight and had been commandant of cadets for twenty-seven years before succeeding General Francis H. Smith, the Institute's first superintendent, in 1890.[14] For General Shipp, unbending and austere in his own life, the primary goal of the Institute was not so much to train officers, chemists, or engineers as to teach discipline. He was himself a soldier who had led the "Baby Corps" into the battle at New Market and had been wounded there. But he prized the soldierly life rather as a builder of men. In his report of 1901 he noted that well-regulated school life leads "to habits of obedience, self-denial, and self-restraint: to respect for lawful authority, and to that self-respect which the consciousness of duty well done carries with it." Under his watchful eye, drills, parades, inspections, and formations dominated the school routine for the two hundred and twenty-one cadets. The academic year lasted from early September until almost the end of June. Classes did not meet on Christmas Day, New Year's, Washington's Birthday, and the anniversary of the New Market battle, and there were no Christmas vacations. Students were excused at that time only by special dispensation of the superintendent.[15] The school week ended at one o'clock on Saturdays. Cadets with no penalty tours to walk off were then allowed two hours in uptown Lexington, a few blocks away. On Sundays they marched to church. Afterward they were allowed to go to the back country, but not to Lexington. They had to be back for evening parade.[16]

Room 88, to which Marshall was assigned with three other cadets, was about twenty-one by seventeen feet and contained four wire-spring cots, straight chairs, a table, a wardrobe, and a washstand on which, during the first winter, the water often froze in the basin. Before the end of Marshall's first year, central heating and inside toilets were installed, but water still had to be brought in buckets from outside hydrants. "Rats" (new cadets—fourth classmen) were commanded by upper classmen to sleep with the large double windows open wide in all seasons. Blankets strapped to the cots against night winds might be covered with snow in the morning.[17]

If not at his first meal, then at his second or third, Marshall met "growlie"—a hash of various and indescribable elements that for years was the mainstay of the VMI menu. The other staple, bread, could be tough enough to be thrown—and sometimes was. "The mess," said the General, reminiscing across a span of sixty years, "was a pretty stern affair."

The new cadet was not to find living conditions fun at VMI, nor did he pretend afterward that they had been. He was fortunate, however, in having as one roommate Leonard Nicholson, a boy of imperturbable good humor and generosity, who with his brother Yorke had inherited the *New Orleans Picayune*. Nick, with whom he lived his whole four years, provided a refuge and a release from the rigors of the Institute. This was perhaps especially important for Marshall, who had no taste for social activities and little pocket money to spend on them anyway. His allowance for the first three years was five dollars a month, and he handed this on to Nick to dole out to him.[18]

To his fellow cadets, Marshall at first seems to have been distinguished chiefly by the Pittsburgh twang in his speech and by his aloofness. These, together with the fact that his room was on the stoop next to those occupied by third classmen, may have accounted for the earliest and most serious incident of the hazing which he and his fellow "Rats" had to endure despite stern Institute rules against it.

He had been in residence only two or three weeks when one evening he was required to squat over a naked bayonet as a test of endurance. Still weak from typhoid, his endurance proved slight. He slipped. The bayonet gashed his buttock. By a narrow margin, he escaped serious injury; the wound at most may have caused him to miss drill for several days. How Marshall explained that disability is not recorded. He certainly said nothing of the real cause.[19]

Toward hazing as toward other trials of cadet life, Marshall took a characteristically stoical attitude that set him apart from many—perhaps most—of his fellows. As he remarked mildly afterward, "I think I was more philosophical about this sort of thing than a great many boys. It was part of the business and the only thing to do was to accept it as best you could."

Years later he came back to VMI to be honored by having an arch named after him. In a speech at his class dinner on this occasion he recalled that he had been hazed throughout his four years for his Yankee accent and remarked in good humor, but with an edge, that while they were nearly all Southerners and had "pretty much kept the pressure on me on account of my northern accent and all, I happened to be the one and the only one there who had an arch named for him down at VMI." [20] It does not appear that he was crowing over his classmates so much as boasting of a defect that he had lived down. Of his unfortunate accent he would later remark that "it improved a little bit" after he got married.

Hazing, chivvying, discomforts, were "part of the business" to be borne. Other parts caught his imagination. The excitement of his first glimpse of military ceremony on the parade ground stayed with him, widened and deepened with familiarity. VMI at this time was saturated with recent and heroic memories of the Civil War. "Stonewall" Jackson had been an instructor there and had left his teaching on the outbreak of war for a brief but brilliant career in battle. On the day of Chancellorsville, where he was mortally wounded, he had seen so many former cadets in the line that he boasted "the Institute will be heard from today." When he died his body was brought back to VMI to lie in state in his old classroom before burial in the Lexington cemetery. His fabled marches, his tragic death, as well as his eccentricities, were already legend in Marshall's time. Jackson Memorial Hall at VMI was dedicated, although not completed, three months before Marshall's arrival, crowning the long struggle of former Superintendent Smith to restore the Institute after it was burned by General Hunter during his raid on Lexington in 1864. Scars on the barracks walls from Hunter's cannon remained as a tangible reminder of the war.[21]

Adjoining the VMI parade ground to the west was the campus of Washington and Lee University, of which General Lee was president after the Civil War.[22] The Lee Chapel, a few hundred yards from the limits of VMI, held his remains and was at least as much a shrine for the cadets as for the university students. For Marshall, both Jackson and Lee were inspiring figures—both great and austere generals, the one an infantry commander of fanatic drive, the other, a soldier-statesman whose brilliance in war was capped by his demonstration in peace of how a general could live honorably and constructively in defeat.

In Marshall's day the VMI college catalogue listed all graduates and distinguished with heavy black type those who had fallen fighting for the Confederacy. On May 15 a formation was held each year to commemorate the battle of New Market, in which ten cadets were killed and forty-four wounded. As the name of each fallen cadet was called, a first classman would step forward, salute, and reply, "Died on the field of honor." Five of those who died at New Market were buried "in a wooded dell" on VMI grounds. And every living cadet knew the story of their sacrifice, how two hundred and forty-one of them, under six officers, marched to reinforce the fifteen hundred men of General J. D. Imboden opposing the drive of General Franz Sigel up the Shenandoah Valley, and how when the flank of the Union forces was turned at New Market, they charged the retreating enemy to their front from the wheatfield north of Bushong Orchard to the Pike Bridge over the Shenandoah. They were credited with having taken up to one hundred prisoners, and at an average age of eighteen—some were only fifteen—they showed the stuff of which great legends of courage are made.[23]

There were at VMI in 1897 still living reminders of the war— General Shipp was one—veterans for whom the lost cause still stirred hot blood. To the Yankee from Uniontown some of the speeches at VMI ceremonies sounded shockingly close to treason.

The past also bred sentiment. "In the archway, the sally port we called it, there was an old fellow with a scraggly beard—so sunburned and dark he looked like a colored man. He sat there and sold nuts and things like that which he had collected up on the mountain. Some one of the cadet officers (once) ordered the old man out of the archway. He was sent for by General Shipp and in the general's very ponderous voice . . . he was informed that the man was a veteran of the Confederate Army, the Confederate Cavalry, with a very fine record, and he could sit in that arch till he died."

Marshall absorbed the lore of history and soldiering and profited by the discipline. "What I learned at VMI," he said later, "was self-control, discipline, so that it was ground in. I learned also the problem of managing men." But he never thought much of the academic instruction. Though he improved steadily during his four years, he remained somewhere in the middle of his class in most subjects and could not afterward remember having liked any of them. Some contemporaries say that they had to tutor him; others that he always excelled in military subjects. Marshall admitted later that as a mediocre student he had no right to criticize the curriculum but he always regretted his lack of training in how to express himself in writing and speaking, the ineffective instruction in foreign languages (he considered the time spent there on French and German almost completely wasted), and the total lack of courses in history and the social sciences which would have better prepared him for understanding national and international problems. Yet one thing he learned well—the art of leadership. At Finals in the spring of 1898, when the names of cadet officers for the following year were read out, George Marshall led the list as first corporal. When he came home that first summer, he seemed taller, heavier, less awkward. He walked erect and proud in his cadet uniform. He was growing up.

So was the nation. The year 1898 saw America at war with Spain and at the beginning of new world responsibilities. Cuba, in whose fortunes we had shown a lively interest for almost a century, had gained our sympathies in a bitter civil war which had broken out in 1895. The repressive measures of Governor General Valeriano Weyler, appointed early in 1896, intensified the struggle and stirred American demands for intervention. Public resentment, fanned by sensational newspaper reports, reached a climax in February 1898, after the sinking of the U.S.S. *Maine* in Havana harbor. President William McKinley, who had been pursuing the moderate policy favored by many of his supporters, now demanded self-government for Cuba. When the Spanish government delayed full acceptance of his requirements, he asked Congress to act. On April 25 the two houses declared that a state of war existed.

Cadets at VMI were able to follow the exciting developments in Lexington's weeklies. One of them, the *Rockbridge County News*, responded to the announcement of the sinking of the *Maine* with an appeal for calm. In the days which followed, the editor reminded his readers that the South knew the heavy costs of war and reprinted former Confederate General Wade Hampton's suggestion that if conflict came the North should be allowed to fight it. A local correspondent noted that if a draft law were imposed a number of the county residents would head for "caves and bomb-proofs" in order to escape the horrors of yellow fever in Cuba.[24] The cadets were somewhat more enthusiastic.

In February 1898 the VMI Dialectic Society chose as its debate topic: "Resolved that war alone will efface the national insults inflicted by Spain on the United States." [25] When Congress announced that a state of war existed the cadets unanimously voted to offer "their services to the government to fight for their country." Adopted at a mass meeting at the Cadet Society Hall on the evening of April 27, the offer was formally conveyed to the Secretary of War, to the Governor of Virginia, and to General Fitzhugh Lee, former Confederate officer who was now consul general in Havana.[26] More to the point, Superintendent Shipp had already told Virginia's governor that the Institute would assist in organizing and training volunteers at Camp Lee. VMI's commandant left for the camp not long afterward.

George Marshall, in voting with his fellow cadets for service against Spain, did not foresee the extent to which the war with Spain and the attendant occupation of the Philippines would affect his own career and the future of the United States. Dewey's destruction of the Spanish fleet at Manila Bay less than a week after the outbreak of war and the speedy, though badly handled, campaign to rid Cuba of Spanish rule announced to the world that the United States had fully reached the status of a great power and raised the question of what disposition this former non-colonial power would make of Spain's conquered provinces.

After word of Dewey's victory, Major General Wesley Merritt was dispatched to the Philippines with a force of regulars and volunteers. His orders were to complete the reduction of Spanish power and administer the Islands for the United States, with respect for the rights of the natives. There was no mention of a native government. General Merritt arrived in Manila at the end of July when the city had already been under close siege for ten weeks by the Insurrectos under Emilio Aguinaldo. The Spanish commander had refused demands to surrender only because he still dreamed of getting reinforcements from home. When that dream faded the Spaniards saw their next best hope of protecting the city and themselves from Philippine vengeance in a deal with the Americans. An American attack was arranged on August 13. Aguinaldo was ordered to stay out of the city. He decided to obey in the hope that the independent government he had declared might still be recognized by the United States. After a sham battle the Spaniards gratefully turned over Manila to United States troops. By a special irony this battle, unnecessary and contrived, took place a day after the armistice with Spain had been signed, ending the "splendid little war."

Among the volunteers sent to Manila with General Merritt was the 10th Pennsylvania Regiment, reputed to be one of the best of the National Guard regiments. And with them of course went Company C from Uniontown. In the months following, Marshall was brought close to the war by reports of casualties or of heroic action by men whom he knew. Besides, three recent VMI graduates, known to Marshall, were off to war with commissions in the volunteers: R. C. Marshall and James Taylor of the class of '98 and Arthur M. Shipp, class of '97, son of the superintendent. A classmate of Stuart Marshall's, Charles E. Kilbourne, later superintendent of VMI, won the Medal of Honor as a captain of the volunteers in the Philippines.[27]

When Marshall returned to VMI in September, hostilities had been halted by the August 12 armistice, although peace would not be signed until December and would be followed by prolonged bitter fighting in the Philippines. The Army meanwhile was much in the news as the nation learned of scandalous blundering in the conduct of the war. Two revelations were particularly shocking: the filthy, disease-ridden conditions of the American camps at Santiago during the siege and the issuance of inedible rations. Even more serious from the standpoint of national preparedness was the scene of utter confusion at Tampa where the Cuban expeditionary force was assembled. The troops came dressed in winter uniforms for tropical duty. No one knew enough about the enemy or the terrain of Cuba to have any precise idea of what their mission would be. The capacity of the ships to transport them had been grossly overestimated. Supplies poured into Tampa in three hundred freight cars and parked along miles of siding without bills of lading. To equip and load their units, officers had personally to find the supplies and in many cases commandeer the ships. While the press had a field day over "embalmed beef," it was the chaos in Tampa that impressed those seriously concerned with the future of the Army, including Marshall, who would study the failure and never forget it.

In September, Major General Nelson Miles returned from Puerto Rico and handed the press a statement of sensational charges against the War Department. Demands for investigation of Secretary of War Russell Alger's conduct of his department became irresistible. The Dodge Commission appointed in September reported its findings in eight volumes. It found not a clear-cut, easy-to-understand indictment against Secretary Alger, but abundant evidence of the need for thorough reorganization of the Army and the War Department. As Marshall himself was to conclude after his later study of the unpreparedness, "It wasn't so much wrong, in a sense, as it was lacking. . . . Roosevelt and Wood and the Rough Riders sort of highlighted the affair and took the painfulness out of the situation [at Tampa]. But there [was practically nothing] in the way of preparation as the troops [were] gotten together from the western posts, company by company, assembled there almost for the first time since the Civil War. . . . It was a sorry dilemma and only the gallantry . . . and the initiative of the men and leaders and the extreme weakness of the Spanish Army . . . made it possible to go through with the early fighting . . . without some great catastrophe befalling us." So clear to those who studied it, the lesson would be learned only slowly and painfully by the nation after many blunders and risks of disaster.

In the same month that the Dodge Commission report was published, news arrived of insurrection in the Philippines. It might have been expected. Indeed, in retrospect it looked as though the United States worked hard to bring it on. Nevertheless the outbreak came as a shock even to imperialists. From the moment the country had known of Dewey's victory at Manila, American leaders had worried over our future policy regarding the Philippines. That our decision might mark a grave turning point in the nation's history was clear to many Americans at the time—to anti-imperialists of both parties who disliked the idea of conquest and feared the implications of American involvement in the Pacific; to Democrats who hoped for an issue to counter McKinley prosperity in the next presidential election; and to the

President who moved slowly under the pressure of his more militant advisers and of the march of events abroad toward a commitment far beyond his original crusade to liberate Cuba.

The immediate American reaction had been to stay out of these little-known and far-off islands, but a small group of expansionists, which included Theodore Roosevelt and Senator Henry Cabot Lodge, influenced by the "big navy" teachings of Captain Alfred Thayer Mahan and by publicists preaching the special destiny of Anglo-Saxons for imperial rule, first urged that we take and hold the city of Manila and then added the whole of the Philippines to the list.

The expansionists of 1898 differed from their ancestors who had pushed to the shores of the Gulf of Mexico and of the Pacific in insisting on island bases as the gateway to Far Eastern trade and on accepting the tutelage of a backward people not ready for self-government. It was this talk of empire, long accepted in Europe's capitals but long deprecated here, which disturbed the traditionalists. McKinley's final decision to demand the whole of the Philippines brought a stirring national debate on the issue of imperialism in which the desire to "civilize" the Filipinos and to prevent another major power from taking the Islands equaled and perhaps outweighed our hopes of gaining economic benefits from the Islands. The ultimate results were the expenditure of more men and money to pacify the Philippines than we had spent on the war with Spain, and the acquisition of military and naval outposts on the opposite side of the world.

Marshall, whose career was to be so intimately involved in his country's altered course toward world power, continued to prepare in his own way. His second year at VMI brought scant improvement in his grades but resulted in his appointment among the first sergeants for the year following. Again he stood first on the list.

Midway in this year he and his fellow cadets got a lesson in what "Old Billy" meant by soldierly discipline. On New Year's Eve, 1898, the entire first class (seniors), with the exception of the first captain who was officer of the day, barricaded themselves on top of the barracks and set off fireworks in defiance of the superintendent's specific orders. They apparently took for granted that "Old Billy" could not punish the whole class. They underestimated him. He could and he did. He ordered every one of them put under arrest at once and shortly thereafter expelled them from school. The expulsion lasted until almost the end of the month. Then, having made his point, he allowed them to return but stripped them of their rank for three months, promoted former subordinates over their heads, took away their first-class privileges, and delayed the granting of their diplomas until the beginning of the following fall term.[28]

That summer (1899) Marshall got a job as a rodman for a surveyor who was mapping the area around Uniontown for the United States Geological Survey. In later years he remembered best the summer dreaminess of an eighteen-year-old on a job whose ultimate relevance to his Army career must have seemed more remote than the woods and mountains in which he had always felt at home. He recalled that time and again the man behind the transit had to remind him to pay attention and hold the rod so that it could be read.

"On one of these occasions I sought an excuse, as a boy always does, and told him I was looking at a bird on the fence. He stopped and, in a scathing tone, said, 'What about that bird on the fence?' Without any idea of what I was doing, I walked over to the fence and picked up a swallow. It wasn't wounded. Yet it didn't fly and I picked it up. That paralyzed my surveyor friend. When I turned the swallow loose and it flew off, he thought I had some mysterious quality which allowed me to handle birds." In fact, whatever magic there was served Marshall just that once. In a long life no other bird ever sat still for him.

The surveying job lasted only two months and Marshall was back in Uniontown at the end of summer in time to join the town's tumultuous welcome for the men of Company C returning from the war. They had given a good account of themselves in fighting both against the Spanish and against the Insurrectos. When their train brought them to Uniontown from Pittsburgh, where their regiment had been received by the President, every whistle and church bell in town blew and rang for five minutes in a pandemonium of local pride.

George Marshall watched with an excitement as great as anyone's as the troops paraded down Main Street, painted red, white, and blue for the occasion and hung with more flags than any local inhabitant had ever seen before. Through arches—one made of a hundred electric lights, another built of coal—the returning heroes and their official escort marched to the fairgrounds. There, perhaps twenty thousand of their fellow citizens gathered to cheer.[29]

Afterward Marshall was to feel that this was his "first great emotional reaction" and that it had "a determining effect on my choice of profession." He was stirred not only by the panoply of parade and visions of glory but by the thought of far-off places suddenly brought close. Neighbors had fought and some had died in Manila, which until then had been just the name for a kind of rope.[30] He had, in fact, though he did not know it then, a glimpse of the new dimensions of twentieth-century America and an intimation of his own career in it. Uniontown cheered and made every member of Company C a hero who "had but to command and his desires were gratified. . . . It was a grand American small-town demonstration of pride in its young men and of wholesome enthusiasm over their achievements. Years later most of us realized that it was much more than that. It reflected the introduction of America into the affairs of the world beyond the seas." [31]

In his third year at VMI, Marshall chose the civil engineering course and did notably better in his standings. He finished nineteenth in his class of forty-seven. At the Final Ball in June, George led the Ring figure with Miss Kate Fauntleroy of Staunton. His mother came down from Uniontown to be one of the chaperones.

Best of all, he won the prize he coveted most and had worked for hardest. By solid recommendation of his tactical officers, and the four cadet captains, the adjutant, and the quartermaster, he was named first captain for his final year. "I tried very hard," he said afterward. "I was very exacting and very exact in all my military duties as I gradually developed from the mild authority—almost none—exercised by the corporal to the pronounced authority of the first sergeant. As first sergeant, I fell the company in, called the roll, kept tabs on it, and marched the detail to guard mount every morning." He did it all so well, with an impressively military bearing and a voice which could be heard the length of the parade ground, that when the end of the term came apparently no one had any doubt that George Marshall had earned the top rank of cadet command.

He had also developed an austerity and coolness of manner that characterized him thereafter. In later years he corresponded with and sometimes visited Taylor Carter, Banks Hudson, Erskine Miller, Charles S. Roller, Morgan Hudgins, Edward Ryland, and a few other members of his class, but at that time, except for his roommates, Nicholson and Philip B ("Buster") Peyton, who joined him and Nick in their second year, he had no intimate friends at the Institute. He wished above all else to command. He found that he had the power to command but that to keep it he could not let himself get too close to those who had to obey.

The cadets found ways to test the first captain's mettle. He was in charge of the corps during meals and sat at a separate table with his staff—Battalion Staff Adjutant Taylor Carter, Quartermaster Charles S. Roller, and Sergeant Major Murray Innes. One evening, perhaps by chance or perhaps by design, "there was complete silence while they were eating and that attracted some fellow's attention." So he shushed, making the silence deliberate and official, "and they all settled down to see what I was going to do. Recently there had been a famous case up at West Point of giving 'a silence' to a tactical officer" (an act mutinous in intent, if not in form, which became the subject of a congressional investigation). Marshall recognized the challenge and made up his mind. He noted that the cadets had just begun to eat their strawberries —a new and rare dessert. He got up, "called them to attention and marched them out of the mess hall when the strawberries were only about a third eaten." So the reflexes of discipline were used to put down the murmurs of rebellion. Marshall emerged master of the situation, secure in the admiration and respect of his fellows. The cadets, he noted later, "would judge you severely if you proved to be a slack performer in the business of your military duties." He did not expect to be loved for it.

In his last year Marshall went out for football. He had played

some football and baseball in Uniontown and perhaps would have
tried out at VMI sooner had he not promised his mother to re-
frain. Mrs. Marshall was afraid that he might do serious injury
to his right elbow, which had been partly dislocated in play and
never properly healed.[32] The boy was also very light; he weighed
only a hundred and forty-five pounds when on the VMI squad.
Released from his promise in his third year, he had played a little
before an outbreak of typhoid fever forced the closing of the
Institute for six weeks, washing out the football season. In the
1900 season his tackling helped VMI tie the University of Virginia, and he starred in the annual Thanksgiving Day game
against VMI's chief rival, the Virginia Polytechnic Institute. The
Rockbridge County News, in crowing over VMI's 5-0 victory,
noted that "the tackling of G. Marshall in backing up the interference was of the highest order." [33]

It was a year of blossoming because it was a year of success. The
boy who wished all his life to be first in everything was now first
in the soldierly ways that to him counted most. He was also
suddenly, completely, in love.

She was Elizabeth Carter Coles, called "Lily." She lived with
her widowed mother in her Grandfather Pendleton's house near
the Limit Gates of the Institute. Despite this propinquity and
the fact that Lily had dated Marshall's brother Stuart years before, George did not meet her until early in his last year, possibly
because he had more freedom then or possibly because he had
more confidence. It came about as a kind of romantic accident.
One evening Marshall was passing her house and heard her
playing the piano. He stopped, astonished and entranced to hear
"some of the airs my mother had played to which I had become
devoted." He thought she played beautifully. Later he said Lily
was "the finest amateur pianist I have ever heard." Indeed he was
so impressed that he brought one or two of his cadet friends back
on other evenings to stand outside the house and listen with him.
On one such occasion the door was opened and the shy young
man was invited in.

Lily was brown-eyed, titian-haired, fair of skin—by common
consent a beauty. Older than Marshall—four years at least—she
was immediately attracted to him and he to her. She had the repu-

tation of being something of a flirt. Popular with young men, she drew sharp comment from some of the girls who knew her. Older women have recalled her as gracious. Marshall found her vivacious, witty, and altogether fascinating. It was said in Lexington that when she first saw the tall young first captain she declared, "I intend to marry him." In any case, within a few weeks of their first meeting they were seeing as much as possible of each other.

In time he was even to forgive her descent from the first families of Virginia, though he commented that Lily's family was not impressed by his forebears and sniffed at his Pennsylvania birthplace. Lily's father, Dr. Walter Coles, was the great-grandson of Colonel John Coles, who had given refuge on his great estate at Enniscorthy to Thomas Jefferson during the Revolution.[34] John's brother Isaac had been a member of the first United States Congress. Lily's mother, Elizabeth Childs Pendleton, was the daughter of Colonel Edmund Pendleton, a member of the first class to have been graduated at VMI in 1842.[35] He was the namesake of that Edmund Pendleton, nephew of Lily's great-great-grandfather, who was a member of the Continental Congress and governor of Virginia[36] at the time of the Declaration of Independence. It was quite enough, combined with native charm, to make Lily one of the leading belles of Lexington society, even though her mother had apparently very little money.

The regimen at VMI was not designed for a young man in love, and even the comparative privileges of a first classman who was first captain to boot did not provide nearly enough liberty. To be sure, Lily was close by: Marshall could see her often, driving her "little horse and Stanhope trap" along the parade ground, sitting up on the slightly raised seat holding her whip with the long lash. He loved, when he could, to drive with her. But that was not often enough. And so the austere young first captain took to "running the block" or, in plain terms, ducking out of the Institute after hours. The maneuver was apparently not too difficult, but the penalty for being caught would certainly have been the loss of his cadet rank and possibly even expulsion. His only defense, when questioned years later, was, "I was much in love." He was not caught, and under Lily's spell he led a much fuller social life in his last year than before. He was vice-president of the Final Ball, although Lily's health prevented her from dancing, and at graduation he was initiated, along with a number of his classmates, into Kappa Alpha fraternity.[37]

At graduation the first captain received none of the academic honors. His quartermaster, "Chief" Roller, gave the class address. St. Julian Ravenal Marshall (no close relation) was picked as the year's most distinguished graduate. George was not one of the six top men to receive the baccalaureate degree, but had to be content with the ordinary degree of Graduate, such as was also awarded at West Point at this time.

Yet he had reason to be proud. With steady hard work he had brought up his standing, and in his major field, civil engineering, finished fifth. He was eighth in military science. More important, he had taken firm hold of himself and his career. "Ambition," he said later, "had set in." But it would be more accurate to say that ambition had hit upon an appropriate goal, or that the young man, driven from his earliest days by the passion to excel, had found in himself as a cadet an excellence that pleased him.

Second Lieutenant

"Many of our graduates hold commissions in the Army. I am sure Mr. Marshall is fully the equal of the best."
—General Scott Shipp to President William McKinley, February 14, 1901.

MARSHALL had applied himself diligently at VMI and acquired focus, skill, and self-confidence. But to become a general he needed in addition the chance to become a second lieutenant. That chance he got most obviously by graduating at just the right juncture, when the Army, after long neglect, was being enlarged and reorganized.

Americans probably do not dislike military service more than other people but they have a historically ingrained and generally healthy distaste for large standing armies as well as an aversion to paying for them in peacetime. The facts of geography and fortunes of history, reinforced by democratic theory, permitted America to develop a tradition of waging war with volunteers quickly raised to fight and as quickly disbanded afterward. Between wars a small professional army was maintained, initially to fight Indians, put down civil disorders, and provide a cadre of trained leaders and men in case of future troubles. In principle the system was not so bad, but in practice Congress tended to treat the Army with neglect rather than wise frugality. The result, by the end of the nineteenth century, was a military organization that could not play even the minimum role that democratic theory assigned it.

The chaotic blundering of the Spanish-American War revealed the inadequacy of the professional Army as an instrument of war. But though the blunders raised cries for the scalps of those thought to be responsible they brought no public demand for essential reform.

For the duration of the war Congress had raised the Army's authorized strength from 28,747 to 62,597 and permitted the President to call up more than 200,000 volunteers.[1] After the peace all the regulars in excess of the prewar establishment were by law to be mustered out. But before the Senate could be brought to ratify the treaty the Philippine Insurrection broke out. Congress then had in effect to extend the emergency, and a new law authorized the retention of 65,000 regulars and recruitment of 35,000 volunteers for service not beyond July 1, 1901.[2]

When 1901 arrived the insurrection showed no signs of abating, and Congress had again to face the politically unpleasant fact that to win and hold overseas possessions required an army sufficient to the task. Another stopgap measure might have served. In fact Congress now faced—or partly faced—the longer-range military needs. That it did so may be credited at least in part to the new Secretary of War.

Alger in 1899 had at last to resign. It is one of the fortunate accidents of history that he was replaced by a New York corporation lawyer noted in the legal profession and strong in the Republican party but with no special background for the job. McKinley picked Elihu Root to be Secretary of War, and Elihu Root accepted the appointment, under the delusion that the War Department was to be preoccupied with the problems of administering America's new colonies. In such guise did the Army find its first civilian chief since Stanton who attempted to learn its problems and who had the courage and skill, as well as the presidential backing, to solve them.[3]

Alger had plainly deserved his reputation for bungling and

complacence. But he was not the prime author of his own and the nation's misfortune. He inherited a military organization that the ablest chief could not have made to work in war. The Army at this time had a dual directorate: the commanding general, who by law was responsible directly to the President for military operations and discipline; and the Secretary of War, who was charged with supply, recruitment, and fiscal management and who exercised that control through the War Department bureaus. There were ten bureaus, the most powerful being those of the Adjutant General and the Inspector General. Bureau chiefs were permanently assigned to their jobs in Washington under conditions that encouraged each to build an autonomous empire, protected by political influence, remote from the forces in the field and jealously fenced against any encroachment by rival bureaus. They were not answerable to the commanding general, and he was not answerable to the Secretary of War. The commanding general, who was ordinarily the biggest military name of his day, had unlimited power to meddle but almost no power to command. The ten little unco-ordinated bureau kings had vast capacities to frustrate one another but almost none to direct the establishment. No one was charged with planning for war and no one could direct it when it came.[4]

An obvious answer, often put forward since Civil War times, was the general staff system. Abolish the commanding general, who had nothing to command; establish instead a military executive, under the President and Secretary of War, with a general staff to collect information and see that his decisions were carried out; place under him the bureaus, with their functions reduced to administration.

Secretary Root, after long study, accepted the general staff idea and with the devoted assistance of Adjutant General Henry C. Corbin and his assistant, Major William H. Carter, set out to overcome the considerable political obstacles that had frustrated his predecessors. Step by step he drew the blueprint of the modern military establishment in which George Marshall was to rise to eminence.[5]

In his first report at the end of 1899, Root recommended reorganization and noted the need for public education, which he himself was to push relentlessly for more than three years. The following February he took the first step. Finding it possible to establish an Army War College without congressional approval, he appointed a board to organize it. The War College, which opened in Washington in November 1901, was to serve not only for the advanced education of Army officers but as a co-ordinating agency "through which all means of professional military information shall be at any one time at the disposal of the War Department." [6]

Early in 1900 Root submitted to Congress a bill, approved in February 1901, to enlarge the Army to a maximum of a hundred thousand, which was to be maintained until Congress should vote otherwise. The President was allowed to exceed the maximum when men were being recruited for service in the overseas possessions.[7] The bill provided for thirty infantry regiments (one of which was the 30th, in which Marshall was to serve), fifteen cavalry regiments, and an artillery corps. Each regiment was reorganized to include three battalions of four companies each—the basic combat structure that persisted through World War II. The bill also took one small cut at the underbrush in the way of a general staff: it provided that officers assigned to staff positions henceforth would serve tours of duty of four years and not be eligible for reappointments until they had spent at least two years with the line regiments in which they were commissioned.[8] It was an edict of celibacy for the bureaus; the incumbents were safe but they were to have no bureaucratic heirs.

In 1902 Root sent to Congress the General Staff bill, which abolished the post of commanding general, established the position of Chief of Staff, authorized a general staff under him of forty-four officers, and gave him supervision over the bureaus (Adjutant General, Inspector General, Judge Advocate, Quartermaster, Subsistence, Medical, Paymaster, Ordnance, Corps of Engineers, and Signal Corps). Though Congress balked in 1902, the next year (February 1903) it passed the bill. The importance of that Act of 1903 for the future of the Army and for the fate of this nation can hardly be exaggerated. Although it was a long time before the old bureaucracy was forced to yield and the reforming principle became effective in practice, the act laid the groundwork for a military organization.

Hardly less significant than Root's reorganization of the War

Department was his inauguration of a system of Army education designed primarily to train officers for the increased responsibilities which the nation's enlarged commitments would put upon them and which the reformed organization would permit them to accept. At almost every Army post throughout the country he ordered a prescribed training course for junior officers, aimed particularly at officers commissioned from the ranks during the war and those taken in after the February 1901 act had permanently doubled the size of the Army. But Root also believed that even West Pointers might profit by continued "intellectual exercise." He wished, moreover, to discover the livelier minds among the officer corps fit for further training in higher command and staff work. These were to go on to special service schools for artillery, engineer, medical corps, and cavalry officers —schools which had functioned before the war but had atrophied. Now, by being placed in an educational hierarchy, they were for the first time made relevant to the officer's career and so very slowly they gained prestige and began to deserve it.

In 1902 Root reopened the old infantry and cavalry school at Fort Leavenworth, which had closed during the war. Within two years there was functioning there, besides a basic field command course, a small Army Staff College to begin special training of officers of the General Staff. Finishing school for the latter was to be the Army War College.[9]

Finally, in the Militia Act of 1903 (the Dick Bill), Root brought the citizen army into the educational system and imposed on it professional standards. Candidates for commissioning in the National Guard were required to pass federal examinations. Guard regiments were to be instructed by regular Army officers (George Marshall was one of the earliest and most successful of the instructors) and were to join regular troops in maneuvers. To qualified officers of the Guard the course at Leavenworth was to be open for advanced training.[10]

That the Army was thus reformed along lines to encourage and reward the true and devoted professional was critical for the ultimate success of George Marshall, but the fact that the Army was enlarged was what immediately counted. The Act of 1901 authorized an additional twelve hundred officers, at least one-fifth of whom were to be selected by examination at once and commissioned.[11] As soon as the terms of the pending bill were reported, Marshall pointed his course toward taking the examination. His parents remained opposed to his choice of a military career. But his father, obliged to recognize that George's "whole heart was in it," now put aside his own doubts and harnessed himself to his son's cause with remarkable devotion and drive. He wrote to Superintendent Shipp to ask whether the superintendent really felt sure George had "the qualifications so essential to the making of an officer that would be a credit to the Institute." [12] General Shipp was more than encouraging. George, he wrote, was "as well qualified for officer of infantry as any man who has been turned out here." He could assert "with complete confidence that if commissioned in the Army, young Marshall will in all respects, soon take his stand much above the average West Point graduate." [13]

What more could a father ask? Mr. Marshall, who boasted he had "many warm and influential friends in the administration," set out to pull all the strings he could.[14] The vigorous campaign he now launched on behalf of his son showed him in the light of a devoted, or at least devotedly ambitious, father. He thought of everything. He buttonholed everybody who could conceivably help. He fussed over details of tone and timing, fearful that the slightest slip might lose the cause.

Even before the final approval of the February 1901 bill, Mr. Marshall turned to a graduate of VMI who had the ear of the President, John S. Wise, and asked him to write personally to McKinley on George's behalf. The son of a former governor of Virginia, Wise was himself one of the cadets who had fought at New Market and the cousin of Henry Wise who had succeeded Shipp in command of the "Baby Corps." He was—luckily for the Democratic Mr. Marshall—a converted Democrat, having left the party after a factional fight in Virginia, and as a Republican had moved to New York, where he had organized support for McKinley in the 1896 convention.[15] With reason, therefore, to favor the ambitions of an able VMI cadet (especially one with the illustrious name of Marshall), and with claim on the President's gratitude, Wise sent a personal note to McKinley. "This boy's kinsman, the illustrious John Marshall," he wrote, "was a captain in the 11th Virginia . . . commanded by my great-grandfather in the Revolution, and the records fail to disclose since then one of the name who was either fool or coward. They are filled with instances of intelligent brave gentlemen of this name, and this boy bears it most worthily—I heartily commend him." [16]

Apparently he sent this to Mr. Marshall, who then wrote again to Superintendent Shipp to ask him for a similar note to the White House. This, he thought, "will have great weight—particularly as it comes from VMI,—the West Point of the South." He intended to present the letters "in person and do the talking for VMI." His purpose then was to take George with him to Washington to insure the proper backing.[17] He does not appear to have made the trip. Instead, he advised George to go by himself and provided him with letters of introduction.

In April young Marshall used the letters, along with one of his father's cards and a large measure of his own gumption. He saw Philander C. Knox, newly appointed Attorney General, whom he had never met, though Knox, a fellow Pennsylvanian, was a friend of his father's. He burst in on a reception to try to see John A. Hull of Iowa, chairman of the House Military Affairs Committee. Mrs. Hull took him upstairs to the congressman's den where the congressman was resting. Hull "took time to talk with me although he didn't promise anything much."

With characteristic drive and directness, Cadet Marshall went to the White House. "I had no appointment of any kind. The office was on the second floor. I think the President's bedroom, as I knew it in Mr. [Franklin] Roosevelt's day, must have been Mr. McKinley's office. The old colored man (the head usher) asked me if I had an appointment and I told him I didn't. He said I would never get in, that there wasn't any possibility. I sat there and watched people, some ten or fifteen, go in by appointment, stay ten minutes, and be excused. Finally a man and his daughter went in with this old colored man escorting them. I attached myself to the tail of the procession and gained the President's office. The old colored man frowned at me on his way out but I stood pat. After the people had met the President they also went out, leaving me standing there. Mr. McKinley in a very nice manner asked what I wanted and I stated my case. I don't recall what he said, but from that I think flowed my appointment or rather my authority to appear for examination."

One would like to confirm that history did indeed turn on that moment of charming brashness and informality. But unless McKinley, as a result of the interview, asked a certain Pennsylvanian to recommend his constituent, it seems unlikely. As soon as the bill enlarging the Army was approved in February, it became clear that quotas for applicants had been assigned to each state and that appointments for the examinations from Pennsylvania had to be approved by Senators Penrose and Quay, both noted for their party regularity in a partisan age. Perhaps the elder Marshall sent copies of the letters of Shipp and Wise to Quay or more likely had him approached by some Republican Uniontown friends. In any case, Quay in early February commended Marshall in a letter to Secretary Root. In April he wrote the Secretary of War "to recommend the appointment of George C. Marshall," the present "Captain of Cadets at the Virginia Military Institute," whose name, he noted, "was not upon the list handed in by Senator Penrose," but whose papers were on file. "He is a young man of excellent connections and marked ability," Quay wrote, putting first things first, "and I am assured will be an ornament to the service." [18]

The day after the letter was written the other Pennsylvania senator, Penrose, who was technically senior at this time, submitted a supplemental list of recommended candidates, noting that Quay had asked in particular for the consideration of three men, of whom one was George Marshall. In his list, arranged in order of political urgency, Marshall's name was eighth.[19] It was lever enough to win him a nomination among the twenty-three Pennsylvania candidates selected to be examined for commission. The selections were published on June 17 in time for the Lexington newspaper to announce it before Finals.[20]

Applicants were first instructed to appear in New York in early September before a board headed by Major General John R. Brooke, commander of the Eastern Department, but the examination was delayed by the death of President McKinley. Gen-

eral Brooke, as senior military officer in New York, was detailed
to head the military escort which accompanied the President's
body from Buffalo to Washington.[21] It was therefore late September before Marshall came to New York and put up at the Marie
Antoinette Hotel at 66th Street and Broadway, ready to take the
examinations, which were now set for the twenty-third on Governors Island. Still determined to leave as little as possible to
chance, he was fortified with a letter from a family friend, James
A. McGonigle, to Lieutenant Colonel C. A. Woodruff, a member
of the examining board. In New York he called on John Wise to
ask him to put in a good word with General Brooke. In good
humor, Wise wrote of the aspiring cadet that "General Shipp
regards him as one of the fittest pieces of food for gunpowder
turned out by his mill for many years." [22]

For three days the applicants were put through a course of
academic hurdles which may have tried their nerves but were set
so low intellectually as to make one doubt the seriousness of the
exercise.[23] Marshall emerged with a final average of 84.8 per cent
—one of the highest scores. In it was included a mark of 100 for
physique and another 100 for moral character and antecedents.
His other grades, considering the elementary level of the questions, tend to confirm his own strictures on the defects of his formal academic education. While he scored 89 in history, in which
he had partly educated himself, he could get only 75 in English
grammar, 65 in geography, and 86 in mathematics, where his
success in simple arithmetic, algebra, and geometry outweighed
a 70 in trigonometry and a 44 in logarithms. It is notable that
nothing in the examination demanded more than high-school
training with the possible exception of a few problems in trigonometry and logarithms and the paper on international law (on
which he had a mark of 42).[24]

After the examination Marshall went to Danville, Virginia.
During the summer he had hedged his bet on a commission by
accepting an appointment as commandant and instructor at the
Danville Military Institute (a military elementary and prep
school). His duties there—which included teaching arithmetic,
algebra, history, English, drill regulations, and discipline—kept
him busy if not absorbed while the weeks passed and he heard

nothing from the examinations.[25] His father applied to the faithful John Wise, who made inquiries at the War Department. The explanation was simple enough: Marshall had, of course, passed—high enough, indeed, to be recommended for the artillery, his first choice—but the board had decided to delay his commissioning until after December 31 when he would become twenty-one. Somehow someone had just neglected to let him know.[26]

The news nevertheless made a "very acceptable Christmas present," as he wrote General Shipp. The young applicant promptly resigned as general factotum at Danville. He spent Christmas at Lexington and talked about the future with Lily. Now that he was practically a second lieutenant they could get married, and they intended to—as soon as possible.[27]

Indeed, all the dilatoriness and uncertainties of the past months were suddenly swept away and Marshall's career moved with a breathless rush. On January 4, 1902, orders were issued making him a second lieutenant with date of rank from the approval of the enabling act, February 2, 1901. The appointment was confirmed on January 13 and Lieutenant Marshall was assigned to the 30th Infantry, stationed in the Philippines.[28] Surprised at assignment to the infantry when he had asked for the artillery, he inquired and was told the artillery was not taking officers newly commissioned from civilian life. It might be possible to change places later on with an artillery officer who might prefer assignment with the infantry. Marshall swallowed the slight disappointment and soon no longer felt it. The exchange was never made and the general's destiny continued along its charted course.[29]

In Uniontown, Marshall received his commission on February 3 and took his oath at once before a notary public. Five days later he had orders to report to Fort Myer, thence to go immediately to Columbus Barracks, Ohio, to accompany recruits to San Francisco, where they would all take ship for the Philippines. He had until the thirteenth to check in. And before that date he had to get married.[30]

Arrangements were made in haste. He arrived in Lexington on the ninth. Mr. and Mrs. Marshall, Stuart and Marie, and his best friend, Andy, came the following day. Edmund Coles was on hand to give his sister in marriage. The wedding was to take place the evening of February 11 in Mrs. Coles' home on Letcher Avenue, where the young cadet had first been charmed by the music of Lily's piano heard through the windows on an autumn night.[31]

Though the bride was dressed in white and the ceremony performed by the pastor of the Episcopal Church, the Reverend R. J. McBryde, there was little formality in the gathering of family and friends. They say in Lexington that the guests and the bride and groom chatted a few moments in the parlor and then Lily turned to the young lieutenant and said, "Come on, George, let's get married."

Bride and groom the next morning took the train to Washington for a honeymoon they expected to last one day. They took a room at Washington's most fashionable hotel, the New Willard, recently built on the site of the first Hotel Willard, in which Lincoln had stayed before his first inaugural.[32] Soon after his arrival George walked the three blocks to the baroque old War Department building on Pennsylvania Avenue. There he reported to the office of the Adjutant General with his orders and word that he had just been married. Later that day an understanding officer extended for five days the date at which he had to report to Fort Myer just across the river. The letter was signed by Major Carter, who at that moment, with his chief, General Corbin, and Secretary Root, was embarking on the first and unsuccessful fight to get the general staff bill through Congress. Carter personally noted that in addition to a copy of amended orders to be sent to Fort Myer, a special copy was to be delivered to the young lieutenant at the Hotel Willard.[33]

Those five days of grace must have been filled with the exquisite pain of happiness under the sentence of time. They knew, of course, that they would have to part and that George would be gone two years or so. Even if wives had been permitted to accompany junior officers, Lily could not have gone. The Philippine Insurrection was over, but a lieutenant assigned to the Islands could expect rugged duty with troops under war conditions even if not actually in a state of war. Lily, moreover, was in poor health. She had a heart condition (mitral-regurgitation) which she believed had been brought on by excessive strain of social engagements, particularly a series of weddings of her friends in St. Louis, several years before Marshall met her. Although she was not in the ordinary sense an invalid, Lily's physical limitations were always to circumscribe her activities and to enforce when they were together a pattern of quiet domesticity to which Marshall in any event was not averse.

One would like to know what was in the heart and mind of the young lieutenant when February 18 arrived; his honeymoon was over, and he reported for duty across the river at Fort Myer. He had with extraordinary force of will and singleness of purpose fought for and won a wife and the start of a career. As the events would show he had chosen well, but he could have had no easy sense of success achieved or of a comfortable course ahead.

Lily went back to her mother's home in Lexington. George stayed five days at Fort Myer, three weeks at Fort Slocum, New York, to which he was sent instead of to Columbus Barracks, and then with seven other officers took a troop train west. On arrival in San Francisco, Marshall was quartered in the tented area at Tennessee Hollow in the Presidio while awaiting his ship. On April 12, 1902, he boarded the transport *Kilpatrick* for Manila.[34]

The Mettle of the Man

"There isn't anything much lower than a second lieutenant and I was about the junior second lieutenant in the Army at that time."

A YEAR before Marshall arrived in the Philippines the rebel leader, Aguinaldo, had been captured. He was persuaded to take an oath of loyalty to the United States and to urge his followers to yield. During the summer of 1901 some four thousand rebels actually did surrender. General Arthur MacArthur, then in command of United States forces, informed the War Department that the insurrection was over except for rebel holdouts on the island of Samar and in Batangas Province of Luzon, south of Manila. His army of about seventy thousand men was reduced to about forty-two thousand; the rest went home.[1] In July, William Howard Taft took charge of the conquered land as its first American civilian governor.

The rebellion was defeated but not ended. Taft's authority at first extended only to one-third of the provinces and about half the population. Elsewhere the natives were considered insufficiently pacified and remained for varying periods under military rule. On Luzon, General Miguel Malvar, cunning and intransigent, still had some five thousand guerrillas in Batangas and commanded what organized resistance remained. He directed at least one effective raid against the Americans before a punitive force under Brigadier General J. Franklin Bell, during the winter of 1901-1902, literally wiped out his forces by sweeping the province bare of food and natives. It was a bitter-end fight on both sides, attended by massacres, torture, and utter ruthlessness, until virtually all the warriors left were on one side. Malvar himself surrendered in April 1902, just four days after Marshall's ship left San Francisco.[2]

The chronology is important, for while the insurrection as a military problem had long since been solved and, by most people in America, put out of mind, the spilling of blood was still fresh in the Islands. In fact, peace was not officially proclaimed by President Theodore Roosevelt until July 4, 1902. Even after that guerrillas continued to raid and kill in remote areas. The American occupying army in the summer of 1902 still numbered thirty-four thousand, or a little more than half the peak strength.[3]

Marshall, on arrival, was assigned to Company G of the 30th Infantry. It was one of six companies of that regiment which about a year before, during General Bell's campaign to clear Luzon, had occupied the island of Mindoro, to which some Luzon Insurrectos were fleeing. Though the fighting was now over, the 30th Infantry remained in occupation. Marshall was to reach his post by inter-island steamer. Discovering on the morning of his second day in Manila that the boat was about to sail, he barely had time to collect his luggage from the Oriente Hotel and an unfinished tropical uniform ordered the previous day from a Manila tailor before dashing for the boat dock. In his haste he dropped a pocket of the blouse and one leg of the pair of trousers but caught the last launch that would take him out to the *Isla de Negros*. This singularly unattractive 250-ton ship, chartered by the Army, set sail at once across Manila Bay. But off Bataan Peninsula it dropped anchor and there in the steaming heat lay for five days. The delay was forced by quarantine regulations designed to prevent the spread among the islands of cholera, which was then epidemic in Manila.

So exhausting were the heat and tedium of those five days that, when they were up, the captain resumed the voyage despite typhoon warnings. Heading out past Corregidor, he turned down the coast and in a very little time ran into the "damnedest typhoon you ever saw." The General recalled it vividly a half-century later.

"I am not exaggerating when I say that the boat would tilt over until the longboats on the upper deck would go into the water. It would just poise there for a little bit as if it would never go back again. Then it would roll to the other side. The captain got frightened or sick. Anyway he left the bridge and went to his stateroom, where he knocked about in a sea chest which was rolling around from one side to the other. The Filipino at the wheel got his ribs mashed and he was gone. That left nobody to steer and nobody to command.

"So a young fellow, Lieutenant Daly, who was going back to his station at Calapan (on Mindoro), and I took over the boat. The two of us got the wheel and, of course, turned it in the wrong direction. We were heading toward a forbidding-looking mountain before we got straightened out and turned the other way.

"We battled it until about three o'clock in the morning. Then the first mate came up from the lower deck. He climbed up the stanchions on the outside and would go under water every time the boat tilted over.

"The water also poured into the engine room through the open ventilated space in the middle section of the deck. During the worst of it the Filipinos started to leave the engine room. We leaned over the hatch and with our guns threatened them and, as I recall, shot once or twice. I wouldn't have stayed myself if I had been in that position. It was a nerve-wracking experience but finally with this Spanish mate we made it."

Perhaps after such an ordeal even Mindoro looked good, but it was in fact a forbidding place, an island of about four thousand square miles of mountains and jungle. The towns, such as they were, spotted the coastal perimeter and were inhabited by Tagalog, Visayan, and Ilocano natives. In the wild and unexplored interior lived the primitive Manguianes, a tribe of light-skinned nomads. The jungles, in which they hunted even in Marshall's time, still sheltered armed bands of *ladrones*, outlaws, some of whom were former Insurrectos.[4]

The 30th Infantry had occupied the towns of Mindoro in the late summer and autumn of 1901. Company G, to which Marshall was assigned, had headquarters at Mangarin, but Marshall was ordered to join a detachment of the company stationed at Calapan with the battalion command.

Put ashore by small boat, the storm-tossed lieutenant was met by one man, possibly Second Lieutenant Henry Hossfeld (later to become one of his close friends), who had brought a pony to carry the luggage. Since no one had made clear just how primitive was the post to which he was going, Marshall had arrived with nearly full garrison gear. It was as much as the pony could carry, and the two men had to walk up the jungle trail, past an American outpost that stood guard at the foot of the mountains and made Marshall think he was going to war, then on to Calapan. There he came upon an American sergeant teaching a group of native children how to speak English and sing English songs. That, too, was part of the American occupation, and, Marshall thought, "typical."

Though Calapan, the island capital, boasted five thousand inhabitants in 1902, it was little more than an overgrown jungle village. The houses were mostly the typical native huts set on stilts, the ground floor left open, the second story roofed and sided with Nipa palm leaves. Marshall from his billet on the main plaza looked across at a church and convent built like fortresses; company messes occupied one side of the square, a row of native houses the other. There were, of course, none of the amenities of even a small city. The relatively large garrison— besides battalion headquarters it included a company of infantry, a company of Philippine Scouts, and various detachments— found Calapan deadly dull. Minimum guard duty, an hour or two of drill a day, military housekeeping chores—these hardly filled the soldier's day. Marshall, indeed, was to find that his day's work was normally finished by nine-thirty or ten in the morning. The rest of the day was a struggle with idleness and ennui. At this time, moreover, the morale of the Calapan garrison had been badly bruised by an unstable "tough" commanding officer, Lieutenant Colonel W. L. Pitcher, who had had enlisted men thrown into the guardhouse on whim and officers confined for disagreement. Pitcher, called "Billy Danger," [5] was relieved early in May. His replacement, Lieutenant Colonel Charles B. Hall, a Civil War veteran, would in time effect improvement, but on arrival he was as green to the problems of an unruly command of bored men as was young Marshall. The men at Calapan, the General said later, were "about the wildest crowd I've ever seen before or since."

Colonel Hall had scarcely time even to become acquainted with his problems when, without warning, cholera struck the village. Somehow native fishermen had managed to elude the quarantine net around Manila, and one day Calapan, hitherto untouched, was caught in the epidemic. The sickness was noted in the morning, and that afternoon Marshall helped bury three of its first victims—three sisters whom he and his fellow officers had met only a short time before.[6]

The great cholera epidemic had struck Manila about two months before Marshall's arrival in the Philippine capital. Despite preventive work by health authorities and the Army, the disease raced from island to island, aided by ignorance, superstition, inadequate supply of pure water, and the lack of proper medical facilities. By the time it had run its course in September 1903, there were more than a hundred and fifty-seven thousand reported cases and a hundred thousand reported deaths, with probably not more than two-thirds of each recorded. Dr. Victor Heiser, who arrived as chief quarantine officer of the Islands about the same time as George Marshall, has described the swift, ugly, deadly visitation: "A cold, clammy sweat is upon [the victim], his skin shrinks and grows dark gray from the terrific purging. Cramps of unbelievable intensity occur in the calves of the leg and in the arm. His thirst is unquenchable. His circulation literally grows so sluggish that even cutting the vein fails to produce a flow of blood." [7]

There were no known cures and no known method of immunization; the usual palliative for the suffering—one which Marshall recalled hearing that his grandfather used in a cholera outbreak in Kentucky forty years before—was to inject a saline solution to reduce the cramps caused by the drying up of body fluids. Mortality rates were close to 100 per cent. The only defense against the disease was to avoid it. Fortunately it could be avoided by taking care. Spread not by contact with the sick but by contamination of food and drink, it could be checked by meticulous cleanliness. Men in Calapan were confined to barracks; everything they ate or drank was boiled; hands had to be scrubbed, mess kits scoured and thoroughly rinsed. These procedures were rigorously enforced by military discipline lest the soldiers, like soldiers everywhere, take shortcuts. "A very little skimping could cost you your life." [8]

While protecting their own command, the officers at Calapan tried also to help check the disease among the Filipinos by establishing a cholera isolation camp about two miles off, where there was a good, clean water supply. Marshall's roommate, Fletcher Gardner, the only doctor in the area, spent day and night at the camp, and Marshall went up often to help his friend in addition to his regular stints at the camp as officer of the day.[9]

"The first time I went I found the soldiers peacefully eating their supper off a pile of coffins. Later on, there weren't any coffins. The deaths came too rapidly and they were buried by dozens in a trench. A sheet was put over them and disinfectant poured on them. It was a tragic sight. The sides of the tent were rolled up so you could see the patients on these gold metal cots without any sheets, their legs drawn up almost under their chins, generally shrieking from the agony of convulsions. But they didn't last long. . . . I don't remember anybody recovering at that time."

One evening Marshall, exhausted, was lying on his cot when Gardner came in, also ready to drop from his around-the-clock work, and reported that he had the cholera. He laid out some personal papers and personal possessions and was describing how he wished them to be disposed when Marshall fell asleep. "Next thing I knew, I woke up and it was morning. . . . I thought this was a dream. Then I realized it wasn't . . . and I was horrified that I should go to sleep while a man was telling me that he was getting the cholera and was going to die. So I got up—and looked around the corner to his bed; it had been used and he wasn't there. I breathed a . . . sigh of relief. . . . I went to the lattice window and looked out, and he was coming across the plaza with some friends from breakfast. He saw me and shook his fist and said, 'There's the damn fellow who went to sleep when I told him I was dying.' "

In fact no soldier died on Mindoro during the epidemic, which took the lives of several hundred Filipinos. Discipline had been effective, but the prolonged confinement did not improve the temper of the men. The quarantine was lifted just before the Fourth of July and the command decided to make that an occasion for a gala party. It fell naturally to Lieutenant Marshall as the newest and most junior officer present to take charge of the entertainment program, which was worked out by Sergeant Enoch R. L. Jones. But the assignment turned out to be something more than routine.

Still sore at their treatment by the previous commanding officer, the men spontaneously or by arrangement decided to sulk. Names were to have been entered the day before for the athletic events, but when the men turned out on the morning of the celebration, none had entered. Some of the older officers waited in amusement, expecting to see the green lieutenant discomfited. But Marshall had one trump: the prize money which he had already collected from the officers in generous amounts. (There was so little to buy in Calapan that money was relatively easy to part with.) He called for competitors for the hundred-yard dash. Two men stepped forward. When they had run the race, the lieutenant without comment divided between them the prize money intended for the first four who crossed the finish line. There was no holding back thereafter; the program went on from enthusiasm to hilarity and finished in the evening with impromptu entertainment supplied in part by a soldier whom Marshall persuaded the commanding officer to release from the guardhouse for the occasion. All this was highly satisfactory to the men and the command. The young officer was proving—at least in the minor crises—highly resourceful.[10]

He had another quality invaluable in one so green with so large a destiny: the ability to learn quickly and while learning to depend on the experience and skills of subordinates. When presently he was transferred to his company at Mangarin he found himself pushed into the deep water of military responsibility. Two weeks after his arrival he was in command of the company and of the post and acting as civil governor for the southern end of Mindoro Island. He was, in fact, the only officer anywhere around. This was in July, and it was not until mid-September that Captain H. E. Eames appeared to take over the company from him. In this spot he was grateful to VMI for what it had given him through its traditions, its standards of conduct and responsibility. "At retreat formation in some isolated company garrison in the Philippines," he told the Corps of Cadets forty years later, "I would find my thoughts going back to evening parade with the background of the Brushy Hills and the sunset over House Mountain," and he would recall "what the Corps, the Institute, expected of a cadet officer in the performance of his duty." Nevertheless he was "a little vague about matters pertaining to the cooks and kitchen police," and there had been nothing in his courses to solve scores of practical problems he now faced.[11] To at least one member of Company G, the "mild-mannered, soft-spoken" young lieutenant, only six months in uniform, "appeared very green in military affairs." [12] But with the "super-confidence of a recent cadet officer" and the help of two seasoned noncoms, First Sergeant William Carter and Sergeant August Torstrup, he managed to survive. During the summer of 1902, until his relief arrived, he struggled with Army routine, improvised forms to make out his reports because the forms provided had been kept in a barrel and ruined by a typhoon, managed his post, struck up a friendship with Eduardo Lualjadi, "the most natural boss I ever met," the *presidente* of a village on the nearby island of Ilin, and planned and conducted several patrols into the back lands and nearby islands to search for *ladrones*.[13]

On one of these patrols occurred an incident that he long remembered and often told with relish. He took seven men by native boat (*banca*) to a small offshore island where an armed band had been reported. After landing on the island, the patrol passed through a village on its way into the jungle and there came upon some natives sewing up a pony which had been bitten by a crocodile. Shortly after leaving the village the men had to cross a stream, narrow but deep for fording. The lieutenant was in the lead and all the men in the water when there was a splash and someone yelled, "Crocodiles!" In panic the men shot forward, knocked Marshall over and trod him into the mud in their haste to reach the shore. He picked himself up and waded up the bank. Standing before his men, wet and bedraggled, he realized the need promptly to reassert control. He decided very quickly that "it wasn't a time for cussing around." Instead he formally fell them in, gave them right shoulder arms, and faced them toward the river they had just crossed. He gave the order to march. Down they went, single file, into the river, Marshall at their head, and across it and up the other side. Then the lieutenant, as though he were on the drill field, shouted, "To the rear—march!" Again they crossed the crocodile river. When they were back on the far bank "I halted them, faced them toward me, inspected their rifles, and then gave them 'fall out.' " [14] That was all. Not another word was ever said about the little jungle drill by the men to the lieutenant or by the lieutenant to them. Once more he had used the reflexes of discipline to restore the substance of command.

Expeditions of this sort into the interior and brushes with the primitive Manguianes, a people so shy that one had to approach cautiously or risk being shot with poisoned arrows, were a relief from the boredom of the post and, for Marshall particularly, its loneliness.

Calapan had been primitive; Mangarin did not exist. The village had been abandoned years before, after fever had killed most of its inhabitants. There remained a convent of the Recollect Order with extensive land holdings and cattle. A few natives who before the insurrection had worked nearby on a cattle ranch or in a local coal mine lingered in the area without visible means of support. It was chiefly to safeguard the convent that a military post was set down in this otherwise isolated and desolate spot.[15]

So long as he was the sole officer in Mangarin, Marshall, keeping such distance from his men as he felt necessary to command, lived altogether alone except for the companionship of a lay brother, Padre Isidro Sanz. Though welcome, that association was sadly limited by the padre's ignorance of English and Marshall's only rudimentary acquaintance with Spanish. But at least they dined together almost every night and made of the meal a prolonged ceremony that helped to pass and partly to civilize the tedium. By exchanging and combining rations they contrived to eat well, and each evening "had dinner served when the sun was almost halfway down on the horizon across the China Sea. Then we would stay at the table until twelve at night."

Once a month the *Isla de Negros* delivered supplies and mail. Marshall, reading and rereading Lily's letters, amused himself by keeping track of the number of pounds she reported losing since she last wrote. At one point, he noted with glee, she had a minus weight.[16] He recalled years later the sense of isolation: "In those far-off days the soldiers of the regular Army got little attention or consideration from the government or the public. As I recall, the ration was sixteen cents and privates (there was only one class) got thirteen dollars a month plus 10 per cent on foreign service. There was no turkey, chicken, or fresh vegetables. Fried peaches and apples and desiccated potatoes were a daily ration. No ice in a tropical hot sun. The only contribution to recreation I recall during my first year was a box of forty books from Helen Gould." [17]

In December, Company G, now under command of Captain Eames, who had arrived in mid-September, was alerted for a move to Manila at the end of the month. Most of the unit departed three days before Christmas, but Marshall, as the junior officer, was left with twenty-six men to garrison the station until replacements arrived. On December 25 there was so little in the tropical setting to remind anyone of home that it was afternoon before anyone realized that a celebration was in order. Someone found a young pig, and the animal was killed and roasted for the holiday dinner. Two days later the replacements arrived, and Marshall and his detachment were transferred to Manila, where the young lieutenant celebrated his twenty-second birthday. Billeted at first in temporary barracks of the 3d Reserve Hospital, they moved in January to Santa Mesa reservation eight miles east of the capital. Here Marshall, sharing a house with ten to twelve other officers, found a pleasant garrison life with time and facilities for recreation. It was here that he first learned to ride, beginning a lifelong recreation that he would always prefer to any other. In off-duty hours Manila, with a theater and an Army and Navy Club, was readily accessible by horseback or carriage.

The lieutenant's horse fell on him near the end of March, severely spraining his right ankle, so that he was excused from duty and had to use crutches for several weeks. While immobile, he was assigned to help the inspector of the headquarters examine the property accounts of officers awaiting financial clearances before they could return to the United States. Working through masses of receipts and vouchers, he received a postgraduate course in Army accounting and accountability.

Among miscellaneous duties that Marshall performed at this time was a week's trip by *banca* to post signs on various small islands in Manila Bay which the Army proposed to take over as military reservations. One of the islands was El Fraile, from which the Spaniards had fired the first shots at Commodore Dewey's fleet four years earlier. The names of all of them would appear in history later when the Japanese conquered the Philippines in World War II and would awaken forty-year-old memories in the Chief of Staff. But at the moment the very junior officer was a little fed up. When his report of the accomplishment of his mission as agent of the United States was received by the authorities as merely routine, he was moved to reflect on his low estate. As he put it later, "There isn't anything much lower than a second lieutenant and I was about the junior second lieutenant in the Army at that time."

Another lasting impression of these first years as a soldier was more significant. While learning the techniques of a company officer, Marshall was observing something of the large problems of occupying a foreign country, new of course to him and also largely new for America. So long as the insurrection continued, the Philippines were administered by the Army under military law. A commission in 1899 had studied the capacity of the Islands for self-government and concluded that any native government would collapse if American forces were withdrawn, leaving the Islands at the mercy of conquest by another foreign power. Nevertheless President McKinley and Secretary Root were eager to re-establish civil government as soon as possible and took the first steps while the insurrection was still in progress. The second Philippine Commission, headed by Taft, was authorized to assume legislative responsibilities from the military governor as early as September 1900. Taft, as civil governor, replaced General MacArthur at the head of the Philippine government in July 1901. General Adna R. Chaffee became military governor under him, with responsibility for areas not yet pacified. This kind of mixing of civilian and military authority would, in the easiest of circumstances, have been a source of friction. The Army's experience in the Philippines intensified misunderstandings. Fighting against a foe who had no respect for the conventions of war, many high officers had become convinced that they dealt with a savage nation and that their own survival depended on keeping the country in tight subjugation. They were not sympathetic to Taft's efforts to speed the return of native self-government to the conquered provinces. They were particularly embittered by the civilian government's action against Army officers who on occasion answered brutality with brutality.[18]

Marshall heard much of the story of the early occupation from his fellow officers and studied it later from official reports. He concluded that both sides were wrong. The junior officers commanding expeditions against towns were often outrageous in their actions, he recalled. He added: "I remember distinctly one officer reporting that he had three men wounded in an encounter and he had burned the town down. . . . It showed how men are likely to get out of hand when they are on their own in critical situations. Near Manila, a cathedral that had what was considered to be the best library east of Suez was burned. Some of the Americans had taken the robes of the priests and the silver service from the chancel and were executing a dance outside. So, however quiet you may be in your home district, when you get abroad on a wartime basis under conditions that are extremely difficult, you are likely to do things that you would utterly discountenance at another time. Of course, the discipline was very loose because these things were hastily organized and [men] were serving under most difficult and trying circumstances."

On the other hand, he thought, "maybe the civil officials [went] too far too fast. . . . It is hard for the military who have suffered so much [to accept] all the overtures of peace. . . . The Civil Commission was rather impatient with the troops. Both sides are wrong. Both reactions are perfectly natural. One of the best things would have been to discharge the fine officers they had and to have made them civil officials. . . . They would have had a much better understanding of the point of view of these fellows who . . . suffered the torture of the damned, as it were, . . . than would the man who had just come out from the States, who had never gone through any of it." He appreciated the reasons for the "tough" attitude of the Army, the excesses of reprisals, and the water cure to make captured Insurrectos talk. He did not approve them and never doubted the principle of re-establishing civil control as soon as practicable.

The last of Marshall's assignments in the Philippines he found especially distasteful. Company G in September 1903 was ordered to join the detachment guarding military prisoners on Malahi Island in the Laguna de Bay, some of them men who had committed the sort of brutality of which he had heard so much. Just before the transfer he had had temporary command of the company for a week while Captain Eames battled malaria. Just after the transfer Marshall himself came down with dengue fever and had to delay joining the company for two weeks. He had barely recovered when Captain Eames was ordered to report to the 10th Infantry, and so for the third time command of the company devolved on him.

Malahi Island was isolated and all but unfit for human habitation. It boasted a lake whose waters were so contaminated as to be ruled unsafe even for bathing. Shortly government inspectors would recommend that the Malahi post be abandoned. But for a while longer the "scum" of the Army, murderers, deserters, and the like, were imprisoned there and kept busy quarrying rock for Fort William McKinley, then under construction just outside Manila.[19] Among the officers of the prison guard when Marshall arrived was Lieutenant Walter Krueger (later to be General Krueger and commander of the Sixth Army in the Pacific in World War II). Krueger recalls young Marshall as a green second lieutenant who reported for duty in a fresh uniform and with evident distaste for his new surroundings. Krueger, having been commissioned from the ranks, was experienced in the tougher realities of Army life. He remembers that Marshall asked the officer of the guard where to sleep and that he, Krueger, pointed to a pile of straw on the floor, evidently with a certain satisfaction.[20]

Actually, of course, Marshall was less green than Krueger thought and had already acquitted himself well in rugged circumstances. Yet he retained (as indeed he would always retain) a fastidiousness which the prison grossly offended. "The prisoners," he said later, "were the dregs of the Army of the Philippine Insurrection; they were the toughest crowd of men I have ever seen. You had to count them twice every night. To go through the barracks where they were lying stark naked on those gold metal cots was a very depressing sight."

Happily the duty was soon over. Near the end of October, Marshall's company was relieved by elements of the 7th Infantry who had just arrived from the United States. "Their depression when they saw the place was very great. Our elation when we left was even greater."

The 30th Infantry was being ordered home. In early November the men assembled in quarantine on Bataan and on the thirteenth embarked on the Army transport *Sherman* for California. The ship made stops at Nagasaki, Japan, and Honolulu, Hawaiian capital situated near Pearl Harbor. Names for history. But in 1903 for the homecoming lieutenant they were just way-stops where it was possible to shop for souvenirs to take back to Lily, the final ports of call in foreign lands before assignment in the still wild heart of America. Marshall's next post was to be Fort Reno in Oklahoma Territory. It would continue his education in the rugged life and test his stamina and love for the Army.

It is not clear just when Lily joined him at Fort Reno. Her health was still not fully equal to Army life, and it may have been eighteen months or more before she came out.[21] In the meantime he continued the bachelor life he had lived ever since getting married.

Fort Reno, relic of the frontier, lay west of Oklahoma City in a reservation sixteen miles square along the north branch of the Canadian River. Across the river were reservations of the Cheyenne and Arapahoe Indians, where men of the post were permitted to hunt. The hunting was "superb." "There was hunting every day of the year," Marshall recalled. "At that time I was a pretty good shot and we would get out and camp ten days on the Indian Reservation. . . . We would get channel cat, which is very good eating, in the river. I shot ducks that would fall on the tents. On one occasion [after Lily arrived] when Mrs. Marshall and I were early for breakfast, we heard quail calling in the sumac grove near us and I went out there and in about thirty minutes I had ten or twelve quail. Actually, I think I had fifteen, but I don't want to claim that."

Assigned to Fort Reno were four companies of the 24th Infantry, two companies of the 30th Infantry, and a troop of the 8th Cavalry. The young lieutenant, still with Company G, seems to have been no busier than was customary with garrison routine—drills, inspections, administration—which at most posts during this period was over for officers and men by noon each day. In March, Marshall became the post ordnance officer, and in June the engineer officer as well. The duties were not exacting, but the commanding officer Marshall found "exceedingly difficult" and hard to please.[22]

Fort Reno in 1904 was dominated by the "old Army" and its traditions. These were essentially the traditions of spit and polish, preoccupation with the look of a soldier and the precise ordering of the military society by the rules of rank and discipline. "The immaculate uniform," wrote one officer who knew the Army well at this period, "the varnished wheel spokes, the glistening metal work, the shining pots and pans, that shocking speck of dust on a locker shelf—all these were the things occupying the mind of our 1904 officer." Even the garrison schools through which Elihu Root hoped to reawaken the professional interest of officers in the art and practice of war concerned themselves less with the tactics of battle than with the techniques of the model officer. "Methodical precision was the rule; close-order drill, the alignment of a row of tent pegs; the parrot-like memorizing of the Manual for Interior Guard Duty; the exact respective dimensions and use of garrison, post, and storm flags; . . . the layout and drainage of a campsite; the customs of the service. Such things were paramount." [23]

Marshall himself had a strong feeling for neatness and order and a care for his personal appearance which many of his associates thought remarkable enough to be worth special comment. He would always uphold the military forms but only as the basis for effectiveness in the military profession. At Reno he got by rote the assigned work of the garrison school and passed the examinations. He was found to be proficient in military law, field engineering, military topography, international law, hippology, troops in campaign, and security information. It was an impressive list until one finds that all he read for the examinations were: Root's *Military Topography* and *International Law; Military Field Engineering,* Winthrop's abridgment of *International Law;* "some in" *Horses, Saddles and Bridles;* and *Security and Information* and *Troops in Campaign.* He had previously studied the *Guard Manual, Infantry Drill Regulations, Firing Regulations for Small Arms* and a "portion" of *Army Regulations.*[24]

There began at Reno a long struggle to stretch his Army pay to cover his living expenses. The starting salary of a second lieutenant of $116.67 a month was by the standard of the day generous enough, but out of it he had to pay for uniforms, food, "the required arms and equipment, from saber and revolver and field glasses to mess kit and bedding roll, as well as the civilian clothing he needed." [25] Much of the time he had to support not only himself and his wife but his wife's mother. He recalled the constant battle of the budget. "A spring hat was $3.50 and the spring suit was $14.00. I can remember that quite well. I had to keep track down to the last dime. My struggle was to come out ahead. I really wasn't so much interested in whether it was $1.50 or $10.50 ahead for the month, but it was to be ahead and not to get behind. I always struggled in those days to have a month's pay ahead and live on that." The turns that his own career took made it particularly hard. He was to be moved frequently and he had to pay most of the costs himself. "In those days the government didn't move our wives or families and we got a very limited allowance for packing our things. We had to pack ourselves . . . and get hold of the lumber for crating." What appears in the history books under the head of national unpreparedness, the officers—and particularly the young officers —felt keenly as enforced penury. "A citizen army can vote and get the attention of the press and the attention of Congress; . . . an Army such as I served in then, the President wasn't interested in . . . , the Congress wasn't interested in . . . , except to keep down the appropriation as closely as they could."

It was characteristic of Marshall's career that the few relatively routine assignments he had were interrupted for special duty. So in June 1905 he was abruptly plucked out of the garrison routine, pleasant enough if neither affluent nor stimulating, and set a job which he later called "the hardest service I ever had in the Army."

Several posts had been asked in the spring of 1905 to detail young officers to Fort Clark, Texas, headquarters of the 1st Cavalry, to assist in mapping two thousand square miles in the southwestern part of the state. The duty was to take three or four months. According to Marshall, it was because some units in Texas reported they had no officers available that "they brought an infantryman from Oklahoma to do the job." Marshall actually was one of ten officers from Oklahoma Territory assigned in June to the mapping expedition. His part was to start in an area just west of Del Rio, two days' march from Fort Clark.

Fort Clark assigned him two riding horses. "One belonged to the quartermaster, was very good-looking and a runaway, which was the reason I got him, and the other came from [Captain] Malin Craig's troop. Fort Clark also supplied me with an escort wagon and a four-line mule team driven by Nate Cox of Brackett-ville, whose father brought Nate when he was six years old through Dead Man's Pass near Shumla, Texas, then to Silver Lake. His earliest recollection was watching his father stand in the doorway of the cabin with a rifle to keep off a band of Comanches, his mother loading the rifle. I was also supplied with twenty pack mules under a packer about fifty-eight years old, one assistant packer—a soldier named Davis of the 1st Cavalry—a cook from the 1st Cavalry, and a sergeant also of the 1st Cavalry, to assist me in sketching. The sergeant was a soldier of twenty-four years' service, as I recall; had long drooping cavalry mustaches and was a very fine man but would drink after he got paid off." [26]

In the country through which Marshall was to travel both forage and water were scarce. In fact he was told there was practically no water in the area at all "except in the small portion near Devil's River." The only place to buy food for men or mules was Langtry, and very little could be bought there. He wished therefore to have the post quartermaster ship rations and forage to points along the railroad between Del Rio and Sanderson, Texas. It was a simple and reasonable request, and therefore Marshall found it particularly frustrating when it came to nothing.

The paper was to shuttle back and forth between headquarters in search of authority like a laboratory mouse making its first trip through a maze.[27] Through channels it proceeded from Fort Clark to the engineer officer of the Southwestern Division, Oklahoma City, to the commanding general, Southwestern Division, who in correspondence signed by Lieutenant Hugh A. Drum approved Marshall's request for pack mules, ignored the request for rations, and sent it on to the commanding general, Department of Texas, San Antonio, who forwarded it to the commanding officer, Fort Clark. There it was noted that no authority had been given for shipping rations and so off the letter went again to Oklahoma City. The military secretary "respectfully returned" it to the commanding general, Department of Texas, "within whose province lies the authority requested." And so, no doubt, it did, but before the correspondence at last got back to Fort Clark someone had discovered an easier way and had given Marshall voucher forms with instructions to buy forage in the field.[28]

July, Marshall recalled, was the hardest month as he and his men hiked from Comstock to Langtry. "The thermometer would go up to 130 and I had to walk the track and count the sections of rails. That would give me an exact measurement which I needed as a sort of base line. I got my distances otherwise from the odometer on the wheel of the wagon and from the time scale on the walking of my horse." The difficulty of finding food was as great as he expected. Not many days after they set out they had exhausted their supply of potatoes and onions and had to subsist almost wholly on bacon and canned meats. "I would have the effect of too much acidity from the bacon without fresh vegetables of any kind and get heartburn so badly that I could barely drink without gasping. As I recall, I went in there weighing about 165 or 170 and I came out weighing 132 pounds. . . . At one period the old packer and I were without water for eighteen hours and had to travel pretty nearly fifty miles. This was an endurance contest of the first class."

By the end of July, moving ten or fifteen miles a day, they had pushed beyond the Pecos to Langtry, named for Judge Roy Bean's favorite entertainer, "the Jersey Lily," when pay day arrived. Marshall was cheered by both prospects, for it meant a chance to get some fresh food. For his sergeant it meant a chance to wash out of his system a month's accumulation of Texas dust, and that, he anticipated, would take a good bit of drink. So, drawing his pay, he found himself a house with girls and bottles and settled in. The girls, he announced, were all for him, and he declared the place off limits for anyone else.

Certain citizens were outraged. Indeed the situation had the ingredients of a riot and was simmering when Marshall heard about it. Trying diplomacy in place of command, he talked the sergeant into agreeing to share his domain and drink in peace, and that the sergeant proceeded to do, so long as his pay lasted.[29]

During August the mapping detachment apparently turned north, parallel to the river, and then doubled back eastward. Reports at the end of August were dated from a point "30 miles due north of Ry., on Devil's River, Texas." Here two vouchers with which he had bought supplies in late June and early July were returned to him unpaid with instructions to furnish headquarters with certificates in duplicate stating the emergency that caused the purchases and his authority for making them. He found the request irritating enough and the tone of it, suggesting that the purchases might be disallowed, exasperating. He sat down and composed a full statement of explanation, concluding patiently and respectfully, as a lieutenant should, that "there seems to have been some misunderstanding about the supplying of my detachment and I respectfully request that I be informed as to whether I have been at fault or not, though my instructions are so clear as to hardly permit being misconstrued." Five weeks later he had an answer—in fourteen endorsements— which in effect said that he was not at fault but neither was anyone else. The bills were paid and the monumental correspondence concerning them came to rest first in the headquarters of the Southwestern Division and then in the National Archives, where they remain eloquent of congestion in bureaucratic minds and of exasperation in the field.[30]

Back in Fort Clark, the lieutenant reported to the headquarters of Captain Malin Craig whose troop had furnished one of his two horses. Marshall came in wearing "an old Panama hat which a mule had bitten the top out of and I had tried to sew . . . together. I was burned almost black. When the sergeant took in the horses, Captain Craig met him . . . and wouldn't look at me. He didn't think I could be an officer and talked entirely to my old sergeant. . . ."

For the lieutenant, however, there were two expressions of thanks to compensate for the bruises of body and spirit he had suffered in his travels through rocky desert and Army red tape. The chief engineer officer of the Southwestern Division told him his map "was the best one received and the only complete one." [31] At the headquarters of the commanding general of the Department of Texas he was warmly welcomed back by the military secretary, Captain George Van Horn Moseley. "When I came into your office," he wrote Moseley afterward, "a young lieutenant who had been mapping on the Pecos, feeling that I had a pretty hard time, not only as a result of the climate and a harsh terrain, but largely because of the dyed-in-the-wool spirit of the commissary staff—we darn near starved—I have never forgotten your kindly greeting at that time." [32]

The commanding general at San Antonio also granted him four months' leave. It was a chance, among other things, for a reunion with Lily in Virginia and for a visit with his parents for the first time since he had left for the Philippines three years before. There was no question of a long visit. The Marshalls had moved out of the Main Street house shortly after George was commissioned and were now living in the "Skyscraper," eleven stories of offices and apartments, which Andy Thompson's father had built farther east on Main Street in 1902. Marie was to be married in mid-November to Dr. J. J. Singer of Connellsville, and to move to Greensburg, Pennsylvania. Stuart in 1907 married Florence Heaton of Virginia. Their son Stuart was born in 1910.

The return for George Marshall was poignant. Four years had already made startling changes in the town of his childhood. The house on Main Street had been torn down, the yard leveled with fill, and on the site now stood the West End Theater. Coal Lick Run where the Marshall ferry once plied was partly choked with rubble. The Thompsons no longer lived across the way. Andy's mother was dead; his father, J. V., had become one of the wealthiest men in the area, and in 1903 had married a lively widow who persuaded him to buy the old estate of Congressman Boyle west of town and remodel it at a rumored cost of one million dollars. In addition they bought Friendship Hill, Albert Gallatin's great house on the banks of the Monongahela at New Geneva.[33] Mr. Marshall by contrast, though somewhat better off financially, had begun to fade. He was stouter, slower, no longer a householder or man of affairs.

For the young man the mood of melancholy deepened as he searched the town for the familiar. He went to visit the mother of an old playmate. The friend had died, but Marshall was delighted to find his dog, a short-haired terrier named Trip, lying "on the stones by the old pump in the sun, . . . his black coat . . . turned almost brown." Fifty years later, the emotion of that moment remained vivid in memory. "He paid no attention to me—he didn't bark at me—he was so old he was just indifferent. . . . That was quite a blow because Trip was one of the close companions of my youth. So I sat down on this long flagstone that was around the pump and succeeded in petting him, although he rather resented it. . . . I talked to him quite a long time, trying to renew my youth, and was very much distressed that he didn't remember me at all. After, I suppose, five or ten minutes, he took a careful sniff of me, then he sniffed at me two or three times, and then he just went crazy. He had finally gotten a scent in his old nostrils and he remembered me. That was the most flattering thing that occurred to me on that short visit home after many years of not being there."

Marshall spent the remainder of his leave at Esmont in Albemarle County, Virginia, with Lily and her Coles relations. By the end of January 1906 they were back at Fort Reno, with only a few months to stay there. From this last period, he told a story revealing of his kindliness toward the less fortunate which constantly broke through his normal reserve. While acting as commander of the post during the absence of all the other officers and most of the men on a march to Fort Riley, he was making a routine inspection of the houses on the post in which wives, and widows, of the soldiers lived.[34] The houses were miserable shanties and the Army did nothing officially to maintain them. On this day one of the women approached him to ask if he could not have her kitchen sink fixed. He promised he would, but noting the disreputable state of both house and yard "an idea struck me and I made a proposition to the lady." Pointing out the yard of beaten-down clay strewn with tin cans and rubbish, he said, "If you fix your yard and make it look like something, I'll fix your house up. I'll come back here in about two weeks."

Two weeks later he found the yard cleaned, the tin cans painted green and made into flower pots, the whole place transformed. She waited anxiously for his approval. "I looked it over very carefully—I'm quite [given] to that kind of performance—and I congratulated her. Then I went into the house to see what was to be done."

He thought paint would do a lot and promised to send a painter so that she could select her own colors. A little later the astounded painter reported that the woman had selected pure, undiluted colors, red for the living room, blue for the kitchen. "Well, it was very hot down there in the summer, and this red was just like lighting a fire. The blue was the kind that created a haze in the room unless it was diluted." Nevertheless Marshall decided that if these were the colors she wanted she should have them. She had carried out her part of the bargain. So it was done, and Marshall went to see it. "Well, actually when you opened up the front door . . . the living room almost knocked you down. It was an intense red, a terrible red. The kitchen was this vivid blue. [But] she was just pleased to death." And so were her neighbors, and all down the line of "Soapsuds Row" they "started to fix up their lawns."

In the spring Marshall was offered a chance to attend the Infantry and Cavalry School at Fort Leavenworth and gladly accepted.[35] He left for Leavenworth in August to begin a one year's assignment that stretched into four and gave clear direction to his career.

VI

Professional Training

---

*"It was the hardest work I ever did in my life. . . .
I learned a thoroughness which [later] stood me in
good stead through all the clamor and push and excitement [and] lack of time. . . ."*

A G A I N Marshall had extraordinary luck in timing. In retrospect it appears that he had to get his appointment to
Leavenworth in 1906 or miss his career. In 1903 Brigadier General J. Franklin Bell had become commandant of the reopened
schools at Leavenworth. Bell took great interest in them and
worked hard to give them high professional quality and standing
in the Army. Among other things, he insisted that regimental
commanders, some of whom regarded Leavenworth as a convenient place to shuffle off deadbeats, select better qualified officers to attend the first course. That insistence may have helped
Marshall get his appointment. In 1906 Bell became Chief of
Staff. Still intent on upgrading Leavenworth, he directed that
henceforth only officers in the rank of captain be assigned to
the course. Marshall was appointed just before this order took
effect. He did not become a captain until 1916 and then it would
have been too late to have been named to Leavenworth until
after the beginning of war. Had he missed out in 1906, he would
have missed the ten years of intensive training and experience in
staff work that prepared him for the important staff positions he

held during the war and brought him into close association with General Pershing, so important to his career. No doubt other paths could have led him to the top, but the course he actually followed was opened to him just briefly, just that once.

At the outset there was a small disappointment. Lily could not go with him right away. Additional quarters for married officers were under construction but would not be ready until mid-October at least. Meanwhile, the school adjutant suggested, Mrs. Marshall and her mother, Mrs. Coles (apparently then living with them, as she did off and on during all their married life), might "visit some rich relative." [1]

So Marshall came up by himself in the middle of August and took bachelor quarters. He was not long in discovering that he had a hard road ahead. If the entire entering class of fifty-four were not top caliber, most were older and more experienced than he. They included, with him, nine future generals,[2] the most outstanding of whom at that time appeared to be Captain Charles D. Rhodes, graduate of West Point, veteran of the Philippines campaign, and former member of the War Department General Staff. Rhodes, nearly everybody thought, would certainly stand first in the class. George Marshall had another opinion. Finding himself a definite underdog acted as a spur to his ambition. When he overheard two classmates guessing who were most likely to be kept on for the second year and found his own name missing from the list he reacted as he had long ago on hearing Stuart run down his prospects at VMI: he would show them.

When Elihu Root had reopened Leavenworth in 1902 as General Service and Staff College his aim, it will be recalled, had been to develop a training course for officers tabbed for higher command and General Staff duty. In 1906 Leavenworth was still not that, but the transformation had gone far, considering the novelty of the whole concept of postgraduate professional training in the American Army. Two exceptional officers were largely responsible, General Bell, commandant of the school from 1903-1906, and Colonel Arthur L. Wagner, instructor at Leavenworth from 1888 to 1904.[3] Wagner, "the first of our military men to write anything readable on tactics, was a kindly, friendly old man who looked like a farmer dressed up in uniform." Bell was tall (six feet two), large-boned, a vigorous, extroverted man who participated in sports with the younger officers and called them and their wives by their first names—an unusual informality in those days and particularly in the Army, which maintained an extra reserve between ranks.[4]

Bell's great quality was his vast store of energy. Born in Kentucky in 1856, and commissioned in 1878 after graduation from West Point, he was still a lieutenant of cavalry at the outbreak of the Spanish-American War. Besides the usual garrison duty, he had served as professor of military science at Southern Illinois Normal University, where he had picked up a law degree. He had also been secretary of the Cavalry and Light Artillery School at Fort Riley. When the war came he was quickly promoted to temporary major of volunteers and in 1898 went to the Philippines. There he acted successively as chief of the Office of Information, chief engineer, and acting judge advocate, and made his way up to temporary colonel. At that point he was given command of a volunteer infantry regiment and had a chance to prove himself as a tough, able soldier. He won the Medal of Honor and within a year was promoted to brigadier of volunteers. In 1901 while in command of the Department of Luzon, where he destroyed the rebel forces of General Malvar, he became brigadier general in the regular Army. When he took over as Chief of Staff in April 1906 he was not quite fifty; it was just eight years since he had discarded his lieutenant's bars.[5]

Leavenworth in the early days of its renaissance needed both the professional and thoughtful spirit of Colonel Wagner and the protective and stimulating enthusiasm of General Bell to survive the indifference or even hostility of Army conservatives, who called the school "Bell's Folly" and found it unmilitary of Colonel Wagner to write books. Opposition on the part of older officers to "any studious preparation" Marshall recalled as having been "decided," and he thought it "quite outrageous." [6] So did General Bell, who responded gladly to Colonel Wagner's request, only a few months before the latter's death, that the War Department "cause a ray of light to penetrate the skulls of some of these superannuated individuals, who have not kept pace with the march of events, and who will give the detail at Leavenworth to the regimental idiot." [7] As Chief of Staff, 1906-10, a period which coincided with Marshall's four years at Leavenworth, Bell kept an uncomfortably close watch over his two successors as commandants of the Army Service Schools, Colonel Charles B. Hall (who was Marshall's first regimental commander in the Philippines) and Brigadier General Frederick Funston (who had captured Aguinaldo and was to win later fame for his activities in Mexico).

The old Infantry and Cavalry School became within a year or two of reopening a general service course which in 1907 was renamed the Army School of the Line. It was to this course that Marshall and all of the other officers appointed to Leavenworth were first assigned. By 1906 it was the rule that approximately the top half of the class of the School of the Line was eligible for the second-year course in the Army Staff College.[8] This was the core of Leavenworth training and the goal of the ambitious officer student.

Marshall was, of course, determined to be among those who stayed a second year. He taught himself to study hard and to take nothing for granted. "I finally got into the habit of study, which I never really had before. I revived what little I had carried with me out of college and I became pretty automatic at the business . . . [but] it was the hardest work I ever did in my life."

Much of the work consisted of committing facts and formulas to memory and recalling and applying what was memorized in classroom recitations. The marking on this work was stringent and meticulous. Each student found his performance constantly weighed to hundredths of a percentage point and stacked competitively against the performance of his classmates.[9] Differences could be minute, yet critical. One day, for instance, when Marshall made 100 on a map exercise, his friend, Second Lieutenant Fay W. Brabson, with a grade of 95.17, ranked forty-seventh.[10] Under the strain Marshall had difficulty sleeping at night. "I used to get up and shine my boots. I had very shiny boots at that early period." But there was no question that he was making the grade. Steadily throughout the year he and four classmates—Captain Rhodes, Captain Monroe C. Kerth, Second Lieutenant Royden E. Beebe (one of Marshall's closest friends in the class), and Second Lieutenant Harry L. Hodges—jockeyed for position among the first five.

Then, in the middle of things, Marshall, along with Beebe, Brabson, and three first lieutenants, had to take time out for examinations for promotion. Not to interrupt their classes, these were scheduled for the Christmas holidays. Brabson's diary was eloquent with the misery of it all. Noting that he and a Lieutenant Hennessey had had a "dandy meal" with the Marshalls on Christmas Day, he reported back to the grind at once for the first of the written exams in engineering on December 27. On the twenty-ninth they were making road sketches. "So foggy we couldn't see the bottom of the hill. It rained all day. A big drop would fall off your hat on your pencil as you wrote. . . . We were wet, muddy, and hungry while other people were doing what they pleased." And the indignity was compounded on December 31, which was "Sunday but not a day of rest." Indeed on Sunday there were two papers: military law in the morning, theoretical topography in the afternoon. The test on drill regulations wound matters up on January 2. Everybody passed.[11] Marshall, promoted to first lieutenant as of March 7, was not sworn in until October 28.[12]

Concentration on grades and ranking had perhaps only a tenuous relation to education or even professional training, but since it had a close and demonstrable relation to career, Marshall characteristically applied himself without distraction to the task at hand. After Lily arrived at the post he found in her frail health an excuse, whenever he wished it, to stay home and study. The routine of the Marshall household seems to have been quietly domestic, as he liked it, and keyed to his hard work.

A classmate recalls that Marshall never dallied after work. When tactical problems might require a ride several miles out from the post Marshall would always lead the way home. "We never bothered to find the shortest way—all we did was to watch George Marshall, and he would go off as straight as a bee to a beehive and we would follow him. Except once we were stopped at one of those western streams that run way down in the ground. They are narrow and wind around in that country. The banks were fifteen feet high and there were no bridges there except a railroad bridge—one of those narrow-gauge railroads. It had a couple of twelve-inch planks laid across it for people to walk across. . . . When we got there Marshall rode his horse across that bridge. Nobody followed him." The classmate, Major General Charles D. Herron, was to know Marshall all his life and find that this was a lifelong habit. "He never fooled around and he knew exactly the way home." [13]

School was not all grind. There was stimulus, too, above all from a remarkable teacher, Major John F. Morrison, who at about the age of fifty had just begun an instructorship in tactics that was to leave a mark on the American Army. For years to come an officer who could say, "I was a Morrison man," had a kind of professional pedigree that commanded general respect. Morrison, a West Point graduate, had failed to ride the wartime expansion of the Army to rapid promotion, perhaps because he never got along very well with other men. A captain when the war broke out, he advanced only one grade during three years in the Philippines, was still a major when he was assigned as military observer to the Japanese Army, which was fighting the Russians in Manchuria. Not until he came to Leavenworth as assistant professor in the military art department did he find the right place for the development of his considerable talent. A prickly original, he was happiest in the master-student relationship and made his greatest appeal to young uncommitted minds.

"The students all took to Morrison immediately," Marshall said. "He spoke a language that was new to us and appealed very much to our common sense." The new language was in fact the language of thought applied to military problems in place of the traditional language of regulations. "After listening to him it began to appear that the others were talking about technique and calling it tactics; that he talked the simplicities of tactics and cared (or maybe knew) nothing of technique. In the making of problems we [had been] given minute cuts on dozens of little errors in technique, until we came to him, and then we lost shirt, pants, and shoes in one swat, for violating a fundamental tactical principle which none of us had recognized as such. Heretofore we could recite the principle but rarely recognized it in action.[14]

"His problems were short and always contained a knockout if you failed to recognize the principle involved in meeting the situation. Simplicity and dispersion became fixed quantities in my mind, never to be forgotten. . . . He spoke a tactical lan-guage I had never heard from any other officer. He was self-educated, reading constantly and creating and solving problems for himself. He taught me all I have ever known of tactics."

Morrison was, of course, exceptional. But Leavenworth would increasingly accept his lead away from the cut-and-dried learn-ing by rote, to emphasize the solving of operational problems. In 1903 the school had adopted a method of map exercises newly developed by the French. Two officers out of a class were given problems to work out on a large glass-encased map and at the end of an hour or so were required to explain and defend their solution before the class, which also heard a critique from the instructor. In Marshall's time classes used maps of the Franco-Prussian War based on Griepenkerl, whose work had been freshly translated at Leavenworth. Captain Matthew F. Steele, author of the classic *American Campaigns,* taught them strat-egy and military history.[15]

From March through May each student worked on twenty problems in the tactics of combined arms. They had, for in-stance, to plan a change of direction in a march, a retreat after defeat, a rear-guard action, an attack on a prepared position, an advance-guard action, the forcing of a river line. Marshall ranked third in these exercises, behind Captain Rhodes and Lieutenant Beebe.

But when the year ended and all the rankings were averaged out, Marshall stood first in the class, as he had intended from the beginning.[16] He was assured, of course, a place in the Army Staff College for the following year, but, even more important, his performance caught the eye of General Bell, who came from Washington to address the graduates. The General was at Leav-enworth when a request came from the Pennsylvania National Guard for a regular Army officer to instruct the citizen soldiers during the summer. Bell recommended they be assigned several instructors (five in fact were detailed) and that George C. Marshall be one of them.[17]

Marshall knew nothing about the prospect when he left Leavenworth with his wife at the beginning of July, planning a month's vacation at a resort in Buffalo, Minnesota. Orders reached him on July 4 and directed that he report at once to Mount Gretna, Pennsylvania.[18] There he was assigned to the 13th Regiment, commanded by Colonel F. W. Stillwell.

Although only a week's duty, it was of crucial importance. Marshall was such a success as an instructor, particularly in making the volunteers like their work and wish to excel in it, that he was asked to come back the next summer.[19] And so began an association of several years with the National Guard from which Marshall picked up invaluable experience in directing the maneuvers of large units. His success also vindicated General Bell's faith in him and advertised the virtues of Bell's old school. The young lieutenant's stock stood high with the Chief of Staff.

The second year (1907-1908) at Leavenworth in the Army Staff College was a good deal less of a grind than the first, less fiercely competitive and more stimulating. Though Marshall continued to work hard it was no longer necessary to struggle for rank in class, and in fact no standings were given. Leavenworth was working against a weight of tradition to train officers not only to understand the principles of war but to apply them. One of Marshall's classmates recalled the struggle. "It took a long time to make senior officers realize that if they didn't make junior officers go through a process in which they alone must make decisions or make recommendations on which decisions could be based, they hadn't done much." For the first time students at the Staff College trained with the responsibility of a staff officer always in mind. Their papers were prepared for action with recommended solutions for command decision. "We were there in the midst of transformation and we knew it." [20]

About half the hours of instruction were spent on military art. The class studied the duties of the General Staff, Von der Goltz's book on the conduct of war, and the organization of foreign armies. They read some military history. They worked very hard on solving tactical problems and problems of troop leading.

They wrote papers on tactics and history and criticized them. (Marshall's paper was on "Infantry Tactics in Defense.") They reconstructed the Peninsula Campaign of the Civil War from official documents and plotted troop movements on large-scale maps especially prepared for them by the school's engineering department.[21] As chief of staff for General Lee they wrote orders for his withdrawal after Antietam; as General Meade's chief of staff they submitted plans for action as of the evening of June 30, 1863. They became almost as intimately familiar with the details of the Franco-Prussian War. So well did they come to know the military topography of the battlefields around Metz that graduates who later fought there in World War I found they could sketch maps for their own actions from memory. Out of more recent history Major Morrison reported his own observations of the Russo-Japanese War, stimulating an interest in Marshall which he was to pursue on his own.

Of his experience at the Army Staff College, Marshall said: "My reading of course was pretty helpful, as was my study of past operations. I learned how to digest them. . . . My habits of thought were being trained. While . . . I learned little I could use . . . I learned how to learn. . . . I began to develop along more stable lines. Leavenworth was immensely instructive, not so much because the course was perfect—because it was not —but the association with the officers, the reading we did and the discussion and the leadership . . . of a man like Morrison had a tremendous effect, certainly on me, and I think on most of my class."

At the close of the school year in 1908 Major Morrison led the members of the Staff College class on a staff ride through the Shenandoah Valley to Gettysburg. Thirty-four officers, including Morrison and Captain Steele, took horses from Manassas Junction and between July 3 and 15 rode to Bull Run, Gainesville, Delaplane, Front Royal, Middleburg, Harpers Ferry, Sharpsburg, Williamsport, Allegheny, and at last to Gettysburg. At each major stop instructors and students discussed the fighting that had taken place there. Six lectures at Gettysburg ended the tour, and Marshall gave the last, a review of the battle as a whole.[22]

While in Rippon, West Virginia, Marshall and a companion

had stopped at a house for a drink of water. The residents, people named Osborne, asked them to stay for dinner. Something about the occasion made it especially heartwarming and memorable to the young lieutenant. Perhaps it was the unexpected touch of home life in the midst of the camping trip, or perhaps it was the charm of an excited little girl who was twelve and couldn't get over the fact that soldiers on horseback had stopped at her house. In any case Marshall every year thereafter sent a note or gift to the Osbornes. Years later when he became Chief of Staff, he found that the little girl, now grown up, was working as a secretary in the Pentagon, and he made her the receptionist in his office.[23]

The staff ride ended the school year, but Marshall presently learned that he was to stay on at Leavenworth as an instructor. One of five from his class unanimously proposed by the Academic Boards of the Leavenworth Schools, he was to teach engineering and military art. There was one difficulty: he was only a first lieutenant (and a very junior one at that); by the order of 1906 all of next year's students would be captains. Major Morrison undertook to get around the difficulty by asking the War Department for special permission. Permission was given, Marshall understood, by General Bell himself.[24]

As he indicated by his work with the Guard in Pennsylvania and now in the next two years demonstrated at length, Marshall had unusual talent as a teacher. He might perhaps have been a great one, and he himself sometimes regretted that he had not set out on an academic career. It is arguable at least that a good part of his impact on the Army was actually as a teacher. Besides Leavenworth, he had extremely influential teaching assignments later at the Infantry School at Fort Benning and with the National Guard on several occasions. More than that, his method, his style, in staff and command posts was to direct men by trying to make them see the way to go. "He had the ability to make everybody understand"—so said one of the lieutenants in the 13th Regiment of the 3d Brigade of the Pennsylvania Guard in which Marshall was an instructor during the summer of 1908. The National Guard lieutenant, M. W. Clement, who later became president of the Pennsylvania Railroad, remembered more than fifty years later the fresh wind of new ideas that blew into the regulation-stuffed Guard with Marshall and his fellow regular Army instructors. "A new world in military affairs opened itself up to the minds of the militia men." [25]

Like every good teacher, Marshall was also learning. At Leavenworth two more years of association with Morrison, as well as with such other distinguished instructors as Captain Steele and Captain Clarence O. Sherrill of the engineering department, deepened and extended the lessons of his student days. In the summers he went back for duty with the Pennsylvania militia, where he had a chance to apply his theories, work out the problems, or some of them, with actual bodies of troops. It was ideal grounding for a staff officer.

Of his experience in putting on maneuvers with very limited time, restricted maneuver areas, and volunteers who had to be treated with rather more than regulation courtesy, Marshall said: "I learned a tremendous amount about how to do a great deal in a short time. Troops were arriving one day and going into maneuvers the next. We were running eight to ten maneuvers on the road. I shall never forget the lesson I learned from the human reactions and from what goes to make attacks, apart from maps." [26]

He also learned something of the unreadiness of the militia generally for war. From Pennsylvania, which was one of the few states having well-organized and fairly well-trained units, he went to Fort D. A. Russell outside Cheyenne, Wyoming, to take part in one of eight combined regular Army and National Guard exercises held in the summer of 1908. The maneuver was not large—all eight that summer involved less than fifty-five thousand men altogether—but it drew Army units from posts in South Dakota, Minnesota, Nebraska, Wyoming, Utah, Colorado, Kansas, and California, and militia from Colorado, Utah, and Wyoming. The Wyoming maneuvers went badly, and the umpire commented that some of the militia "never had a sufficient number of companies together for battalion drills, much less regimental drills, and camps." As for the regular Army, many of their officers showed a clumsiness in handling troops that betrayed their lack of experience. [27]

The umpire recommended further encampments and maneuvers. Many others had been recommending the same thing for many years. Yet, for the most part, both the states and Congress remained more sensitive to the expense than to the military need. Some state maneuvers were held every year, beginning in 1902 (except 1905, when Congress voted no money at all), and combined Army-militia exercises took place biennially and would continue up to World War I. Every Secretary of War since Root recognized that the militia—not the regular Army—would constitute the bulk of the nation's defense forces at the outset of any war. The regular establishment was, as Root put it, "the mold of form and the guide of practice for that greater army of citizens which will take up arms in case of war." [28] General Bell, and after him General Wood, urged the use of the Army as instructor for the citizen army. Early in 1908 a Division of Militia Affairs was set up as part of the War Department General Staff, to plan and supervise the organization and training of the National Guard. If General Bell had had his way, Lieutenant Marshall would have been made assistant to the chief of that division and put in charge of National Guard training plans, but Bell was overruled by the Assistant Secretary of War, who felt that the job should go to a West Pointer.[29] The quality of the militia gradually improved. Yet the intent of the War Department to make of it, by federal regulation and training, an effective adjunct to the regular Army continued to be frustrated by inadequate resources, not least the inability of the Army itself to spare the instructors.[30]

For George Marshall the relationship with the National Guard was a mutually happy and constructive one, and would continue. At Leavenworth the young instructor had achieved an eminence—if a relatively humble one—had proved himself and found work that he enjoyed. He could relax a little. "I went out to some of the dances and saw people around. I was not working at night as I had before. But most of the profit to me came out of experience in dealing with other officers, with whom I am happy to say I got along very well. I did some hunting. I had hunting dogs to which I was much devoted. I rode practically every day.[31] I bought a horse and trained it. I wanted to learn how to do that.

That required a great deal of time, of course, particularly in the riding hall, which I didn't like very much. But I undertook to try to train the horse." His old arm injury apparently handicapped him in training because he could not check the horse when it stumbled. For the same reason he was never rated an expert horseman.

In the summer of 1909 Marshall, while on duty with the Pennsylvania National Guard at Somerset, found time for a brief visit with his parents at their home in the adjoining county. It was the last time he saw his father alive. His father's affairs were in better order than they had been four years before. An effort by stockholders of the Percy Mining Company to show that he had misused funds of the company over a period of several years was met with a detailed accounting in January 1909 which apparently satisfied the court.[32] In 1908 George Catlett had been selected as one of the state's delegates to the Democratic National Convention on a slate pledging all-out support to William Jennings Bryan.

That same summer of 1909 Lieutenant Marshall and his wife visited her relatives in the "Green Mountain section" of Albemarle County, "as they called that isolated part . . . beyond Carter's Bridge fifteen miles south of Charlottesville." It was one of those seemingly magic times when mood, circumstance, and experience combined to make him unusually susceptible to his surroundings, and he found himself yielding to the enchantment of the old South. All during his boyhood his Virginia and Kentucky ancestry had been drilled into him and he had seemed to resist it. For four years at VMI he had absorbed much of the military lore and spirit of the Confederacy while he was set apart as a Yankee. In his marriage he had heard much about his wife's Virginia family and had been moved to defend the antiquity and gentility of Uniontown. Even now in Albemarle he thought he was viewed with some reserve as a Yankee and recalled that to Uncle Julian, the family retainer, he was in particular "Miss Lily's" husband, a dubious quantity, until one day when he performed a routine trick of campcraft and Uncle Julian decided that he "would do." [33]

They stayed, he and Lily, in "a large but plain Reconstruction-era white clapboard dwelling, . . . then the home of Miss Sally Coles" (Lily's aunt). To this house, in which Lily's mother was then also living, came cousins, neighbors, friends—Coleses had lived in the county for a hundred years—to talk, mostly about old times, which in the changeless atmosphere of this isolated area seemed not so very old. Their talk measured a tiny but complete world. They discussed and solemnly debated how far it was "between 'Woodville' and the post office at Esmont, between 'Old Woodville' across the way and the little old red brick Episcopal church near Keene, where all of them attended services, between the ancient portals and great spreading yews of their ancestral homestead, 'Tallwood,' and 'Warren,' a disputed nine miles south of the James. Miss Sally recalled that, standing in the churchyard at St. Ann's, she had heard distant cannon on that Palm Sunday morning of April 9, 1865 (the day of the battle of Appomattox Courthouse). There had been a rumble as of thunder far away, across the river to the southwest. They were sure it was Lee's army. As they entered church the firing was becoming desultory. It was quiet when the ladies, and the children, and a few old men returned to their paint-chipped, mudflecked carriages and to their old, uncurried saddle horse. . . . As they scattered to ride homeward, they did not know they had heard the last guns before the surrender." [34]

The young lieutenant fell in love with this little world, its graciousness and hospitality, the charming serenity of the country, the horseback rides down tree-lined country lanes, the canoe trips on the James. He expressed his devotion in characteristic fashion, in action. He borrowed a buggy, "tied a handkerchief" on one wheel, measured the circumference of the wheel, and with the help of some neighbors set out to map the county. Day after day he pursued his project, measuring the distances "between plantations and crossroads, between infrequent hamlets, and innumerable fords, by counting the revolutions of this wheel." Then from his computations he drew a map which still exists, a singularly energetic tribute to a romantic moment.[35]

From the years 1908-10 come almost all of Marshall's military writings—a surprisingly meager and routine production. He helped prepare a manual on *Cordage and Tackle* and contributed to Captain Sherrill's *Map Making and Topography.* As an associate editor of the *Infantry Journal,* he collected material about the school and articles by its instructors. He himself wrote only one piece—an account of the preparation under his supervision of a detailed contour map of the Missouri National Guard camp near Nevada, Missouri. Although Marshall had a lifelong interest in professional military writing and would often go out of his way to encourage it, he had little facility in writing himself. This deficiency he tended to attribute to poor teaching. Yet it may be assumed that in any case his bent was not in that direction; his creativeness remained that of a teacher, stimulating and supporting others.

In 1910 he completed his four years at Leavenworth, a period in which many of the strands of his future career were woven. Among the officers he came to know well was Captain John McAuley Palmer, grandson of the General Palmer of Civil War fame. Palmer, who became a lifelong friend and exerted considerable influence on Marshall, was one of his students. So were Captains James W. McAndrew, Le Roy Eltinge, and George Van Horn Moseley, who held the posts of chief of staff, deputy chief of staff, and chief of Supply (G-4) at General Pershing's GHQ in World War I. When he initially came to First Army Headquarters he found that he had taught the chief of personnel (Bugge), the chief of intelligence (Howell), the chief of operations (McCleave), and the chief of the Air Service (Billy Mitchell). The chief of supply (DeWitt), the deputy chief of staff (Kerth), and the senior troop movements officer in operations (Fuqua) were former Leavenworth classmates. An associate on the Leavenworth staff, the only other teaching lieutenant, was Walter Krueger, with whom he had served in the Philippines. In the engineer company stationed on the post was another lieutenant, nearly a year older than Marshall but his junior in rank, Douglas MacArthur. The two men were of course brought together from time to time in the social life of the post but they did not know each other well. Marshall knew much better an older officer, Lieutenant Colonel Hunter Liggett, who commanded a battalion of the 13th Infantry stationed at Leavenworth. After class Colonel Liggett would frequently work through some of the lessons with the lieutenant, of whom he became very fond.[36] Six years later Marshall was his aide in the Philippines; ten years later his chief of operations in the First Army in France.

VII

The Making of a Staff Officer

---

*"The teacher was being educated at the same time he
was instructing. . . . I was able to experiment. . . ."*

IN September 1909 George Marshall senior died. For several
weeks he had been ill enough to have a nurse; then he improved and the nurse was dismissed. The end came suddenly. On
the morning of September 21 he was talking on the telephone in
his apartment when he had a massive stroke. Paralyzed and
within the hour unconscious, he lived only until that afternoon.
Mrs. Marshall, Marie, and Stuart were at his bedside when he
died; George could not get there.[1] The Knights Templar performed a short memorial ceremony for their brother Mason. In-
terment was in the Allegheny Cemetery at Pittsburgh, where
Mrs. Marshall's maternal family, the Stuarts, had a plot; it was
her decision that she and her husband should be buried there.
Mr. Marshall left no will, but his estate of some twenty-six thousand dollars—the children assigned their legal shares to their
mother—was sufficient to support Mrs. Marshall during her remaining nineteen years.[2] She kept the apartment in Uniontown
but visited Marie in Greensburg, Pennsylvania, spent some time
in Washington after World War I when both George and Stuart
were there, and took regular long holidays in Atlantic City.[3]

In the General's reminiscence of his youth, his father was a

strong and dominant figure, more prominent, more vividly realized and remembered than his mother, for whom he reserved his
expressions of love. The elder Marshall's death marked for the
younger another break with his past toward which he already
felt a stranger. His hometown had so changed that it no longer
looked or felt like home. Now the loss of his father locked one
more door on the house of boyhood.

There was also about this time a pause in his career. Nearing
the end of his four years at Leavenworth, he had clearly finished
for the time being one phase of his professional training. Now
what? Would he find some immediate use for it? Would he perhaps have further assignments to teach? Would he go back to his
regiment, to garrison routine, and bide his time? It was a moment which in the career of a civilian would have seemed like
a crossroads, calling for earnest analysis and prayerful decision.
But in the Army decision was made by someone else, and the
lieutenant had already done all he could to guide it, although
not necessarily as he would have willed.

With four months' accrued leave and the first real opportunity
since his marriage to have a true honeymoon, he asked for the
whole of his leave beginning in mid-August 1910 to take a trip
with Lily to Europe. He got it (as well as a subsequent one
month's extension at half pay) despite the disapproval of the
commanding officer of the 24th Infantry, who pointed out that
Marshall had not yet served with the regiment to which he had
been assigned in 1907.[4] Before taking ship Marshall put in another few weeks of instruction with the militia, a week at summer camp in Karner, New York, and two weeks at the Massachusetts Militia Camps in Hingham and South Framingham. At
his own request his leave was delayed to the end of August in
order to allow him to spend the month at the National Rifle
Matches at Camp Perry, Ohio.[5]

The Marshalls toured Europe in leisurely fashion—more than
a month in England, two weeks or more in the Paris area, a
month's journey in the château country, three weeks in Florence, about two weeks in Rome, then to Austria. On January 7,
in Trieste, they caught a slow boat home that stopped in Patras
and Algiers on the way. Typically he took time in England to
see British Army maneuvers at Aldershot.[6] He rented a bicycle,

"went through" the whole exercise, and believed that he saw more of it than the American military attaché, since he was free of official restrictions. He enjoyed recalling years later that at Versailles he and Lily had managed a forbidden picnic on the palace grounds by inviting an *agent de police* to share it with them. In Rome he talked his way into the Quirinal Palace, where he was taken upstairs to the room in which the royal family had just dined and in which, nine years later, he was himself to dine with King Victor Emmanuel in the company of General Pershing. He also indulged with zest in some ancient history. An expert, whom the Marshalls had met on the Florence-Rome express, took him on tours of the Roman ruins, and in the evening Marshall would report the day's lectures at the *pension*, where two archaeologists and an Oxford don were also staying. "That would lead to an argument that would last about all evening."

On his return at the end of January, Marshall took command of Company D of the 24th Infantry, which was stationed at Madison Barracks near Watertown, New York. But that proved to be little more than touching home base (and a bitterly cold one that winter) before he was off on another assignment for which his talents and training especially fitted him.[7]

Major General Leonard Wood was now Chief of Staff, having succeeded General Bell in the spring of 1910. Like Bell, Wood had come to Washington filled with ideas of what needed to be done to reform the Army and the War Department and affirm the authority of the Chief of Staff, which remained in practice a good deal less than it appeared in law. A year before his appointment he had observed that the War Department bureaus, supposed to have been brought by Root's legislation under central control and subordinated to the General Staff, seemed "to be becoming more and more disorganized." "Orders," he continued, "emanate from different sources, and there seems to be little control or centralization." Wood was resolved to end that diffusion of authority and become himself the sole uniformed boss of the Army. In a memorable fight with the most powerful of the bureau chiefs, Major General Fred Ainsworth, he won his point, though only in principle.[8]

Wood's other major concern was to reorganize the Army to

fight. It was with this that Marshall became directly involved. Despite the experience of the Spanish-American War nothing had been done to assure, in case of war, rapid and effective concentration of the Army in units prepared for combat. The largest tactical unit was still the regiment, and in practice even the regiment existed largely on paper. Troops were scattered throughout the continent in forty-nine posts in twenty-four states. The average garrison was smaller than a battalion (less than seven hundred men). While regimental commanders were responsible for discipline and training of their troops they had no effective way of discharging that responsibility. To assemble a balanced fighting force to cope with an emergency of any size still required the War Department to issue scores of separate orders to commands all over the country.

The best solution would have been to abolish many of the "hitching post" forts, which were in any case useless relics of Indian fighting. Concentration at fewer places would have saved money as well as promoted more effective training and efficient administration. But when General Wood made the first tentative proposals along this line he touched a political nerve. Congressmen with Army installations in their districts or in their friends' districts, along with some admirers of General Ainsworth, responded by trying to pass a law to prevent Leonard Wood from continuing as Chief of Staff.[9] Frustrated on that tack, Wood and Secretary of War Henry L. Stimson managed at least to simplify tactical command channels by an executive order in 1913, organizing the continental Army into divisions and brigades without, however, shifting any troops.

In the meantime maneuvers could accomplish something in providing commanders and staff officers with occasional experience in handling comparatively large bodies of troops. Marshall, as has been noted, had taken part in maneuvers and camps of instruction regularly for four years. Not surprisingly, when one of the largest of them was scheduled in the spring of 1911, someone in the War Department thought of him. The exercise was the first attempt since the war to concentrate a division. Since there were then no regular Army divisions, the unit was designated simply the Maneuver Division, to be commanded by Major General William H. Carter (the man who as assistant to the Adjutant General had done much of the drafting of the General Staff law) and assembled in the vicinity of San Antonio, Texas. Though publicly explained as a training exercise (and actually amply justified on that ground alone), it was also intended as a show of force along the troubled Mexican border. The Mexican Revolution had broken out the year before. The revolutionary leader, Francisco I. Madero, had fled to Texas and issued from there his call for the overthrow of Dictator Porfirio Díaz. Washington, uneasy over inflamed feelings on both sides of the border, ordered officers taking part in the maneuvers "to render the civil authorities any aid that might be required to secure the proper observance of an enforcement of neutrality laws on the Mexican border." [10]

Marshall arrived in San Antonio in March in the midst of heavy rains and cold winds. Assigned to duty with Company D, Signal Corps, he organized a communications center at headquarters, then worked out "a brief plan of having maneuvers with . . . the staffs . . . using communications details . . . instead of the troops at first." This appears to have been a precursor of what was later to be a common method of staff training, the "Command Post Exercise" (CPX), in which troop movements are simulated by messages. As assistant to the chief signal officer, Marshall drew up the plan and selected the three pilots assigned to the signal company to represent generals commanding two infantry columns and an independent cavalry brigade. These officers then reported by telephone and wireless to Marshall, acting as chief of staff of the exercise.[11] He had one portable wireless transmitter, whose generator required two men to crank, and this he sent with the cavalry on the first tactical problem. It was perhaps the first time wireless was used in maneuvers. The historic first message that came back to headquarters was from the cavalry commander, who reported, "I am just west of the manure pile." What manure pile he was west of no one at headquarters ever found out.[12]

In addition troops had field telephones and airplanes for observation and messenger work. Major George O. Squier, the chief signal officer, finding the communications work impressive, was moved to some predictions. On the future of aircraft he reported: "If there was any doubt in the minds of individuals of this command as to the utility of the aeroplane for military purposes, that doubt has been removed by aeronautical work done in this division." [13] And in the larger view he had a vision of the future of generalship. He thought it conceivable that with large armies the communications systems they had demonstrated would permit the commander to remain from ten to thirty miles in the rear. It was possible for a man to "attain eminence in the military profession at present without ever having been actually under fire." [14]

Most comment was a great deal less sanguine on maneuvers which in fact revealed serious weaknesses. A plethora of orders from the War Department had produced a "hodgepodge concentration" of troops in the field, and at the end of ninety days the division was still not fully assembled.[15] Foreign observers noted that units were seriously under strength and officers green to command. German critics blamed the volunteer system and the low esteem in which the military profession was held in America—so low, in fact, that Congress in 1911 had to order managers of inns, restaurants, and other public places not to discriminate against soldiers under penalty of a five-hundred-dollar fine.[16] American officers tended to blame the archaic dispersion of the Army in frontier posts. General Wood himself took the occasion to write an article for *McClure's,* early in 1912, in which he attacked the widespread scattering of troops in posts (though he had already lost that battle) and the excessive power of the bureaus in Washington. The Texas maneuvers, he wrote, had "demonstrated conclusively our helplessness to meet with trained troops any sudden emergency." Secretary of War Stimson contributed another article—one of a series of seven that the *Independent* published on "What Is the Matter with Our Army?"—in which he proposed the establishment of a council of national defense consisting of members of Congress and civilian and military leaders to draw up an intelligent national military policy.[17]

Congress could not be moved to any such basic reappraisal of America's military needs and resources. It would, however, be persuaded to vote a little more money as the Mexican crisis persisted. It also enacted another law to improve the quality of the militia along lines already laid out by Elihu Root. The law, passed on March 3, 1911, permitted the President to detail Army officers for regular tours of duty with the National Guard as instructors, one for each militia regiment or separate battalion of infantry, and proportionately for other branches.[18] As early as the autumn of 1910 when the bill was being considered, Governor Eben S. Draper of Massachusetts asked the War Department to assign Lieutenant Marshall to his state's militia if and when the bill passed. As soon as the measure was approved the commanding general of the Pennsylvania National Guard and the adjutant general of the state pressed General Wood to let them have Marshall, but the Chief of Staff ruled that it was only proper to yield to Governor Draper's earlier request.[19]

Marshall left San Antonio in May, under orders to report to Massachusetts. But he had first two short assignments with the National Guard: one in Luray, Virginia; the other at Mount Gretna, Pennsylvania. The latter turned out to be a rugged week. And he bequeathed in his reminiscences a vivid picture of the young lieutenant, mounted on a black horse borrowed from a Lebanon undertaker, galloping across the rugged countryside around Mount Gretna among groups of militia officers who were working out tactical problems he had assigned them. This gallant and very military spectacle was marred only by his most unmilitary horse, which, never having been off a paved street in his life, could not keep his footing; seven times he stumbled and fell in the five days. "If I hadn't been young," the General commented, "I never could have stood it." [20]

On reporting in Boston to Brigadier General Gardner Pearson, Massachusetts adjutant general, Marshall found his first task was to organize a school program for militia officers for the end of June and thereafter to assist Captain Matthew Hanna in drawing plans for state maneuvers.[21] He had known Hanna at Leavenworth, where the captain taught during Marshall's last year. Hanna, now on the War Department General Staff, was one of the intellectuals of the new Army. His *Tactical Principles and Problems* was a required text at the Army School of the

Line and was besides well known in foreign armies, which were
not accustomed to looking to Americans for military theory. The
Massachusetts maneuvers which he planned with Marshall's help
were among the largest militia exercises so far attempted. Con-
centrating six thousand state troops in Essex and Middlesex
counties at the end of July, they stirred the pride of local patri-
ots. Ten thousand citizens of Boston and vicinity watched the
beginning of the exercises before torrential rain drove them
from the field. Local newspapers delightedly covered the whole
affair. Hanna was also enthusiastic; he believed the maneuvers
were "beyond doubt the best [for militia] ever seen in this country." [22]

In September, Marshall, who had been almost constantly on
the move, and much of the time in camps, tried to set up his
domestic base once more. He rented quarters in Boston and Lily
again unpacked their things. But as it turned out he was to find
himself seldom at home. During the autumn and early winter he
conducted a brigade school, lectured to officer groups on the lessons of the summer maneuvers, and prepared problems and
other teaching materials for six schools to be held in 1912. Between January 22 and March 8, 1912, he inspected forty-two companies in twenty-five cities and towns in eastern Massachusetts.
He was in Lawrence during the I.W.W. strike, staying one to
three days at a time to inspect units there on strike duty, though
he had, of course, no responsibility for their performance under state control.[23]

It was hard work and kept him on the go but he did it with
relish. He found that while the men sometimes complained at
the load of work they were responsive to his lead. "This was an
educational treat to me. The teacher was being educated at the
same time he was instructing. . . . I was able to experiment
and enlarge and subtract and so on."

In the spring of 1912, after a week's assignment to a camp of
instruction at St. Augustine, Florida, Marshall was detailed to
Governors Island, New York, to work with Brigadier General
Tasker H. Bliss on still more ambitious exercises. It was planned
that summer to assemble for a two-state exercise some fifteen
thousand men of the National Guard from Maine, Vermont,
Massachusetts, Connecticut, New York, and New Jersey, along

with twenty-three hundred regulars. The Boston newspaper which hailed the maneuvers as "the greatest military event of its nature held in peace in the United States" was exaggerating slightly.[24] Maneuvers at Manassas in 1904, in which General Bell had commanded one force, had involved considerably more troops (26,296). Nevertheless the exercises, for which General Bliss, later to become Chief of Staff, acted as chief umpire with Marshall as his assistant, were of national significance and brought both Secretary of War Stimson and Chief of Staff Wood to witness the final stages. Bliss was pleased with his assistant and wrote him afterward: "It is recognized that a very great measure of the success . . . is due to the skillful manner in which you planned the various situations of the campaign." [25]

Perhaps, had Marshall himself been able to choose, he would at this time have gone on in the teaching that he found so stimulating. If so, he would have had a choice between setting up a kind of "baby war college" in Massachusetts, as the new adjutant general, Charles H. Cole, wanted him to,[26] or becoming commandant at VMI, which had put in its second request for him in three years.[27] But he had no choice. In August, Congress passed the so-called Manchu Law, which stiffened the restrictions on detached service laid down in the law of 1910. Under the law, line officers below the rank of major in time of peace could not at any time be on detached service unless they had served two of the preceding six years with the regiment to which they were assigned. Commanding officers responsible for abrogating the law whether intentionally or not were to forfeit pay and allowances during the period of their disobedience.[28]

Marshall went back to troops, to Company M of the 4th Infantry Regiment, stationed at Fort Logan Roots outside Little Rock, Arkansas, a post of eighteen officers and two hundred and ninety-one enlisted men,[29] and one of those that Congress had been asked in vain to abolish. Militarily the high point of his six months' stay came with the organization of a postgraduate garrison school, which won praise in the Inspector General's report on the post as "a model course of instruction." [30] Personally the experience which he recalled with greatest relish was a Christmas party he put on for the children of the post.

He discovered on the Thursday before Christmas Eve, which

fell on Tuesday, that no celebration had been planned and that in fact Fort Logan Roots had had none for years. In Army fashion the commanding officer, having heard his complaint, gave him permission to remedy it himself. With no more backing than that, he took on that Christmas party, to make some other people's children happy, with the same drive, ingenuity, and persuasiveness he had applied to New England maneuvers. He collected the money. He talked the toy merchants of Little Rock into giving him bargains on the things they had so little time left to sell. He found a Santa Claus and persuaded him to build his own chimney in the post gymnasium. He had himself made officer of the day three days running (a privilege no one protested) so that he could get some prisoners to volunteer to decorate the gymnasium. In the end all of them turned out, and he rewarded them by allowing them on Christmas morning to give out the presents. The party was a success, and there was a sequel—a reward for the unsentimental lieutenant himself: Christmas night, as officer of the day, he made the required check of the guardhouse. He found the prisoners gathered in the corridor. One stepped forward to make a little speech. Only one man among them, he said, had ever had Christmas in his home. Now the lieutenant had given Christmas to them all. Their chances of ever doing anything for the lieutenant in return seemed remote, but they would always hope for such a chance, and if he ever called for any of them they would come, if possible, from wherever they might be.[31]

After Christmas there was more moving, of which Mrs. Marshall at least was heartily sick. The 4th Infantry was transferred to Fort Snelling, Minnesota, arrived there in mid-February, and ten days later was ordered as part of the 2d Division to Fort Crockett, near Galveston, Texas, some twenty-six hundred miles away. The latter move reflected the emergency created by revolutionary developments in Mexico. President Madero, who had succeeded Díaz in 1911, was ousted by General Victoriano Huerta and a few days later (on February 22) murdered. To guard against border incidents in the resultant turmoil, President Taft wished to concentrate troops in Texas. The recent reorganization of the Army into divisions now proved its usefulness.

Instead of the usual swarm of War Department orders to each regiment or separate battalion, Secretary Stimson was able to boast that with a single order and a five-line letter he had been able to direct the concentration of the 2d Division under General Carter. Within a week 11,450 men (half the division's authorized wartime strength) were on their way to Texas City and Galveston.[32]

Marshall spent four months in Texas in command of Company M. On May 28, 1913, he had orders to move again, this time overseas. He had had nine years in the States and now was to go back to the Philippines to be assigned to the 13th Infantry near Manila. Mrs. Marshall was to accompany him but she would spend the hottest part of the year away from the Islands.

A twenty-six-day trip aboard the old transport *Logan* took them from San Francisco to Manila, with stops at Honolulu and Guam. They arrived on August 5, 1913, and Marshall joined his regiment at Fort McKinley, which had been under construction when he left Manila a little less than ten years before.[33]

Ten years had changed the whole character of military service in the Philippines. In the southern islands the Mohammedan Moros were still in rebellion but even they were at the end of their rope. Elsewhere the insurrection was history. American governors like Taft and W. Cameron Forbes had made considerable progress in preparing the Islands for self-government. In 1907 Taft, while Secretary of War, had come to Manila to inaugurate the first Philippine legislature. Wilson's Secretary of State, William Jennings Bryan, was on record as favoring early independence, and shortly after Marshall reached Manila a new governor (the first Democratic one), Francis Burton Harrison, arrived with orders to speed the process.[34]

As for the American Army, its view was turned outward, on guard against the possibility of invasion of the Philippines, especially from Japan. Japanese aggressiveness, displayed in the Russo-Japanese War in 1905, together with the cooling of relations with the United States after the victory, had made Japan a Pacific neighbor to be watched. Her annexation of Korea in 1910 sharpened the danger. Relations with the United States were strained in 1906 and again in 1913 by California anti-

Japanese legislation, which the Japanese assumed the federal government should be able to control. Although the cloud over the Pacific was not very dark,[35] it was sufficient to prompt the Philippine garrison to hold maneuvers designed frankly to test island defenses. It was one of those that was soon to provide George Marshall's career with a myth of the kind familiar in the lives of heroes—the moment when suddenly his native genius was supposed to stand revealed and one could no longer doubt that he was marked for the highest success.

Despite the vague menace of Japan, life in the Philippines was relaxed. There was no sense of imminent peril to the Islands or to the world. At Fort McKinley, where four to five thousand officers and men were billeted in buildings only completed in 1904, life was much like peacetime Army life in the States if one ignored the occasional green lizard that dropped into the soup, ants sometimes on parade over the living-room floor, the tarantula on the bridge table, plagues of grasshoppers, and, of course, the heat. From a professional point of view McKinley was superior to many, perhaps most, continental posts. Relatively large, it had a full regiment of infantry (the 13th), a regiment of cavalry (the 7th in 1913, later the 8th), a field artillery battalion, and attached signal and engineer units—all maintained at combat strength. It was possible, therefore, to carry out war games on a scale more nearly realistic than at any mainland United States post.[36]

Fort McKinley was tailor-made for an ambitious young staff officer in training, and particularly for George Marshall, who found himself once more under the eye and wing of General Bell, now commanding general of the Philippine Department. After a few months Company F, to which Marshall was assigned, got a new commander. He was Captain E. J. Williams, who had been a student of Marshall's at Leavenworth and had subsequently worked with him on maneuvers.[37] Lowly as was the niche he filled in the tables of organization, the lieutenant was special, a marked man, and he knew it. It was not entirely a comfortable situation. Educated and experienced above his rank, he was caught, like many of his fellow officers, behind the hump of officers produced by the Spanish-American War. Having directed the movements of thousands of troops, in his daily job he took orders from the commander of a hundred. Marshall recalled rather bitterly in later years that despite his teaching at Leavenworth and his work in maneuvers he was assigned to a post where for the first six months he never commanded a company for one day. "And yet the company commander was a dear friend of mine and had been a student under me at Leavenworth." There were moments of frustration. It was perhaps at such a time, feeling both bored and cocky, that he made a foolish wager. He bet that the officer who next inspected his company would catch three minor faults and miss three major ones: that he would note the soldier who was unshaved, the soldier whose blouse was unbuttoned, and the soldier who lacked a bayonet, but miss three grave tactical blunders in a field exercise Marshall himself would arrange. The bet was won and regretted thereafter.[38] A momentary triumph over a stuffed shirt proved not worth that officer's lasting enmity.

Actually Marshall was very soon engaged on the project that, through a combination of accident, talent, and extraordinary devotion of energy, was to make his fame. He had arrived in August. In September he was assigned as adjutant to the "White Force," scheduled to simulate an invasion of Luzon in January maneuvers, and was set to work with one of two planning detachments. Planning proceeded toward a target date, but the day of the attack was kept secret at General Bell's headquarters until the last minute.[39]

The last minute proved to be the morning of Janury 22. Orders were given to the commander of the White Force, a senior colonel on the brink of retirement, to concentrate his 4841 officers and men in the Batangas Bay area beginning immediately and finishing by January 25. The troops were to be gathered from various posts in northern Luzon, transported by ship to Batangas, and put ashore by small boats. Once assembled, White Force was to move to attack Manila against 3245 defenders assigned to the opposing Brown Force.[40]

Initial difficulties were typically of the kind that commonly mar any relatively green unit's first leap into battle. A scarcity of small boats delayed the concentration forty-eight hours. The

White Force commander proved to be "a courtly gentleman, a very nice fellow" (in his young adjutant's words), and quite incompetent. "He rode in the spring wagon," Marshall said, recalling the first days of the maneuver. "Every time we would stop [his zinc-lined] suitcase would be brought out and he would refresh himself against the Philippine heat." It was clearly no way to go into even a mock battle, and General Bell's headquarters proposed to relieve him. Lieutenant Marshall then demonstrated his own unusual position and influence by arguing successfully against the move, which he feared would result in his getting a new commander more difficult to work with. The amiable colonel was left in command but under instruction to leave his adjutant free to act on his own.

Still larger responsibilities followed. The White Force chief of staff, Captain Jens Bugge, fell ill and had to be taken back to Manila. That happened on the second morning, just after Bugge and Marshall had arrived in the maneuver area. Since only Marshall had comparable knowledge of maneuver plans, it seemed logical that he should take over. So it seemed to General Bell's representative with White Force, Captain E. E. Booth, who was also aware that Marshall had been Bugge's teacher at Leavenworth. Disregarding the matter of rank, Booth named as acting chief of staff the man whose abilities he knew so well. General Bell confirmed the assignment.[41] The highly unusual consequence was that a junior lieutenant wound up for all practical purposes in command of nearly five thousand men.

Lieutenant Henry H. (Hap) Arnold, who would be Chief of the Army Air Forces in World War II, was there in Batangas and has recorded a memorable picture of Lieutenant Marshall lying on his back in a bamboo clump, glancing at a map and dictating precise field orders for the advance. Arnold was so impressed that he wrote his wife that he had just seen a future Chief of Staff in action.[42]

Because of the lack of boats White Force could not begin the advance toward Manila until January 29. But for the next five days the invading troops moved smoothly to occupy successive objectives against a disorganized defense. The umpires did not declare a winner and the exercise was terminated before Manila fell. In the official report White Force was criticized for putting inadequate forces on its first day's objective, but commended for thereafter keeping the units intact so that subsequent attacks could be made in strength. The chief umpire of White Force praised the field orders of the detachments and singled out Marshall's work, noting that "sudden changes . . . placed upon Lieutenant Marshall . . . a severe task which he carried out successfully and for which he deserves great credit." [43]

Certainly it was a job well done and represented the acceptance by a junior lieutenant of unusual responsibility. But the myth born in Batangas did not come out of an umpire's report. It had the breathlessness of rumor and the touch of extravagance such as to make General Hagood "remember" quite erroneously later that General Bell at the close of the maneuver called his staff together and said of Marshall, "This, gentlemen, is the greatest military genius since Stonewall Jackson." Bell did not say that and probably didn't think it.[44] He knew what Marshall had learned at Leavenworth. He knew that for the job done the lieutenant had had probably better and longer special training than any other officer in his command; the intelligent, even brilliant, application of lessons well learned was admirable but not necessarily Olympian.[45] Furthermore it could be observed that Marshall had planned more complex maneuvers in New England, involving more troops, and as assistant umpire and instructor had had intellectually more difficult assignments. Nevertheless, in respect to his performance in the Philippines, history has to reckon with two facts: a solid achievement and the appearance of a miracle. The achievement demonstrated the development of a fine staff officer; the extra glamour of the demonstration gave a dazzle to Marshall's name that helped in the future to make sure that his associates and superiors did not forget him.

Marshall had not found the performance easy. The strain under which he had worked for many weeks brought on an attack of "neurasthenia." It was his second warning of the consequences of overwork. The first had come some eighteen months earlier at the conclusion of the Connecticut maneuvers in which he had similar responsibilities and long working hours. On a visit to his wife's uncle, Thomas Coles, in Brooklyn in August 1913, he had collapsed and was found unconscious on the street. Treated by a civilian doctor, he had been found to have "acute dilatation of the heart." Later Marshall described the malady to an Army doctor as being "a tight dry feeling" of increased tension and inability to relax.[46] He felt himself that it was a warning to take it easy, but it was some time before he could learn to do that.

Directly from the maneuvers he went to a Manila hospital and stayed there nearly two weeks. General Bell on February 15 granted him two months' sick leave, which was later extended by two months' regular leave. Most of that time he spent with Mrs. Marshall in Japan, Manchuria, and Korea—in part a busman's holiday. He spent part of a month studying the Manchurian battlefields of the Russo-Japanese War. Despite the edginess of Japanese-American relations, "Japanese officers . . . treated me royally." He was "entertained by General Baron Fukushima, the Governor of Manchuria at Port Arthur, and by Lieutenant General Akiyama, their greatest cavalry leader, at Liaoyang. . . ." From Dairen, he visited nearby Nanshan Hill and Port Arthur, and then went to Telissu, Liaoyang, the Shaho, Mukden, and Antung at the mouth of the Yalu River. He then went to Seoul and Pusan before returning to Japan. He rode horseback sometimes twenty-five to forty miles a day and walked long distances besides. He found "the weather was perfect, the scenery in some places was magnificent," and altogether the trip was tonic for muscles, nerves, and spirit.[47]

Feeling that what he had observed was important for the Army as a whole, he reported in detail to the Adjutant General. While at Leavenworth (no doubt under the influence of Major Morrison), had made, he said, "a serious study of the events of the Russo-Japanese War" and had kept at it since then "with considerable energy." After visiting the battlefields, talking to Japanese officers, who apparently freely discussed their own training methods, and witnessing Japanese troops in exercises, he "came away with a new idea of those fights and entirely different ideas as to the proper methods to follow in peace training." For instance, he admired the Japanese handling of the bayonet. Unlike the Americans, he noted, the Japanese did not fence but rushed skillfully in such a way as to make "utmost use of the momentum of the man." He admired, too, Japanese training in the hand grenade, which he felt would be particularly important in any attack on, and defense of, the Philippines. Yet our own Army, he thought, had all but neglected grenade training; he doubted that there was a private soldier on Corregidor "who ever heard of a hand grenade." Finally he thought an important lesson of the Manchurian War was the value of attack at night, involving special techniques and tactics in which Americans had not been schooled.[48]

As a result of the report he had a lecture to give the officers of Fort McKinley on his return. But despite his unquenchable professional enthusiasms, he came back resolved to reduce the intensity of his life and teach himself to relax. He began the habit of riding an hour or so before breakfast and of playing tennis in the afternoon. When he could he went hunting. Among his hunting companions were "Hap" Arnold and Lieutenant Courtney Hodges, who would command the First Army in World War II.

Fort McKinley for the most part followed the tropical routine, getting the bulk of the day's work out of the way in the comparative cool of the morning, napping in the worst heat of the early afternoon. But it was not a routine to which the children on the post always took kindly. Marshall's next-door neighbors had "very young, very little" children who customarily played between their house and his and organized baseball games during the hour of siesta with all the kids in the vicinity. "They made so derned much noise nobody could sleep." The lieutenant may have been annoyed, but he took the way out of a man who liked children: he didn't try to lick them; he got up and joined them, "pitching for both sides and umpiring."

"The catcher," he recalled, "used a coffee strainer as a mask. I was very much afraid he would get hit on the coffee strainer, and it would take the skin off all around his head where the thing rested. The little children were out in the field, about two players for each position, one deep infield and one 'way out' infield. When they got the ball they would get so excited they couldn't throw it. All they could do was yell. It used to get very exciting, and when the man at home base would plead with them to throw the ball in, they would throw it about twenty feet from him; with his coffee strainer he could never get the ball."

In the evenings there was the usual garrison social life, frequent dances at the club, strolling and visiting, usually in formal dress, officers in white, their wives in dinner gowns. Soon after Marshall got back from his leave he bought a Model T Ford from Major Sherrill, the engineer officer who had taught with him at Leavenworth. The car helped break the monotony of life on the post. "We ride from twenty to sixty miles almost every evening," he wrote a friend. "The roads out here are wonderfully fine—so much better than the roads in the States— and the scenery is magnificent." [49] As if to make sure that his enjoyment of motoring should be matched by learning something useful, he proceeded to take the engine apart to see how it worked. "I was not at all mechanical," he explained, "but I just had to do it."

In March 1915 the 3d Battalion of the 13th Infantry, to which Marshall was assigned, along with the 1st, was transferred to Corregidor. Not long before the transfer Brigadier General Hunter Liggett, who had known Marshall both in Leavenworth and on the Connecticut maneuvers which he umpired, arrived in the Islands to command the Provisional Infantry Brigade at Fort McKinley. General Liggett had Marshall detached from his company and assigned to him as aide.[50] Less than a year later Liggett succeeded Bell as commander of the Philippine Department, and Marshall accompanied him to his new headquarters in Manila. In both assignments he worked with Liggett's other aide, a former Leavenworth classmate and close friend, Lieutenant Beebe. Both men helped Liggett in the tactical instruction of his command. An aide usually went with him on inspections, taking notes as to points to improve. At other times he would send one of them to check on exercises or instruction. In a sense, they were continuing their staff and field training under a man whom Beebe considered one of the finest tacticians and strategists in the Army, "with the quickest and best answers to tactical problems of any officer I ever met." [51]

Japan's swift action after the outbreak of the European war in 1914 to improve her position in China by seizing the former German concessions in Shantung and by making a number of heavy demands on the badly divided country increased American fears for the safety of the Philippines. In an effort to see how a Japanese invasion from the direction of the Lingayen Gulf might be stopped or delayed, Liggett at the end of 1915 ordered a staff ride for his officers up the central valley of Luzon to the gulf. Marshall, who had spent some months poring over the War Department's reports on the battles during the Philippine Insurrection and had visited many of the battlefields, worked out a plan for a two weeks' ride, January 14-29, 1916.[52] Reinforced by maneuver experience, it led to the general conclusion that the Japanese could successfully land if they wanted to risk the invasion.[53]

Liggett, in this past year, was having another and closer look at the young officer he had long admired and becoming convinced that in case of war he would like very much to have Marshall under his immediate command. That in fact would happen soon—sooner than anyone then expected.

VIII

The Coming of the War

---

*"He [Marshall] should be made a brigadier general in
the regular Army, and every day this is postponed is
a loss to the Army and the nation."*
      —Johnson Hagood in Marshall's Efficiency
      Report, December 31, 1916.

IT happens to many—perhaps to most—ambitious men: a day
comes when they reckon their birthdays and their accomplishments to date and they see suddenly that not only is the time
left in which to realize their dreams short, but it may not even be
time enough. In October 1915 Lieutenant Marshall was fresh
from his most considerable and conspicuous triumph as a military
tactician; he was occupying a role of prominence and promise as
aide to General Liggett. He had powerful friends in the Army at
home and an unbroken record of high distinction in his career
so far. Yet it was in that month that he sat down and wrote to his
friend, the superintendent of VMI, General E. W. Nichols, that
he was not getting anywhere and felt he ought to make a change.
"The absolute stagnation in promotion in the infantry," he wrote,
"has caused me to make tentative plans for resigning as soon as
business conditions improve. Even in the event of an increase as a
result of legislation next winter [this was to develop as the National Defense Act of 1916, which considerably enlarged the

129

Army], the prospects for advancement in the Army are so restricted by law and by the accumulation of large numbers of men of nearly the same age all in a single grade, that I do not feel it right to waste all my best years in the vain struggle against insurmountable difficulties." Clearly he thought he had already wasted a few of the best years. He was almost thirty-five, still a first lieutenant. And though by current Army standards he had by no means been an unusually long time in grade, it seemed to him, considering his age, that he was terribly near the bottom still. He had apparently thought so two years earlier. In the interim he had worked hard and achieved success but without, it seemed, the tangible reward of pushing up ahead. That drive to excel which had goaded him incessantly since boyhood was at him with peculiar intensity. He had, he thought in these last years of youth, a moral obligation not to rest. "The temptation to accept an absolutely assured and fairly soft living, with little or no prospect of reasonable advancement, is very great when you consider the difficulties and positive dangers of starting anew in civil life at my age. However, with only one life to live, I feel that the acceptance of my present secured position would mean that I lacked the backbone and necessary moral courage to do the right thing." [1]

Superintendent Nichols, of course, replied as a friend, with the facts that Marshall knew very well: that he was an assured and recognized success at his profession and that the Army would soon be enlarged and Marshall would then have a chance at a captaincy. "I would advise you to stick to it. If you do, I am sure in time you will be among the high ranking officers in the service." [2] It was modest prophecy but good advice. Probably Marshall did not really need it, but perhaps it helped soothe that moment of nightmare when a sense of failure coincided with a sense of advancing age.

It is remarkable that in this correspondence neither Marshall nor Nichols mentioned the outstandingly relevant fact of the time: the great war in Europe, with its threat to draw America in and provide Army officers with opportunities for promotion to overmatch their most extravagant dreams. The fact was that neither man, like the overwhelming bulk of his fellow citizens, had any notion that the quarrels of the Central Powers and the Allies would involve the United States in war.

While in Europe in 1910 Marshall had had no presentiment of the coming conflict. Four years later in Japan he was shocked to hear a young German bitterly attack the British and sensed for the first time the hatred between peoples of Western Europe. Yet though the incident impressed him, it came into focus only in recollection afterward. Even after the war began he seems to have followed its course chiefly through various presidential proclamations of American neutrality, which it was his duty to read to units of the regiment, as country after country entered the war. Throughout his stay in the Philippines it was Mexico, not Europe, whose belligerence seemed relevant and threatening to him and to his fellow officers.

It will be recalled that when President Madero was ousted and murdered by the forces of Victoriano Huerta in February 1913 the War Department ordered the 2d Division to duty on the Texas-Mexico border. From that time until the eve of American entry into World War I the bulk of United States tactical forces was concentrated on the border or engaged in expeditions into Mexico. To that extent, at least, the military posture of the nation was more alert than it had been before the Spanish-American War. The total United States regular force thus disposed was never more than the war strength of a division of regulars. With the calling out of the National Guard in the summer of 1916 this number was increased.[3]

Despite advice that General Huerta as a strong man was the best guarantee of the restoration of order in Mexico, President Wilson refused to recognize his regime. He believed that both morally and in our own practical interest America should offer no help to a usurper whose object was to destroy constitutional Mexican democracy and return to the dictatorial system of Díaz He recommended a policy of "watchful waiting." When in the spring of 1914 one of Huerta's officers arrested a paymaster and several crew members of an American warship who had come ashore at Tampico and declined to make the full apologies re quired by the United States after their release, Wilson asked Congress for authority to enforce his demand "for unequivocal amends." [4] Before Congress could act the American consul at Vera Cruz reported that a German merchant ship was about to land ammunition in that port for the Huerta government. The President thereupon ordered the Navy to seize Vera Cruz. Marines were landed within a few hours and Army units were dispatched at once from Galveston under Brigadier General Frederick Funston. At the head of a combined Army and Marine force of some seventy-five hundred, Funston occupied Vera Cruz until near the end of November. Well before that time Huerta had been forced to resign, largely because of United States hostility, and Venustiano Carranza had taken over the capital city.

Yet nothing was solved. There remained a general expectation in the United States that war might come. Congress regularized the status of volunteer enlistments and appointment of volunteer officers in case such troops might be needed, and appropriated two hundred and fifty thousand dollars for airships and other aerial craft.[5]

In Mexico revolutionary groups continued to struggle for power. Violence continued to spill across the border. Marshall, watching events with keen interest from his post in the Philippines, shared the opinion that war was imminent. His old friend and patron, General Bell, then in command of the 2d Division, had passed on to him a promise from the Chief of Staff of the Army that Marshall would be ordered home to serve on Bell's staff if the General went to Mexico. Still in the Philippines a year later, the lieutenant wrote a friend that he feared he would miss "an advance on the City of Mexico" but hoped that he might "still be in time." [6]

In October 1915 President Wilson recognized Carranza as *de facto* head of the Mexican government. While Carranza was to prove relatively durable (he remained in office until 1920) he was unable effectively to assert national authority over the factional leaders. In January 1916 America was shocked by a rebel raid at Santa Ysabel, and this was followed in March by a still more outrageous attack by Francisco Villa on American soldiers and civilians of Columbus, New Mexico.

It was an unusual case of acts of war perpetrated not by order or even sufferance of a foreign government but despite it. America's response was a similarly extraordinary military incursion into the territory of a friendly government, directed against some of its citizens but not against it. Six days after Villa's raid, on orders of the new Secretary of War, Newton D. Baker, a punitive expedition under Brigadier General John J. Pershing crossed the border in pursuit of the bandit chief. Pershing was to remain in Mexico eleven months, without catching Villa and more remarkably without precipitating war with Mexico.[7]

The Pershing expedition made its commander's name (he was promoted to major general in 1916) and revealed the country's military weakness. Although Pershing's force had only one brush with Villa's soldiers and a few minor engagements with Mexican government troops, its long march into Mexico under orders to avoid towns, and denied the use of Mexican railways by the Carranza government, stretched communications to the breaking point. To reinforce the expedition the War Department within two months stripped the United States of its mobile fighting force. In May the President therefore ordered the National Guard of the border states to federal duty. In June the order was extended to all states. By the end of August more than a hundred and forty thousand National Guardsmen were on active service.[8]

While the Mexican crises showed up the thinness of the nation's border defenses, concurrent violations of our neutral rights at sea by both Britain and Germany raised larger questions of our ability to maintain our sovereignty. German submarine warfare, which took American lives in the sinking of the *Lusitania* in February 1915 and continued to inflict casualties on our nationals traveling the Atlantic in 1916, roused some Americans to demand intervention on the side of the Western Allies, and many others, more moderate, to urge a stronger Army and Navy to back the President's stiffening policy toward both Britain and Germany. Public concern, thus variously stimulated, helped to drive the National Defense Act through Congress on June 3, 1916.[9] The act resolved the crucial and acrimonious debate over whether the United States in the twentieth century could continue to depend for defense primarily on the state militias. Wilson's Secretary of War, Lindley M. Garrison, argued vigorously that it could not. Despite the Dick Act of 1903, by which the militia had been required to conform to certain federal standards of training and officer fitness, it remained essentially an Army of the separate states. Even if one were to get around Attorney General Wickersham's opinion of 1912 that the militia could not constitutionally be sent out of the country, there seemed to be insuperable constitutional obstacles to bringing it under effective control and discipline. President Wilson, like Garrison, became convinced that the nation needed a genuinely national reserve force and that the state levies could not supply that need. He favored the scheme advocated by the Secretary of War and a considerable body of regular Army opinion for a volunteer "continental" Army (modeled after the conscript armies of Europe), to consist of four hundred thousand reserves called up nationally by classes and periodically retrained.[10]

But for various reasons the majority of Congress balked at this thoroughgoing national solution. The National Defense Act worked out a compromise, which Wilson accepted (though Garrison would not and resigned in consequence). The compromise set the national defense on a tripod: to the regular Army which was to be gradually expanded, and the National Guard which in case of war was to be drafted into the federal service, it added an organized reserve to consist of an Officer Reserve Corps and an enlisted reserve. The body of the enlisted reserve was to be drawn from regulars furloughed to it; the officers were to be trained at various approved colleges or at citizens' training camps and commissioned on examination.[11]

Neither of these ideas for a reserve component was new. A section of the Army Appropriation Act of 1912 had laid the legislative groundwork for an enlisted reserve by changing the term of recruitment from a straight three years on active duty to a term of seven years, four in the Army and three in the reserve. Veterans were also permitted to enlist in the reserve. Few men, however, were tempted to sign up for such a long period at a time when Army pay and conditions of service compared unfavorably with the opportunities open to even untrained civilians. In the summer of 1915 the enlisted reserve numbered just seventeen men.[12]

Creation of the Officer Reserve Corps accepted and extended experiments in training civilians which General Wood began in 1912 when he was Chief of Staff. In the summer of that year he opened two summer camps to give six weeks' military training to students. Although the students had to pay their own way, they came in such numbers that more camps were opened the following year, and in 1915 similar training was organized for business and professional men as well. Best known of these latter camps was the one at Plattsburg, New York, which General Wood established when he became commanding general of the Eastern Department and which he publicized so effectively with his usual dash and enthusiasm that the whole scheme of citizen-officer training became known as the "Plattsburg idea."

With the National Defense Act and the summer camps the nation by the summer of 1916 had psychologically at least turned to face the possibility of war, but not the war that in fact was only about nine months away. The comparative vigor with which Congress legislated a defense establishment and the enthusiasm with which the young men trained in their summer camps were in response primarily to the challenge of Mexico. These expressed a national consensus in that direction that was especially welcome in contrast to the bitter division of opinion over the European war.

When Marshall sailed for home in May 1916 he expected to go shortly after his arrival to a regiment at Colonia Dublán in Pershing's command.[13] Instead he found himself assigned at the Presidio of San Francisco on the staff of General Bell as the General's aide. Bell, no longer poised on the Mexican border, was commanding the Western Department and was, among other things, deeply involved in the new citizen-training program.[14] It was for that he needed Marshall's help. Before reporting for duty Marshall was ordered to appear before a promotion board at Fort McDowell. The procedure, after the long wait, was swift. Unanimously recommended for his captaincy without examination—waived as a result of his Leavenworth training—he actually received his commission on August 14, nine years after he had become a first lieutenant, fourteen years after he had entered the Army.[15]

The new captain plunged into a job that had familiar ingredients but a wildly unfamiliar setting. On behalf of General Bell he was to look into and recommend changes in the summer training of civilian volunteers at Monterey. The camp had been set up on the grounds of the Del Monte Hotel, "a beautiful and ideal spot," the *San Francisco Examiner* commented, "although an incongruous one. The country and its natives seem to radiate peace and ease and the comfort of life. There is luxury and wealth at the Del Monte Hotel. There is romance and glamour and decaying idealism at Monterey. There is classic literature and artistry at Carmel. There is the joy and sunshine of the vacation season at Pacific Grove and Santa Cruz." [16] And in the midst of it all, twelve hundred trainees, aged eighteen to fifty-three, fashionable young men, ministers, lawyers, brokers, merchants, newspapermen, doctors—men whose idealism, though not decaying, was sometimes mixed. "They were all the hot bloods of San Francisco," the General recalled. "I saw more Rolls Royces and other fine cars around there than I had ever seen collected . . . before." It was quite the thing to do, to come to Monterey for a month, where one experienced a fine blend of patriotic stimulus and holiday air, drills by day and the gaiety of the Del Monte Hotel at night.[17]

Since they were not only volunteers but were paying for the privilege, they had been treated gently—too gently—by their instructors, many of whom were regular officers recalled from retirement. General Bell wanted the training made much stiffer, but he was also aware of the political dangers of clamping down too hard. Marshall approached the problem with the experience of the National Guard behind him and with just the right combination of professional poise and humor.[18]

He pitched his tent on the first day along the path leading to the hotel and began to unpack his bedding roll that had been delivered straight from the ship. As he worked, a circle of curious trainees gathered. "I suppose there were fifteen to twenty lined up watching me, making a few clever remarks, to which I paid no attention." He continued his unpacking though by now he knew what was coming. "The first thing on top was my saddle. But under it were two of Mrs. Marshall's nightgowns, which had been packed at the last minute. Then [came] a long string of stuff of hers which didn't look anything like a bedding roll arrangement for the field. I finally got my stuff out, a heterogeneous combination of everything that was left at the house. . . . That made me famous. . . . Some of the men escorted me [to the hotel] for dinner [that night]. They made speeches [about] my field equipment." And how did the captain take it? "They were awfully nice fellows," the General recalled forty years afterward. "I came to know a good many of them . . . rather intimately."

He liked their high spirits but he thought they needed—and probably would welcome—some tougher discipline. For two days he toured the camp, making recommendations for changes which he submitted to the camp commandant, Brigadier General William L. Sibert,[19] before reporting to General Bell. General Sibert accepted some and then asked that Marshall be detailed to command a different training company each day so that he could personally check on them all. There may have been some malicious relish in the proposal (Sibert's adjutant at least was "redheaded" at what he considered a junior officer's meddling). If it was a case of giving the cocky newcomer an ornery horse to ride, Marshall's first company filled the bill.[20]

The day began with maneuvers in the morning. Marshall's company was in reserve; the men had almost nothing to do. No one minded; it was the end of the week anyway. For lunch a number of girls and wives drove down from San Francisco, bearing picnic baskets and champagne. They spread their viands under the oaks, and the men dined as soldiers ought. But it was too soon over, for the afternoon program was close-order drill, which was something else. The ground was rough, the picnickers sleepy, and the drill ragged, to say the least. At last Marshall called a halt and made a little speech. "You fellows came down here," he said, "because you were enthusiastic to do something in this time of emergency and you are paying your own expenses. This morning you were in a maneuver and you hardly marched at all. You were in reserve, and sitting around resting. Then your wives and girls all brought out good things and you had champagne, and it has been quite delightful to sit under the trees. Now you are so exhausted from this war service you can't do a damn thing. I'm going to go out there and drill you again, and if you can't drill I am going to march you in and report you as wholly ineffective."

It was tough but good-humored, and it worked. "We had a very strenuous drill," the General recalled, "and . . . they turned around that night and gave me a dinner at the hotel. I remember at the time I was called 'Dynamite' Marshall. But it was really quite a funny thing. . . . I continued friendships with them for many years. . . ."

When the Monterey camp closed, Marshall assisted in establishing another at Fort Douglas near Salt Lake City, Utah, of which he became adjutant under his good friend and most extravagant admirer, Lieutenant Colonel Johnson Hagood.[21] Out of this experience he picked up for his record perhaps the most extraordinary praise any Army officer ever had in those routine efficiency reports on which promotion is based. To the form question of whether he would like to have Marshall under his command, Lieutenant Colonel Hagood wrote: "Yes, but I would prefer to serve *under his command.*" He went on to call him "a military genius" and to recommend that he be made "a brigadier general in the regular Army, and every day this is postponed is a loss to the Army and the nation. . . . He is of the proper age, has had the training and experience, and possesses the ability to command large bodies of troops in the field." [22]

The Fort Douglas camp lasted a month. Toward the end of September, Marshall was back in San Francisco, where he resumed miscellaneous duties as General Bell's aide and assistant to the adjutant of the Western Department headquarters.[23] Here he was to remain until after Congress's declaration of a state of war with Germany.

By the summer of 1916 the United States, in the struggle to defend neutrality, had already moved far toward adopting the postures of belligerency, although there were many at this time who believed we had stronger grounds for protest against Britain than against Germany.

That summer most large American cities staged preparedness parades. The President himself walked in the Washington parade on Flag Day, June 14, 1916. On July 22 Marshall witnessed one

in San Francisco in which trainees from Monterey took part. He
was sitting next to General Bell and General Sibert on the reviewing stand when a bomb exploded in the crowd, killing six people
and wounding forty-four. It was this incident that led to the arrest of Tom Mooney and the long judicial battle to affirm his in-
nocence.[24]

The preparedness movement gained momentum, but in 1916
preparedness measures were still calculated not so much to put
America in condition to fight any particular country as to demonstrate the country's will not to be intimidated. So in the summer
of 1916, along with the National Defense Act, Congress approved a five-year naval-building program, established the Shipping Board—through which the government was authorized to
lease, buy, build, and operate a fleet of merchant vessels—and
tacked onto the Army Appropriation Act a rider to set up the
Council of National Defense to co-ordinate industrial resources
for defense.[25]

At the same time political suspicion of militarism in the War
Department culminated in the virtual destruction of the General
Staff on which Root had counted to avoid the planless confusion
with which the country entered its war with Spain. Although the
General Staff was not blameless for its own near-demise, it received at least no encouragement either in its function of planning for possible war or in its continuing and losing struggle with
the War Department bureaus for centralized control. When war
came, only nineteen General Staff officers were on duty in Washington, about half available to supervise the whole Army establishment, the other half to study a national strategy and prepare
plans for the use of the nation's resources in battle. Needless to
say, there were few plans.[26]

So far as public opinion was concerned, the decision to go to
war against Germany was shaped in the end by the greater brutality of German violations of American rights (particularly
through submarine sinkings), reinforced by inept German diplomacy, like the clumsy bid for a Mexican alliance, and by an increasingly potent image, fostered by Allied propaganda, of Kai-
serism as the foe of humane ideals and civilized order. Following
Germany's declaration early in 1917 of its intent to resume unre-

stricted submarine warfare after February 1, President Wilson broke off diplomatic relations. As sinking of merchant ships continued, he appeared in April before a joint session of Congress to ask that the actions of the German government be declared "to be in fact nothing less than war." Against some bitter-end opposition both houses passed the requested resolution, and on the morning of Friday, April 6, 1917, the United States was at war.

For George Marshall the change meant at first more of the same sort of work at a pace stepped up to fit the emergency. General Bell at the end of April was made commanding general of the Eastern Department with headquarters on Governors Island, New York, and his aide had scarcely unpacked before being saddled with the job of helping to organize two reserve officers' camps in the vicinity of Plattsburg, each to give three months' training to twenty-five hundred officers.[27]

The confusion of the weeks and months following made a vivid impression on Captain Marshall that was to remain and help to shape the thinking of the Chief of Staff in 1939. General Bell reported ill with influenza, and during his absence in the hospital he left the office for some time to his aide, who visited him every day to report what was going on and "particularly to tell him of the displeasure of his senior staff officers with my actions."

The staff was upset because Marshall with directness and energy set himself to cut red tape and solve the problems that had to be solved. The camps at Plattsburg were receiving trainees but they were short of nearly everything the trainees needed. Worst was the shortage of blankets. There were none to be had from the department quartermaster. "I personally sent out to locate where we could buy blankets, mattresses, and things of that sort. Then I would send a message over to the quartermaster, the old colonel, to buy these and ship them by express."

The quartermaster objected to the expense. "Finally, he came over to see me. . . . He wanted to bring to my attention what I was letting the government in for. I tried to make clear what *he* was letting the government in for if he didn't have the proper things there for the men." Express bills, Marshall thought, weighed little against the possibility that the citizen soldiers might freeze to death and the Army be indicted once more by public opinion for negligence, as it had been in the Spanish-American War. What really irritated the colonel was the implication that he and the rest of those long on the job needed to be told how to do it by a young newcomer, even if he did have the extraordinary right to speak for the commanding general.

"You must understand," he said stiffly to the captain, "that we have been here for several years and we originally supplied these camps with what we thought was necessary. Now you come in with different amounts of all sorts of things and about every hour you want a new amount. How can you possibly believe you are right?"

Marshall believed he was right quite simply because he had studied the problems. Another of General Bell's aides had analyzed the supply requirements of the training camps on the basis of the needs of a hundred men and had compiled a careful list of everything from pencils to kitchen stoves and rifles.[28] Afterward he visited the camps to check what they had against the list. He would then telegraph Marshall what the shortages were. Besides these messages, other telegrams were coming in almost hourly from camps throughout the Eastern Department asking for all sorts of things, but mainly blankets.

When the colonel saw the captain's list his manner softened. "He had never seen such a thing and, of course, it was a gold mine of information. He asked if he could borrow it. That made quite a change in him. . . . He was very much reassured and went ahead from that time filling the orders that came in over my desk."

Marshall had other problems. His office on Governors Island was only a pleasant ferry ride from New York City. In the burst of patriotic enthusiasm following the declaration of war the young men who thought they might get commissions besieged the headquarters along with their political sponsors. "Everybody who was anybody . . . was trying to get in [to the training camps] and each seemed to feel that political pressure was necessary. I was trying to demonstrate that it wasn't necessary. . . . I found myself then up against ex-President Taft and others, particularly from the wealthy of New York. J. P. Morgan and Company and other firms [like that] all seemed to think they could get what they wanted right away. . . . I guess I stood [them] off better than General Bell [could have] because I didn't know them and they didn't know me." Nevertheless it wasn't easy. "I was using three phones . . . and being seen by everyone that came to the Island; . . . it was exceedingly hectic and I had to learn how to do business quickly."

The confusion which George Marshall faced on Governors Island was typical of the turmoil in which America at last armed to fight. Nothing was ready; everything had to be done at once. Marshal Joffre, formerly commander-in-chief of the French armies, came to Washington as military head of a French mission[29] to plead for immediate American reinforcements to bolster French forces and French morale severely shaken by the failure of the spring offensive. A British mission under Arthur Balfour was making similar pleas. More than two and a half years of trench warfare on the Western Front had exhausted the Allies. There were ominous signs of collapse on the Italian and Russian fronts. Washington was sympathetic, but, except for some cash and supplies and a detachment of destroyers dispatched under Rear Admiral William S. Sims within the first month, the President could only promise that troops would be sent as soon as possible. After signing the Selective Service Act on May 18, he decided that General Pershing should go to France to set up a headquarters in Paris but for the moment would have no troops.

It was possible that Captain Marshall might go along. He wanted to very badly. When Pershing arrived in New York preparatory to sailing he talked to the captain, who had been recommended by his own chief of staff, Colonel J. G. Harbord. But in the end nothing came of it. The trouble was that Pershing was unwilling to detach Marshall from General Bell's staff, and he would not take Bell, who was also eager to go but in ill health.[30]

Disappointed, Marshall wrote to his friend General Nichols that he would like very much to be sent to France with the first convoy of troops, due to sail soon. Nichols, on the point of going to Washington, said he would do what he could.[31] Perhaps it was in fact Nichols who mentioned Marshall's name at the War Department where they were picking the first troops and officers to go. Across the hall from the office in which Pershing had formed his staff was the assistant chief of staff, General Bliss, whom Marshall had worked with two years before in the New York-Connecticut maneuvers. Finally, the man picked to form the 1st Division was General Sibert, who had been impressed with Marshall's work at the Monterey training camp. And there may have been others who could have named and recommended him. In any case, Sibert on June 3 wired General Bell from Washington to ask whether his aide could be released as "a General Staff officer on my divisional staff and for immediate service abroad." [32]

General Bell was keenly aware of how much such an assignment would mean to Marshall, and he was too interested in Marshall's career to stand in the way. It was, besides, a step toward just the kind of post for which he himself thought Marshall best fitted. "In event of war," he wrote of his aide, "especially well qualified to perform the duty of chief of staff for corps or army or to command same." The transfer was arranged and Marshall was already at work at General Sibert's temporary headquarters on Governors Island when the general arrived from Washington.[33]

The troops General Sibert was to command were to be organized as a division, but in fact neither the division nor a plan for putting it together was in existence. The four infantry regiments selected, the 16th, 18th, 26th and 28th, were all in the Southwest, some on guard patrol duty along the Mexican border. All were, of course, greatly under strength. They drew hundreds of men from other regiments and filled their command staff rosters with provisional, temporary, and reserve officers. They also drew new equipment—the 28th Infantry reported that it was "practically 100 per cent new." The 18th Infantry observed that it had made itself over before sailing into a "strange organization that had never existed before in U.S." [34] All was done in the greatest haste, the object being to get the men across where they could at least be seen by the Allies even if it would take a long time to sort them out later into a fighting division.

Shortly before he left, Marshall found time to extend a favor to ten newly married second lieutenants who had brought their wives with them. Recalling his own honeymoon on the eve of sailing for the Philippines, he told the men they would not be needed for a time and dismissed them, giving them two or three days in New York. Later, when he checked on them after heavy fighting in France, he found that at least eight had been killed in action.[35]

There was little enough time for his own preparations. He saw Lily off in early June for Charlotte, North Carolina, where she was to visit her brother. Then she would go to Lexington and remain there for the duration of the war. He had a few hours for shopping downtown—and then he was on board the *Tenadores*, where he shared a cabin with Frank McCoy and Lesley McNair.

Weary and disturbed by the weeks of confusion, Marshall found himself reassured by the sight of the trim sailors rigging a gun on the forward deck. At least the Navy was ready. But before he sailed even that illusion was shattered. He overheard the petty officer in charge of the gun crew announce that, alas, they had no ammunition. "I thought, My God, even the naval part isn't organized and we are starting off to Europe!"

IX

The First Division in France

"We hadn't even been trained in squads left and squads right."

THERE had been exultation in France when General Pershing and his staff arrived early in June. At last the Americans had come. Parisians lined the streets and showered roses on the open staff cars in which the General and his officers rode from the station to their hotel.[1] Pershing, erect and dignified, assured in manner and with a "fine sense of the dramatic," looked like the military savior that every Frenchman wished to believe he was. Within days of his arrival his chief of staff thought that he had "captured the fickle Paris crowd at any rate." [2]

France was impatient and wanted not the promise of eventual victory but a miracle of immediate deliverance. France was desperate. On April 16 General Robert Nivelle, newly appointed French commander-in-chief, had launched an offensive with twenty-seven divisions against the German lines along the Aisne. Both army and nation were led to believe the attack would break the long stalemate and end the war. It failed. The Germans were ready for it, and the French command lost confidence even before the guns opened fire. There was no breakthrough, only more French casualties, some ninety-five thousand, of which some fifteen thousand were dead. So shattered was the morale of the disappointed army that mutiny infected sixteen corps. Nivelle was replaced by General Philippe Pétain, who in time, by a combination of toughness and understanding, would put the army back together again. Meanwhile the darkness of defeat and of cheated hopes remained like a pall over the whole of France.

It was three weeks after Pershing's staff had settled into Paris headquarters for the long, hard work of planning before the troops of the 1st Division began debarking on June 26 at St.-Nazaire.[3] Then once more the French cheered, and the procession of one battalion of the 16th Infantry in Paris on the Fourth of July rekindled the extravagant enthusiasm of Pershing's own reception. But like rockets in the dark, cheers for the Yanks broke through the gloom of France without lightening it. Captain Marshall, who stepped off the boat just behind General Sibert and so was the second man ashore in the first convoy of American troops, was impressed with the number of women in mourning—nearly everyone—and later with the depressing quiet of the people. "Everyone seemed to be on the verge of tears." Admiral Albert Gleaves, commander of the convoy, thought he detected in the silence an "unuttered thanksgiving." [4] Marshall felt only the grief, the exhaustion of the capacity to hope. "The Canadians had come and were going to settle the war in a month or two and nothing happened." Now the Americans were here and still nothing happened. The war went on.

Indeed, even those who cheered loudest could see that the Yanks who were arriving were at best a promise, hastily collected, of more substantial help still a long way off. The 1st Division set up a reception camp near St.-Nazaire and waited for the three remaining convoys of troops to arrive. Already the grave deficiencies of almost all units were known in part—that many recruits had received their rifles only just before boarding ship in New York, that newly organized units like the howitzer companies, mortar sections, and 37 mm. cannon crews not only had no howitzers, mortars, or cannon but "had never even heard of them." As for their training, even their officers knew scarcely anything about the conditions of battle on the Western Front. Some on board ship had had a look at a single copy of a recently published booklet on trench warfare, borrowed from a British officer.[5]

Veterans of the Mexican expedition were intermingled with the rawest recruits who didn't even look like soldiers. They were "all stiff-legged, pasty, and somewhat unkempt." [6] Marshall one day observed a sentry at the St.-Nazaire camp attempt to salute the French area commander who had come to make an official call on General Sibert. The soldier, a tall, rangy Tennesseean, had his blouse unbuttoned and a watch chain stretched across his stomach. When the French officer, resplendent in a bemedaled dress uniform, stopped, apparently to ask the sentry about his rifle, the latter handed it over and seated himself on a nearby post to roll a cigarette. [7] That incident and others like it created an impression of bumbling amateurism in the minds of many in the French command which for a long time they insisted on believing was typical of the American Army.

In fact it was one more sign of unpreparedness and of the haste with which the first troops were gathered and shipped to "show the flag." They were not a combat division at all, but only the raw material for one sent over for assembly in France instead of at home. Months would pass before the division could be shaped to fight and more months before it could be committed as part of an army capable of sustaining itself in the line. Even before General Pershing arrived, the American Military Mission in Paris had discussed and reached tentative agreement on a training ground for United States troops. The requirement was for a relatively quiet area near the line where the Americans might eventually take over their own combat zone. Since the British and Belgians were established on the left wing and the French inevitably were massed in the center before Paris, the obvious place for the Americans was in Lorraine on the right, where there had been little more than local action since the initial German drive in August 1914. Specifically the training area suggested by the French and accepted by General Pershing was the country around Neufchâteau. For eventual commitment, the thought was that Pershing might consider Metz and the St.-Mihiel salient as objectives.

Pershing intended to bring into Lorraine as rapidly as possible four divisions: the 2d (regular Army to which Marine units would be added), the 26th (New England National Guard units), and the 42d (the Rainbow Division with National Guard units from twenty-seven states), besides the 1st. He wished them all located for training as close together as practicable. In mid-July, after going from St.-Nazaire to Paris to witness the Bastille Day parade, General Sibert with Colonel Coe, his chief of staff, Marshall, and other members of the staff set out by car to establish 1st Division headquarters at Gondrecourt and prepare the way for movement of the division units to billets in a half-dozen surrounding villages.[8]

Marshall was delighted with the area, not only as a soldier but as one sensitive from boyhood to the gentle beauties of rich, rolling country. In a later report to Pershing's headquarters he did not note the haze that mutes the colors of the countryside, the red roofs of the little villages, the trees that lined each road and bounded each field in the way of a land that has been combed and groomed by the peasant's plow for centuries. But his appreciation of the soft and peaceful land on the threshold of war crept in. He wrote of the "broad fertile valleys, bordered by high hills, . . . well watered, not too heavily timbered for military training, devoted largely to hay and grain crops and dotted with villages above the average in appearance." He added, "It appears to be healthful, is beautiful, and seems adequately adapted for training." [9]

The 1st Division headquarters set up in Gondrecourt, a town of two thousand, twenty miles northwest of Neufchâteau, typically with houses crowded snugly on narrow streets, its nucleus a public square and an ancient church, staid and sleepy, even though, since the time the grandsons of Charlemagne quarreled over their inheritance, Lorraine had been repeatedly a battlefield. Not far away was the village of Domremy from whence the peasant girl Jeanne, nearly five hundred years before, had gone off to battle to save her beloved France. Almost every day Marshall passed by the house where she was born and the reconstructed church where she was baptized, and he was reminded of her story.[10]

Marshall was billeted with two other American officers and the French interpreter, Captain Jean Hugo, at the house of M. and Mme. Jouatte on the Rue Saussi not far from American headquarters.[11] Mme. Jouatte, whose son was in service, made her guests warmly at home. Marshall, fond of her and grateful, kept in touch with her until her death years later. When after more than a quarter-century American troops came once more to Lorraine, General George Patton paused for a moment in his drive through France to inquire, at the Chief of Staff's direction, how she had fared under the Germans. Four years later it was the American Secretary of State who, with Mrs. Marshall and three aides, stopped in Gondrecourt to bring gifts and recollections of long ago.[12]

Before he could become settled in his new billet, Marshall was on the move by order of Pershing headquarters. His old friend Colonel John McAuley Palmer, Pershing's chief of operations, had decided to borrow him to survey the whole region of Neufchâteau to locate training areas and suitable billets for the three divisions which were to come over later in the year. Palmer's whole instructions were to "do what you think best." [13]

At Neufchâteau the town officials arranged a lunch. As Marshall and his sergeant were the first Americans to make an official visit a crowd gathered outside their restaurant and after the meal there were speeches of welcome to which the captain was invited to respond. Calling on the uttermost resources of his VMI French, he said all that he could find words for. Later he could not recall having used a single verb, but it didn't matter. The crowd, "voluble, friendly, and excited," applauded and cheered. The schoolchildren of Neufchâteau, let out for the day, then formed an escort to conduct him on his tour of inspection.[14]

He was on the whole pleased with what he found and thought the accommodations better than those in and around Gondrecourt, where there was no shelter for the kitchens and the men would have to eat out in the weather. Even comparatively good billets were meager enough. Soldiers generally were to be housed in the lofts of stables with a single mattress and blanket supplied for two men. For that the charge normally was about five cents a day; for a roof only—whether for man or mule—the rate was less than a penny.[15] At the end of July, Marshall reported his findings and was ordered to return to his division to begin at once planning its training program.

Eager to get soldiers in the line as soon as possible, the French wanted training in trench warfare to begin at once. Marshall believed it necessary to begin further back on elementary drill, to make soldiers of the recruits and military units out of the collections of men. General Sibert agreed, and the initial training order laid down that "all possible means will be employed with the utmost vigor to improve the appearance, military bearing, and spirit of the officers and soldiers of this command." [16] A month would be devoted to the task. Junior officers of the command took over this part of the training while General Sibert and most of the officers not involved in the drilling joined French units in the line near Verdun. It was during the Second French Army's attack in support of General Sir Douglas Haig's offensive in Flanders that Marshall, with the Foreign Legion regiment of the 1st Moroccan Division, observed the battle on August 20 in which the Germans were driven back, leaving some ten thousand prisoners.[17]

There was still at this time no firm plan for the use of American troops. From the moment of the declaration of war, when the French and British missions in Washington were urging the Americans to come quickly, the Allies had been arguing for the integration of American soldiers in French and British units. The generalship of the past three years had accomplished nothing more successfully than to kill off the young manhood of Europe. Now that the manpower reservoirs of Britain and France were so low that neither could any longer make good the losses of daily attrition in the trenches, much less build up for offensives, the Allies looked hungrily at America's untapped supply. When the immediate and urgent need was for soldiers to fill the trenches, man the guns, and be fed to the slaughter of enemy guns, they thought it foolhardy to take the time to form a complete and self-sufficient national army. Furthermore, why take the unnecessary risk of committing them to battle under inexperienced American command when the British and French had plenty of seasoned officers begging for men to command? General Pershing was well aware of both risks—the delay and the inexperience—but he remained adamant against integration, both because politically it would, he thought, submerge the American effort and bind America absolutely to French and British war aims, and because he believed that as the war continued, the American contribution would become increasingly large and even dominant. All through 1917 and into early months of 1918 he and his staff fought off an ingenious variety of integrating schemes.

As a unit, the 1st Division could not be put into the line until at least one other trained division arrived to support it. The normal procedure was to rotate divisions between line and reserve every three or four days. Since, furthermore, casualties might be very high (in extreme cases three-quarters of a division could be put out of action in a day), General Pershing did not want to commit any until the four he had planned to concentrate were ready. It was to be a long, difficult, and often exasperating wait.

Impatience meanwhile tended to become focused as through a burning glass on the 1st Division. At the end of August, training for battle began under the tutelage of the 47th Division of the Chasseurs Alpins, the crack unit known as the "Blue Devils." General Pershing's headquarters had moved out of Paris to the casern at Chaumont, only about an hour's drive from Gondrecourt. From this time on the 1st Division was under the constant critical eye of both General Pershing and the French high command. Pershing came over frequently on short notice to check on the progress of training, often with a distinguished French guest. These were difficult moments, made more difficult by general headquarters' doubts as to General Sibert's competence and corresponding suspicions at 1st Division headquarters that Pershing was trying to establish grounds to relieve him. There was a strong feeling at GHQ that an engineer officer, however able, ought not to have an infantry command and that, besides, Sibert was unmilitary in his bearing and weak on discipline.[18] Nevertheless, at the division, Sibert commanded the loyalty of his staff, and notably of Captain Marshall.

So a sense of injustice was stirred early in September when Pershing ordered a review of the division at Houdelaincourt for President Poincaré. Notice of the review reached the division only the afternoon before it was to be held and found units scattered over an area twenty to thirty miles distant. Two units, on the road all day, had to march most of the night to arrive on time.

Marshall, in charge of arrangements, did not get around to selecting the ground until late evening and so failed to notice that the hillside he picked was already churned by previous drills and ankle-deep in mud. Two-thirds of the men and half the officers had had in all their lives only the month's drilling they had just completed; all were now hard at work on combat training. In these circumstances the review was understandably ragged and General Pershing afterward duly noted the extenuating difficulties, but at the moment he was only aware that the troops could not have made a good impression on the French President and he took out his chagrin on General Sibert.[19]

This was a prelude to the blow-up of October 3 when Pershing visited "Washington Center," where the French were conducting training in trench warfare. On hearing of the forthcoming visit Marshall arranged to have Major Theodore Roosevelt, Jr., who commanded the 1st Battalion of the 26th Infantry, demonstrate a method he had developed for attacking an entrenched enemy. After the demonstration Pershing asked General Sibert to conduct a critique. Sibert had witnessed the demonstration for the first time himself and his comments evidently reflected that fact. Pershing then listened to a discussion by a junior officer and then "just gave everybody hell." He said the division didn't show much evidence of training, had made poor use of its time, and had not followed directives. The worst, in Marshall's view, was that "he was very severe with General Sibert in front of all the officers." Finally, turning to Sibert's chief of staff, who had arrived only two days before, Pershing grilled him on matters that Marshall, as acting chief of staff, had been handling. Again there were faltering replies. Pershing dismissed the chief of staff with an expression of contempt and turned to leave.

Marshall, stung at the manifest injustice, tossed aside the caution that a junior officer could be expected to feel on such an occasion. He decided that, whatever the cost to him, he had to explain some things. He began to talk. Pershing, in no mood to listen, shrugged his shoulders and turned away. Marshall, "mad all over," put his hand on the general's arm.

"General Pershing," he said, "there's something to be said here and I think I should say it because I've been here longest."

Pershing stopped. "What have you got to say?"

Exactly what the irate captain had to say was not recorded and afterward he could not remember. An associate of these days has said that in anger Marshall talked very fast and overwhelmed his adversary with "a torrent of facts." Marshall himself recalled that he "had an inspired moment" and that his fellow officers standing by "were horrified." When he finished General Pershing remained calm. He walked away, saying, "You must appreciate the troubles we have."

Marshall, aware that he had "gotten into it up to my neck," gave no quarter. "Yes, General," he replied, "but we have them every day and they have to be solved before night."

Then General Pershing was gone and tempers cooled. General Sibert was sorry that Marshall had got into such hot water for his sake. Some of Marshall's friends were sure he was finished and "would be fired right off." Marshall himself had no regrets. To those who tendered sympathy he said, "All I can see is that I might get field duty instead of staff duty, and certainly that would be a great success."

No retribution came. On the contrary, thereafter when Pershing visited the division he would often take Marshall aside to ask him how things were going. In the months following, it was clear that the general's respect and liking grew. Pershing—Marshall was to discover—was always willing to listen to honest criticism and to an extraordinary degree was able to detach himself from it. "You could talk to him as if you were discussing somebody in the next country. He never [held] it against you for an instant. I never saw another commander I could do that with. . . . It was one of his great strengths that he could listen to things." [20]

The truth was that they were something alike, at least in their professional approach—the man who commanded American troops in World War I and the man who was to direct the American Army in World War II. Pershing at West Point, like Marshall at VMI, had been a mediocre scholar but had throughout his four years held the top cadet rank in each class. He was, like Marshall, aloof, and for the same reason, holding himself apart from intimacy with those he wished to command. Like Marshall, too, Pershing had an unusual aptitude and fondness for teaching. He had taught elementary school for two years before going to the Military Academy. In the Army he had been an outstanding success as professor of military science and tactics at the University of Nebraska, where he took a law degree in his spare time, and as an instructor at West Point. Born too soon to have attended the new Leavenworth, although he had attended the War College, he had been a member of the first War Department General Staff and shared the professional interest of the new Army. Personally they were quite different. In many ways Pershing was the typical cavalryman, hard fighting, hard living. He had commanded troops in Cuba, where he won the Silver Star for gallantry, and in the Philippines.[21] If perhaps he was no more fond of riding and good hunting than Marshall, he had had greater opportunities to indulge them. He was a more dashing figure, popular with women, capable of self-dramatization, a skilled diplomat despite the tough and distant mien he usually assumed.

For the 1st Division the end of preliminary training came with a final review before Marshal Joffre on October 14. The next day they were attached to the 18th (French) Division for experience in the line. One battalion from each regiment was to go into the trenches at ten-day intervals and on relief would return to Gondrecourt to practice with the reality fresh in mind.[22]

It was going to war but no one expected it to be in earnest yet. The sector north and west of Nancy, which General Edouard de Castlenau had held against the Germans in the fall of 1914 with such success that he remained one of the two French high commanders still in command in 1917, had been quiet ever since. Peasants in the area went about their business within range of German guns. Through field glasses one could see the Germans in fine weather sitting outside their trenches. It was of more concern to the men of the 1st Division that on the evening of October 21, when the first of them went into the trenches, the weather was anything but fine. The men in summer uniforms were made more uncomfortable by a cold, driving rain. Winter clothing, requisitioned in July, had not arrived. The Quartermaster General's office in Washington had reported, with notable lack of tact, if nothing worse, that some items asked for could not be sent because they were needed for troops in the United States.

Two weeks later the quiet sector erupted and the Americans had their first touch of battle. It happened to the 2d Battalion of the 16th Infantry, which at ten o'clock on the evening of November 2 relieved French units near Bathelémont "along the rim of the bald hill that jutted out toward the Rhine-Marne Canal." The night was black and quiet except for an occasional crack of a rifle. Then just before three in the morning, German shells ranged in on the American position and for almost an hour bombarded the line. As the Americans ducked into their trenches and dugouts, German infantry advanced and exploded bangalore torpedoes under the barbed wire in front of the trenches. A gap about sixty yards wide was blasted and marked with white tape. The enemy —forty to fifty—waited for the signal lifting the bombardment and then rushed in from two sides. Three soldiers of Company F were killed; one had his throat cut, one was shot by a revolver, the third had his head smashed. Twelve Americans were taken prisoner as the raiders retired.[23]

The news came into the headquarters of General Paul Emile Joseph Bordeaux, commanding the 18th Division, within an hour. Marshall was there. With the general and his billet-mate, liaison officer Captain Hugo, he went up at once to the line. From the top of the communication trench leading into the deeper front-line trench he could look out over the half-mile-wide No Man's Land and see clearly marked the gap in the wire through which the Germans had attacked and withdrawn. In the main dugout he found blood, and, in the open, bodies of the three dead. At the dressing station in the rear where he and the general went to question the lightly wounded there was a moment of hot temper. Finding that General Bordeaux by his questions was implying doubt as to the courage and ability with which Americans had defended themselves, Marshall demanded to know why they had been forbidden to send patrols beyond the wire. He warned that General Pershing would be very much interested in the questioning. Bordeaux got "stiff" under the attack, and Marshall left him to visit by himself the more seriously wounded in the front-line hospital.[24]

Next day came handsome amends. To the funeral of the three Americans in Bathelémont the French sent a battalion of infantry, a troop of cavalry, dismounted, and miscellaneous troops to represent every unit in the French Corps and do the Americans full military honor. General Bordeaux himself made an eloquent speech, which so impressed Marshall that he asked the general to dictate it to Captain Hugo. These words he found undimmed some thirty years later when, as chairman of the American Battle Monuments Commission, he offered them for an inscription on a more imposing memorial to be erected to these first Americans killed in France.

"We will therefore ask," General Bordeaux said, concluding his tribute, "that the mortal remains of these young men be left here, be left to us forever. We will inscribe on their tombs: 'Here lie the first soldiers of the famous United States Republic to fall on the soil of France, for justice and liberty.' The passer-by will stop and uncover his head. The travelers of France, of the Allied countries, of America, the men of heart, who will come to visit our battlefield of Lorraine, will go out of the way to come here, to bring to their graves the tribute of their respect and of their gratefulness. Corporal Gresham, Private Enright, Private Hay, in the name of France, I thank you. God receive your souls. Farewell!" [25] There was little enough of *la gloire* left in the trenches of the Western Front, but it endured in eloquence.

X

In the Line

"War and training is mud and rain and cold."

BY the end of November the 1st Division, in accord with its
schedule, was out of the line and back in training at Gondrecourt. Meanwhile the build-up of American forces in Lorraine
had begun. Headquarters of the 2d Division, which like the 1st
was being shipped in separate units (including two regiments of
Marines to form one brigade), arrived in October. First elements
of the 26th Division had appeared in September. Before the end
of the year the 42d was also assembling, and elsewhere in France
the 41st training and replacement division was coming in. There
was already perceptible momentum in the build-up toward the
twenty-four divisions that Pershing had asked to have sent him
before the end of June 1918.[1] Yet to the hard-pressed Allies the
process still seemed maddeningly slow.

All the war news was bad, and the need for American reinforcements in quantity became ever more urgent. Field Marshal
Haig's offensive in Flanders (July-November 1917) had cost him
a quarter of a million men and gained only a few miles without
effecting a breakthrough. The British Expeditionary Force at the
end of 1917 was nearly one hundred thousand men smaller than
it had been the year before, and there were not enough men left
at home to make up the deficit.[2] The French, in the same cruel

state of exhaustion, had had to disband one hundred separate battalions for lack of replacements.³ In October the Italian front was shattered as Austro-German forces at Caporetto broke through to a depth of sixty miles and took two hundred and seventy-five thousand Italian prisoners. Worse still was the word from the East. While the armies of the Czar had demonstrated their incompetence in the first month of the war, it was expected at least that they would be able to hold their own, tying down substantial German forces which could otherwise be shifted to the Western Front. When the March 1917 revolution forced the Czar to abdicate, that expectation brightened, but the Kerensky government proved to have neither the hoped-for political vigor nor the capacity to stiffen the Russian armies. The Russian summer offensive failed, and in the fall the Bolsheviks overthrew Kerensky and at once began negotiating for an armistice. General Pershing estimated that Russia's withdrawal would permit the Germans to concentrate two hundred and fifty to two hundred and sixty divisions in France against an Allied force of one hundred and sixty. He reiterated his earlier request for twenty-four divisions (with supporting troops amounting to about one million men) by next July.⁴

Against this requirement the troops actually on hand seemed even to him discouragingly few. The British Prime Minister, David Lloyd George, seized this moment of desperate impatience again to urge integration. He proposed that American reinforcements could be got into action much faster if the Americans would ship only infantry and machine-gun units to be permanently absorbed in British units. The French countered with fresh suggestions that American battalions and regiments be attached to French divisions for periods of two to three months, for full battle service, not, as was being done, for training only. Pershing found the French move easy enough to reject, even though he was conscious that in withholding his troops from battle he accepted the heavy responsibility that while he waited the war might be lost. The British gambit was harder to meet, for they offered a *quid pro quo*—additional British shipping sufficient to transport six divisions over and above the twenty-four already scheduled. Eventually a compromise was worked out to ship six extra whole divisions (not just infantry) but to commit the infantry battalions and regiments with British units for battle training, pending the arrival of supporting troops.[5]

Under this kind of pressure General Pershing felt it necessary to get the 1st Division into action quickly. He was determined to relieve General Sibert. This was done by War Department orders on December 12, and two days later Brigadier General Robert Lee Bullard, who had been commanding the division's 2d Brigade, replaced him.[6] Marshall by this time had taken a leap up the wartime promotion ladder. Recommended in September by Sibert for promotion to lieutenant colonel, he was made a major by orders received in November and would have his silver leaves just after Christmas.[7] He was also in line for appointment as chief of staff to the new commander. This he did not know, and he was so infuriated by Sibert's relief, which he considered unjust and unwarranted, that once more he expressed himself with great vehemence. He thought that Pershing's staff was to blame and that, in response to the boss's severity, they were outdoing him without even knowing "what they were being severe about." He discovered later that Bullard learned of his anger and decided that Marshall had no business being chief of staff as long as he was in that state of mind. The top place on the staff went to Lieutenant Colonel Campbell King. Marshall remained chief of operations, sobered and resolved in the future to curb his temper.

Bullard was a slim, tough, aggressive, self-confident Southerner, born in Alabama, who had fought Indians in the West and had served in the Philippines and in Mexico. With a warning to his subordinate commanders that they would be relieved without hesitation if they failed to measure up, Bullard at once set the division a final stiff training requirement designed to make it, in his own words, "a machine that will work independently of the quality of the man that turns the crank." [8] By mid-January the men were ready and the 1st Brigade relieved the French 1st Moroccan Division of the First French Army in the line north of Toul, between St.-Mihiel and Pont-à-Mousson. The 18th Infantry went into the line on January 16 after an exhausting march over ice-glazed roads through a heavy cold rain.

War is many things, and the poets and novelists have taxed their imaginations to re-create its terrors, its boredom, its spiritual triumphs, its miseries. But for the foot soldier war is above all mud. All other sufferings are intermittent: mud is the condition of existence. There never was a war more deeply mired in mud than the war on the Western Front. The trenches taken over by the 18th Infantry were awash and the soldiers manned them in hip boots, shivering in a defensive line under direct observation of the enemy atop Montsec.

As a staff officer Marshall did not live in the mud but he was up at the front frequently and acquired a deep and abiding sympathy for the infantrymen that he never lost. "The poor devil in the Army," he said later, "marches tremendous distances; he is in the mud; he's filthy dirty; he hasn't had a full meal . . . and he fights in a place he has never seen before. . . ."

About a month after the 1st Division troops moved into the line German artillery fire, which had been light and sporadic, began to register on an area near Seicheprey. The fact was noted and reported by the regimental intelligence officer, Captain Charles Coulter. It happened also to be observed by Marshall on one of his frequent trips to the division's forward headquarters at Mesnil-la-Tour, this time in company of French liaison officer Captain Germain Seligman. Marshall at once prepared a warning directive for General Bullard's signature. Thus fully alerted to probable enemy action, the 18th Infantry pulled back from the forward trenches, leaving men only in the automatic rifle pits. As expected, Germans attacked with gas on the twenty-sixth and followed on the morning of March 1 with a raid in force.[9] The men of the 18th Infantry, like veterans, had ducked the one and strongly countered the other. With few casualties themselves, they took heavy toll of the attackers. Though not a large action, it was handled skillfully and the French were delighted. Premier Georges Clemenceau himself came down two days later to award the Croix de Guerre and express the gratitude of France. The promptness with which the French rewarded valor in contrast to the slower American system—Marshall discovered that the men decorated by Clemenceau were not given medals by their own units until weeks later—made a deep impression on him. From this and other episodes grew his determination that if he at any time in the future controlled the giving of awards, he would see that they were distributed promptly. It meant more, he insisted, when the award was made in the presence of those who had shared in the action.[10]

The pressure on the 1st Division did not let up. Bullard ordered a number of raids, small ones, but prepared with meticulous care under the critical eyes of higher command. Pershing so closely followed their efforts that Marshall, determined to prevent any slips, wrote out for one important raid a four-page order for Bullard's signature and followed it up with detailed instructions for the leaders of the raiding parties. To make certain that they were completely informed of the division's wishes, he kept an officer on his staff in constant touch with the raiding party commanders.[11] Of the close supervision from First Army, Bullard later wrote: "I never expect to see as much counsel and advice taken upon the subject of a military operation, great or small." [12] American behavior in the attack was of particular concern to General Pershing, who continued to believe that the hope for ultimate success lay in freeing the infantry from the trenches. He thought the Allies in three years had become so wedded to the principles of static warfare that their offensive spirit was dulled. He insisted on emphasizing mobile tactics and hoped that American skills and aggressiveness might at last contribute materially to a decision. So the 1st Division raids were fully reported and studied by other American units in training. In March, Marshall was detached from the division to lecture on them at the American General Staff College at Langres, the most advanced of several officer schools that Pershing had established in France.[13]

It was now almost nine months since the first American troops had arrived in France. Five combat divisions and one training division were on hand. The I Corps under Major General Hunter Liggett, which, according to Pershing's plan, was to establish an American combat zone, had been formed in January. But the corps with its supporting troops would not be ready to fight for another six months. The divisions were still in training and, except for the 1st, had had no experience with independent action in the line. This was the moment of crisis. While the Atlantic Ferry was stepping up delivery of troops (85,000 in March, 120,-

ooo in April, well over an average of 250,000 a month during the summer), promising a possibly decisive increment to Allied strength in the course of the year, the Allies in the spring of 1918 were at their weakest.

It was obvious to the German command that this was the moment to try for a decision. It had been just as obvious to the Allied command that the blow could be expected as soon as weather permitted. In January, General Tasker Bliss, recently retired as Chief of Staff, and then American military representative on the Supreme War Council, thought the British were already jittery. "They all seemed to be badly rattled," he wrote to Secretary of War Baker, "They showed me their information indicating that the Germans have already secured a decided superiority in men and guns on the Western Front. They anticipate a tremendous effort by the Germans early in the year." [14]

What they anticipated came on March 21, with the first of the German offensives aimed at smashing the Western Allies before the AEF could get into action.

Marshall was at Langres when the blow struck and was almost immediately ordered to rejoin his division. The German attack, carefully planned and massive in execution, hit the British Fifth Army of General Sir Herbert Gough and the Third Army of General Julian Byng along a fifty-mile front from Arras to the River Oise. The enemy objective was to split the French and British forces, roll up the British flank against the Channel, and so leave the road to Paris open. It gained early success. Gough's army was pushed back. As a gap threatened on the French left flank, General Pétain, concerned with the defense of Paris, pulled General Debeney's First French Army out of the Toul sector. He asked Pershing to stretch the 1st Division into the hole around Toul and to bring up the 42d and 26th Divisions as quickly as possible. By March 28 people were beginning to leave Paris under sporadic shelling from German long-range guns. There was talk that the government might move to Bordeaux—the first such speculation since August 1914. Pershing, who had always qualified his insistence on a separate American Army with the proviso that in an emergency he would not withhold his troops, now went to Pétain and offered his divisions for use wherever the

French general felt he needed them. But, for the moment, Pétain asked only that the 1st Division be moved from Lorraine to the front in Picardy.

The move, begun on March 31, took place after the German drive had been checked. The troops were unloaded at Méru near Paris and marched to the training area near Gisors. Marshall, detailed to meet the French troop trains and supervise the unloading of men of the 1st Division, was deeply impressed by the skill of the French in handling great masses of troops—"a great demonstration," he said later, "of the highest form of troop movement."

The 1st Division was engaged in exercises in open warfare when on April 9 a second German offensive hit the British left flank in Flanders between the La Bassée Canal and Armentières. Again there was thought of immediate commitment, but again the emergency passed.

Recognizing the crescendo of the German effort, the Allies were driven at long last to submerge their mutual jealousies and fears and establish a unified command, the lack of which had plagued the whole conduct of the war and perhaps deprived them of earlier victory. At the height of the first crisis (March 26) Marshal Foch was given the authority to co-ordinate action on the whole front. On April 3, in anticipation of the next German drive, he was given "strategic direction" pending his formal appointment on April 24 as Allied commander-in-chief. In the agreement to set up the supreme command Pershing secured specific mention of the American Army, which he hoped would nail down his long fight to be assured independent action.

But for the moment Allied offensive ideas had to be shelved. General Foch awaited the third enemy drive and tried to guess where it would come. On April 24 the 1st Division with the 16th and 18th Regiments went into the line in Picardy, relieving French units west of Montdidier. This was at the tip of the salient which the Germans had driven into the Allied lines in March but had been comparatively quiet since. Foch was not reinforcing the line but freeing French troops with which he hoped to build a reserve.

Quiet was a relative term. In fact during the first month in the trenches the division took heavy punishment from German artillery and gas. One mustard gas attack in particular on May 3 forced the evacuation of eight to nine hundred soldiers to the rear. Division forward headquarters located in the manor house at Mesnil-St. Firmin, within a mile of the railroad station and an ammunition dump, was under almost constant enemy shell fire. Marshall, trying to escape from the damp airless cellar where the staff worked, slept at first upstairs, "but they drove me down when they began hitting this building with eight-inch shells which sounded like the end of the world."

Marshall at this period was working hard, accepting, as usual, at least his full share of responsibility. General Bullard leaned on him perhaps more than he ordinarily would have because, though full of fighting spirit, Bullard was not well. He had had a bad attack of neuritis in his shoulder just before the division went into the line—so bad that he was hospitalized for several days.[15] He got himself out just as Foch was asking Pershing to name another officer to command the division. Thereafter Bullard was in almost constant pain, of which he wrote later: "All my life I had known sickness and suffering; nothing equal to this"; adding with characteristic assurance, "but for it a livelier story, I am sure, would have been enacted to be written of the war where I was."[16] As his chief of operations, Marshall was not only the mainstay of his planning staff but to a large extent his executive, constantly visiting front-line units, seeking information, often riding horseback through areas where shells were falling, explaining patiently to lower commanders what they were to do and why. He was officially commended for his bravery in carrying out his duties under fire.[17]

Marshall was a superlative staff officer—the job for which his whole career had been a preparation—but he was not altogether happy about it. Prominence and promotion were to be had at the front in command of troops. Some of his colleagues of the earliest days in France who had been given commands already wore generals' stars. It was decidedly uncomfortable for a professional whose branch was infantry to remain at headquarters, and not simply because there tended to be up front a feeling that officers of the General Staff, branded by a distinctive band around the sleeve, had easy, safe jobs. Troop-leading was after all the real business of war, to which everything else was ancillary. Marshall, furthermore, despite his excellence as a tactician, had been drawn into the Army through a taste and aptitude for commanding men. Finally the staff job, whether relatively safe or not, could be tedious. Marshall, as he later confessed, was beginning to get tired out "from the incessant strain of office work." [18]

He could make no serious move to change, however, until he could be spared. At the moment he had his hands full. In mid-May it was decided that the 1st Division should make an attack. The objective was the village of Cantigny, little more than a cross-roads, four miles north and west of Montdidier. Occupying a plateau, Cantigny provided a good observation point for German artillery: this was the tactical justification for trying to take it. But far the more important reason for the attack was psychological—or, more accurately in military terminology, moral. Pershing was eager to prove the mettle of American troops. A success in attack would give them confidence, and the Allies confidence in them, and so would further strengthen his insistence on independent American action. It would boost morale in France and at home. It might correspondingly appear to the Germans discouragingly like the beginning of the end.[19]

The attack was meticulously planned. Marshall did at least some of the basic work,[20] and on May 19 when General Pershing visited division headquarters Marshall expressed his own confidence in success. One regiment, the 28th Infantry, was to make the attack with the support of French tanks, French and American artillery, and French planes. Detailed orders from division, regiment, and battalion assured that each man knew what he was to do. In addition the 28th Infantry rehearsed for a week behind the lines. In the early morning of May 28 supporting artillery laid down a heavy preparation, and the regiment, under command of Colonel Hanson E. Ely, jumped off at five forty-five. The enemy was surprised. Resistance was light, and before breakfast the village was in American hands.[21]

Hard fighting came later as the Germans for three days launched determined counterattacks to retake the village. In the course of these battles a lieutenant came angrily into 1st Division headquarters to ask why his machine-gun company had been ordered in to repel the Germans when it had only just been relieved from the line. Marshall, patient and understanding as he ordinarily was, except when faced with injustice or stupidity, talked quietly to him. The reason his men were sent back in was because it was so vital to hold Cantigny and it was thought that his company could do the job. "I left," the lieutenant said long afterward, "with a feeling of added pride in my outfit, which I transmitted on my return to my unit, [and this] restored officers and men to top combat efficiency." [22]

All the German attacks—there were seven before the end of the month—were beaten back, and the Americans consolidated their new line. Considering the gains in ground—from 300 to 1600 yards on a 2200-yard front—1st Division losses of 199 killed, 652 wounded, 200 gassed, and 16 missing constituted a heavy price.[23] But as the first American success in the open warfare for which they were being especially trained the attack seemed to General Pershing well worth while.

He saw to it that a prompt communiqué reached the newspapers at home and cabled his enthusiasm to the War Department: "The affair at Cantigny on the twenty-eighth was well planned and splendidly executed. Our staff work was excellent. . . . The Allies are in high praise of our troops." The job, he thought, had fully justified his faith and stubbornness. "This action emphasizes the importance of organizing our own divisions and higher units as soon as circumstances permit. Our troops are the best in Europe and our staffs are the equal of any." [24]

For the French, as it turned out, Cantigny was only a tiny bright spot in general gloom. For the day before the 1st Division jumped off, the Germans had begun their third great offensive with immediate and deeply alarming success. Selecting a sector of the Allied front that had been considered too rugged to be attacked successfully, the Germans achieved complete surprise. The Chemin des Dames ridge, to which tired French and British units had been sent to recuperate, was overwhelmed in the first hours. Within eight days the Germans reached the Marne, from which they had been driven back in 1914. Pétain threw in all available reserves including the American 2d and 3d Divisions,

which fought well to blunt the cutting edge of the German attack at Belleau Wood and Château-Thierry. The 1st Division,
scheduled to be relieved by the 2d, was forced instead to extend
its sector to the left as far as Grivesnes in order to free French
units for use along the Marne. Considerably west of the German
penetration, the 1st Division was not under attack but, aware
that this was the climactic enemy effort, the combat units prepared for the worst. Marshall organized the division's noncom-
batants from the supply trains and technical services into two
scratch battalions, one commanded by the division adjutant, the
other by the judge advocate.[25] When the new commanders reported for instructions Marshall's assistant took them to a window from which they could see a valley and a railroad. Pointing,
he said, "You are to die east of the railroad. That is all the order
you need."

Despite the touch of melodrama, that was fair measure of the
grimness of the Allied mood. But the crisis was overestimated.
By the first week in June the enemy penetration was contained
and the Marne salient, deep and threatening as it looked on the
map, became a German liability. Hard fighting at the tip prevented a breakout; hard fighting at the shoulders, at Reims on
the east and later in the valley of the Oise on the west, prevented
the Germans from widening the base of the attack. In these circumstances the abundance of combat troops in the salient was an
embarrassment to the German command, committing it to pursuing this battle and no other and consequently inviting the Allies to concentrate in defense and in time to fall in against the
flanks. The time for counterattack was to come after a last-ditch
enemy attempt to widen and deepen the penetration in July had
failed.

Before that happened the 1st Division, showing signs of strain
and fatigue, had been pulled out of the line. Its losses in two
months, mostly in static defense, came to 38 officers and 728 men
killed; 75 officers and 1789 men wounded; 43 officers and 1733
men evacuated as the result of gas.[26]

Although he did not know it at once, Marshall had seen his last
service with the division with which he had lived and fought for
a year. Four months earlier, on March 9, General Harbord, Pershing's chief of staff, had sent Major Hjalmer Erickson down to

the division to be trained as chief of operations so that Marshall could be released for duty in the Operations Division of GHQ.[27] The shift was to be made, however, only when General Liggett's I Corps and General Bullard agreed. Meanwhile Marshall himself had been trying for troop duty. On June 18 he had written asking to be relieved from the General Staff and assigned to troops. He wrote under the impetus of special frustration, knowing that General Bullard's attempt to get a full colonelcy for him had just been turned down on grounds that the War Department was opposed to giving this rank to anyone but combat commanders. General Bullard forwarded the June 18 letter but did not add his approval. Marshall, he thought, was far too valuable in staff work. "I doubt," he wrote, "that in this, whether it be teaching or practice, he has an equal in the Army today." [28] It was hard to be penalized, in effect, for special excellence, especially when there were others who wished to see him in command of troops. Major General George B. Duncan (commander of the 77th Division, organized and commanded briefly by General Bell before age and health made it necessary to give the unit to a younger man) in early July proposed to GHQ that Marshall be given a star and command of a brigade. Brigadier General Wilson B. Burtt, chief of staff of the newly formed V Corps, at the same time listed Marshall among several other officers recommended to First Army for regimental command.[29] It was not to be. (He had to be content with a full colonelcy, which he received at First Army September 21, 1918.)

When Marshall's letter reached I Corps, its chief of staff, Colonel Malin Craig, noted in an endorsement that he would be glad to have Marshall's services at corps. The letter then passed through channels to GHQ and there reminded its new chief of staff, Brigadier General James V. McAndrew—Harbord had meanwhile been given command of the 2d Division—that Marshall had been spoken for some months earlier. So he renewed the request for transfer, to take place as soon as the division was relieved. There was no difficulty about this release. General Bullard was leaving himself soon to take over the III Corps. Orders to duty with GHQ came on July 13.[30]

XI

St.-Mihiel and the Meuse-Argonne

---

*"If we had fought by the book rules, we would have
wrecked ourselves about every twenty minutes."*

WHEN Marshall reported to Colonel Fox Conner, chief
of the Operations Section of GHQ at the barracks of
Domremont in Chaumont on July 17, 1918, the Germans were in
the midst of what proved to be their last offensive on the Western Front. It was an attempt to broaden and deepen the Marne
salient won in the May attack, and it was foredoomed. There
was no possibility of surprise and no possibility of local superiority on such a narrow front now that Foch had the reserves to concentrate against it. The attack ground to a halt on July 18, and
the French, with American divisions in the spearhead, began at
once a counterattack. This battle, which the French called the
Second Battle of the Marne, failed in its object of pinching off
the salient as the Germans executed a skillful withdrawal. It
began, however, the series of Allied offensives which steadily
drove the enemy back all along the line and finally cost him not
just ground, as in the past, but his power to resist. This was the
final reckoning for the failure of the German spring offensives—
the time when the balance of forces on the Western Front
changed decisively and irreversibly in favor of the Allies. The
Germans knew it.

But the Allies were not disposed to take victory for granted. Victory had been glimpsed before, only to be found a mirage. In the minds of the Allied commanders the decisive battle had still to be waged, and there remained strong disagreement over where and how it should be fought. At GHQ, Marshall set to work on plans to commit an American army in Lorraine initially to reduce the so-called St.-Mihiel salient. The idea was a year old and had been on the GHQ drawing boards ever since. Colonel Conner, Marshall's new boss, a towering, imperturbable, concise, Mississippi-born West Pointer, had himself selected the zone of attack and with Pershing and Colonel Drum defended its importance. Conner, fluent in French, had served with a French artillery regiment in 1911 and as liaison officer with the French mission to the United States shortly before we entered the war. At conferences with the French and General Pershing he had argued that the area, besides being off the main lanes of attack toward Paris and therefore ideal for independent American action, offered worthwhile prizes for offensive drives. Lorraine was one of the three historic invasion routes into France from Central Europe (the others being the lowlands of Belgium and the Belfort Gap). A successful attack here could threaten envelopment of the German line, provided the attackers could get past the formidable fortifications of Metz. More immediate prizes were the iron deposits in the region of Briey, which had been vital in sustaining the Kaiser's war machine through four years of war, and the communications system—the Paris-Nancy railroad, which the French wanted cleared for their use, and the roads and railroads to the north, which were main German supply lines.

The St.-Mihiel attack had long been accepted by the Allies, though reluctantly, for planning purposes. On July 24 General Foch at his headquarters at Bombon formally assigned Pershing the task. Pershing completed the organization of his First Army, which became operational on August 10. Pershing himself was in command, and Colonel Drum was his chief of staff.[1]

This was not, however, the end of the matter. The turning of the tide in the second Battle of the Marne, along, of course, with the steady build-up of American forces, now flooding into France at the rate of more than a quarter of a million men a month, had given Pershing his opportunity. But he had to fight again to keep it when presently it became apparent that the Germans had not just been halted but were mortally weakened. An Anglo-French offensive, beginning August 8 east of Amiens, in four days "gained a success unparalleled in their previous offensives within a similar period of time." [2] This was followed on August 18 by a French attack up the Oise and by British and Belgian attacks all along the left flank, undertaken in accordance with Foch's directive of July 24 to probe everywhere for German weakness. In fact German weakness appeared to be general, and so critical that on August 14 (unknown of course to the Allies) Ludendorff had recommended immediate negotiations for peace.

With the enemy retreating (though still in orderly fashion) all along the line, Foch wished above all to keep up the pressure to turn retreat into rout. From that point of view the American enterprise at St.-Mihiel, which had once appealed as a thrust capable of exploitation if it succeeded, now seemed only a diversion from the main battles. Foch near the end of August pressed Pershing to give it up and instead mix his troops with the French for a drive northeast from the Meuse-Argonne sector. Pershing, more determined than ever after the year's long wait to command his own army in battle, flatly refused. The meeting at Bombon became stormy. Foch pointedly asked the AEF commander, "Do you want a part in the coming battle?" Stubbornly Pershing replied, "Only with an American army." Foch observed that an American army could fight only if the French furnished supporting troops, above all artillery. Pershing reminded him that he was dependent on the French in that respect only because the French and British had insisted that he move chiefly infantry into France.[3]

Three days later, on September 2, the high command came together again and found a way out. Foch agreed that the First Army could go ahead with the St.-Mihiel battle but with limited objectives. As soon as the salient was flattened out, the army should be ready to take over a twenty-four-mile sector along the Meuse River and Argonne Forest, prepared for an attack in the direction of Sedan in conjunction with the French Fourth Army on its left. This was to be followed by a British-

French push on the general line, St.-Quentin-Cambrai, as Foch in his general order of September 3 directed unremitting attacks all along the line to keep the Germans on the move.

Since the Meuse-Argonne offensive was set to open on September 26 and the St.-Mihiel operation could not be ready before September 12, American staffs had to plan simultaneously for both battles and work out complicated movements of troops and supplies to nourish both. The problem would have taxed the most seasoned staff. First, it was essential that the St.-Mihiel attack succeed. Even though it had been downgraded to something like a sideshow, it remained the setpiece in which the American Army and General Pershing were to prove themselves. It didn't look easy. The salient had been created by the initial German drive in 1914. Two German corps advancing from the Woëvre plain had been checked at Verdun, north of St.-Mihiel, east of Commercy, and north of Toul. The resulting wedge, or "hernia," had resisted French counterattack in 1915 and had been fortified at leisure by the Germans since.[4] Second, even with the best of battle good fortune, troops used in the attack could obviously not be shifted to the Meuse-Argonne sector in time for the scheduled offensive there. That meant that reserves would have to be moved across the rear of the attacking army—a difficult maneuver at best, especially when all movements had to take place at night without lights in order not to disclose the concentration to the enemy. Third, although there were troops enough—a half million in the First Army and reinforcements arriving daily—few were battle-tested and many not even wholly trained.

Plans for the St.-Mihiel attack emanated from both GHQ and the newly formed First Army headquarters. Many staff officers worked on them, and the plans were frequently changed; many were scrapped before they could be completed. But the chief impetus at this stage came at GHQ from Conner, who has been generally considered one of the more profound students of military history and doctrine in the Army.[5] It was Conner who had Pershing's ear and his assistants who did the initial work on the St.-Mihiel plans. Marshall, promoted to full colonel on August 27, was associated closely in the early drafting with Colonel Walter S. Grant at GHQ. The two men submitted separate outlines on August 9, Grant suggesting a deeper penetration than did Marshall. (Conner adopted Marshall's concept and apparently directed both men to continue their efforts.[6]) In the next three weeks Marshall prepared at least three other versions of an attack on the St.-Mihiel salient, none of them in final form. At First Army the chief of operations, Colonel Robert McCleave, and officers of his section worked independently. In mid-August they were given the two August 9 plans, Marshall's plan of August 13, and a detailed artillery plan by Grant based "on a scheme by Marshall." Shortly afterward Conner also lent Grant to First Army, where he drew together the final package and drafted the battle instructions. Marshall, after reporting to First Army near the end of August, on detached service from Conner's section, reviewed the plan, wrote security instructions, and supervised the preparations of annexes to the field order.[7]

Before he went to First Army, Marshall had been busy on various other projects at GHQ, one of them a deception scheme to counteract the loose talk of American officers and men who, as the time of action neared, were openly boasting that "we are going to take Metz." Pershing's plan was to try to make the Germans believe that an attack was being mounted into the Belfort Gap a hundred and twenty-five miles south and east of the St.-Mihiel area. Marshall drew up the outline for the dummy operation to capture Mulhouse, and near the end of August the commander of VI Corps, Major General Omar Bundy, was directed to establish headquarters in Belfort to continue detailed work on it. He did so in the belief that the operation was in earnest, with orders to conceal his preparations. The orders, of course, were issued in full recognition that concealment of sudden battle preparations in that hitherto quiet sector would be impossible. Rumors, as expected, spread rapidly and shortly were given substance by an intelligence officer's calculated indiscretion in writing of the Mulhouse attack to General Pershing and leaving the new carbon paper he had used crumpled in his wastepaper basket. It was duly stolen. The Germans suspected a trick but felt they could not count on it; they recommended therefore that the Mulhouse area be reinforced.[8]

Much more important to the success of the First Army attack, however, was the fact that the retreating Germans no longer valued the St.-Mihiel salient as a base for offensive action and recognized it instead as a defensive embarrassment. They were actually planning to evacuate it when the Americans attacked.

The main First Army effort was made against the southern face of the salient by the IV and I Corps with seven American divisions in line. On the west the V Corps with one French and two American divisions was to press in the hinge of the German line, while the all-French II Colonial Corps in the middle was to keep up pressure on the tip of the salient. Marshall's old division, the 1st, along with the 2d and 42d, led the main attack, which was immediately successful. By nightfall of the first day units in the main drive were beyond most of their second-day objectives. Progress on the west was slower but sufficient, so that Pershing ordered the 26th Division at the west hinge to join with the 1st advancing from the south at Vigneulles to pocket the Germans fighting at the point of the wedge. Vigneulles was occupied in the early morning, and by daybreak the 1st Division had closed off the remaining escape routes. By the end of that second day the salient had been pinched off. The clean-up, lasting until September 16, netted sixteen thousand German prisoners. The cost to First Army was thirteen thousand casualties.

The price of the victory suggests that the weakened Germans fought hard. First Army had reason to be satisfied with this, the first major American action under American command. If one man were to be credited for the success it would have to be General Pershing, who approved the project and assumed responsibility for it. That Marshall had a large hand in the planning, both in shaping the concept and in supervising the detailed orders, is clear enough. But again it was Colonel Conner who had envisaged the operations initially and who had furnished from his Operations Section at GHQ the planners who did most of the work on First Army's plans. Similarly it was Colonel Hugh Drum's responsibility as chief of staff of First Army to see that the staff worked smoothly to get the job done.

Marshall was fortunate to work with Drum, who was only a year and a half older but already a top staff officer associated closely with Pershing for more than a year. As Pershing men they were to remain friends in the postwar years until at last they came into rivalry for the position of Chief of Staff of the Army. Son of an Army officer who was killed at San Juan Hill, Drum received a direct commission in 1898 by order of President Mc-Kinley in honor of his father's sacrifice. (Four such commissions were given.) As a result Drum was fighting in the Philippines while Marshall was still at VMI. He came to Leavenworth the year after Marshall left and was graduated an honor student from the two-year course. In 1914 he was a member of the expedition to Vera Cruz and later an aide to General Funston in Texas. He came to France with General Pershing as a member of his original staff and worked with Conner on long-range plans from the beginning.

Swift success in the salient and some signs of enemy disorder in the region north of the Rupt de Mad suggested the possibility of pushing on toward Metz. Marshall believed it could have been done and that Metz itself might have fallen by the end of September. At least he felt the initial lunge might have been extended had corps commanders sent infantry battalions with artillery support forward of their final objectives as they were authorized to do, and as Colonel Douglas MacArthur, chief of staff of the 42d Division, wished to do. But "none of the others had gathered themselves," and in view of Foch's insistence that the attack not be continued in force, Pershing and Drum "thought they should let well enough alone." [9] From the commander's point of view the main prize—an offensive success—was in hand.

Furthermore it was only ten days to the Meuse-Argonne drive, for which preparations were already far along. Nine divisions were to be used in the initial three-corps attack from the Meuse-Argonne line. Altogether fifteen divisions had to move to the front before the jump-off. Supporting troops, including French and American artillery, air service, and tanks, as well as the manifold combat service units, swelled the number of men to be moved into position to about 600,000, of which at least 400,000 came from the St.-Mihiel sector. Altogether 428,000 were transported by truck; the rest walked. Since none of the infantry in the line could be pulled out and refitted in time for the first attack, fifteen fresh divisions were to be brought up. Of these, four were in close reserve in the Lorraine battle area and three more came out of Army reserves stationed to the south. The others moved from elsewhere in France. Some of the artillery was to be shifted from St.-Mihiel even before the battle there was over. Some 3000 guns in all were moved into the line along with 40,000 tons of artillery ammunition, which had to be replenished at the rate of 3000 tons a day. Since the Americans were taking over a sector from French and Italian troops, 220,000 foreign soldiers had to be moved back over part of the same road net. And the roads to be used to shift the First Army west were just three, feeding through St.-Mihiel, Commercy, and Bar-le-Duc into the new battle area.[10]

General Foch and General Pershing both had doubts that the maneuver was feasible. Colonel Drum gave Marshall the job of doing it. He was to plan and supervise the shift of all troops out of the St.-Mihiel sector to the zone of the French Second Army, then holding the line the Americans would take over. Colonel Monroe C. Kerth, classmate of Marshall's at Leavenworth and now First Army deputy chief of staff, was charged with finding billets in the Meuse-Argonne. Colonel Grant was to make arrangements for the relief of the French Second Army.[11]

Two days before the St.-Mihiel battle began, the units to be transferred were notified of the order in which they would pull out. But battle, even when successful, disrupts all neat plans. Changes had to be made at the last minute and units hurriedly alerted to move before their time in order to keep the allotted transports and road space filled. Since horse- and tractor-drawn artillery was much slower than the infantry in trucks, army, corps, and division troops were mixed in order to keep solid columns on the road. Even so, congestion was inevitable as worn-out horses—more than ninety thousand animals took part in the move—lagged or dropped dead in their traces.[12]

Marshall's office, where he sat nightly by his telephone, issuing orders and meeting emergencies, was upstairs in the town hall of Souilly, Pétain's headquarters during the fight for Verdun in 1916. Almost at his front door was the "Sacred Way," over which Pétain had moved 190,000 men and 25,000 tons of supplies in eight days to make good the promise: "They shall not pass." [13]

The move Marshall now handled with the help of Colonel Grant, Captain Gorju (French Army Regulation Commission officer at Bar-le-Duc), the troop movements officers of First Army, II and IV Corps, and French staff officers, was larger if not so immediately critical.[14] It required all his fine staff training and maneuver experience and something more—the ability to throw the book away when crisis or common sense demanded.

Many of the trucks used were borrowed from the French, and agreement for their use was often made *"en principe."* It was a phrase of slippery meaning Marshall discovered one day when a commitment *en principe* to move an entire division left part of the unit behind. He insisted thereafter on having his French colleagues spell out in writing precisely what they had in mind. Grateful for the French drivers who, already desperately tired from driving in support of recent French offensives, now had again to work day and night, he was disgusted to discover that some American staff officers objected to feeding the drivers at American messes. "We had to deal with them very drastically," he said later, "to make them wake up to the fact that we couldn't move our troops unless we fed these drivers." Whenever possible he tried to plan also to let them rest an hour or so between trips.

Some American officers were impatient with the makeshifts, which offended their sense of military order. An old friend from Leavenworth stood by one day while the chief of staff of a division explained to Marshall certain changes in the division's orders that he thought would facilitate its movement. Afterward the friend commented impatiently that in his view orders were issued to be obeyed and not thereafter to be discussed and altered. Had any such rigid formula been followed, Marshall commented later, "we would have wrecked ourselves about every twenty minutes." More serious was the sense of the fitness of things which led one division commander to reject French trucks when he discovered there were not enough to lift both of his brigades at once. The French obligingly reclaimed their trucks, and Marshall informed the division commander with crisp understatement that General Pershing would never forgive him.[15]

Despite all difficulties the job was done, thanks in large part to Marshall's energy, drive, skill, and perhaps above all his ability to

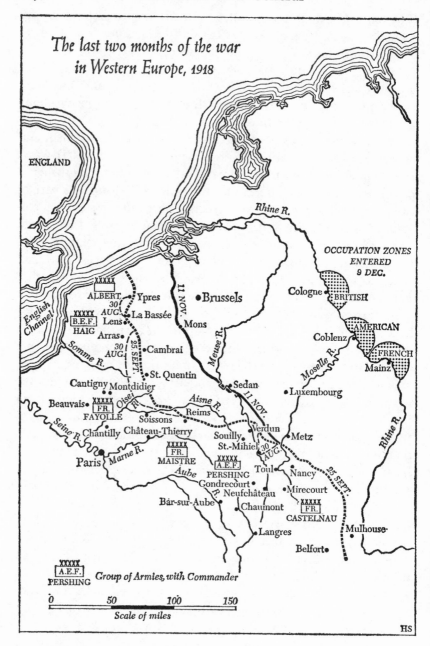

The last two months of the war
in Western Europe, 1918

ENGLAND

English Channel

Rhine R.

OCCUPATION ZONES
ENTERED
9 DEC.

Cologne
BRITISH

AMERICAN

Coblenz

FRENCH
Mainz

XXXXX
ALBERT
30
AUG.
Ypres
La Bassée
Brussels
11 NOV.
Mons

XXXXX
B.E.F.
HAIG
Lens
Arras
30
AUG.
Cambrai
St. Quentin
Meuse R.
Sedan
11 NOV.
Luxembourg

Somme R.

Cantigny
Montdidier
Beauvais
XXXXX
FR.
FAYOLLE
Oise R.
Aisne R.
Reims
Soissons
Chantilly
Château-Thierry
Souilly
St.-Mihiel
Verdun
Metz
Moselle R.
Rhine R.

Seine R.
Paris
Marne R.
XXXXX
FR.
MAISTRE
Aube
XXXXX
A.E.F.
PERSHING
30
AUG.
Toul
Nancy
25 SEPT.
Gondrecourt
Neufchâteau
Mirecourt
Bar-sur-Aube
Chaumont
XXXXX
FR.
CASTELNAU
Mulhouse
Langres
Belfort

XXXXX
A.E.F.
PERSHING   Group of Armies, with Commander

0   50   100   150

Scale of miles

HS

improvise coolly when things went wrong. Reporting the move a week after the war ended, he wrote with considerable satisfaction: "Despite the haste with which all movements had to be carried out, the inexperience of most of the commanders in movements of such density, the condition of the animals, and the limitations of the roads, the entire movement was carried out without a single element failing to reach its place on the date scheduled, which was, I understand, one day earlier than Marshal Foch considered possible." [16] The job earned for him the nickname "wizard" and made another Marshall legend to add to that of the brilliant young tactician of the Philippines.[17]

The Meuse-Argonne offensive was planned as a two-army attack (the French Fourth on the left, the American First on the right) to cut the Lille-Metz railroad in the vicinity of Mezières-Sedan, or at least get close enough to interdict German use by artillery fire. If successful, it would push the Germans against the rugged Ardennes country and deprive them of their ability to move troops and supplies east and west behind their lines. In conjunction with French, British and Belgian offensives on the west, it could make the Germans unable to conduct an orderly retreat.

In recognition of the importance of the railroad, for four years the Germans had constructed and reinforced defensive positions to an average depth of 13 miles. Behind the first lightly held front line were other well-prepared positions of field fortifications, wire entanglements, trenches, and machine-gun emplacements: the first of these ran through Montfaucon to the Argonne Forest; back of it the Kriemhilde position, part of the Hindenburg Line, took in the Cunel Heights; the last line, Freya, extended along the ridge of the Bois de Barricourt, from which the ground sloped down toward Sedan sixteen miles away.[18]

The First Army report, which Marshall helped write, noted that "the region was ideal for defensive fighting, as it presented unusual difficulties from the viewpoint of the assailant. On the east the Côtes de Meuse commanded that river valley, and on the west the rugged, high hills of the Argonne Forest dominated the valley of the Aire River. In the center the watershed between the Aire and the Meuse Rivers commanded both valleys, with the heights of Montfaucon, Cunel, Romagne, and of the Bois de Barricourt as natural strong points in observation stations for the enemy." [19] Broadly the American attack was to drive into the double defile of the Aire and Meuse Rivers under the eyes and guns of the enemy on high ground on each flank and in the center. The advance would be all uphill and through patches of heavily wooded country until the Americans reached the ridge north of Buzancy. Success of the attack as a whole for both French and American armies depended on success along the four miles of the front through the Argonne Forest. Marshall in 1919 described this as "the hinge of the entire Allied offensive, then pounding the Germans at various parts of the front. . . . The enemy must hold this part of the line or the withdrawal of the rest of his armies with four years' accumulations of plants and material would be gravely imperiled." [20] Consequently the Germans made doubly strong what nature had already shaped—in the words of General Liggett—as "a natural fortress beside which the Virginia wilderness in which Grant and Lee fought was a park." [21] Because of the difficulty and importance of the Argonne, the battle there, though involving only a small portion of the attacking force, overshadowed the rest. It was in the Argonne that Alvin York and the "Lost Battalion" won immortality.

On September 26, before daylight, twenty-seven hundred guns pounded the German defenses for three hours. First Army moved forward at five-thirty, nine divisions abreast, General Liggett's I Corps in the Argonne on the left, General Cameron's V Corps in the center, General Bullard's III Corps pivoting on the Meuse on the right. Half an hour later the French Fourth Army attacked. Both flanks advanced. Bullard's Corps captured the Germans' second defense line; Liggett moved two or three thousand yards through the forest. That was something of a surprise. Marshall wrote later: "We drove right through [the enemy] barbed-wire entanglements and mastered the first-line defenses. . . . Our troops walked right over" the wire. Pétain could not believe it and afterward sent staff officers down to investigate the report. They found it true and, Marshall said, marveled "until they saw the size of our feet." In fact the wire was found to be so low and tightly massed that the infantry had no need for the bangalore torpedoes they carried to blast lanes through.[22]

The value of the flank advances, however, was nullified by the inability of Cameron in the center to get up on the terrible "Mount of the Falcon" until the second day. By then the Germans had brought up reserves, so stiffening their defense that at the end of the month the attack everywhere was virtually stopped. Part of the trouble was the inexperience of some divisions. Six of the nine, in fact, had had little or no testing in battle before. Marshall observed that "young officers did not know how to regroup their men after the initial advance, . . . and when the time came to push on, they were unable to carry out their mission. . . . With better-trained divisions in line much greater progress would have been made at this period." [23] That was a penalty paid for the St.-Mihiel attack in which many of the more seasoned American troops had been committed. First Army suffered also from the weakness of its tank support. Of the 189 tanks (all light) attached for the assault, only 18 remained ten days later, because of battle casualties, mechanical difficulties, and the withdrawal of French units. Colonel William Mitchell's air force had 821 planes flying at the outset and controlled the air over the battlefield. But this advantage dwindled as the American forces moved farther away from the airfields.[24]

For their massive attacks touched off by the Meuse-Argonne offensive the Allies could now draw on 217 divisions on the Western Front, of which 39 (with 3 more to come before the war's end) were American. Inasmuch as the American division was about double the size of the British division and the French division, which were also below strength, the American units in France near the end of the war looked impressive beside the 102 French and 60 British divisions and the 16 other Allied divisions. Opposed to the Allies were 197 German divisions, of which only 51 were classed by British Intelligence as fit—and all these were below strength.[25]

Foch used his advantage in a series of drives which allowed the enemy no chance to rest. The American-French attack on September 26 was followed on the twenty-seventh by the French-British strike at the Cambrai-St.-Quentin line and on the twenty-eighth by the Anglo-Belgian offensive in the Ypres sector. The Germans fell back along the Channel while in the center the Allies drove through the Hindenburg Line in the first week. Ludendorff and Hindenburg, having nothing left with which to reverse the tide, proposed that the German government ask for an armistice. A council of war beginning on the twenty-ninth led shortly to the resignation of Chancellor Hertling and his replacement on October 4 by Prince Max of Baden, who almost at once telegraphed President Wilson that he was prepared to negotiate peace on the basis of the President's Fourteen Points.

For the Allied command and Allied armies, however, this was not surrender and not the end. Pershing was to find the early days of October in some ways the hardest of the war. He was faced with the fact that only in his zone had the Allied forward movement been checked. There were good reasons which he was to cite in extenuation later: besides the greenness of some of his troops and the handicaps of bad weather and terrible roads, German reinforcements, he thought, had concentrated a third of the whole German defense force against him. He could point out, moreover, that Foch himself before the attack began doubted whether the Americans could get beyond Montfaucon before the end of the year.[26] In fact they did better than that in four days. Nevertheless he would have to agree that his attack must move again if he were not to hold up the progress of the whole front. He did not agree that the fault lay with the American command and firmly rejected Foch's proposal that the Second French Army be committed between the French Fourth and the American First to take command of American divisions in the Argonne.[27] Instead he decided to throw seasoned troops into his center corps where the advance had been slowest. Marshall was again charged with the movement. To get the fresh divisions in and the relieved units out it was necessary to build a road across the morass of no man's land. So vital was this road that when a regiment of heavy artillery used it against orders and tore it to pieces, the resumption of the attack had to be delayed a day and a half. Newly arrived American supporting units were also moved in to relieve some of the French groups. As the relief proceeded, Marshall was struck by the contrast between the French who were "very, very tired and the Americans who were very, very cocky."

When the fresh attack jumped off on October 4, the veteran 1st Division, under command of Major General Charles P. Summerall, did particularly well in the Aire valley, while I Corps completed the clearing of the Argonne on the left. Summerall, Marshall said later, was "the nearest approach to the Jackson type that I saw in the war. And he was a wonder to watch when the fighting was on. . . . I never saw anything to beat him on a battlefield. I remember once he took around the British division commander who was going to relieve him. And when he got through walking around and talking like a cathedral, as he did, with shells breaking all over the place, this Britisher—who was accustomed to pretty hard fighting—came back and said he never wanted to make another inspection with General Summerall. He was really unconscious of any feeling of fear."

"The purpose of the battle between September 26 and November 1," Marshall wrote immediately after the war, was "to maintain a constant pressure against the Germans." Under that pressure the Germans steadily built up their forces from the fourteen divisions originally in line to about thirty-four in line and reserve by the end of October. Nevertheless First Army maintained a considerable superiority and by October 10 commanded over a million men (900,000 Americans, 135,000 French). The enemy had constantly to shift reserves to meet successive First Army attacks. "In this particular fighting," Marshall said, "while we could not launch attacks as co-ordinate as they might have been, given longer preparation, at the same time, by continually attacking the enemy he was becoming more disco-ordinate in his defense. . . . His regiments were being thrown into the defense as fast as they arrived, and so confused was he in his defensive tactics that elements of his divisions were scattered far apart and intermingled with other units." [28]

By October 16 First Army had taken the Romagne Heights within the Hindenburg Line. There the general advance halted, though probing attacks continued to keep the Germans off balance while Pershing planned a fresh offensive to capture Buzancy and the high ground to the east.

He now had two armies in the field. The Second Army, created on October 12 with General Bullard in command, was assigned the sector between Fresnes-en-Woëvre and Port-sur-Seille east of the Moselle. Pershing on the sixteenth turned over First Army to General Liggett, a big man who had proved by his performance as I Corps commander that he was not, as some had alleged, too fat for field duty. Pershing himself assumed full-time duties as AEF commander-in-chief. General Liggett, Marshall's boss from Philippine days, moved Marshall up to First Army chief of operations, replacing Colonel McCleave. The change only recognized the fact that from the outset Marshall had been working closely with General Drum, and these two, for most practical purposes, had been functioning as the commanding general's chief tactical advisers.

During the preparation for the new attack scheduled for November 1, Marshall and General Drum were frequently at the front, going forward sometimes on horseback but more often by car along the "Sacred Way" from Souilly to the sector north of Verdun. There were additional units to get into place and problems of holding in position "exhausted, heavily suffering troops" already in line. And, as always, there were late changes in plan. A friend of Marshall's, the chief of staff of the 1st Moroccan Division, observed that the Americans, continually writing plans and amendments, were fighting *"une guerre des papiers."* He was reminded by Marshall that he had earlier made the same complaint against his own, the French Army. That was true, "but," said the Frenchman, "you do a better job of it than even we do."

To force a quick decision, with the expectation that victory was within grasp, Foch gave the order for the November drive. Objectives were not to be limiting. "Troops thrown in the attack," he ordered in his instructions of October 25, "have only to know their direction of attack. On this direction they advance as far as possible, attacking and maneuvering against the enemy who resists, without any attempt at alignment, the most advanced units working to assist the advance of those who are momentarily halted." [29]

Foch's optimism, which Pershing shared, was at once borne

out. On the first day the Americans broke through the German lines. More remarkable, the momentum continued on the second day. A correspondent at First Army later wrote: "Staff officers in the front room of the Souilly *mairie* almost capered before the wall map as the thumbtacks and red string went forward to places that had seemed once as far away as Berlin. The drawn, sleepless face of Colonel George C. Marshall, chief of operations, lighted up as he went over with us the colored penciled lines on his own map and talked with happy sureness of where we would be next day." [30]

Success at the front multiplied supply problems behind the lines. Chronically short of transportation, the American armies "had tremendous supplies to bring up to the front" over roads that "were practically impassable," and at the same time had, Marshall reckoned, "176,000 sick and wounded to evacuate." "At one period," Marshall said in describing the battle, "we found ourselves running short of ammunition for some of our batteries. There were no trucks available to haul ammunition, and even if we had had trucks we could not have gotten them through on account of the terrific jam. But the problem was solved. A regiment of infantry going into line was turned around and marched back twelve miles to an ammunition dump. Every man in this regiment . . . came back carrying a shell on his shoulder. . . . When the 6th Division detrained at Clermont to be rushed up to the front they were faced with such an insufficiency of horses that it was impossible to haul all their equipment. . . . The men of this division took the place of the horses . . . and pulled their carts and wagons with them right up to the front." This, it turned out, was all in vain. Their heroic efforts brought them in position on the day the war ended, and they had to haul it all back again.[31]

The last days before the armistice had two points of special interest for Marshall. One was the night march of the 2d Division under Major General John A. Lejeune on the night of November 3, which pushed one regiment through the Forêt de Dieulet and surprised the Germans at Beaumont. The maneuver paralleled the action of the German Army at this spot in 1870, when they too surprised the enemy asleep in Beaumont. Philip Sheridan, an observer with the Germans advancing from Bar-le-Duc toward Sedan, left an account of the attack which Marshall had studied at Leavenworth.[32] The other point of interest was the mix-up over who should take Sedan.

With the fall of the Beaumont ridge and arrival of American troops within light artillery range of Sedan, the Germans began a general withdrawal. Pershing ordered pursuit "without regard for fixed objectives and without fear for their flanks." [33] Nearest to Sedan at this point was the 42d Division under I Corps, command of which had passed from Liggett to General J. T. Dickman. To the right of the 42d was the 1st Division under control of V Corps, now commanded by General Summerall. But Sedan itself lay within the French zone of action. Foch had in fact altered boundaries to assure that French units would liberate the city where France had suffered her bitterest defeat in 1870. In a pursuit situation, however, rigid boundaries could hamper the action, and General Pershing and General Maistre, commanding the Group of Armies of the Center, had agreed that if American forces outran the French, boundaries between them could be ignored. Maistre in fact, on November 4, had suggested that Americans might cross into the French Fourth Army zone on their left to help deal with German resistance.[34] The records do not show a clear understanding on Sedan, but it was Marshall's recollection shortly after the war that the French general had conceded that the military importance of Sedan was such that the Americans should occupy it if they could.[35] In any event Pershing wanted very much to take it; it lay dead ahead in the path of the American advance and it had been from the beginning the prize at the end of a long, hard road.

In the late afternoon of November 5 General Conner, Pershing's chief of operations, came into Colonel Marshall's office in Souilly and after some discussion of Pershing's wishes dictated this message: "General Pershing desires that the honor of entering Sedan should fall to the First American Army. He has every confidence that the troops of I Corps, assisted on their right by the V Corps, will enable him to realize this desire." Preparing this message for relay to the corps commanders involved, Marshall added: "In transmitting the foregoing message, your attention is invited to the favorable opportunity for pressing the advance throughout the night." He then held the message until either General Liggett or his chief of staff, General Drum, arrived. It was Drum, in fact, who came into the command post about an hour later. Assuming that Pershing and Maistre were in agreement on Sedan, Drum made the message clearer by adding: "Boundaries will not be considered binding." He completed the message in the usual fashion: "By command of General Liggett" and signed it himself with Marshall authenticating it. It went out by telephone at once to I and V Corps.[36]

Under the circumstances the message had a heady effect on the commanders who received it. They were in pursuit of a beaten enemy. They had earlier been told to ignore exposed flanks and move fast. They had just witnessed the spectacular success of the 2d Division's night dash ahead of the main line and were advised now specifically to consider repeating that maneuver. As a result, Drum's amendment, intended merely to authorize a shift westward by the I and III Corps, was interpreted by both corps as an invitation to stage a race toward Sedan. Marshall said later, "It did not authorize a free for all, although that is what happened." [37]

General Summerall, not one to hold back when invited to dash forward, on November 6 took his orders in person to Brigadier General Frank Parker, commanding the 1st Division. General Dickman the same day alerted General Menoher's 42d Division, one brigade of which was now commanded by Brigadier General Douglas MacArthur. Parker notified Menoher that he was going to move on Sedan the next day without, however, making clear that he would cross into Menoher's zone. In fact Parker began moving that night. By morning 1st Division men, with Theodore Roosevelt, Jr., limping along on a partly healed wounded leg at the head of his 26th Infantry, were streaming through both the 42d Division and the French 40th Division on their left, in whose zone the prize, Sedan, actually lay. Troops of the 1st and 42d Division were soon mixed and the roads jammed. General MacArthur went forward to check. He ran into a 1st Division patrol whose commander, Lieutenant Black, thought MacArthur in his floppy garrison cap and non-regulation muffler looked like a German officer and arrested him. When word of this reached General Menoher he complained to First Army. His chief, General Dickman, was already exploding with rage, fed by the suspicion that the dashing V Corps commander was trying to grab some additional glory at his expense. The French seemed calmer, but they reported to First Army that they might have to fire artillery into Sedan even if the 1st Division was in the way.

It was the French report that gave General Liggett his first news of what was happening. His temper flamed. He sent an order to his corps commanders to get their divisions back in their own zones at once and then ordered an investigation of the whole affair. But with the end of the war the inquiry was dropped. No one took Sedan. The French were unable to get in before the guns were silenced on November 11.

Since the consequences were nil, the incident reads in history like a kind of heroic farce. So General MacArthur apparently regarded it. He harbored no ill feelings against First Army officers for their part in the mix-up,[38] and Marshall said of MacArthur, "the main thing was that [he] was up there trying to press the attack and get it ahead." There were others, however, whose tempers never cooled. "The fight between Summerall and Dickman," Marshall commented long afterward, "was very intense and it went back to all sorts of jealousies. The real factors in the case were largely ignored, and it kept on in a senseless way for almost the rest of their service. It started from jealousy: They were jealous of General Summerall's great reputation which he had made in the hard fighting. The whole thing to my mind was out of place. The thing was, we were succeeding. We weren't there to fight each other. I didn't have much patience with it. But I wasn't the one receiving the animosity."

Even before the armistice was signed Marshall was scheduled to leave First Army. His new assignment was to be chief of staff of VIII Corps being formed at Montigny-sur-Aube for occupation duty. Pershing had put his name on a list in mid-October for promotion to brigadier general.[39] When the list reached Washington, Congress decided to delay approval until the Meuse-Argonne fight had ended. But the fight ended only with the war's end, and thereupon temporary promotions ceased. So it would be eighteen years before Marshall received the star which many of his 1st Division associates, some once subordinate to him, won through positions of command.

He emerged from the war a temporary colonel, almost forty years old. He had lost ground to contemporaries in the race for rank—Drum, for instance, and MacArthur. For once, it might be said, his luck in timing had failed him. A few more months of war and he would have taken the biggest rank hurdle of them all into the company of generals. On the other hand he had solidly built his career and his reputation as a staff officer. In both tactics and logistics—in the planning of battle and in the organization and maintenance of large bodies of troops—he had developed a competence probably unexcelled by any other officer of his age in the Army. Having come over with the first convoy of troops and dealt with combat training and planning for the nearly eighteen months before the war ended, he was familiar with every major problem the fighting forces faced. As chief of training and operations of the 1st Division in its first year in France he had applied to training and combat his long experience in the handling of small units. As a member, and later as chief, of the Operations Division of First Army he had a key role in planning and supervising the movement and commitment of more troops in battle than any American officer would again achieve until General Omar Bradley established his 12th Army Group in France in 1944. It had been his job, one of Pershing's principal staff officers would later write, to "work out all the details of the operations, putting them in a clear, practical workable order which [could] be understood by the commanders of all subordinate units. The order must be comprehensive, yet not involved. It must appear clear when read in poor light, in the mud and rain. That was Marshall's job, and he performed it 100 per cent. The troops which maneuvered under his plans always won." [40]

If the immediate rewards seemed meager, the record was solid, exceptional, and enduring. The three chief contenders for nomination as Chief of Staff in 1939—none a graduate of West Point—had all worked in the top jobs on the staff of First Army: Drum, the chief of staff; DeWitt, the chief of supply; and Marshall, the chief of operations.

Armistice—1919

"Both the British and American governments would
be very loath to involve their armies in a further advance into Germany. . . ."
            —Letter drafted by Marshall for Conner to Chief
            of Staff, February 15, 1919.

T H A T moral singleness, simplicity, and intensity of purpose which is unique to war was the first casualty of peace.
The huge American Army—almost two million men on November 11—were suddenly out of the job for which they were
trained and to which they had steeled themselves.[1] Orders to
the First Army on November 11 were "to hold the front now
attained while preparing for further advance and to cease hostilities until further orders." Presently they began to move out of
the line. Only the Third Army, formed while the Meuse-Argonne battle was going on, was to remain for occupation duty
under command of General Dickman. For all other troops the
ensuing weeks and months were a purposeless, exasperated
wait to get out and go home. For the command it was a period,
hardly less exasperating, of holding together a military organization while speedily demobilizing it[2] and simultaneously preparing against the contingency of more fighting if Germany proved
intransigent. The battle cement of common purpose and life-

and-death urgency that united professional and recruit in a citizen army leached out in the silence of the Western Front. For professionals like Marshall the rest was patchwork; he was thrust into scores of small emergencies, making plans that came to nothing, filling in for departing colleagues, straightening out injustices, working to keep up discipline.

For two months—until near the end of January 1919—he served as chief of staff at VIII Corps under Major General Henry T. Allen. Allen, a cavalry man with a good fighting record (he had commanded the 90th Division), was charged with training units for use in Germany. Apparently Pershing suggested Marshall to him for that purpose. The tall, straight, serious, businesslike infantry colonel seemed markedly out of place in this headquarters of boots and spurs. He actually stayed only long enough to carry out some training exercises, gaining the commendation of General Allen as a staff officer who had "few equals." [3] Then he was called back to Pershing's headquarters as a member of the Operations Section and set to work on a study of how to move an American army into Germany in case negotiations at Paris broke down. In spite of estimates and information already compiled by GHQ Intelligence, he had little firm basis for planning. He had to suppose various eventualities in which the Allies might elect to use force and the Germans to resist. If the object was to occupy the German capital, to force on the German government the reality of unqualified military defeat, then he proposed that the Allies occupy the North Sea and Baltic ports and send expeditions to Berlin from Hamburg and Stettin. If, on the other hand, the Germans were disposed to resume the fight in the West, he outlined a broad advance between Mulhouse and Wesel to sweep the Rhineland and western Germany. As a final objective of such an advance he proposed occupation of an arc from the Baltic northeast of Lübeck on the left to Leipzig and Lake Constance on the right. The center—interestingly, in the light of what happened in World War II—would hold at the line of the Elbe, and if it were necessary to move into Berlin, that would be done by advancing the left flank to Stettin. [4]

It was a portion of the center that Marshall selected for the American army. From a line of departure in the occupation zone between Bonn and the Lahn near Koblenz, three divisions in the lead, followed by four more for clean-up and occupation duty, would move on the axis, Koblenz-Kassel-Helmstedt-Stendal. At the Elbe the American sector would be widened to about sixty miles from Wittenberge to Schönebeck and would require an additional three divisions in line.

Having made the plan, Marshall along with General Conner regarded the whole project with distaste. Some such show of force might indeed be desirable if internal disorders in Germany threatened to open the way for the Bolsheviks. Yet Marshall was inclined to doubt the wisdom of American participation. "Both the British and American governments," he wrote in a letter prepared for Conner's signature, "would be very loath to involve their armies in a further advance into Germany, particularly in view of the earnest desire of the two governments at the present time to carry out the rapid demobilization of their armies." Furthermore there was some question as to the political aims and consequences of an occupation, which, he was aware, the French, in particular, were pushing. Marshall warned that a move in force into Germany, if done at all, "should only be carried out to such extent as is deemed necessary in order to maintain the present dominant position of the Allied governments and to definitely cripple the power of the German government." He was anxious, in other words, that military operations should go only to the point of fully achieving the military aim of crushing the enemy's power to resist. Beyond that he was thinking of reconstruction. The purpose of putting down civil disorders within Germany was to avoid the destruction of its national wealth. He recommended that the Allies take steps to send more food into the defeated country.[5]

His final objection to the march into Germany was doubt that we could do it successfully. Not only was the Army rapidly slipping away, but it was hard to find transportation for even the few divisions that might be left. To move a few United States occupation forces to Koblenz a few weeks before, Marshall had had to "unhorse brigade after brigade of artillery and leave them on their fronts near the railroads and take their horses for units that were going into Germany." Had it been necessary to move on in force to Berlin, there might have been logistic nightmares. Marshall did not afterward change his skepticism of the wisdom of a march into Germany, but he did feel that the Germans should have been sufficiently "licked" to scotch the myth that their government accepted peace without defeat in the field.[6]

From planning operations that would not happen Marshall turned to describing those that were finished, first in writing— he worked on General Pershing's final report—then in talks. Along with General Drum and the First Army G-2, Colonel Willey Howell, he was ordered on a lecture circuit of division camps.[7] The idea was that if the troops waiting to go home were told of what America had done in the war their pride in past achievement would stiffen them against their present discontent. The project had been ordered by Pershing and the men had been personally selected by him, as the Operations Staff at GHQ discovered when they tried to get Marshall excused from the assignment. The Allied commander-in-chief was moving to answer criticisms stemming from returned officers and men and spreading in Washington. Frederick Palmer, the war correspondent, and Martin Egan, one of Pershing's old friends from early Philippine days, both wrote to urge that he meet the attacks by telling the AEF story; Egan particularly emphasized the need of giving close attention to returning divisions, in whom he had found a "woeful lack of understanding" of the campaign and a failure to grasp the simplest facts behind certain policies and actions.[8]

Because of General Drum's subsequent shift to the Services of Supply and Howell's duties elsewhere, Marshall ended by giving more of the lectures than the other two. As delivered, they must have been a good deal more interesting than they appear in surviving notes. At least some officers asked for repeat performances. How the troops reacted is uncertain. Colonel Howell, anxious to be rid of the job, was of the opinion that the men began with the assumption that they were being fed "headquarters propaganda" and scarcely listened.[9] Marshall, however, persisted. For his diligence he was rewarded by assignments to deliver his general lecture complete with maps and charts at Chaumont to members of the House Military Affairs Committee, among whom was Fiorello LaGuardia, then a major recently elected to Congress.[10]

On his tour Marshall did more than try to talk the soldiers into a better frame of mind: he inquired into their grievances and at the request of the AEF chief of staff, McAndrew, made recommendations for relieving them. Some he dealt with himself. It was a mission with which he had particular sympathy. The substantial grievances—and there were many—were largely complaints against two kinds of officers who flourished in the rear: the martinet and the bureaucrat. It exasperated Marshall to find a "Prussian-type officer" conducting a rigid training program just to keep the men busy while they waited for a boat. He thought that was the abuse of the idea of training both in principle and practice. The men "were going out into the cold and wet and slime and going through these [special drills] in some godforsaken little village which didn't have a pavement in the place or a thing to see after dark. With this severe program . . . they were embittered in a way they never forgot." To make matters worse, regulations governing their after-hours activities were arbitrary and inconsistent.

Lecturing officers and men of the 27th Division on board the *Leviathan* at Brest just before it sailed, he found officers resentful over a directive to fill out complicated forms and repeat in Brest shakedown inspections that they had already gone through at Le Mans. As time for a remedy was short, Marshall went after it himself. He talked to the general and chief of staff of the Base Section at Brest who had demanded the forms and inspections. They said only that they had to do it "because it was an order." Marshall dropped his lecturing and went to the Embarkation Center at Le Mans, where he knew the chief of staff. The reply was the same: Sorry, but those were the orders. It was useless to explain how damaging was the effect on morale, particularly serious and unnecessary when the division was on the point of going home. The general treated Marshall like an intruder and would hardly listen. Taking the bit in his teeth, Marshall then drove to the headquarters of the Services of Supply at Tours. Again he talked to the commanding general, whom he knew, and again he was brushed aside as an intruder. Even the

G-4 who was an old friend, "a very nice, gentle friend," said he could do nothing and urged Marshall to "talk to them at Le Mans." He said he had but agreed anyway to go back and try again. It was no use. At Le Mans they said they could do nothing without an order from Tours.

Marshall then picked up the phone and called the chief of staff of the Services of Supply and told him the whole story of his frustrations and the reasons given him. The chief of staff said he was sorry.

At that Marshall exploded. "You may be sorry," he said, "but that doesn't cure anything. Now I have reached the point where I am going to . . . communicate directly with the chief of staff, AEF."

The SOS chief said, "Give me two hours."

Marshall snapped at him, "I will give you an hour and a half and no longer."

It was enough. Tours talked to Brest and then to Le Mans as Marshall waited. Then his call came: "It's all cured."

Some of the bureaucratic troubles, Marshall thought, were caused by the precipitation of "class B officers" in the rear echelon when their incompetence could not be tolerated at the front. More—like the rigidity which he fought through for the benefit of the 27th Division—were due not to incompetence but to the reluctance of even fine officers to meddle with the workings of the machine of which they felt themselves, often rather helplessly, a part. They feared "changes which would complicate things [in a way] they couldn't foresee." They also tended to resent the intervention of outsiders, the "visiting firemen" from higher headquarters.

But if their attitude was understandable it could not be tolerated. There were already grumblings at home, some just, some unjust, all boiling up in the headlines and in the halls of Congress. Marshall, from his view of the staging and embarkation camps, suggested changes, a number of which Pershing ordered into effect. His suggestions eventually reached Secretary of War Baker, who made use of them in answering some criticisms of the Army's handling of men in the port areas.

There were a lot to answer—from the complaints of disgruntled officers who thought they had been unfairly passed over for promotion or decoration to more serious charges of blundering in supply and of brutality to military prisoners. The acting Judge Advocate General of the Army joined in grave complaints against the Army's system of military justice.[11]

Perhaps the most general and bitterest attack fell upon the civilian welfare organizations, the YMCA in particular. Investigating some of the charges later, Marshall felt the criticisms of the Y, which for a time threatened to dry up contributions, were largely unjust. For one of the more venomous gibes, that the Y had sold gift cigarettes, he blamed Army shippers, who mixed packages marked as gifts with others consigned for sale. He thought also that the more general complaint concerning the shortage of canteen goods should properly have been made against the Army, which provided less shipping space than it had promised. With a keen sense of injustice, Marshall persuaded General Pershing to come publicly to the defense of the Y and later he himself took every chance he got to set the record straight.[12]

Along with the peculiarly frustrating problems of these final house-cleaning days in France, there were also rewards and exuberant moments. Near the end of April, Marshall went to Metz to receive, along with other members of Pershing's command, the French Legion of Honor for distinguished service.[13] Before the ceremony one of Pershing's staff members, Colonel James L. Collins, a former aide in the Philippines and Mexican campaign who had been with Pershing early in the war and had recently returned to his headquarters, brought an offer from the American commander. Walking beside Marshall and fitting his words to the cadence of the step, he said in a low voice, "How would you like to be the General's aide?" Whether Marshall altogether liked the idea or not, he made up his mind quickly that he should accept. He told Collins so after the ceremony.[14] He knew, of course, that he was not being picked as a social secretary but as a personal adviser and executive—the capacity in which he had served General Liggett briefly in the Philippines and General Bell for a longer time. In later years he was to have a strong feeling that his service as an aide had been a handicap to his career by keeping him from troop duty, and during his years as a general on active duty he seldom had an officer detailed as aide.[15]

The moment of his decision, however, was celebrated with rare gaiety. Following the award formation, Marshal Pétain, whom Marshall knew well and for whom he had a high regard,[16] invited the American officers to join him and his staff at lunch in the villa of the former German commander of Metz. After they had eaten and drunk and talked like old comrades at ease, Marshall recognized two brigadiers he had known in the 1st Moroccan Division, to which he had been attached in 1917. They were delighted to see him, kissed him on both cheeks, and talked of old times. "One fellow was standing with his arm around me and I had my arm around him. We were having quite a time (we had had a lot to drink) when Pétain came up and said, 'I'm very glad to see you on such intimate terms with my fighting generals.'" Then Pershing joined them and announced that Marshall had just consented to be his aide. On this relaxed and harmonious note Marshall embarked on one of the longest tours of his Army career. For more than five years—to within three months of Pershing's retirement in October 1924—Marshall would stand at his right hand as a kind of personal chief of staff.[17]

At Chaumont the myriad details of winding up the affairs of the AEF occupied Marshall for a little while longer, until shortly after the signing of the Treaty of Versailles, when Pershing transferred his small remaining headquarters to Paris.[18] Marshall, along with the rest of the personal staff, moved into the Rue de Varenne house that was owned by American banker Ogden Mills. Their days thenceforth, and a good part of their nights, were devoted to the ceremonies of victory, which were to take Marshall at Pershing's side on a grand tour of the Allied capitals and introduce him to the leaders of Europe.

Paris set the pattern and the standard. On the Fourth of July, President Poincaré reviewed American troops in the Place de la Concorde. Then on the French holiday, Bastille Day, Paris in perfect weather put on what Marshall called the greatest victory parade he ever saw. Early in the morning, when the marchers began gathering near the Porte Maillot and the Avenue de la

Grande Armée, spectators already thronged the line of march from the Place de l'Etoile down the Champs Elysées to the Place de la Concorde, thence past the Madeleine, through the Place de l'Opéra to the reviewing stand at the Place de la République. Symbolically the chains placed at the base of the Arc de Triomphe were removed so that the troops might march through after the solemn ceremony of commemoration, in which President Poincaré and Premier Clemenceau placed wreaths on the casket in the center dedicated to those who had died. With them stood a sailor and soldier of France, representing the victorious armed forces, a girl from Alsace and a girl from Lorraine, symbolizing the recovery of the lost provinces, and a member of the Lafayette Escadrille, included in tribute to the ally whose help was at last decisive.[19]

The parade itself began on a solemn note as a thousand lame, mutilated, and blind veterans led the procession. Then followed military splendor to which the huge crowd responded with wild cheering. After Marshal Joffre and Marshal Foch came Pershing and his aides, followed by thirty American generals on horseback at the head of an American composite regiment of men whose combat records and soldierly bearing earned them the honor. Troops of the other Allies came next—the British, the Italians, Japanese, Portuguese, Serbs, Czechs, Rumanians, and Poles—then the French.

Just behind Pershing and Harbord, Marshall, mounted on a white horse, rode abreast with his fellow aides, Colonel John G. Quekemeyer and Major John C. Hughes. He was deeply moved by the great military spectacle of which he was now a part. The broad expanse of the Champs Elysées, which even in its daily shabby flow of civilian vehicles conveyed some of the breadth and flow of civilization, was now a breathtaking triumphal way. The banks of cheering crowds, the statues representing Alsace and Lorraine in the Place de la Concorde decked in flowers in place of the mourning crepe that had clothed them for nearly half a century, the Madeleine with rich red drapery hung behind the white columns in a startling burst of color—these remained vivid memories through Marshall's life.[20]

Then the triumph and exultation passed. The cheering ceased, and France remembered. Wives, mothers, fathers, brothers, sisters of men who had fallen in the most terrible of humanity's wars to date marched single file through the quiet Arch of Triumph, each to drop a single flower on the casket there. All afternoon they filed past, and into the night, leaving a great mound of blossoms to mark the place where the casket lay.

With the cheers of Paris still fresh, Pershing, his staff, and the victory regiment boarded British destroyers at Boulogne to cross the Channel and then take a train to London. Among the political and military great of Britain who greeted them at Victoria Station was Winston Churchill, Secretary of State for War. In the course of the next week of festivities Marshall spent one day as Churchill's escort when, in Hyde Park, Pershing held a review for the Prince of Wales and Churchill and later decorated a number of British officers.[21] It was Marshall's first close look at the man whom he would come to know intimately as stanch ally and brilliant adversary in the great debates over how to defeat the enemy in World War II. That same evening Churchill presided at a dinner in the House of Commons in honor of the Americans, attended by many of the top British political and military leaders.

With Churchillian eloquence the Secretary of State for War warned of the Bolshevik threat that might join Germany and Russia and force the English-speaking peoples to stand together. "It was inevitable," he said in both tribute and prophecy, "that the struggle should terminate victoriously for freedom from the moment that the United States entered the war. Until then the fearful equipoise of the conflict gave no certainty that even if every effort was made a decisive victory would be attained. From the moment the Germans in their vanity and folly drove the United States to draw the sword there was no doubt that Germany was ruined, that the cause of freedom was safe, and that the British and American democracy would begin once more to write their history in common." [22]

London's victory parade on July 19 was chiefly memorable for Marshall because of a "devil of a horse" he had to ride. The horse had been assigned to General André Brewster, the inspector general, who was unable to manage him. Marshall offered to swap mounts. The parade assembled at Hyde Park and from Albert Gate marched along Sloane Street through Belgravia and across the Thames by Vauxhall Bridge. They marched then to Westminster Bridge, recrossed the river, passed through the Admiralty Arch in Whitehall, and thence along the Mall before the royal pavilion on the steps of the Queen Victoria Memorial. All the way Marshall fought his horse. At the Admiralty Arch the animal reared and went over backward. Marshall, falling, broke a small bone in his hand. Nevertheless he remounted and continued past the reviewing stand. Thereafter he was invited to sit in the royal pavilion to watch Haig, Beatty, and Foch lead British and French troops through the remainder of the parade. Years later General Brewster, writing to Marshall, recalled the parade and said with little if any exggeration that Marshall by trading horses had saved his life.[23]

Back in France there were more parades and more parties. General Pershing and his staff visited the 1st and 3d Divisions in Germany and made a nine-day tour of the old battlefront from Belfort to Nieuport on the Belgian coast. Partly a sentimental pilgrimage, it involved also some study of the places where Americans had fought. With scarcely a pause, Pershing's party swept on to Italy, where in four days they visited scenes of Italian victory, were fêted in Venice, Treviso, Vicenza, Milan, and Turin, and entertained by King Victor Emmanuel in Rome. Among the guests at the royal dinner in the Quirinal Palace were some leading figures of the time—Nitti, president of the Council, Albricco, war minister, General Diaz, commander-in-chief—and some of the future: Count Sforza and General (later in less happy circumstances Marshal) Badoglio.[24]

It was near the end—nine more days in Paris for packing, shopping, and farewells, including Clemenceau's reception on the last day. On September 1 they were in Brest ready to board the *Leviathan* along with members of the victory regiment and some men of the 1st Division selected to march in the parades still ahead at home. Among them appeared suddenly, for Marshall, a familiar face: Sergeant Torstrup, the noncom on whom Lieutenant Marshall had leaned long ago on his first assignment in Mindoro, when he was just beginning to learn his business as an officer. It was a curious reminder of the beginning on a day which marked such a dramatic ending. There was also a reminder of the future when Marshal Foch, personally bidding farewell, remarked on the pier: "We have cemented our ties of friendship, and if ever in the future we shall find it necessary to unfurl our banner, then we know that we shall continue as brothers-in-arms." [25] The banner would be unfurled almost twenty years to the day from that morning. Twenty-five years later, less one week, American forces would parade again down the streets of liberated Paris.

New York might find it difficult to outdo Paris and London, though the tumult began at high pitch as the *Leviathan* moved past Ambrose Light and guns fired and sirens screamed the news to the waiting city. But New York had what nearly every returning hero wanted most, wives and families—home. Lily was there at City Hall, waiting while Pershing's party made their way up Broadway. At the Battery they had been met by Vice-President Thomas R. Marshall, representing the President (already on his crosscountry tour to try to get public support for the League of Nations), Secretary of War Baker, the Chief of Staff, General Peyton March, General Bullard, Governor Alfred E. Smith, and Mayor John F. Hylan. This was at last the moment of completion —the end of war.[26] Marshall and his wife were put up at the Waldorf, along with other members of the staff and their families, and there must have been in the course of the next wildly festive days some quiet times to talk and knit over the two-year gap in their married life.

New York, of course, had its official reception, its banquet followed by a special program at the Hippodrome, and its parade, this time all American, with the veteran 1st Division in the lead just behind Pershing, his staff and aides. From New York they entrained for Washington, with a stop at Philadelphia, where Pershing and his party were driven through cheering throngs, dined at the Union League Club, and then put back on their train.[27]

Washington found hundreds of thousands of persons lining the route from the Peace Monument down Pennsylvania Avenue to the White House for the last of the victory parades on September

17. Altogether twenty-five thousand troops marched by.[28] There were cheers for them all, but Marshall recalled that the hero who pleased the crowds best was an Army mule who lapped up some soup spilled from one of the field ranges. They were home. This was peace. And to make it official a joint session of the Senate and House of Representatives convened the next day to do honor and say thanks to the general.[29]

XIII

Aide to Pershing

"My five years with you will always remain the unique experience of my life."
—Marshall to Pershing, September 18, 1924.

WHILE America rushed back—as it thought—to normalcy, the Army renewed its usual postwar struggle for survival. The test of war had exposed grave faults of American military organization. Clearly once again the country had been caught seriously unready to meet its military commitments. Despite advance warning and, indeed, some advance preparation during 1916, a year passed between the declaration of war and the entry of an American division into battle. The great American industrial machine never did get into full war production. At the Armistice, almost no United States artillery ammunition except shrapnel and not a single American-made gun corresponding to the 75mm. gun or 155mm. howitzer, the workhorses of World War I artillery, had reached the front. Fewer than a thousand American-built airplanes—of some fifty thousand which it was at first estimated could be produced—got into action.[1] Because there were at the beginning no plans and no organization in existence either to mobilize industry or recruit and train men, much of the extraordinary effort put forth by industry, the armed forces, and the citizenry at large was expended in improvising techniques before the job could be done.

Once more, as after the war with Spain, Army leaders were determined to profit by experience and reform the defense establishment so that it could be much more rapidly effective if needed again. And once more the reformers were to meet resistance, actively from those who read the lessons differently and passively from many more who could not be bothered to think about next time, especially when even thinking about it was likely to be expensive. Marshall, at Pershing's side in Washington for the next five years, was to see at close hand and take some part in the Army's struggles, gaining invaluable experience in dealing with congressmen and congressional committees. It was to be training not only in the political art of the possible but in the temper of democracy.

Immediately after the Armistice the War Department had asked that Marshall's old friend Colonel John McAuley Palmer be sent home to take part in discussions on the future organization of the Army. Palmer, then in command of a brigade of the 29th Division, reported to Chaumont for Pershing's instructions. There were none in detail. GHQ had made some tentative sketches of a future Army but none had Pershing's approval, and he was wholly absorbed in the thousand details of providing for the occupation, demobilizing, setting the record straight, and getting the story told.

Palmer had his own ideas. As a member of the War Department General Staff in 1911 he had worked on plans for a small regular establishment conceived essentially as a ready force for small emergencies and as machinery to recruit, organize, and train the citizen army that would fight any major war. This was still his basic concept. By the time he reached Washington, however, he found that the Chief of Staff, General March, had settled on a different approach.[2] March, thinking in terms of maintaining a skeleton organization for combat which in case of war would absorb into its own structure the citizen levies, had decided to ask for a standing army of half a million men. Secretary of War Baker accepted the plan, and a bill embodying it was introduced into Congress early in 1919.

Seldom has any bill had such various and powerful opposition.

On the basis of cost alone it was hardly credible that Congress would authorize a permanent Army more than five times the size of the prewar establishment. Besides that, in the aftermath of the war the anti-militarist movement was rapidly gaining momentum and fresh recruits. Revulsion to war fed the movement. The usual postwar attacks on Army mismanagement and injustice furnished fuel. Organized labor, traditionally opposed to a large standing army as a menace to labor's freedom to strike, joined the attack on the militarists. A growing sense of the need for economy in government was to make many businessmen, including leaders of big steel, champions of disarmament. Liberal groups added scattered but unusually articulate protests against enlarging the influence of the military, which they traditionally regarded as a move toward the garrison state. For Americans generally, the war had been a victory over Prussian militarism; it was better to cherish the democratic virtue we had made prevail than to imitate the ways of our enemies. The editor of the *New York World* just before the Armistice rejoiced that "the disciplined forces of militarism yield at every point to the hurriedly assembled hosts of democracy." [3] So unpreparedness itself could seem like a virtue, recalling the traditional view that all the nation needed for security were citizens with stout hearts and a fowling piece over the mantel. Finally, political suspicion of President Wilson's international ideals led some opponents of the administration to charge—and perhaps believe—that the large Army was wanted in order to send forces abroad.

The mood of the nation, turning its back on war, became the stuff of partisan politics. While the Army was trying to work out its future, the key political fact was that in the elections of November 1918 the Democrats had lost control of Congress. The lame-duck session therefore made no serious attempt to deal with the March-Baker plan. Congress in the appropriations bill for the fiscal year 1919-20 authorized an Army with an average strength for the year of 325,000 men. To come within that figure it would be necessary to reduce the actual number in uniform to about 225,000 by October 1919. General March at once took steps to do so. But he did not alter his ultimate goal of 500,000.

Beginning in the summer of 1919, committees of the new Congress held hearings on the March-Baker proposal and a number of other measures which in the end gave a thorough airing to the military problem.[4] A procession of experts testified before the Senate Committee on Military Affairs, headed by Senator James W. Wadsworth of New York, and the House Committee on Military Affairs, under Representative Julius Kahn of California. Almost no one supported the War Department's request for half a million men. Palmer, who on orders had worked on modifications of the original March-Baker bill, came before Senator Wadsworth to argue that not only was the force too large but that the concept was "not in harmony with the genius of American institutions." He believed that democracy's defense should be not only militarily effective but politically congenial, and he spelled out in some detail his own ideas about the regular establishment as the core and mentor of a citizen army. It was a reasonable position and, as it happened also to be close to the committee's own, Senator Wadsworth promptly asked that Palmer be assigned to the committee to help write a bill to substitute for the War Department's.[5]

This was early in October and for all practical purposes signaled the death of the five-hundred-thousand-man Army some weeks before General Pershing was scheduled to testify. Yet it was of course inevitable that Pershing's views should be sought and probable that they might weigh in the final decision of what alternative shape to design for the postwar Army.

To rest and prepare for his appearance before the Joint Committee, Pershing in the latter part of September took Marshall and a few members of his personal staff to Naushon Island off New Bedford, Massachusetts, where for about three weeks he was the guest of W. Cameron Forbes, former governor-general of the Philippines. At Naushon one of the ways these usually serious, dignified Army officers found to relax was to write and perform a play. Marshall collaborated on a little farce as full of impersonations as *Charley's Aunt* and in it played the role of a policeman named George Marshall. Pershing improvised verses and sang.[6] From there, in early October, Pershing, Marshall, and Colonel Quekemeyer (the General's social aide) joined General Conner at a camp belonging to Mrs. Conner's father on

Brandreth Lake in the Adirondacks, where in almost complete isolation they stayed for another three weeks, hunting and fishing and working nearly every night until midnight on the presentation Pershing was to make to Congress. Marshall managed to shoot a buck slightly smaller than the one Pershing killed—an achievement of both skill and tact for which he was congratulated by his guide but in which he himself took no pleasure.[7]

At the working meetings there were technical problems and still thornier political ones to discuss. One of the most difficult was the relations between Pershing and March. Pershing on the way home from France had received word that a grateful Congress had given him the permanent rank of General of the Armies, carrying four stars. March's four stars were temporary— his permanent rank carried only two—yet as Chief of Staff he was Pershing's superior. This would have created difficulties between the most forbearing of generals. In fact March was an autocrat in the mold of General Ainsworth, determined to yield neither substance nor shadow of supreme authority. He was, Marshall believed after intimate dealings with him and study of the record, a great administrator "with a weakness for antagonizing everybody and, in particular, in having men about him who were curt, almost rude." Pershing was not the man to suffer such treatment patiently. He enjoyed supreme authority himself and was used to it as commander of the AEF. In France he had exercised virtually independent military command, treating the War Department rather as a service agency than a superior headquarters. Furthermore he had acted as personal representative of the President in many matters of high strategy that were quasi-political. March had very recently been his subordinate, serving under him as director of a field artillery training school at Le Valdahon near the Swiss border until February 1918.

Hostilities between the two Generals broke out almost as soon as March took over as Chief of Staff on May 24, 1918, and began issuing orders to the AEF commander, as General Harbord put it, "in a tone which might have been used by a commander-in-chief of all the armies of the United States, if there had been any such authority except Wilson." [8] Marshall, who came into the middle of the bitterness after it had already hardened, admired both men and thought both were at fault, "because it was essential that they get together and they didn't." He later deplored the harsh tone of March's memoirs and tried in vain to get Pershing to omit similarly bitter statements from his. Quite probably Marshall's distaste for the subsequent public controversy shaped his later fixed aversion to writing his own autobiography.

Newton Baker, for whom Marshall had unbounded respect, calling him in later years "the most penetrating observer of Army facts and fancies" and "the greatest American or the greatest mind that I ever came in contact with in my lifetime," did his best to mitigate the antagonism of the two generals or soften its consequences. "He rode a very difficult horse," Marshall remarked, "there between General Pershing and General March and he did it extraordinarily well." He managed at least the very difficult task of being friend and chief to both men. The question of the command relationship between the two he resolved temporarily by permitting Pershing to remain as AEF commander with his own staff until he could make his official report. So Pershing had taken office space at 8th and E Streets and in form remained an overseas combat commander so far as the War Department some ten blocks away was concerned.[9]

His co-operation on any project of General March's was not to be expected. In any case, he could see another weighty reason for rejecting the five-hundred-thousand-man Army, quite apart from any technical objections: it was sure to be highly unpopular. Whether or not at this time Pershing entertained active political ambitions, he was having them thrust upon him by the usual American search for presidential timber wherever a hero grows. He had no politics, had never voted, but he was the son-in-law of Republican Senator Warren. It was obvious enough that the Republican party behind the intransigent leadership of Senator Lodge was not going to be saddled with advocating a big Army or with any other issue that unpleasantly might recall Wilson's war to the American voter. It was not apparent that the Democrats were any more eager to buck normalcy in 1920 with an issue of preparedness. Indeed, from any politically sensitive point of view, whether in furtherance of personal ambition or in quest of the most effective military organization that Congress would accept, defense of the War Department scheme was impossible.

Pershing, moreover, was sympathetic with the conservative economic view which opposed such a large army as an undue burden on the country's resources. He knew intimately the temper of the business conservatives from wartime association with industrialists and bankers who had visited him at Chaumont and Paris and from such close friends as Charles G. Dawes, Chicago banker, and Martin Egan, member of J. P. Morgan and Company. Their conviction that the budget must be balanced and taxes reduced was also his conviction; as a soldier he tried to shape an Army establishment to fit fiscal needs yet provide what he could reasonably and honestly defend as an adequate defense.

In making final preparations for his testimony Pershing, Conner, and Marshall rounded out their study with formal talks with twenty key officers, including General March. Marshall had already made Pershing familiar with Palmer's presentation.[10] His homework done, General Pershing went before the Joint Senate and House Military Affairs Committee meeting on October 31 to begin three days of testimony.[11] Conner and Marshall were there to assist. It was for Marshall his first taste of a democratic procedure of which he himself was later to become a master.

Committee members treated Pershing with great deference and gave him every courteous opportunity to shoot down the administration bill. Despite some apparent shifting of ground in the course of his testimony, he did so. He thought a regular army of two hundred and seventy-five to three hundred thousand was large enough and that its primary job should be to train the National Guard and the organized Reserves. He also defended a program of universal military training, which Palmer was writing into the Senate Committee bill. For Palmer such training was the heart of the matter—the kind of military preparedness which was suited to democracy and which would permit the nation to grow militarily strong without suffering a large standing army. But it too was very unpopular. Before debate on the Hill was over, organized labor, farm groups, liberals, would all set up a cry against UMT as the essence of militarism. And even inside the Army there was strong resistance from champions of the National Guard and traditional proponents of military professionalism. Nevertheless Pershing made a spirited defense. Before the joint committee he advocated eleven months' training for every able-bodied young American, as called for in the Senate draft bill, followed by service in the reserve for four years. He believed the service not only necessary for national defense but good training in citizenship for young Americans and especially for the large number of foreign-born.[12] The latter, he believed, could be soundly grounded in American principles during their Army training and so protected against the appeal of non-American influences. It was not, on the whole, the sort of argument best calculated to disarm anti-militarists, though it fitted the postwar mood of 100-per-cent Americanism that was about to float through Congress the most stringent of our immigration bills and spill into a nationwide effort to flush out the Reds. Two less controversial matters he also approved were for the adoption of a single list for promotion, with some freedom of selection other than by seniority, and the retention of a strong General Staff system with an effort at long last to make of it the machinery for over-all planning and supervision that Elihu Root intended.

If there had been any doubt as to the fate of the March-Baker scheme, Pershing's testimony ended it. The *Washington Post* pronounced it dead as early as November 4. Congress, however, adjourned without taking action.

As the debate continued in the country Marshall and other members of Pershing's staff turned to finishing the report of the commander-in-chief, AEF. Its release in December 1919 marked the completion of Pershing's assignment, but Secretary Baker found for him at once another congenial job: he wished General Pershing to tour Army camps and war plants throughout the United States to recommend those that should be retained in peacetime. Two special railroad cars were put at his disposal. Most of the key members of his overseas staff went along.[13] On Conner, Moseley, and Marshall fell much of the responsibility for organizing the expedition and preparing the report.

The trip, which began December 3, developed into a kind of triumphal tour, combining formal inspections, minutely prepared in advance, with receptions for the hero, speeches favoring

preparedness, and unmistakable overtones of politics. Whatever
the intentions—and one must assume that Baker did not propose
to build up a possible Republican candidate—the framework
was ideal, the occasions irresistible, for placing the general before the people as one who might be worthy of high office. As the
Pershing train moved through the South and Middle West, officials and citizens turned out at every stop to welcome the wartime commander, put on parades for him, entertain him at
lunch, at dinner, at receptions, at balls.[14] The most important lesson Marshall learned from this social and official whirl was how
to survive it. He managed to stay clear of whatever he could gra-
ciously avoid. He learned to dig a little into each locality, get a
quick briefing on local problems, prejudices, and personalities.
(His whispered asides to the general on who was who at various
receptions, Pershing found invaluable.) And he did, as usual, at
least his share of the work.

There was a lot to do. At each Army post the local commander,
following instructions sent ahead, held a briefing on the facilities
of the post, troops in residence, methods of administration, and
was prepared with his staff to answer questions on morale, recreation, training capacity, land available for maneuvers, buildings,
supply, hospital, sanitation, health. All these things Pershing and
his staff would survey, and each officer was then responsible for
writing a report on certain findings. Before Christmas, posts in
eleven states had been inspected. From each post in this way was
gathered a complete accounting not only of its physical capacities
but of its present effectiveness and future usefulness in the pro-
jected citizen-training program. Citizen training became one of
Pershing's major concerns. In major speeches in Savannah, Atlanta, Nashville, Louisville, Cincinnati, and Chicago he stressed
the need for a citizen army, while praising local heroes and dropping warnings against the menace of Bolshevism.[15]

So far as the speeches took on the general coloration of a political candidacy, Marshall strongly disapproved. At least later he
thought it too bad that Pershing had let himself be touted for the
presidency. It was, he believed, soon after Pershing's return that
"some of his friends deluded him" on his chances of becoming a
candidate. "I know one group came from Tennessee and I sent

them back home. He was away at the time, [and] I didn't even consult him. He was furious with me." The bug had already bitten. But Marshall, aloof from the contagion, thought the chances were never good enough. "I knew pretty well what the general reactions were [to Pershing] and I thought it was a shame that he might in some way cut down his prestige by being involved, unless it was . . . almost by acclamation."

There was probably never any serious possibility of Pershing's nomination by acclamation; most of the Republican party leaders were confident of victory and did not want an amateur to lead them. In the circumstances Pershing's indication that he would accept the nomination if offered was not enough. Yet not until after the Republicans had made their final choice and the Democrats put out feelers did he at last issue a denial of "political ambitions," saying with belated forthrightness that "in no circumstances whatsoever would I think of being a candidate for the presidency." [16]

Unquestionably Pershing hoped for a different conclusion as in the early months of 1920 he continued his triumphal tour. There was a break for Christmas which enabled Marshall to spend the holidays with his wife and his mother in Atlantic City. On January 2 he reported to Chicago to board the Pershing train again and begin visits to twenty-one more states during the next two months, traveling to the Far West, back through Texas and the South to Boston and New York.[17] If politically the trip failed to touch off a Pershing boom, it had long consequences for the Army. It gave three future Chiefs of Staff, Pershing, Marshall, and Craig, who joined the tour in January, a detailed view of the peacetime Army and its local problems; and it put Pershing solidly on record in favor of universal military training. Incidentally it brought Craig in a close association with Marshall, the man whom he, as Chief of Staff, would later name his deputy.

In the report on his inspection, submitted March 23, 1920, Pershing recommended that nearly all existing posts be retained if universal military training should be adopted. Concerned about morale, he proposed better pay, more equitable handling of rank, and a number of schemes to develop pride of organization.[18]

Work on the reorganization of the Army had meanwhile proceeded and two bills were before the first regular session of the
66th Congress. The Wadsworth bill in the Senate, which had
been largely drafted by Palmer and his assistant, Colonel John
W. Gulick, contained a provision for universal military training
to be given all able-bodied young men between their nineteenth
and twenty-first years. To reduce political opposition the training period was cut to four months—a schoolboy's summer. But
even this much was under increasing attack. Members of Congress were being bombarded with letters and telegrams from
constituents who objected to the cost, to the implications of militarism, to the futility of preparedness when war had been
abolished, and, of course, though they seldom said so, to the
direct burden and discomfort of sending their sons into service
or going themselves. So strong was the tide that, when it was
reported that the Democrats were going to make a party fight
against the program, Senator Lodge decided that the Republicans
could not afford to support it. Anticipating that retreat, Palmer
already had redrafted the Wadsworth bill to substitute "volun-
tary" for "compulsory" citizen training.[19] He was ready to accept
the change because he felt that he could still save the concept of
the regular Army as a training establishment and the machinery
for the peacetime organization of the citizen army. These, he
thought from the long view of preparedness, were the essentials.
The amended Senate bill passed and on reconciliation with a companion House bill became law on June 4, 1920, as the National
Defense Act. Written as an amendment to the National Defense
Act of 1916—Palmer remarked that this was like Jefferson writing the Declaration of Independence as an amendment to the
Book of Job—the new law was in fact a new charter for the
peacetime Army. The authorized strength of 297,800 officers
and men conformed with Pershing's estimate of what was adequate.

Under wide latitude to reshape the field force, the War Department shortly created by General Orders the new military
establishment. To a small standing Army organized for immediate tactical use were closely linked National Guard and organized Reserve divisions ready to be mobilized if needed.[20] Instead

of the old geographical military departments, the country was divided into nine corps areas, in each of which one regular Army division would be stationed. With each regular division was to be associated one reserve division (a paper organization) and two National Guard divisions whose component units would be contributed by the states within each corps area as they themselves determined. The nine corps with their regular troops and citizen components were grouped in three armies. Provisions for federalizing the Guard in war and for training it in peace were held over from the 1916 act. The General Staff was strengthened, though Congress cut the number of General Staff officers on assignment in Washington from the two hundred and twenty-six requested by the War Department to ninety-three.[21] Congress also betrayed lingering suspicions of the general staff idea, associated with threats of militarist domination, by creating a War Council of the War Department to consider military policies. To it, General Pershing was assigned along with the Secretary and Assistant Secretary of War and the Chief of Staff.

Under the Act of 1920 was established in all essentials the Army which Marshall would head in 1939. On paper the establishment was sound and flexible. Its great weakness was that as a military structure it rested ultimately on a body of trained citizenry, but the provision to ensure such a body was dropped out. Surrender on universal military training, as it turned out, paved the way for other surrenders. It was difficult to maintain the urgency of Army training centers when there were only a relatively few volunteers to be trained. So in subsequent years when Congress, normalcy-bent on economy, successively cut the number of men whose keep it would pay for, the General Staff itself recommended giving up the training centers. In practice, therefore, the Army lost its position at the core of a citizen organization and reverted to a skeleton combat force which in case of war would again have to try to flesh itself out largely with another generation of raw recruits.

Although Marshall had little to do directly with drafting the reorganization bill he found himself sympathetic to both its philosophy and its principal authors. In the course of the hearings he had made a friend of Senator Wadsworth and become more closely associated than ever before with Palmer, for whom he developed a deep personal as well as professional respect. Not long afterward he persuaded Pershing to name Palmer as an aide with specific responsibility to continue research and writing on the development of our national military policy.[22] In later years he saw much of the Palmer family in Washington and tried hard to get Palmer some official recognition for his work in reshaping the Army. Marshall would write in 1935 that he knew of few people who had done so much and had received so little credit.[23]

Two days before the bill passed Congress, Marshall went to Maine with Pershing and was there when the Republican National Convention in Chicago seemed to be threatened with deadlock. Pershing cut short his tour and returned to Washington a day earlier than he had planned. He wrote Secretary Baker, recalling an earlier conversation, in which he had expressed the thought that he might resign from the Army. "I feel," he wrote, "that after the completion of the work contemplated by the Army Reorganization Act, I could relinquish military duty without detriment to the service and thus be free to engage in something more active." The timing of the letter and its prompt release for publication by Pershing's headquarters led some newspapers to speculate that the general was standing up for the lightning from Chicago to strike him.[24] Yet whether it struck him or not, the fact was that Pershing had indeed come to the end of the period when he could plausibly function as a quasi-independent field commander. General March still had a year to go as Chief of Staff, and it remained unthinkable that the General of the Armies should serve happily and effectively as his subordinate. (The incongruousness was underlined when, in July, March reverted to his permanent rank of major general while Pershing, of course, kept the four stars Congress had awarded him.)

June ended political uncertainties with the nomination of Harding. Pershing, after making clear he was not interested in overtures from the Democratic National Convention—some Brooklyn politicians had proposed a Pershing–Al Smith slate—attended the graduating exercises at West Point and then at Marshall's behest went down to Finals at VMI.[25] Marshall was gratified by the visit and wrote Pershing afterward that his gra-

ciousness and tributes to VMI and Southern leaders had made
a profound effect on the people of Lexington who were "painfully conservative" and still lived in the Civil War. But one
Southerner, at least, remained impervious and unreconstructed.
On the ride down from Washington they stopped near New Market. Marshall, anxious to point out to Pershing exactly where
the VMI cadets had made their famous charge, approached an
old resident on a farm nearby, "a tall, angular, Lincolnian individual with beard and cheeks stained with tobacco. I went in,"
Marshall recalled, "and asked him if he had been there at the
time of the Battle of New Market. He said he had. . . . I asked
him if he had seen the cadets. He said, 'Yes, I watched them
march by on that hillside right there.' " They talked a little
about his memories, then Marshall said, "Outside here, waiting
to be shown some of the battle scenes, is General Pershing. He
commanded all our troops in Europe." The old man spat but
said nothing. Marshall said, "I said outside here is General Pershing who commanded all our troops in Europe," and added that
they were on their way to VMI. "The fellow looked at me and
said, 'I heered you the first time.' " Told by Pershing in Lexington, it made a good story for the cadets and a suitably modest introduction for the Yankee general.

All during the summer the War Department worked on reorganization plans. Pershing stayed on with some of his old staff at
the Land Office Building. Marshall himself was detailed to a
committee with Conner, Drum, and eight other officers to consider a new shape for an infantry division. Like Pershing, he
believed the great square division with two infantry brigades and
four infantry regiments—totaling some twenty-eight thousand
men—while perhaps justified for the trench warfare of World
War I, was unnecessarily cumbersome. Pershing wanted a much
smaller "triangular" division of about seventeen thousand men,
and Marshall strongly urged it in committee. But he was overruled largely by General Drum, who "was the ardent proponent
of the large division." [26] That part of the reorganization could
wait.

Marshall that summer found himself back in the familiar
position of a very junior officer with responsibilities co-equal to

those very much his superior. With the ending of wartime ranks, he slipped back to his permanent rank of captain and then on orders the following day was promoted to major. By a curious twist of fortune, and the intervention of Secretary Baker and General March, Brigadier General MacArthur—now the superintendent of the Military Academy—had been named to one of four vacancies in the list of permanent brigadier generals submitted to Congress in February.[27] So the men who had been lieutenants at Leavenworth ten years before were now three grades apart and separated by the immense chasm that existed between general officers and all others. There is no evidence that Marshall felt any resentment at his own bad luck or at the better fortunes of others. Indeed, apparently on his own, he prepared a list of older officers for Pershing to consider for possible promotion. In response to Pershing's request for more information, Marshall submitted lists which he and Conner had worked out, arranging the men in the "proposed order of merit." When near Christmas of 1920 it appeared that Congress might adjourn without approving a number of promotions, Marshall interrupted Pershing's vacation to ask whether he should not intervene with Senate leaders to speed confirmation to general's rank of officers "who played an important part in the AEF" and "will rather expect you to put up a fight for them." [28]

As time came for the change of administrations, Pershing's own future was uncertain. Though the obvious job for him was Chief of Staff, that had to wait until General March had reached the end of his term. Briefly there was talk of raising him to the position of Secretary of War in Harding's cabinet; then, after John W. Weeks got that post, further speculation that he might be shelved altogether. Weeks, in April 1921, announced that the General of the Armies would head a special staff to draw plans against the contingency of another war. The scheme, duplicating War Department General Staff functions and fouling lines of responsibility, was on the face of it unworkable, although it had actually been proposed earlier by General Conner to Pershing himself as a means of putting the AEF commander in a top position but free from the routine duties of the Chief of Staff's office.[29] Coming now from Weeks, it had other connotations: the idea struck some as not only unwise but probably mischievous. Weeks was a Massachusetts man. Massachusetts opinion, the *Boston Transcript* in the van, was still boiling over Pershing's relief of General Edwards, commander of the 26th (Yankee) Division, just before the war ended. The *Transcript* now hailed Weeks' proposal as a device to eliminate the taint of Prussianism from the American Army by sidetracking Pershing. As for Pershing, he declined absolutely to go along with the proposal, threatening to resign if Weeks insisted. Apparently the President intervened. Within a few days the proposal was dropped and Pershing was announced as the next Chief of Staff to take office on July 1. While the *Transcript* scented a political payoff to the general for helping stop Leonard Wood as a presidential candidate and a potential cabinet member, most of the press remarked the obvious: that the appointment was altogether fitting and had been expected.[30]

As Chief of Staff, Pershing occupied the huge office in the State, War, and Navy Building given up by the Secretary of Navy when the Navy Department moved out of the building in the fall of 1921. With General Harbord as his Deputy Chief of Staff (followed by General Hines in January 1923), Pershing promptly made over the War Department General Staff in the image of Chaumont. The five staff divisions he established—G-1 (Personnel), G-2 (Intelligence), G-3 (Operations and Training), G-4 (Supply), and War Plans—remained through World War II. War Plans Division, which Pershing expected to furnish the staff for the commanding general in any new conflict, in World War II became the Operations Division of General Marshall's command post.

Marshall was installed in an office near his chief, where he could be called on for many assignments not usually given an aide. Pershing, easily bored with the routine of the peacetime Chief of Staff job, sent many proposed letters, draft reports, and staff recommendations to "Major M" for comment. On many matters the aide gave his opinions to his chief privately in order to avoid friction with some of the division chiefs. As the years passed and most of the other subordinates who had been with Pershing in France went on to other posts, Marshall drew more and more assignments. Pershing visited France nearly every year, and between October 1923 and March 1924 was gone for six months. In these intervals he depended on Marshall to prepare reports for his signature, carry out special assignments, and keep him in touch with the situation in Washington.

As one who knew Pershing's views, Marshall was appointed to various boards during the period of Army reorganization. In the fall of 1921 when Congress asked for an investigation of the alleged inequities under the Army's single-list promotion system, a board under Major General D. C. Shanks with Marshall as recorder was established. On the major, in General Shanks' words, "fell the important duties connected with securing, tabulating, and preparing the voluminous records required by the board." After more than thirty meetings the board recommended that the system be retained as essential to the efficiency of the Army.[31] Marshall's work in examining the service records of hundreds of officers gave him detailed background on the careers of many men who would serve under him in later years.

So far the Army had fared remarkably well. After precipitous demobilization, which had rushed draftees back to civilian life (many into the ranks of the unemployed), discharged the National Guard, and mustered out even all the regular enlisted men and noncommissioned officers who wanted release, it had recovered an organization capable of rebuilding an effective defense and a chief whose prestige stood high. But this, which from the Army's and General Pershing's point of view was a good fresh start, in fact was to mark the high point of preparedness. From 1921 on, the generation which admired public frugality, hated war, and shunned collective security was easily persuaded to neglect its own defense. Congress found the coincidence of anti-militarism and saving money irresistibly popular. The special session of the 67th Congress in 1921 cut wartime taxes. Corresponding cuts in the budget, it was clear, would have to be chiefly at the expense of the Army and Navy. At the Washington Naval Disarmament Conference, ending in February 1922, the United States negotiated a treaty with its World War I Allies limiting naval armaments and reducing sources of possible friction, which seemed to make it safe for the United States to let its seapower decline even below treaty limits. While the Senate promptly ratified the treaties, the House passed an Army Appropriations Act which would have reduced the number of enlisted men to 115,000—less than half the strength authorized in 1920. Pershing in a speech in March protested the cuts as disastrous. They would leave the United States an Army scarcely any larger than the Allies had permitted less populous Germany under the treaty intended to disarm her. General Harbord, in a statement not likely to allay labor's militarist fears, warned that the increase in strikes raised threats of radicalism against which the regular Army might have to act. Congress retreated a little but nevertheless cut appropriations so far that the Army's actual strength by the end of the fiscal year 1923 was 131,254—93,625 in the continental United States.[32]

Clearly the 1920 organization plans, based on twice that many men, could not be carried out. Palmer wished to absorb the cut by scaling down the 1920 plan, maintaining fewer regular divisions but keeping them at approximately full strength and above all holding on to the training centers. But the War Department, under pressure to keep the paper army as large as possible and the command and staff positions correspondingly numerous, decided instead to skeletonize the existing establishment and abolish the corps training centers altogether.[33]

Marshall apparently agreed with Palmer. At least he was more concerned than ever, as the standing Army shrank, with the importance of citizen training and the responsibility of regular officers to keep that task in the forefront of their thinking. He strongly urged Pershing to make the point in a speech to the Army War College in June and drafted for him these key paragraphs, which Pershing delivered.

"In no other Army is it so important that the officers of the permanent establishment be highly perfected specialists, prepared to serve as instructors and leaders for the citizen forces which are to fight our wars. The one-time role of a regular Army officer has passed with the Indian campaigns and the acquirement of colonial possessions. Our mission today is definite, yet so broad that few, if any, have been able to visualize the possibilities of the new fields opened up by the military policy now on the statute books.[34]

"In serving on the War Department General Staff or at corps area headquarters, it is difficult to avoid a detached and impersonal attitude which soon carries one out of sympathy with the subordinate organizations and, especially, with the humble worker in the ranks. It is hard for the man at the desk to see with the eye of a troop commander or of a businessman struggling with self-imposed duties as an officer of the National Guard or Reserve Corps. Unintentionally misunderstanding arises and co-operation fails. It is the special duty of the regular Army officer to avoid this possibility. As a matter of truth, the establishment of a sympathetic understanding is more important than the performance of any routine duties."

No doubt Pershing agreed, but it was Marshall talking out of the heartfelt lessons of his own experience. The earnestness came from the conviction of a teacher who accepted the concept of a citizen army not because it was the best that could be got out of a democracy but because he believed in it and believed in the pre-eminent mission of the military professional to make it effective. He said the same thing on his own behalf at a speech to the Army War College in the fall. And he would get Pershing to return to the theme near the end of his tour as Chief of Staff when he spoke at Camp Merritt, New Jersey, at the dedication of a memorial to the citizen soldiers trained there for the last war. There Pershing emphasized what he hoped would prove the contrast between the unpreparedness of 1917 and the opportunity under the 1920 Act to "enroll and train the framework of a citizen army, with officers prepared for their work and thus not to be left at the mercy of chance." [35] In the same spirit Pershing and Marshall in the summer of 1923 undertook to visit all the fifteen summer training camps in the country.

They had called at eight and were in San Francisco when the sudden death of President Harding made it necessary for them to return with the funeral train to Washington. The change in Presidents made no easier the struggle to keep something of the shape and function of the Army as envisaged in the reorganization act. Calvin Coolidge proved the perfect guardian of Harding's normalcy. While he did not ask for further Army cuts he was perfectly willing to let the spirit of economy hack where it would. Pershing's annual report for 1923, which Marshall was in charge of during the Chief of Staff's six months' European trip beginning in October, pleaded for a small increase in the regular Army's force (to 150,000 men and 13,000 officers) and asked that they be suitably housed and be given funds for annual maneuvers. As for the citizen army, the National Guard, then numbering 160,000, should be enabled to build up progressively to 250,-000. Funds, besides, were needed to maintain a skeleton of the organized Reserves, to permit reserve officers to have an average of fifteen days' training every three or four years, to develop ROTC units, and to increase the number of trainees in the Citizen Military Training Camps.[36] The modesty of the requests was eloquent of how tight the congressional pursestrings had been drawn.

Nothing came of the plea, and nothing came of efforts at about this time to unify the armed forces for the sake of economy. Representative Walter Brown of Ohio had suggested a Division of National Defense. One of Pershing's closest advisers, General Moseley, proposed a Secretary of National Defense to co-ordinate Army and Navy policies and a Secretary of Munitions to supervise procurement for both services.[37] The idea, though stillborn —both Army and Navy chiefs were opposed—did lead to some study of ways to avoid waste in separate Army and Navy purchasing.[38] The problem was one which had exasperated General Charles G. Dawes when he was Director of the Budget in 1921, and he had once demonstrated in a furious burst of sweeping that two brooms, bought separately by the Army and Navy at different prices, did the same job.[39] Marshall recalled the lesson when he was selected to meet with the Assistant Secretary of Navy, Theodore Roosevelt, Jr., on the subject. In the course of a number of meetings he advocated preliminary steps to help Army and Navy officers to understand each other's problems. He wished to exchange officers "from every section of the General Staff with equivalent officers of the Navy Department"—a scheme not of liaison but of actually swapping jobs. He would have liked to apply it also to the "supply departments, ordnance, and communication service," but he found solid opposition from both Army and Navy—solid and durable, for fifteen years later he wrote: "I seem to be out of step with the rest of the world in this

particular idea, but to me it is fundamental, and the only effective lead-up to the proper co-ordination of the two services." [40]

Unification was not practical but exploring it was educational
for the future Chief of Staff and Secretary of Defense. There was
education, too, in the last of the major projects Marshall completed as Pershing's aide: a complete revision of the First Army
report first distributed in 1919 and then at Pershing's request recalled. Marshall had made some changes in it before he returned
from Europe and had sent them to Drum, who had distributed
the initial draft, for suggestions. In the fall of 1920 Pershing
found time to make suggestions, which Marshall attempted to
incorporate by rewriting entire sections of the text. Continuing
to work on it at spare moments during the years and keeping up
an intermittent correspondence with Drum concerning maps, ap-
pendices, and various phases of the report, he finally found time
during Pershing's long absence in Europe to prepare it for publication in 1924.[41] At the same time he was gathering data for
Pershing on the wartime meetings of the War Council in Washington and on the Army's handling of personnel and supply.[42]
Although the final report was dry, factual, pedestrian in style, and
without evaluations, it provided its author with a thorough review of the war experience and, as a source for the memoirs of
both Pershing and Harbord, helped establish the accepted story
of American operations.

Marshall's five years with Pershing inevitably involved him in
a miscellany of activities to which in retrospect it was difficult to
assign any coherent pattern. From the point of view of his career
the years were perhaps most fruitful in terms of exposure to
politics and to personalities of politics and business, not only in
Washington but in the course of his frequent travels through the
country with his chief. He sat in on a number of informal talks
between Pershing and President Harding. When the trip to
inspect citizen-training camps in the summer of 1923 was broken
off at Harding's death, Marshall returned on the funeral train
from San Francisco and became acquainted with Secretary of
Commerce Herbert Hoover. Hoover, he recalled, spent a lot of
time in the observation car and did not say much. With General Dawes, Marshall developed a close relationship during

Dawes' year in Washington as Director of the Budget. An old friend of Pershing's, Dawes often dropped in on the Chief of Staff and frequently took time to talk over with Marshall his ideas on governmental finance. Later Marshall visited Dawes at his home with Pershing and accompanied the two men on an excursion by special train to some of Dawes' properties in West Virginia. He kept in touch with Dawes for the rest of his life, and at one of their last meetings rode with him in the funeral procession for their mutual friend, General Pershing. In the fall of 1922 while on a trip through Louisiana, Pershing and Marshall joined the state's Governor John Parker and Bernard Baruch for duck shooting at Pass-a-Loutre.[43] In the years between wars Marshall wrote and talked to Baruch from time to time and kept up the acquaintance until his own death. In 1933 he told Pershing "I always enjoyed talking to Mr. Baruch and Mr. Baker more than any other prominent characters of my tour in Washington with you." [44]

One story of his encounters with notables that Marshall liked to tell concerned Senator Moses of New Hampshire. Pershing and Marshall were traveling together in a drawing room from Boston to Washington. The senator, they observed, had a Pullman berth in the next car. The general and his aide sat up talking and finishing a bottle of real Scotch the general had been given. Well after midnight Pershing remarked that there was just enough left in the bottle to give Senator Moses a drink. Whereupon they poured a glass and together went down the aisle, Marshall, like a good junior officer, carrying the glass and leading the way. On reaching the space they thought was the senator's, Pershing scratched at the green curtain, whispering, "Senator Moses." When there was no answer he lifted the curtain a little, at which point the woman occupying the berth said sharply, "What do you want?" The general in his shirt sleeves, without identifying collar, dropped the curtain and, as Marshall told it, "ran against me and we spilled the Scotch between us and over us as we raced down the aisle. I had a hard time keeping out of his way because he was running right up my back. But we got to the stateroom and got the door shut. Then he just sat down and laughed until he cried. There was still a little bit of

Scotch and he suggested that I go back with it. I told him he would have to get another aide; I wasn't going back out there again." The next morning they emerged from their drawing room to find Senator Moses waiting for them with the young woman next to him. She had told the story and he had guessed the culprits. "We had an amusing back-and-forth in regard to it."

Marshall liked the story because it showed Pershing in the gay, relaxed, and "youthful" after-hours spirits which were in strong contrast to the public image of him as a "very severe character." In fact both Pershings existed, and the gulf between them was absolute—as Marshall found after the hilarity of the Boston train. "When we got back to Washington and after he had gone home and changed . . . and come back to the office, I came in to see him; he was just as stern as though we had never been together at all."

Stern he was, and often stubborn and autocratic, but his mind was not closed. Not long after he became Chief of Staff he proposed a change in the procedure of the War Department which General March had initiated. The proposal—as many such proposals did—went to Major Marshall for comment. Marshall this time wrote his disapproval in a memorandum, sent it to Pershing, and shortly thereafter was summoned.

"I don't take to this at all," Pershing said. "I don't agree with you."

Marshall said, "Well, let me have it, General; let me have it again."

Marshall went back to his office and wrote a fresh résumé of the affair and another more careful explanation of just why he thought Pershing's proposal was wrong. Again Pershing sent for him.

"I don't accept this," he said.

Once more Marshall took it back, rewrote it again, restating his objections.

"No," said Pershing when he saw the third memo, and slapped his hand on the desk in an angry gesture the aide had never seen him use before, "No, by God, we will do it this way."

Marshall stood his ground. "Now, General," he said, "just because you hate the guts of General March you're setting yourself up—and General Harbord who hates him too—to do something you know damn well is wrong."

Pershing looked at his aide, handed him back the paper. "Well, have it your own way."

And that, Marshall recalled, "was the end of the scene. No prolonged feeling—nothing—that was the end of the affair. . . . General Pershing held no [grudge] at all. He might be very firm at the time, but if you convinced him, that was the end of it. He accepted it and you went ahead." [45]

That was tribute to Pershing, but tribute also to the aide himself, who knew not only when but how to stand his ground. Pershing for the official record called Marshall "a very exceptional man" and urged that he should be made a general officer "as soon as eligible." Personally the two had got along from the beginning and developed and retained genuine affection for each other. From his next post Marshall wrote his old chief in a note of unusual warmth: "I have a hard time realizing that everything I do is not being done directly for you. My five years with you will always remain the unique experience of my career. . . . Not until I . . . took up these new duties . . . did I realize how much my long association was going to mean to me and how deeply I will miss it." [46]

The years in Washington were also relatively settled and domestic years, despite the frequent excursions. As senior aide to the Chief of Staff, Marshall had Quarters Number 3 at Fort Myer, a short automobile or streetcar ride from downtown Washington. Lily continued to be bothered by her bad heart and suffered particularly in crowded social gatherings when the air was heavy with smoke. Nevertheless she accompanied her husband to most of the dinners and receptions which the aide and friend of the Chief of Staff was expected to attend. Sometimes she even went alone to represent him when he could not make it himself. They entertained a little themselves. Pershing from time to time dined informally with them.

Marshall's mother spent part of each year in Washington at the Grafton Hotel a few blocks from the War Department. In her middle seventies, she was bedridden part of the time. Marshall stopped to see her once or twice a day, usually sitting and talking to her while she had lunch. Occasionally he brought General Pershing for a visit, and the sight of him or word of his presence rustled the ladies resident in the Grafton like an autumn wind. It was the first time since he had left Uniontown for VMI that Marshall had been able to see his mother for more than brief and occasional visits. It was also to be the last time.

Pershing's tour as Chief of Staff was drawing to a close in 1924 and so was Marshall's eligibility for General Staff duty. In the spring of the year he applied for an assignment he had long desired, with the 15th Infantry in China. His request was granted and he was told in April that he could leave in two months. Pershing, who would be in Europe in the summer on a tour of the French battlefields as chairman of the Battle Monuments Commission, gave the Marshalls a farewell luncheon at the Shoreham Hotel on June 8. But it was actually not until July 12 that Marshall boarded the U.S.A.T. *St. Mihiel* at New York with Lily and her mother, Mrs. Coles.

The trip out was long but pleasantly broken on the way. At Panama the Fox Conners entertained them "with lots of champagne." At San Francisco they were made warmly welcome by General and Mrs. Hunter Liggett, with whom Marshall had kept up an affectionate correspondence. In Honolulu they visited General and Mrs. Summerall. So his friends from the days in France had scattered. And Marshall himself, on his way to Tientsin, with both affection and nostalgia cabled good-by to Pershing across the world. From Paris his old chief replied to the U.S.A.T. *Thomas* out of San Francisco: "Au revoir, Affectionately, Pershing." [47]

XIV

Lessons in Chinese

*"Out here the pot boils over and appears to grow daily
more involved."*
—Marshall to Pershing, October 30, 1925.

ASSIGNED as executive officer of the 15th Infantry, Lieutenant Colonel (he had been promoted to that rank in August 1923) Marshall on arrival in Tientsin actually took acting
command and held it for two and a half months until the new
commanding officer, Colonel W. K. Naylor, came from Washington. The regiment with headquarters and service companies and
two of its battalions totaled about a thousand men.[1] One rifle
company was in Tangshan; the rest of the men were in barracks
in the American compound in Tientsin, where they had been
for twelve years and where they would remain until 1938 on a
mission unique in the American Army.[2]

The Americans occupied buildings which until the War of
1914 had belonged to Germany, on what had been the Kaiser
Wilhelmstrasse and now was Woodrow Wilson Street. In the
same compound was the headquarters of Brigadier General
W. D. Connor, commanding United States Army Forces in
China—a command that had existed only about a year and had
been set up principally to keep the Army in close touch with the
American Minister at Peking and with various foreign and Chinese officials.[3]

Down Woodrow Wilson Street, which as it went along became
Victoria Road, Rue de France, and Via Italia, were the concessions of Britain, France, and Italy respectively, each quartering
its contingent of troops. Adjacent was a detachment of the Japanese Army, which occupied a patch of Japanese ground. Until
the Bolshevik Revolution there had been Russians in that vicinity too. Yet all these men in foreign uniform did not constitute
an international force or, in the proper sense, even an occupation
force. They were rather an extraterritorial police, each separately engaged in defending the lives, property, and commercial
interests of its own nationals and in keeping open the lines of
communications from Peking to the sea. All but the Americans
had taken up residence in Tientsin in 1901 in accord with the
Protocols that the powers imposed on China after the defeat of
the Boxer Rebellion. The United States acquired similar rights
under the settlement but, except for leaving a small legation
guard in Peking, did not exercise them until the revolution of
1911 again raised threats of anarchy and a fresh effort to drive
the foreigners out.[4] It was then, early in 1912, that two of the
three battalions of the 15th Infantry moved in from the Philippines, occupying quarters for which they paid rental instead of
claiming a particular area as a concession. In the First World
War the Germans were forced to give up their concessions; the
Russians after the Bolshevik Revolution voluntarily relinquished
theirs. Britain, France, Italy, and Japan held on to their respective areas, while the United States undertook generally to
guard the quarter once assigned to the Germans.

For Tientsin itself the foreign garrisons, providing an effective defense of the city amid the chaos of civil war, were more
obviously blessing than burden. The strategic and commercial
importance of Tientsin was its position between Peking and the
sea on the Hai River (Hai Ho) and on the Peking-Mukden Railroad. The railroad ran southeast from the capital through Tientsin to Taku, a port on the Gulf of Chihli; thence it turned
northeast to Mukden in Manchuria. Lying thus athwart the main
highroad to the Chinese capital, Tientsin was entirely without
natural defenses. It was built on an alluvial plain sixty miles
from the sea but only seven feet higher and was swept by floods,
dust storms out of the Gobi Desert, and periodic bands of war-

ring provincial leaders. After the Boxer Rebellion its ancient wall had been torn down and the city largely rebuilt. Foreign troops thenceforth became its main security and in defending themselves and their nationals provided peace for the citizenry. Tientsin flourished. With nearly a million people in 1924, it was China's second greatest commercial city, second only to Shanghai.[5]

But foreign troops were also a symbol of China's tragedy and a badge of her humiliation. Incapable of defending the lives and property of foreigners, the Chinese government was forced to yield a portion of its sovereignty to alien commands. The chaos born of factional fights and civil war had made imminent the partition of the country among the great western powers and Japan. The United States, interested in the China trade since the 1790s and in the salvation of Chinese souls since the early 1800s, had persistently refused to take part in the scramble for special concessions. Instead, while demanding respect for our national interests, we tried to strengthen the Peking government. This, however, did not save us in the 1920s from being listed among their nation's oppressors and exploiters by Nationalist leaders. Nor did it avoid the clash of interest when nationalist boycotts and riots threatened American lives and property no less than the lives and property of the Europeans and Japanese.

In the four years that followed the overthrow of the Manchu dynasty and the establishment of a republic early in 1912, the government of Yüan Shih-k'ai maintained a semblance of national unity under despotic and increasingly corrupt rule. Dr. Sun Yat-sen, the first provisional President of China, who had stepped aside in the hope that Yüan could provide the leadership so desperately needed, broke with Yüan in 1913 when the latter took steps to make himself emperor. Sun's party, the Kuomintang, was expelled from the parliament in Peking. Some of them moved south to Canton, where in time the revolution would be reborn.[6]

On the death of Yüan in 1916 China fell into a long period of anarchy and confused civil war. Peking, for more than a decade, remained nominally the capital city and the parliament there claimed to be the source of political authority. In fact, however, the President at Peking often exercised no real power outside the circle of his own retainers. The provincial military governors, whose aid had been sought by the national government, fought for political and military control of North China and for domination of the Peking regime. In the provinces warlords (*tuchuns*) recruited mercenary armies and fought and betrayed each other in a kaleidoscopic pattern of conflict in which few of the *tuchuns* suffered decisive defeat and none was ever quite victorious. South of the Yangtze the Kuomintang set up in 1918 a rival national government, which in 1921 elected Sun Yat-sen the President of the Chinese Republic. But here, too, effective political power proved elusive. The Kuomintang moved in and out of control almost at the whim of local warlords, and such allegiance as the provinces yielded to Canton remained also nominal. It was only on Dr. Sun's return to power in 1923, after being ousted the previous year, that the nationalist movement in Canton began to take effective shape.

The shape was tragically misunderstood in the West. Despite the weakness of Peking, most foreigners in China continued to hope that a strong conservative leader, a new Yüan Shih-k'ai or a super-*tuchun*, would arise to unify the country. Dr. Sun with his visionary principles and demands for the immediate end of special treaty rights seemed an obstacle to unity as well as a menace more or less serious to life and property.[7] That point of view was widely shared by foreign diplomats, who incidentally remained accredited to whatever regime took up the reins in Peking, and was conveyed strongly to foreign capitals, including Washington. When Dr. Sun sought foreign aid for his movement the United States was cool. So were Britain, Canada, Germany, and Japan, whom he also approached. Only Moscow listened. From the beginning Lenin had been sympathetic, approving in particular the Kuomintang's militant stand against foreign imperialists.

In the autumn of 1923 the Soviet Union sent Mikhail Borodin to Canton to advise Dr. Sun and to cement an *entente cordiale* between the Soviet Union and the Kuomintang. Borodin, an unusually able and persuasive agent of the Communist International, began by reorganizing the Kuomintang, already a one-party government in southern China, along the lines of the Communist party. He also negotiated the admission of Chinese Communists on the proviso (which proved worthless) that they must accept Kuomintang principles and work loyally for the Chinese revolution, which it was agreed was not Communist.[8] Under Borodin's tutelage the Canton government became vigorous and efficient. It caught the imagination of idealistic and ambitious young men. Through organization of peasants and workers it laid roots for popular support. It developed a revolutionary fervor that spread its reputation far beyond Canton.

Since the first task of the revolution was the conquest of power, Kuomintang leaders set about creating an army. In 1923 Chiang Kai-shek, one of Dr. Sun's early supporters, who had received the bulk of his military education in four years at the Preparatory Military Academy in Tokyo, was sent to Moscow to study Soviet political and military organization. A few months after his return (in mid-1924) he was put in charge of the newly created Whampoa Military Academy in which he was to train officers for the revolution—and would in the process create an outstanding reputation for himself.

Soviet in form, nationalist in aim, Dr. Sun's government began in 1923 to develop an increasingly promising amalgam of idealism and discipline. Yet the contradictions—the essential incompatibility of Kuomintang and Communist aims—that were in the end to destroy the Chinese Republic were already present in the instrument being forged in Canton to create it.

At Tientsin, when Marshall arrived in 1924, the ambitions of the Kuomintang (soon to be known as the Nationalists) seemed remote. (It is unlikely that Marshall in the beginning even knew who Chiang Kai-shek was or was aware of the existence of a Soviet Military Mission, headed by General Vasili Blücher, which had been sent to southern China in the same year.) The immediate concern of the 15th Infantry was with the confused struggle of the *tuchuns* in the north, particularly the triangular wars among Chang Tso-lin, whose base of power was in Manchuria, Wu P'ei-fu, who dominated the relatively helpless government at Peking, and Fêng Yü-hsiang, called the "Christian

General," whose adroit shifts from one camp to the other effectively kept either Chang or Wu from holding the upper hand. By the middle of 1924 Wu had achieved military dominance of most of China except the tier of three southern provinces and the province of Chekiang on the coast south of Shanghai. Chekiang was in the hands of a *tuchun* who was at the time allied with Chang Tso-lin. In August, a month before Marshall debarked in China from the U.S.A.T. *Thomas* out of Manila, the *tuchun* of Chekiang tangled with his neighbor, the *tuchun* of the province of Kiangsu (in which Shanghai is located). The boss of Kiangsu was an ally of General Wu, and the dispute was soon widened to include war between Wu and Chang Tso-lin. Wu, attempting to block Chang's forces near Jehol northeast of Peking, was forced to flee when his momentary ally, General Fêng, defected and used the opportunity to seize Peking.

As Chang and Wu battled in the north during September and early October, the 15th Infantry stood guard, ready to keep warring factions out of Tientsin, hold the railroad, and defend themselves—all without fighting if they could possibly avoid it. Marshall, almost before he unpacked, put the regiment on special guard duty. His own daily ride for exercise was "converted to an inspection of a four-mile outpost line established three miles south of the compound and in patrolling a little for my own information." [9] When Fêng seized Peking, Marshall telegraphed Captain Henry H. Dabney, who commanded the company stationed in Tangshan, well up the railroad toward Manchuria, to be ready for a crisis in the next few days. He sent a small reinforcement and put additional guard detachments along the railroad. To hold rolling stock that might be needed in transporting Marines to Peking to strengthen the legation guard, he sent a corporal and five men to the East Station in Tientsin with orders to shoot only in self-defense. For all detachments the deployments were military but the weapons with which finally the defense was to be made were psychological—bluff and persuasion. [10]

The testing of the 15th began when Wu's army, deserted by Fêng and under heavy attack by Chang, fell apart and the pieces drifted toward Tientsin. Some stragglers were drawn, as toward an oasis, to one place in the war-torn country where there were still food and plunder. More came simply because Tientsin was on the line of retreat. The pursued and their pursuers, perhaps amounting to a hundred thousand men altogether in a single week, poured down by rail, steamer, horseback, or on foot.[11] The 15th Infantry's job was not to halt but to disarm them. Five outposts were set up where the fleeing soldiers were offered rice and cabbage and tea in exchange for their arms or were persuaded to take the long way around the city. Frequently the troops had to carry out their missions "with guns and knives pointed at their stomachs," but the job was accomplished. There was no shooting and no armed Chinese got loose in the city. Villagers around Tientsin were so grateful for the protection which the regiment thus provided them against potential loot and rape that the following spring they presented to the Americans a white marble memorial "gate," which remained with the regiment until it left China in 1938 and then was set up at Fort Benning. As for Marshall, he wrote an old friend: "I snaffled a nice letter of commendation out of the affair which is worth my three years in China." [12]

In the game of bluff, officers of the 15th Infantry had found more useful than bullets the working knowledge of Chinese picked up in the regimental language school. General Connor, an able diplomat as well as soldier, had established the school shortly after he came to China and had made attendance compulsory for all officers in his command.[13] Marshall encouraged noncommissioned officers to attend and arranged for the preparation of simple exercises in conversational Chinese which would be useful to soldiers.

Marshall, whose experience with VMI and AEF French had done little to persuade him he was a linguist, had plunged into the intricacies of Chinese on his arrival, determined not only to learn the language but to learn it faster than anyone else. The others had been at it since February 1924—some six months before he got there—but by March of 1925 he was reporting to Pershing that he had caught up. "At my present rate," he wrote, "I should be well ahead of them in another month. Yesterday," he went on, "while conducting a summary court trial [martial],

I drew a Chinese witness who could not speak or understand English. Rather than hold over the case until an interpreter could be secured, I took his testimony in Chinese and did not have very much trouble in handling him." [14]

He was delighted to discover this undeveloped talent, but there were moments of stress when it failed him. The regimental chaplain one day overheard him say something to his Chinese chauffeur. The chauffeur looked blank. Marshall said it again, louder, and then again, and louder still. No comprehension.

"Oh hell," said the student of Chinese, "send my car!" Then, looking up, he saw the chaplain. "You heard?"

"Yes," said the chaplain.

"Will it go all over the Army?"

"Yes, sir," said the chaplain. "It will go all over the Army." [15]

There was, after those first few months of bracing against the gusts of civil war, a period of comparative leisure for Marshall in which he reverted to the role of executive officer, attending to the myriad details necessary to carry into effect the regimental commander's policies. He continued his project of procuring shaggy little Mongolian ponies to mount a regimental detachment of "a sporty-looking cavalry troop," sponsoring horse shows and riding formations until the officers, listed as infantrymen, began to feel, in the words of their regimental poet, that they had joined the "Foot Hussars." [16]

Perhaps Marshall proceeded too much as if he were still in acting command. In any case the 15th's new commanding officer, Colonel Naylor, author of a book on the *Principles of War* which was used by both the American and Japanese armies, proved to be jealous of his prerogatives. Not long after signing in, late in November, he issued a directive narrowly circumscribing the authority of his executive.[17] Marshall had worked with difficult superiors before, and if he felt the strain unduly it is not recorded. Physically he was in good health, heavier by some twelve pounds before the end of his tour, and still an enthusiast for regular and vigorous exercises—his ride in the morning and a couple of hours of squash tennis before dinner in the evening was the usual day's routine. He played, of course, to win. "Squash tennis," he wrote, "is pretty lively, especially when I undertake to beat these young fellows, which I usually do, but it is not like straight running, and you can pause for a needed breath." [18]

Mrs. Marshall's health was, as always, much less robust, but the years in China were probably the happiest of her married life. They rented large and comfortable quarters on Woodrow Wilson Street near the compound and employed at least five servants. (The regimental commander in 1926 had fifteen. Nearly every officer had one or more.) As was the custom of the Army of that time, they took a paternal interest in the younger officers and their families, displaying the fondness they had always felt for children. Lily saw more of her husband than she had since before the World War, and the household chores were taken off her hands by their "perfect" number one boy, C. H. Hsieh, who twenty years later would get an appreciative letter from the General and enjoy on the strength of it a few moments of reminiscing for the press.[19] There were visitors—some big names and some good friends. Roy Chapman Andrews stopped at the post on one of his trips to the Gobi Desert, gave a lecture there, and donated the proceeds to pay for the carpet of the post chapel which Marshall had encouraged Chaplain Miller to buy on credit.[20] Dr. Victor Heiser, health officer in the Philippines at the time Marshall was serving his first Army assignment there, spent a single evening with the Marshalls, talking into the early morning hours about the memories and interests they had in common, including their meeting not so long ago at Governor-General Forbes' home at Naushon. Governor Forbes himself also made a visit.[21] When Senator Hiram Bingham came through and asked to see the deposed boy emperor, Henry Pu-yi, then living in Tientsin (and later to be the Japanese puppet ruler of Manchukuo), Marshall arranged the interview and produced a newly assigned American major, Joseph W. Stilwell, to act as interpreter.

Despite the convulsions shaking China which constantly threatened to engulf all foreigners there, life in the American compound was as relaxed and pleasant as any Marshall had known in years. Many of the informal parties on the post were sparked by the wit of Major E. Forrest Harding, a man with an

interest in military history and a knack for doggerel, who became one of Marshall's close friends and would serve with him
later at Fort Benning. Stimulated by Harding's irreverent verse,
Marshall on one occasion wrote one of his own called "Retaliation" and recited it one evening. Mercifully Marshall's only published sally in rhyme, it began:

> Night after night we sit abject,
> Our good wives sit adoring
> While Forrest, Poet Laureate,
> Another hit is scoring
> A little fun at our expense,
> With laughter as a recompense.

And for nine more verses recounted Harding's poetic triumphs
and alleged success with the ladies of the post. Harding tactfully
had it printed at the end of his own privately circulated collection of regimental verse, *Lays of the Mei-Kuo Ying-P'an* (the
Chinese words meaning "American compound").[22]

In the autumn of 1925 Tientsin again found itself a precari-
ously neutral island in a turbulent flood of war. The fighting was
essentially another round of the battles of the previous year,
again involving Chang Tso-lin of Manchuria, Wu P'ei-fu, and
General Fêng, the latter playing his old role alternately on both
sides. Marshall wrote to Pershing at the end of October: "Out
here the pot boils over and appears to grow daily more involved.
An American gunboat with Marines is due here today to reinforce our garrison for the defense of the Tientsin concession and
this possible port of entry. No one, official Peking or elsewhere,
knows just what the present situation is leading to. There are
three military leaders now in the field and their possible alignment with or against each other is continuing to be a matter of
conjecture. Fighting has started south of this province, but reports are too conflicting to judge of results." [23] For the 15th Infantry the job once more was to try to hold the railroad open from
Peking to Tientsin and from Tientsin to Shanhaikwan while
keeping Chinese armed forces of all sides out of Tientsin.

When the new troubles moved close to Tientsin, Marshall was
taking increased responsibility for the regiment and in the last

week in December actually took command. Colonel Naylor, who had found the opportunities for conviviality in Tientsin irresistible, had been charged by General Connor with neglect of duty during summer and fall. Although the charges were eventually dropped and Naylor's subsequent career not damaged, he was relieved nevertheless. Marshall had inevitably assumed some command duties even before he replaced Naylor, and again commanded the regiment for two months until a new full colonel arrived.[24]

During most of November and December a *tuchun*[25] who professed to be neutral in the struggle between Wu and Chang deployed his forces south of Tientsin, where they fired on Chinese troop trains trying to pass reinforcements to the north to fight against the Manchurian warlord. General Connor and the other commanders now ordered the International Train, with guards furnished by the foreign powers in Tientsin, to make special runs to the Chinese capital and to the sea. Several such trains, carrying the flags of Britain, France, the United States, Japan, and Italy, made the run from Tientsin to Shanhaikwan during November and December but none was able to get through to Peking between the fifth and twenty-fifth of December. As Christmas approached, another Chinese force arrived in the Tientsin area. On December 23, the day Marshall took acting command of his regiment, General Fêng—now fighting against Chang and his allies north of Tientsin—moved south to throw his army against the "neutral" warlord who had been harassing the trains. The maneuver put the 15th Infantry uncomfortably in the middle.[26]

In the early afternoon of Christmas Eve, General Connor had word from a Chinese official that Fêng's troops had already moved into a part of the former German concession in which the 15th Infantry was quartered and had taken over the police barracks and municipal headquarters. Connor sent Marshall with a platoon of men to demand that the Chinese leave. Marshall proceeded to the police barracks, which he entered with Captain Frank R. Hayne and an orderly, and informed the Chinese officer in command that in conformity with treaty regulations Chinese were forbidden to come armed into the area. He asked that they surrender their arms and leave. The Chinese, after only a few moments' hesitation, complied. Marshall was back with his mission accomplished less than an hour and a half after the news of the Chinese "invasion" had been received.[27]

Eager as most of the Chinese were to avoid trouble with the foreigners, each confrontation was fused for explosion. The avoidance of trouble depended sometimes on the coolness and nerve of noncommissioned officers like Sergeant William Hambrick, who, in charge of one of the outposts, turned aside considerable bodies of armed Chinese troops; sometimes on junior officers like Captain William B. Tuttle, regimental adjutant. On Christmas Day, Tuttle with nine enlisted men moved out in a truck to confront some five thousand Chinese who had crossed the Hai Ho and entered the American defense sector. As Tuttle's truck approached, the Chinese, who were marching in column, deployed with fixed bayonets and kept coming. Tuttle dismounted, leaving his nine men boldly on guard against the advancing five thousand, and walked forward alone. Good-looking, athletic, with a cavalryman's ease and toughness, he took charge at once, giving in Chinese the order to halt. The Chinese halted. One of their officers came forward. For a considerable time, while the men waited on either side, the two officers tested each other. That prolonged discussion was a strain on Captain Tuttle's command of the language but his nerve held. The Chinese at last agreed to withdraw. Tuttle was formally commended by Colonel Marshall and informally immortalized by Major Harding in a doggerel epic, "Tuttulius at the Dike." [28]

These displays of courage and cool judgment were creditable to the individuals and gratifying to the command, but they underlined the dangerous anomalies of the 15th Infantry's position. In the game of bluff General Connor was impressed in particular with two weaknesses in the American hand: although the 15th Infantry, like the other contingents of foreign troops in Tientsin, had an assigned defense sector, it did not have a concession into which to withdraw in case of trouble; second, it was all too obvious that the responsibility for practical decisions for or against armed clashes with the Chinese rested on a comparatively large number of junior officers and noncoms, any one of whom might lose his head or act tough for fear of being thought cowardly by his fellows. These weaknesses so impressed Connor that he proposed that American ground troops be pulled out and the defense of the area left to the Navy unless the Army was given a specific concession and its position strengthened. Although his recommendation was not accepted, all the foreign powers, as the civil war continued, came to confine themselves narrowly to the defense of their own nationals.[29]

Before the new year was far along, the Tientsin area had become quiet again and remained so during most of 1926. In March, Colonel Isaac Newell arrived to take command of the 15th. But Newell, an easygoing Georgian winding up his Army career, was content to leave the details of running the regiment to the executive who had already amply demonstrated his competence. There was a quip in the regiment that "let George do it" was born in Tientsin at that time.

What George did for the most part was the work common to regimental commands everywhere. To help keep his men out of the clutches of "cheap liquor and cheaper women"—the 15th for years led the Army in venereal-disease rate[30]—he worked to develop the athletic and recreation facilities. He encouraged the presentation of amateur shows, pressing into service any officer who showed aptitude for organizing such programs. He backed the chaplain's program for setting up a recreation room for the soldiers and conveniently looked the other way when the chaplain arranged a comfortable place for some of the old-timers to do their gambling. So much pressure was put on company commanders to keep down the venereal-disease rates in their units that some provided free rickshas to bring back the men from bars at closing time.

At Nan Ta Su, some hundred and seventy-five miles northeast of Tientsin near Shanhaikwan, the point at which the Great Wall enters the sea, the regiment in 1924 had built a range firing camp. Marshall undertook to improve the living conditions there so that it might be used more widely as a combined training and recreation area. The tents were fixed up to accommodate families, and units were sent in turn to the camp during the summer on training assignment, with time off for swimming, sightseeing, and drinking beer at "Denny's Dump." Marshall took his turn with other regimental officers in commanding the summer camp and carrying out the training. These were all small matters in contrast to the great swirling chaos of China in revolution, yet in fact they were the matters in which the colonel was deeply and nearly continuously involved, and on which the affairs of China only impinged now and then. But it was service with troops and he was satisfied.

A young lieutenant, assigned as language officer in Peking, visited Nan Ta Su in the summer of 1925 and was dismayed to find a colonel who he knew had been an important figure in the Army in the war here condescending to instruct sergeants and corporals in the simplest routine of training. "It seemed," the lieutenant recalled much later, "to be a great comedown, and I began to wonder what the Army held for me [when] almost ten years after a great war . . . one of its large figures was busily engaged in teaching little groups of eight men how to handle themselves on the field. Secondly, I think I was a little surprised that he didn't feel that sort of thing beneath him. . . . It was a considerable time afterwards that I realized that that was really part of the essence of George Marshall, that basically when he thinks there is something that should be done . . . he follows it right down. . . . It was only, as I say, after I had been there some time that it really began to dawn on me that . . . this is a strength and not a weakness that he's showing." [31]

At about the same time that Colonel Newell arrived, General Connor was replaced as head of the United States Army Forces in China by Brigadier General J. C. Castner, a change disruptive of headquarters and regimental routine. Castner was of that irritating breed of military men who pride themselves on being simple, rough, and blunt old soldiers. A Rutgers graduate with an excellent record in World War I, he affected a private's unpressed trousers and rumpled, sweaty shirt and was convinced that the way to turn out a well-disciplined, rugged command was by hard drill and long hikes, the latter led by himself at a pace that forced the men at the end of the column to run most of the time. (He proudly reported to the Chief of Staff at Washington after one hike that he had sweated thousands of pounds of fat off his command.) Castner's bluntness caused something of an international stir when, on being greeted at a reception by the wife of a British official with a polite "delighted-to-meet-you," he replied, "Lady, tie that bull outside." [32] In regimental affairs Castner insisted on intervening in the smallest details. Marshall decided to try a mixture of diplomacy and strict adherence to military protocol. On Castner's arrival Marshall called in Lieutenant McCammon of the regimental staff, informed him that the new CO was as interested in hunting as in hiking, and gave McCammon the permanent assignment of keeping the general happy. Marshall himself would see Castner punctiliously every morning, salute, and ask for instructions. But he declined all invitations "to sit down and chat." If there was nothing more, sir, he would say, he must return to his duties. So he made it difficult for the general to impose and impossible for him to criticize.[33] The tactic worked: Castner gave him highest ratings at the end of his service in China.

In both North and South China the civil war continued in 1926. In the north shifting alliances of the warlords continued to frustrate any conclusion. By the spring of the year the Peking government, never strong, had collapsed. Weary and endless, these struggles among Chang and Wu and Fêng and their fickle provincial allies revealed the absence of a nation but did nothing to create one. It was in the south that a force less feudal and more hopefully national was being shaped. Early in the previous year Dr. Sun Yat-sen had come north to confer with the northern warlords in a vain effort to put together a coalition that might conceivably unite the country. Already ill, Sun died in Peking in March 1925. His death curiously gave new life to his cause, for in legend he began to be remade into the ideal leader and symbol of Chinese nationalism that he had never been able to make of himself in life. His party meanwhile fell into the hands of living leaders more effective in grasping power than he. At first there were two: Borodin and Chiang Kai-shek. They had openly split by the beginning of 1926, but the differences and antagonism between Communists and anti-Communist Nationalists within the Kuomintang were patched over temporarily pending the conquest of power. Chiang set about that early in 1926. He won the southern provinces in succession and then began to carry out Dr. Sun's long dream of the "Northern Expedition." Military success was swift, and by the end of the year Chiang's armies were threatening Shanghai. Marshall at that time reported to Pershing the uneasiness of the foreign diplomats: "Officials in Peking have their wind up pretty badly, fearing the southern part will leap into control of North China any month, through successes in the field and treachery on the part of leaders in this section. They fear that the Kuomintang (Southerners) will sweep into power and calmly disregard all treaty stipulations as to concessions and extraterritoriality, in the enthusiasm of conquest and in the belief that the Powers are really unwilling to risk actual fighting over the question." [34]

The Kuomintang had, of course, made no secret of its wish to kick the foreigners out of China as quickly and with as little ceremony as possible. Although this was necessarily a promise made by every Chinese leader who sought popular support, the Nationalists had been most militant about it. Furthermore, despite Chiang's obvious disagreement with the Communists, the whole southern movement remained frighteningly Red in the eyes of most foreign observers.

Marshall himself was not inclined to oversimplify the issues or the problems for the future, which some twenty years later would fall in part into his lap. "How the Powers should deal with China," he continued in his letter to Pershing, "is a question almost impossible to answer. There has been so much wrongdoing on both sides, so much of shady transaction between a single power and a single party; there is so much of bitter hatred in the hearts of these people and so much of important business interests involved, that a normal solution can never be found. It will be some form of an evolution, we can only hope that sufficient tact will be displayed by foreigners to avoid violent phases during the trying period that is approaching."

This was the time—at the end of 1926—that the split between Chiang and the Communists headed for a showdown. Borodin shifted the Kuomintang capital from Canton to Hankow, ignoring Chiang's demands that it be set up at Chiang's own base in Nanchang. From that time on, relations between the two leaders became increasingly strained until, in March 1927, while Chiang was occupying Shanghai, the Hankow government declared that he was deposed from his party position. Chiang responded by establishing his own government at Nanking.

For three and a half years Borodin had been playing a careful game, supporting native Chinese aspirations (which up to the point of the victory of the revolution coincided with Communist purposes) and avoiding any show of the ultimate Soviet aim to subvert and dominate. Now his careful work was suddenly undone. In April a raid by agents of the Manchurian warlord, Chang Tso-lin, on the Soviet Embassy in Peking uncovered evidence that the Communists were planning to take over the Kuomintang. That dropped Borodin's mask a little and made his position more difficult. In June, Stalin sent new and explicit instructions to Borodin to begin at once the communization of China, and these instructions were revealed by the Indian Communist M. N. Roy to a native leftist leader. It was a challenge the Chinese could not ignore. In July, under pressure of disillusioned members of the Chinese left wing of the Kuomintang, Borodin, General Blücher (the Soviet military adviser), and other Moscow agents were forced to leave the country. With their departure the position of the Chinese Communists became untenable and they retired to organize a fresh base of power among the peasantry. Chiang was left in control of the Nationalist movement. Within a year he had captured Peking and in October 1928 formally established the National Government in Nanking.

The direction of these events was clear enough, though they had not been consummated, when the Marshalls sailed home in May 1927. There is no evidence that Marshall formed, before he left, any firm ideas about Chiang himself, though he appears to have shared the typical western concern over the threats of radicalism inherent in the Kuomintang bid to conquer the country. By the time Chiang reached Peking the foreign powers had increased their troop strength in China from the 4800 stationed there in midsummer 1926 to 18,000. Included in that figure were 936 United States Army and 4965 United States Marines.[35] Very shortly after Marshall left China, Major Stilwell reported back to General Castner the results of a three-week observation trip to the eastern and southern armies of General

Chiang. Stilwell's views, with which Marshall certainly became familiar when Stilwell joined him at Benning, were considerably more sympathetic to Chiang. He had found the Nationalist armies badly fed and poorly equipped but imbued with faith in their cause, strongly anti-foreign, led by young student officers convinced they could beat any European army in the field.[36]

Marshall in his three years at Tientsin had at best a glimpse of the beginning of China's long agony. In the manner of Army careers he now moved away from it. He was to go back to Washington to lecture at the Army War College. It was not an assignment he especially relished (he had turned down five previous requests to teach there); he would have preferred to instruct at the Infantry School at Benning, which had asked for him in 1924 and 1925 when he was not available. When the request was not repeated in 1926 he accepted General Hanson Ely's invitation to come to the War College.[37] Mrs. Marshall was pleased with the assignment. Whether or not she encouraged him to accept it, she was "radiant over the idea of a beautiful house at Washington Barracks." She had enough Chinese rugs, lacquers, screens, and brocades to furnish a large place, and she came back looking forward eagerly to setting up housekeeping in style and showing off the acquisitions of her "three-years' shopping trip." [38] They got back to Washington in May or June of 1927, ahead of their household furnishings, and while waiting for them stayed in the apartment of their old friends the Palmers.

In August, Mrs. Marshall became ill. Her old heart condition became seriously aggravated by a diseased thyroid gland and she went to Walter Reed Hospital for a medical examination. An operation was required, but she was so weak that Marshall took her home in an effort to build up her strength for this ordeal. "The joy of her new house, the peace and quiet, did a great deal for her," and she soon wrote General Pershing that she was going back to the hospital where she expected to remain for a long time. "The heart is a slow thing to improve," she added, "but I pray I may be back in my own house at the War College before long." [39]

The operation on August 22 was long and extremely serious. As soon as she was able in early September, she wrote her "Aunt Lottie" Coles that she felt she had been given back her life, but that it was a matter of life and death for her to have complete rest and quiet. In this period of slow and painful recovery she leaned heavily on her husband, who spent on her all the time he could spare from his classes at the War College, which had begun early in September. She told her Aunt: "George is so *wonderful* and helps me so. He puts heart and strength in me." [40]

Despite her slow recovery she thought she could leave the hospital soon for home, where she expected to be confined to bed until Christmas. The doctor apparently told her on September 15 that she could go home the next day. She sat at her desk to write the good news to her mother. But suddenly the pen fell from her hand and she slumped over the unfinished note.[41]

It was a little after nine in the morning. Colonel Marshall had just begun his lecture when a guard entered to call him to the telephone. They left together. The guard stood by while Colonel Marshall took the call. "When Colonel Marshall answered the call," he said afterward, "he spoke for a moment over the phone, then put his head on his arms on the desk in deep grief. I asked if I could do anything for him, and he replied, 'No, Mr. Throckmorton, I just had word my wife, who was to join me here today, has just died.' " [42]

Marshall's grief at Lily's death measured the strength and exclusiveness of his attachment to her. Pershing, who in one tragic evening in 1915 had lost his wife and three of his four children in a fire, wrote: "No one knows better than I what such a bereavement means and my heart goes out to you very fully at this crisis in your life. It is at such moments that we realize that our reliance must be placed in the Father who rules us all." Marshall replied: "The truth is, the thought of all you had endured gave me heart and hope. But twenty-six years of most intimate companionship, something I have known since I was a mere boy, leaves me lost in my best effort to adjust myself to future prospects in life. If I had been given to club life or other intimacies with men outside of athletic diversions, or if there was a campaign or other pressing duty demanding a concentrated effort, then I think I should do better. However, I will find a way." [43]

His way would be through hard work, which was to yield five of his most constructive years in the Army.

XV

Marshall's Men

". . . control of troops closely engaged with the enemy is the most difficult feat of leadership and requires the highest state of discipline and training."

EVEN in his happiest and most relaxed periods, lecturing at the War College would not have offered scope enough for Marshall's energies. In the emptiness left by Lily's death he found the surroundings unbearable. "At a War College desk I thought I would explode." [1] He needed hard demanding work into which he could throw himself full time, and the outdoors to release his spirit. At Fort Benning, Colonel Frank S. Cocheu was completing a tour as assistant commandant of the Infantry School. Marshall was asked if he would like to take that position, go to Governors Island as chief of staff of that corps area, or remain at the Army War College. "I thought it best professionally and in my present frame of mind to go to Benning," he wrote Lily's Aunt Lottie. [2] Orders for the change arrived in October, and he was out of Washington early in November. With the help of his sister, who had come down from Greensburg, he moved into a small house on the post, "actually as old as the hills, 1850, but the nicest one I ever had." [3]

Fort Benning, nine miles from Columbus, Georgia, comprised ninety-seven thousand acres of land, including the houses of some old estates which had been bought by the government as part of the reservation. At the time Marshall was there it had not been adequately developed for its most important activity, the Infantry School, and the Inspector General in 1929 commented on the poor location and "unattractive housing" of the Academic Department and the fact that almost two hundred student officers could not find accommodations at the base at all but had to live in Columbus, where the rents, for lieutenants, proved prohibitively high.[4]

As assistant commandant, Marshall was head of the Academic Department. Under the two generals who commanded while he was there—Edgar Collins and Campbell King, with both of whom he had formerly served—he had almost a free hand to mold the course and direct the methods of teaching as he wished. Although Colonel Cocheu had already done much to raise the level of instruction, Marshall intended to go further. With strong and revolutionary ideas, many of which had been developing in his mind for some years, he had often itched to be just where he now found himself, in position to apply them to the training of young combat officers.[5]

It was a happy circumstance that at his "most restless moment" he was given a teaching job (the work he had always found stimulating) with, for the first time, the authority and scope to make a mark not only on the Infantry School but on the United States Army. At Benning he found for himself "an unlimited field of activity, delightful associates, and all outdoors to play in. . . . The change to Benning was magical. . . ." [6] As for the Army, it found in Marshall one of those rare teachers who make a difference, who open minds in such a way that they never afterward quite close again or forget the excitement of a new idea. The importance of that influence cannot be statistically measured, but a roll call of the Benning staff and graduates of Marshall's five years there (a quarter of the school's history between the great wars) is studded with the Army high command of World War II and after—Bradley, Collins, Ridgway, Decker, Stilwell, Bolté, Dahlquist, Almond, Van Fleet, Huebner, Paul, Bedell Smith, Bull, Terry Allen, Leven Allen, Eddy, Cota, Moore, Hull, Cook, Timberman, Hilldring, Lanham, John R.

Deane, and William Dean. Courtney Hodges, while neither a
staff member nor student, sat with Marshall on the Infantry
Board, which studied new weapons for the infantry. In addition
to the hundred and fifty future generals of World War II who
were students and another fifty who were instructors there during this five-year period,[7] hundreds of future field-grade officers
also felt the impress of Marshall's Benning when they were learning the basis of their trade.

What Marshall intended and at last achieved at Benning was
"an almost complete revamping of the instruction and technique."
But that was not to be attempted overnight. He felt it necessary to
proceed "quietly and gradually, because I felt so much opposition would be met on the outside that I would be thwarted in
my purpose." There was also opposition to be overcome on the
inside, from staff members who preferred "the even tenor of
their theoretical ways." [8] Besides, it had always been Marshall's
style to lead by commanding assent rather than mere formal
obedience. When, some years later, a question arose of changes
at the Command and General Staff School at Leavenworth, he
wrote: "To issue an edict or regulation would probably do more
harm than good. The job must be a personal one, to be effected
slowly as faculty minds, physical means, and other tangible factors are gradually rounded into shape for each step. Sudden
changes in an educational plant are bound to be destructive, and
any material changes must be timed by the men on the
ground." [9]

To Benning, Marshall brought the fruits of his own education. And because Benning was the basic training ground for the
Army's basic fighting branch, the things that Marshall had
learned and thought about he could now transfuse into the
Army's main blood stream. The greatest of his lessons was the
need for simplicity in the techniques of troop leading. He had
caught the enthusiasm for "simplicities in tactics" first from Major Morrison at Leavenworth some twenty years before.[10] In subsequent experience with the National Guard he had been impressed with the fact that a citizen army, which could be led
only in small part by highly trained professionals, must concentrate on learning the essentials of tactics. Its own officers must

know how to think clearly about problems of the battlefield without being entangled in elaborate techniques if leadership was to be effective, particularly in the early stages of a war. In World War I, Marshall had been involved in some of the over-elaborate planning and proliferation of written, "highly paragraphed" orders, which reflected both the American Army's anxiety to show itself professional under the scrutiny of its Allies and the fact that it had time to do so as long as the Allies accepted primary responsibility for conducting the battle. American success in battle, however, he felt did not prove the soundness of American techniques. He warned against being tempted to that conclusion.

The techniques of 1918 suited a particular end-of-war situation in which the Allies had a virtual monopoly of initiative. Errors made by the AEF, Marshall believed, were harmless only because the enemy in those last months could not take advantage of them.[11] After the war, as Pershing's aide, re-examining the Army's peacetime needs, he developed further his conviction that "our equipment, administrative procedure, and training requirements are all too complicated for anything but a purely professional Army." Finally, in command of troops in China, he found his convictions borne out. After five months there he wrote: "I find the officers are highly developed in the tactical handling or functioning of weapons, in target practice, in bayonet combat, and in the special and intricate details of paper work or administration generally, but that when it comes to simple tactical problems, the actual duties of troop leading, they all fall far below the standards they set in other matters."[12] During one of the training exercises in China he observed one bright officer faced with the problem of enveloping the flank of a hostile force. There were no special complications but "nothing happened. Time passed, and the situation finally died. I found this officer on the bank of a canal trying to draft a written order for seventy men, and completely stuck because he could not tie the order to the limited data on the blueprint of General Van Deman's sketch of the terrain. I learned that he had stood first at Benning, and I then and there formed an intense desire to get my hands on Benning. The man was no fool, but he had been taught an absurd system, which proved futile the moment a normal situation of warfare of movement arose." [13]

Part of the campaign for simplicity was negative—a constant struggle to get rid of the petty and merely formal requirements of the traditional technique. "I insist we must get down to the essentials, make clear the real difficulties, and expunge the bunk, complications, and ponderosities; we must concentrate on registering in men's minds certain vital considerations instead of a mass of less important details. We must develop a technique and methods so simple and so brief that the citizen officer of good common sense can readily grasp the idea." [14]

But the drive for simplicity was a battle, too, against a kind of military scholasticism. The image of that theoretically trained young officer by the bank of the canal stumped by a simple battle reality was always goadingly in the forefront of his mind. His efforts to free instructors and students from "the book," in which problems were laid out neatly in the front and solutions cut and dried in the back, called on all his great energies and ingenuity and often wore out those endowed with less.[15] One class of officers was dismayed when the assistant commandant one morning required each of them to draw a sketch map of the route they had followed to the classroom, locating both natural and man-made terrain features. Perhaps it was not an altogether fair demand but it helped to drive home Marshall's point that a well-trained troop commander was one whose eye and mind were alert all the time to the salient military facts of any situation in which he might suddenly be called on to make a command decision.

In the classroom, battle was organized and predictable. "I found that the ordinary form of our tactical problems committed two deadly sins, relieving the student from the greatest difficulties of his tactical task in warfare of movement. The information of the enemy was about 80 per cent too complete. And the requirement called for his decision at a pictured moment, when the real problem is usually *when* to make a decision and not *what* the decision should be." [16] In the field it was the unexpected that was normal; Marshall was constantly trying to toss the unexpected at the student officers. In exercises he would send some of them out with troops to attack an enemy force. The enemy would obligingly withdraw, and about dusk when the student felt the problem was just about wound up, another force would attack from a wholly different direction. In the ensuing confusion Marshall himself would turn up to criticize and explain.

In an annual command post exercise instructors and students took turns commanding regular Army troops of the 29th Infantry stationed on the post along with troops brought in from Fort McPherson. In the exercise of 1930 General Matthew Ridgway (then a captain), who had served under Marshall in China before coming to study under him at Benning, recalls that the intelligence estimates contained an inconspicuous reference to an undetermined number of tanks of unknown type in the enemy force. No one paid much attention. The attack proceeded, and the Blue Force got one brigade partly across a river when hostile tanks suddenly appeared. They came out of a wood behind a screen of smoke and caught the attacking troops in the open. Many threw down their rifles and ran. In the confusion, without prior preparation, the maneuver officers had to make decisions to rally their men and restore their position. This sort of experience in training, Ridgway believed, could result at last in a kind of mental conditioning more important to a combat officer than any number of learned techniques. It "cut down the time in which you have to think things out, so that your decisions come out almost instantaneously, and they are sound decisions, if you have worked your brain through this . . . before." [17]

Students at Benning worked out their problems on the terrain of a reservation that had been accurately and minutely mapped. But battles might have to be fought on unfamiliar ground with inadequate maps or none at all. "In warfare of movement, division or corps staffs will seldom have time or opportunity to see the ground except from a plane. They will usually have to work from small-scale maps. They may secure a mosaic in time, but they will be under the necessity of drafting instructions to be used by the lower echelons with reference to the small-scale map, or no map at all. . . . If you get your mosaics, fine! But the hard thing to learn is how to manage without them." And that, Marshall found, was not even being taught. "Early in my stay at Benning," he wrote, "I accompanied two instructors out with the class for a terrain exercise in a battalion engagement during the development phase of an action, where the hostile dispositions and intentions were not clear. A large-scale map was used. After the students had dispersed to work on their solutions, I asked the instructors to put away their maps and solve the problem for me on the basis of no maps available. They were at a complete loss for a workable solution method (or technique) to handle the affair, and were two hours preparing a solution—a very poor one. Fifteen minutes should have sufficed." [18] Time and again he required that classes work with road maps, foreign maps, maps that were out of date. After World War II an officer who had been one of his students, General Charles Bolté, said: "I think he was so right, because that's exactly what we had—maps of North Africa that were no good, and as far as the Pacific was concerned, if you got a sketch you were lucky. . . . I have never forgotten [his] dictum: . . . 'study the first six months of the next war.' Over and over he put that down." [19]

Marshall's emphasis on training for warfare of movement recalled Pershing's insistence in 1917-18 on preparing the AEF to move out of the trenches into "open warfare." Pershing had argued both that open warfare was better suited to the temper of the American soldier and that it was the one hope of forcing a decision in battle. Marshall was certainly imbued with that point of view. It is not necessary to suppose, however, that he had a fully developed concept of the war of movement that would come on battlefields dominated by the tank and airplane, and there is no evidence that he had any such vision. He remained essentially an infantryman, though one who welcomed and readily recognized the significance of technological changes. He had a special tank company established at Benning. He tried to get an air detachment. Balked in that, he arranged for annual demonstrations of air support techniques by a squadron from Maxwell Field. In a determined effort to improve relations, traditionally difficult, between infantry and artillery officers, he

arranged for the exchange of faculty members and troops between Benning and the Artillery School at Fort Sill.[20] He insisted
that artillery officers be consulted in discussion of infantry doctrine and vice versa.

As a teacher of tactics, however, he was not primarily concerned with theories of war or even with the grand shape of the
battles of the future. He was concerned with methods and principles of command. In almost any battle situation he believed
leaders of troops would be required to make up their minds
quickly with scant information. He sought, therefore, to teach
the art of improvisation, to extricate tactical principles from the
procedural formulas in which they had become fixed by the
schoolmen. One way to do that was to set problems in rapidly
moving situations where even a mediocre solution arrived at
in time was better than the perfect tactic discovered hours after
the opportunity to use it had passed. "I found," he wrote, "that
the technique and practices developed at Benning and Leavenworth would practically halt the development of an open warfare situation, apparently requiring an armistice or some understanding with a complacent enemy." [21]

Most of Marshall's innovations at Benning were designed to
jolt instructors and students out of traditionally leisurely ways
that had emphasized formal perfection. It had been customary
for instructors to prepare written lectures about a month in
advance and submit them to the editorial section, which made
sure that no sentence contravened accepted doctrine. Marshall,
who disliked edicts, issued one on this occasion: no more lectures
were to be read. At first he permitted instructors to use cards
on which they would note the main points to be touched on.
"But when I heard the instructor say one morning, 'I am required this morning to discuss . . .' (it was just a nervous gesture)—I suppressed the card too. I found it was many times
more effective when a man talked off the cuff, as it were, although it was a very well ironed cuff."

For some time before Marshall arrived officer students had
been required to write a monograph on some aspect of military
history. That had always been a time-consuming and nerve-
racking exercise, and Marshall made it harder. He required
that the monograph be delivered orally in a class lecture lim-

ited to twenty minutes. Once when a class insisted that the time
was much too short to allow the subject to be covered properly,
Marshall, on the spot, delivered a lecture outlining the Civil
War in five minutes.[22] He set great store by the monograph as a
device to force officers in training to come directly to grips with
a problem and outline it clearly and briefly. He himself seldom
missed the presentations. But he never succeeded in making
them popular. When Major Harding came to Benning and was
moved to write a short play about student life he ended it with
an officer's prayer:

> Now into my bunk I creep
> To catch an hour or so of sleep
> And dream about my monograph.
> Help me, O Lord, to stand the gaff.[23]

History properly presented could also underline for students
the real problems of decision amid the confusion of battle. Marshall was delighted when one of his staff, Major Truman Smith
(later distinguished as the United States military attaché who
watched and perceptively reported the rearming of the Third
Reich), worked out several lectures in which a historical battle
was described and the part played by a small unit outlined. On
the basis of the actual fragmentary information the students
were required to explain what they would have done had they
been in command. Major Harding's section later carried on the
idea and wrote a book of such examples from history (published as *Infantry in Battle*). Among those who worked hardest
on the volume was a young lieutenant with a talent for writing,
Charles T. Lanham. Marshall marked him as one of the kind of
young officer who should be pushed for advancement. As for the
book, he was pleased with it and with its reception among Army
officers and military writers abroad.[24] After he left Benning he
wrote an introduction praising it as a text that captured the realities of battle: "By the use of numerous historical examples
which tell of the absence of information, the lack of time, and
the confusion of battle the reader is acquainted with the realities
of war and the extremely difficult conditions under which tactical problems must be solved in the face of the enemy." [25]
Because he was so much more interested in thoughtfulness

than in mere correctness, Marshall tended to value—and perhaps even overvalue—the unorthodox approach. Major Bull, who was later to be Eisenhower's G-3 in SHAEF, recalled a map exercise in which he was required to halt an armored force threatening a hypothetical advance of troops under his command from Washington toward Chambersburg. He threw away the book and tried a maneuver of his own. Although he was judged by the umpires to have failed, Marshall was delighted with his display of ingenuity. Years later when Prime Minister Churchill, another enthusiast for the unorthodox, visited Benning during the war, Marshall recalled the experiment.[26] One of Marshall's earliest revolutionary edicts as assistant commandant had been to order that "any student's solution of a problem that ran radically counter to the approved school solution, and yet showed independent creative thinking, would be published to the class." One danger in this approach, which some officers felt Marshall did not always avoid, was a predisposition to admire novelty even when not sound and to prefer for advancement officers whose chief distinction was a willingness to experiment. The virtue, noted by Captain J. Lawton Collins, who would become a corps commander in World War II and later Chief of Staff, was that it helped to create "the spirit at Benning, which was a marvelous thing, because if anybody had any new ideas he was willing to try them instead of saying, 'Why don't you let the thing alone instead of stirring things up.' " [27]

Stirring things up was just what Marshall insisted was essential to his teaching purposes. An infantry lieutenant colonel who came to Benning in 1930 for a short refresher course was struck by the opportunity given officers "to disagree at times on questions of military education, regardless of rank, and an attitude of tolerance of ideas which encourages open and free discussion." The Benning staff, he thought, was "thinking seriously about matters, old and new, that may find application in our Army of the future. They are not afraid to look outside the field of what is generally considered military education for ideas to help in solving the problems of national defense." [28]

That appreciation was written about midway in Marshall's five years as assistant commandant. He had by that time largely effected his quiet and gradual revolution. By the autumn of 1930, beginning his last two years, he had his own staff of chosen men whom he admired personally and who had served recently with troops and found themselves sympathetic with his pragmatic approach.[29]

Heading the Tactical Section at Benning in 1930 was an "old China hand," Lieutenant Colonel Stilwell. Marshall wanted him badly enough to hold the position open for a year until Stilwell became available. The tall, lean, profane man who later became known as "Vinegar Joe" was at least as difficult then as when during World War II he commanded American troops in China and India and acted as chief of staff to Generalissimo Chiang Kai-shek. Intense, intolerant, energetic—many lunch hours he spent racing the clock over long distances—he spared neither himself nor those who worked for him. He was a rebel by instinct, chafed against any and all authority, mocked at those in command, continually burned to remake the situation in which he found himself, and throughout his Army career walked the razor's edge of insubordination. But he was nevertheless a brilliant soldier. Marshall valued him for what he could do, and no doubt also for the very fact that he was a nonconformist. One of the instructors in Stilwell's First Section, another brilliant commander, was Captain Collins.

Marshall's choice of an officer to head the Second Section (logistics, supply, training, equitation, signal communications) was highly unorthodox. Lieutenant Colonel M. C. Stayer was a doctor. But Marshall picked him because he was blunt-spoken, a good judge of men, who could be depended on to say exactly what he thought. The staff under Stayer included two future lieutenant generals, Captain Willard Paul and Major Bull. For Bull, Marshall had a particularly strong and lasting admiration. He gave him credit for creating a simplified supply system for the Army.

"The general supply system of the Army for regiments, battalions, and divisions," he said later, "grew out of the demonstrations at Benning under the leadership of Bull." The system of supply for these units had been so complicated that the manual describing it ran to a hundred and twenty mimeographed pages and a field demonstration of the process took three days. Early in his stay there Marshall asked that the editorial section cut the length of the manual. Under continued pressure it was got down to twelve pages, but he was still not satisfied that citizen soldiers in the early stages of a war would understand the procedures. "I changed the set-up of this supply business," he recalled, "and gave it to Bull and told him to demonstrate this as a mobile supply problem, not as a set-up affair, and to do it as quickly as possible. Bull had paid no attention to supply and was very emphatic in telling me that. And I must say I gave him no ideas at all except time limits. . . . I was working on the proposition that we had to hurriedly train an Army and if we couldn't be precise and brief, there was no hope in the manuals. . . . As I recall he finally succeeded in getting this [supply demonstration] to a day and a half. And as I perfectly recall, he later . . . cut this down to a half-day. This was the supply basis for the Army. . . . From being the most unpopular course in school it became one of the most popular."

The Third Section taught the use of weapons and developed weapons doctrine. Marshall appointed to head it a quiet-spoken man, as different in temperament from Stilwell as it is possible to imagine, Major Omar N. Bradley, who would command an army group in World War II and become Chief of Staff of the Army afterward, and was, in Marshall's opinion, an officer "conspicuous for his ability to handle people and his ability to do things simply and clearly." As an instance, Marshall later recalled that at the time there had been an obsession "with the idea of machine-gun barrages with the 30 caliber weapons, and [many veterans of World War I] wished practically to equip companies with a great deal of the communications set-up of a battery of artillery. I was opposed to this, not that I knew much about the details, but I was certain it was not a good thing to load down an infantry company with so much equipment. I transferred Bradley to [head] of the Weapons Section and told him to take a close look at the machine-gun situation." After careful study, Bradley's section gave a detailed demonstration of the problem. Marshall was delighted to find that the companies "already had enough equipment to do the whole thing," and that the presentation took half of the allotted time. He called it "the best demonstration I ever saw" and ordered that it be repeated for every class that came to Benning as an illustration of how to simplify instruction.

To the Fourth Section, in charge of history and publications, Marshall brought his old friend from China days, Major Harding. He contributed to morale with a lively column for the *Benning Herald.* Another post publication, *Mailing List,* Harding developed into a significant professional aid by publishing tactical problems to be solved by readers. Marshall, in summarizing the state of training at Benning just after he left, singled out the *Mailing List.* "It now has readers," he wrote, "where formerly it only had subscribers. Its small problems make the real picture of a battle. It is being used throughout the country by National Guard and reservists, and not filed or dumped into the wastebasket." [30] As noted, it was also Harding's section that prepared *Infantry in Battle.*

Marshall himself believed that the faculty of the Infantry School during his last three years there "was composed of the most brilliant, interesting, and thoroughly competent collection of men I have ever been associated with." Yet characteristically he was not satisfied with what they were able to achieve. "We all learned together, but we had a devil of a time getting started. We never got to the point of teaching tactics as General Morrison taught it—most of our supposed tactical instruction fell into the domain of technique." [31] For what was achieved he gave the staff the credit, and in telling about the Benning revolution he protested against being "in the embarrassing position of seeming to be the one who knew, when as a matter of fact I am recording my own experience in the AEF and later training in the Army when I was with General Pershing and my own experience in these schools." He did not feel that he had been the originator. "In all this, I must say, in a sense, I had no part. I furnished the directive and the drive and the arbitrary orders it must be done." Yet to Colonel Truman Smith it seemed that Marshall was using his instructors as weapons to carry out his ideas. Harding, too, felt the initiative was Marshall's. "He would tell you what he wanted and then you would do it. There was something about him that made you do it, and of course you wanted to do it the way he wanted—which is the trait of a commanding officer." [32] Marshall kept close to his staff, and with some, including the heads of sections, he met frequently at his quarters to discuss problems of command. Seeking constantly to stretch minds, he would often have Major Gilbert Cook (later a corps commander under Patton in Normandy) act as master of ceremonies and hand out books on psychology, sociology, or military history to read and discuss.[33]

Benning's primary function was to train company-grade infantry officers in the art of leading small units. But it also offered short refresher courses for more senior officers as well as for officers of the National Guard and organized Reserves. Marshall was particularly interested in bringing in the citizen soldiers and among other things arranged to have the Air Corps fly in National Guardsmen and reservists who lived at some distance. Among them there appeared in his last year two Negro officers. This was Georgia in the days before the nation had accepted responsibility for integration. Some officers circulated a petition demanding the Negroes withdraw. Marshall denied it and the two officers remained. One of them wrote him later to say: "Your quiet and courageous firmness, in this case, has served to hold my belief in the eventual solution of problems which have beset my people in their ofttimes pathetic attempts to be Americans." [34]

While at Benning, Marshall found another way to keep up with and influence civilian training. In 1929, at Pershing's suggestion, he was appointed a member of the Mershon Fund Board, set up by Ralph D. Mershon, who had worked with the officials of Ohio State University to develop the concept of the Reserve Officer Training Corps before World War I. The objective of the fund was to promote reserve-officer training and improve civilian-military relationships—aims to which Marshall himself was devoted throughout his life. Marshall continued active on the board for several years and was particularly influential in meetings of ROTC instructors and university officials at Lehigh in 1933, and at Purdue in 1934.[35]

The vigor with which Marshall plunged into his work at Benning was partly an expression of his natural abundance of energy and particular interest in teaching, partly the product of his loneliness after Lily's death. Because he himself craved to be continually active, he kept not only his officers, but his officers' wives, continually on the go. He organized so many hunts and pageants that some on the post would gladly have settled for a short period of ennui.

Beginning about the first of October and lasting until April, hunts were held about twice a week. Sixty or more officers and their wives rode to the hounds. Sergeant Thomas Tweed, whose private pack served the first hunt in 1923, was the permanent Huntsman in Marshall's time and in fact took part in most of the hunts until his retirement after World War II. For less strenuous hunting the Benning reservation abounded in quail, wild pig, and raccoons. During the war Marshall came down when he could to shoot and nearly always took Sergeant Tweed with him.[36]

As always, Marshall was an indefatigable horseman, though he preferred a quiet canter to the cross-country pursuit of foxes. Occasionally he held competitive night rides in which pairs of riders were assigned points to be reached between start and finish but were permitted to make their way between them in any way they pleased. Marshall himself competed and, although a comparatively slow rider, used his intimate knowledge of the terrain to finish well up. One of the legends of the post is of the colonel returning from a treasure hunt on horseback, wearing a Japanese kimono and Filipino hat, and carrying a bird cage.[37]

Marshall's pageants became famous. Staged for visiting dignitaries in place of formal military reviews, which he found tiresome, the pageant consisted of a series of acts presenting the activities of the post. In one of these, students marched by with their weapons, tennis players with their rackets, polo ponies and riders, basketball players, baseball players—and then, as climax, a pack of hounds following a scent laid down earlier in the day burst through the crowd, followed by huntsmen. It was Marshall's favorite show and he repeated it as often as he found occasion.

Marshall's Benning was not only physically strenuous; it could also be intellectually wearing. At official gatherings he risked becoming a bore by suggesting brain-teasing games, testing the ability of his guests to solve problems or recall obscure capital cities and their population. He himself might talk almost steadily through the evening as if by compulsion to let out the loneliness in him. He encouraged dramatic and musical productions, his own favorites being Gilbert and Sullivan. Diversion for him was only another form of busyness. There were, moreover, those who found the assistant commandant lacking in cultural taste, uncomfortably prudish in his tight-lipped distaste for the most modestly told off-color story, and overweening in his paternalistic concern with the leisure as well as the working hours of the post. Well out of earshot they called him "Uncle George."

Under the constant drain of strenuous work and play in his first years at Benning, Marshall lost weight. His lean, bony face, never handsome, was drawn and plainer than ever. A nervous tic from which he had suffered since his days in France and which pulled up one corner of his mouth in a grimace that the unwary often mistook for a smile became more pronounced. It was during these years that he began to suffer periodically from a thyroid disturbance that produced an irregular pulse. It worried him, but Lt. Col. Stayer, to whom he confided the trouble, was able to keep it under control.[38]

Marie Singer, who made several long visits to Benning, was disturbed by the fact that her brother kept the house filled with photographs of Lily so that in moving from room to room he was constantly reminded of his loss. The reminder was made more painful when less than a year after Lily's death, in October 1928, his mother died from a heart attack suffered at Marie's home in Greensburg. Within another year Lily's mother, Mrs. Coles, also died, and the last of Marshall's close emotional ties to the past was broken.

He tried to fill his loneliness in part by sharing the family life of some of his friends on the post. Childless, he and Lily had always been fond of children, and it was one of Marshall's most characteristic poses to unbend, gravely affectionate, to a child. His quarters at Benning were near the tennis courts, and he formed the habit of inviting youngsters in for refreshments after their game. Sometimes he would ask a child to go with him to an entertainment on the post. One little girl of nine won his heart one day by telling him that she had worn a blue dress, which he admired, because it matched his eyes. Remembering her for years thereafter, he wrote letters of fatherly advice to her on the eve of her marriage and later asked that he be allowed to be godfather of her first son.[39]

When he wrote to a child it was with an easy sense of humor and sense of style rare in the rest of his surviving correspondence. A few years later after visiting the young daughter of a friend of his in the hospital Marshall sent her this note:

> I do hope your patience and fortitude will be rewarded with a quick recovery, though I must say I never saw you looking prettier. I found your company of fish, turtles, and guppies quite fascinating —much more attractive than the average group I meet socially— even if one did escape down the drainpipe.
>
> I have been pondering over what might be added to the collection, and hoping to hit on something that will be self-supporting, and not demand so much maid service from your Father. I believe that a chipmunk of the type they have at Crater Lake would be just the thing, because you can feed those peanuts in bed and they have no other interests, sentimental or otherwise.
>
> With my sympathy, and my admiration for your patience, I am affectionately . . .

For more than two years Marshall suffered his loneliness. Then one evening in 1929 he went to dinner at the house of the Tom Hudsons in Columbus, who had as their guests for the evening a widow, Katherine Boyce Tupper Brown, and her teen-age daughter Molly. Marshall arrived first and, it is recorded, was standing by the fireplace when Mrs. Brown, tall and striking, walked in. Marshall quite clearly stared. Mrs. Brown has written of that moment: "I will never forget. George had a way of looking right straight through you. He had such keen blue eyes and he was straight and very military." They were attracted and fell at once into an easy bantering conversation. At the end of the evening he offered to take her home. She was staying with Mrs. William Randolph Blanchard, mother of one of her college friends and Molly's godmother. George assured her that he knew just where Mrs. Blanchard lived. At the end of about an hour, during which they drove through a good part of the city, she observed mildly that he did not seem to have learned his way around Columbus yet. He replied that if he hadn't known his way around so well he wouldn't have been able to drive for an hour without getting on to that street. The next day he asked her to come to a reception at the post. When she demurred he sent a soldier in a car to get her.[40] She came, and he monopolized her so completely that she met few of the guests and the Columbus people at the reception complained that they had no chance at all to talk to her before, ending her brief visit, she returned to her home in Baltimore.[41]

Mrs. Brown was a handsome and unusual woman. Born Katherine Boyce Tupper in Harrodsburg, Kentucky, in October 1882, she was the daughter of a Baptist minister, Henry Allen Tupper, who became one of the most distinguished of his day.[42] His wife, Marie Louise Pender, was the daughter of a North Carolina hotel owner who during the Civil War ran the northern blockade chiefly in trade with Bermuda to supply the southern armies. As Pender and his wife both died during the war, Marie was reared by a relative, another Baptist minister, Jeremiah B. Jeter, who lived in Richmond.[43]

From this strongly Baptist background (her grandfather, Henry Allen Tupper, and her uncles, James Pettigru Boyce and Kerr Boyce Tupper were also eminent divines) Katherine took a new and, to her father, disturbing departure. She wanted to be an actress. After completing her studies at Hollins College she persuaded her father to permit her to study at the American Academy of Dramatic Arts in New York. She stayed for two years and then won permission to go abroad with her sister Allene to continue her study. (Allene was to study art but her true bent was literary, and she would in time write plays, among them *The Creaking Chair,* in which Tallulah Bankhead starred in London in 1924.) The sisters settled in a boarding house in London in 1904, and Katherine, armed with letters of introduction and superb self-confidence, sought an interview with Sir Herbert Beerbohm Tree, perhaps the most Olympian figure of the London stage. He saw Katherine, listened to her, and then gave his opinion that even if she had the histrionic talent of Ada Rehan he could not engage her with her American accent. Undismayed, she applied next, on the advice of the brother of Walter Hampden whom she had met on shipboard, to Frank Benson, who had Shakespearian companies touring Australia, Scotland, and the provinces of England. For him she declaimed the lines of the dying Camille, and when she had finished he looked at her a long time and said, "You know you will have to study English." But he was interested enough to propose that she join his company as a student. He first asked a fee, but when she explained that her father was going to cut off her allowance as soon as she joined the cast, he agreed to waive the fee.

It was arranged that Allene would give up her art and go along with Katherine as chaperone and visible means of support, since she, not being on the stage, would continue to get her allowance from home. For one season they toured England and Scotland, staying in cheap boarding houses, often with little to eat. When not on the stage Katherine spent hours each day practicing her diction. Her first speaking part was as the voice of the ghost in *Hamlet*—a considerable advance from her role in *Macbeth* in which she was required to stand where she could catch Lady Macbeth when she fainted.

In her second season one of the leading ladies married Walter Hampden and left the company. This left parts for Katherine in *The Rivals, She Stoops to Conquer, The School for Scandal,* and five Shakespeare plays, in which she acted on tour in Ireland. At the end of the season she summered with her sister and parents in Lucerne and then returned to London, where she signed a seven-year contract with Benson.

The next year she began suffering severe pains in her side and shoulder which she first attributed to fatigue from practicing continuously for new roles. One night in Glasgow, however, the pain was so bad that she could not go on and the curtain was rung down. After a rest she seemed to recover and undertook the part of Jessica in *The Merchant of Venice* in Newcastle-on-Tyne. Stricken again on the stage, she was taken from the theater to the hospital, where the doctors told her she had tuberculosis of the kidney. She came home. A specialist in Baltimore took a less grave view. Her trouble, he thought, was exhaustion, and he sent her to rest in the Adirondacks. There a childhood friend from Baltimore, Clifton S. Brown, caught the moment to declare his love and urge her to give up the stage and marry him.

She refused. Her career seemed promisingly begun. She had an offer from Richard Mansfield of a place in his company provided she could get her release from Benson, and when she felt well again she accepted. Then she went out to Chicago to play at the National Theater. The familiar pains struck again. She got through two or three performances; then one evening when the final curtain fell she found herself unable to move and had to be carried from the stage. Back in the Adirondacks for another rest, she found Clifton Brown again. To his renewed urging, family and friends added their pressure, and at last she yielded. That decision to turn her back on the stage cost her such heartache that for two years she could not bear even to go into a theater.

But in time she became reconciled. Her daughter Molly was born, and then two sons, Clifton and Allen, and she took on happily enough her second career as wife of a successful lawyer, champion tennis player, and president of the Whist Club. By 1928, like much of the rest of middle-class America, the Browns were prospering. They had bought a house; Molly and the boys were in private schools. With money enough and no worries, Katherine decided to invest some of her own money in a summer cottage on Fire Island. A few days later she called her husband's office to tell him that she had received the final papers for the property. There was no answer. While she was puzzling over that, two men appeared at the door. They told her that Clifton Brown had a little while before entered the building in which he had his office and found there in a hall a former client. The man, aggrieved over the fee he had been charged, was waiting with a gun to settle accounts. As Brown approached the door to his office the man shot and killed him.[44]

Dazed from shock, Mrs. Brown left Baltimore and stayed with her sister in Connecticut for eight months. She sailed then for Hawaii and spent several months with Molly in a cottage on Waikiki. When at last she was ready to return to her life in Baltimore she stopped fatefully in Columbus on the way.

It was on that visit that Marshall met her. Apparently it occurred to both of them, during that first evening, that they might get married. Both agreed firmly that they would not marry again. Nevertheless during the summer of 1929, much of which he spent in Wyoming, Marshall wrote frequently to Mrs. Brown and in the fall suggested that Mrs. Etta Blanchard Worsley invite her on another visit to Columbus. The invitation was extended and accepted only in the spring of 1930. Marshall then cleared his evenings and devoted himself wholly to her. By the time she left they were at least tentatively engaged. She insisted, however, that her children must approve.

Molly, having known Marshall from the beginning and grown fond of him, was no problem. Clifton was also readily agreeable. The doubt was Allen, who was then twelve. Mrs. Brown arranged for friends to come to Fire Island and suggested Marshall join them. The situation was then explained to Allen, who first proposed that things be left as they were. Overnight he had second thoughts and in the morning himself wrote to Marshall. "I hope you will come to Fire Island," he said. "Don't be nervous, it is O.K. with me. A friend in need is a friend indeed, Allen Brown." [45]

Five weeks Marshall spent on Fire Island, and if Allen or Clifton had any lingering objections they were dispelled. Marshall on August 1 wrote to Pershing that he was to be married in mid-October and added that he was acquiring "a complete family" and that Molly was "quite a little beauty." [46]

General Pershing was best man at the wedding in Baltimore at the Emmanuel Episcopal Church on October 15, 1930, his presence being of course the news of the occasion. Mrs. Marshall's sister, Colonel Marshall's sister, and the brother of Lily, Edmund Coles, were among the group at the ceremony.[47] Inasmuch as the school year had already begun and Marshall's presence was required, the couple went directly from the chapel to the train for the trip to Fort Benning.

With a sense of humor and the poise of maturity, the new Mrs. Marshall made the transition readily to Army wife. She does not seem to have balked at the regimented routine of the Marshall household, so rigorous that Allene Tupper, during a visit, was moved to satirize it in a skit.[48] After a time, when horse-back riding became too strenuous for Mrs. Marshall, Molly sub-stituted as Marshall's regular riding companion. Molly and "the Colonel," as the two older children always called him, became good friends. As for Marshall, he fitted easily and gratefully into the role of father and was particularly fond of Allen, who was young enough to accept him most fully and to whom he was not "the Colonel" but "George." To Mrs. Marshall he trans-ferred the solicitude he had felt all his life for Lily, and the emptiness in him was filled. For the rest of his life his letters reflect his constant care for her well-being and her health.

The last years at Benning were contented and productive.[49] Under regulations, Marshall's tour as assistant commandant had to end in 1931, but to keep him longer, at the commandant's request, the War Department arranged to attach him to the 24th Infantry, part of the garrison of the post. The shift was made on paper only and he continued to carry on the same duties as before.[50]

Under Marshall's encouragement, officers at Benning devel-oped simplified procedures, wrote new manuals and revised old ones, worked out better techniques of supply, and experimented with new infantry tactics to fit new or improved weapons. When a member of the Infantry Board wrote of changes that the French had recently made in their drill system, Marshall asked Captain Collins first to study them and then to develop an im-proved drill. The new drill, on completion, was sent to the War Department, where it languished until Marshall, as Deputy Chief of Staff in 1938, took steps to get it adopted. These were tangible products of Marshall's Benning. But more important were the long consequences of education. Classes of company-grade officers of the age to occupy senior command and staff positions in World War II were imbued at Benning with Mar-shall's pragmatism, his insistence on the application of princi-ples and common sense to battlefield problems, his dictum that the only orders worth giving were those that could be prepared and delivered in time and readily understood by troops not long removed from civilian life in the confusion and unreadiness of the first days of war. One colonel, writing in 1935, noted that whereas once graduates of Leavenworth met on the proud ground of having been "Morrison men," now there were many who called themselves "Marshall's men." [51] And when in 1940 and 1941 the Chief of Staff looked for division and corps commanders, he knew intimately scores of officers who had worked with him at Benning and who valued the same essentials of battle leadership.

XVI

The Old Man

"Suggest Lieutenant Colonel George C. Marshall. He has no superior among Infantry colonels. . . ."
—General MacArthur to General Keehn,
September 28, 1933.

S O O N after he came to Benning, Marshall had received a flattering offer to go to Manila. In the spring of 1929 the newly appointed governor general of the Philippines, Dwight F. Davis, asked that he go out with him to the Islands as prospective chief of the constabulary, a post that would carry great prestige and higher pay. Secretary of State Stimson proposed him for the post, and he went to Washington to discuss it with Davis. But in the end he put the temptation behind him, partly because he was not sure he would like to work with Davis but mostly because he thought he should "keep close to straight Army business at my age"—duty with troops. Pershing agreed. "Your future interest," the general wrote, "lies in your continued splendid service with the Army." Not long after, Virginia friends asked that he allow his name to be presented for the superintendency of VMI—again a considerable compliment and a temptation. But again he declined. At the end of his Benning tour he had his chance to be again with troops: he was assigned to command a battalion of the 8th Infantry at Fort Screven, Georgia—a small post but one that he was delighted to get.[1]

When Marshall left Benning in the spring of 1932 the United States was near the bottom of the greatest economic depression in history. The unemployed numbered at least twelve million and guesses ranged as high as seventeen million. In America's great cities the destitute begged, lined up when they could for free bread and soup, slept in parks or in the packing-case shanty towns that were derisively called "Hoovervilles" after the unfortunate President who a few years before had been one of the most popular men in America and now was the goat for all its ills. As in the depression of the 1870s, gangs of idle young men roamed the land. People long without work came to doubt their ability and to despair of their world. People still employed had their wages cut, saw the men beside them let go, and held on with a numbing sense that each pay envelope might be the last.

While men and officers of the regular Army had somewhat greater job security, they were by no means free from the general uncertainty or from the economic pinch. The orthodox administration of Herbert Hoover under the pressure of national misery was trying some highly unorthodox economic experiments to feed federal funds into the stagnant economy, through the Emergency Relief Organization, the Home Loan Banks, the Reconstruction Finance Corporation. But, insisting at the same time on fiscal soundness, which then meant balancing the federal budget, it called also for economy, and the Army, as always, stood high on the list of the dispensables. Even before the crash Hoover had proclaimed that military spending must not "exceed the barest necessity." Now he asked for drastic economies. The House, captured by the Democrats in 1930, was as eager as the Republican Senate to help the President pare the budget—at least where it was politically safe. They agreed to impose on the services an unpaid furlough equal to $8\frac{1}{3}$ per cent of their active duty and barred increases of pay for promotion and automatic in-grade raises. The House also approved a reduction of the officer corps from twelve thousand to ten thousand. Although the Senate, in response to appeals by General MacArthur, Chief of Staff since 1930, and Secretary of War Patrick Hurley, struck out this provision of the bill, both houses agreed on cutbacks in the appropriations for the organized Reserves, the National Guard, and the Citizens Military Training Camps. So strong was the drive for retrenchment that the thirty-year-old proposals to eliminate some Army posts along with more recent schemes for unifying the services were at last gathering support. In the circumstances Army officers could hardly feel sanguine about their careers even if they avoided unemployment.[2]

The post to which Marshall reported in June was rumored to be among those Congress was thinking of abolishing. Located on the northern end of Tybee Island, seventeen miles from Savannah, Georgia, Fort Screven had once housed coast artillery to guard the entrance to Savannah harbor. More recently it had served as headquarters of the 8th Infantry. In 1929 when the regiment moved to Fort Moultrie, South Carolina, one battalion was left at Screven to keep the post alive. The whole establishment that Marshall came to command consisted of less than four hundred men, but he was cheerful enough about the prospect. "However small," he wrote to Pershing, "it at least keeps me away from office work and high theory." [3]

He was happy to be back with troops. Characteristically he plunged into the new job of managing a small post and making it run as harmoniously and efficiently as possible with the same enthusiasm and wholehearted absorption as he had applied to his assignment at Benning. Arriving unexpectedly, he found the officers in the throes of getting several hundred CMTC trainees settled. He had a reputation in the Army as a strict and meticulous taskmaster, and when he suddenly appeared in the confusion at Screven the unhappy officers expected an explosion. Instead they got an apology for his unannounced arrival. When they proposed an off-post informal reception that evening, the colonel not only accepted but suggested they dispense with the formal affair scheduled for later in the week.[4]

Off on the right foot in his new command, the colonel resolved also to lay at once ground work for friendly relations with its civilian community. That Sunday he and Mrs. Marshall made the long drive into Savannah to attend services at an Episcopal church. Members of the congregation were surprised and delighted.[5] Considering that the new commanding officer had put himself out to pay his respects to Savannah, the mayor the next day returned the courtesy and visited Fort Screven and shortly

thereafter had some crepe myrtle delivered to help landscape
the driveways.[6] The good community relations thus launched
Marshall cultivated with special festivities on the post. On the
Fourth of July, he asked the mayors of Savannah and Tybee
Beach to review the CMTC unit at the end of its summer
training.

From these first days at Fort Screven, Marshall cherished
what he called a "ribald" story of how the ice was broken at a
formal post dinner. The new CO, despite the graciousness of
his arrival, still seemed somewhat forbidding—a man who in
discouraging fools often discouraged gaiety, too, among the
majority who lacked his self-assurance. That evening was particularly sticky. The dinner guests crowded at small tables in a
steamy hot room, ate in silence or with subdued conversation,
while waitresses squeezed among them serving course after
course. One waitress, a large colored woman, was particularly
hot and uncomfortable as she pushed among the tables, mutter-
ing, "Excuse me, excuse me." Only after the dessert did she
come with dawning happiness, bearing the finger bowls. It was
nearly over. She had the bowls almost all distributed when she
looked into one and realized that she had forgotten the flower
petals that traditionally floated on the water. Facing another
tortuous journey through the crowd, she cried out in anguish,
"Jesus! The geraniums!" The diners dissolved in laughter and
so did the last stuffiness of the evening.[7]

Work at Fort Screven included training and military housekeeping. Marshall took over the post like a paterfamilias or, as
one of the young officers under him later wrote, "as would a
Southern planter his domain." On his early morning rides about
the post he noticed a spot where a little myrtle might be planted
to improve appearance, a freshly planted garden to be commended. He was a stickler for details. At least once he observed
girls playing tennis with dirty shoes and ordered that henceforth
their shoes be whitened to set his men a good example. He liked
to have things just so but he preferred not to issue orders. He
did more by suggestion or example. (When the CO was seen
fixing up his yard, it was a foolish young officer who did not take
the hint.) Along with his insistence on an outward perfection

he concerned himself with the welfare of his men. He arranged, with the help of a local civic organization, to buy a captured rum runner which he made available to officers and men and their families for picnics or fishing.[8] To combat the effects of the recent legislative economies he personally saw to the laying out of vegetable gardens and chickenyards and had the troop messes prepare extra portions of food and put them up in containers for sale at cost to men with families. Those who knew what he did in those days never forgot him. For all his austerity the role of "the old man" suited him.

The New Deal would soon provide larger scope for his paternalistic concerns. In March 1933, when President Franklin D. Roosevelt was inaugurated, Marshall was in Washington at a meeting of the Mershon Fund Board. He was impressed, as were so many others, with the fresh air of excitement. "Washington was a remarkable-looking place," he wrote to General Pershing, who had been prevented by illness from taking his place in the ceremonies as grand marshal of the inaugural parade. "Seemingly every deserving Democrat . . . was there—streets crowded, hotels overflowing, and every crowd sprinkled with the uniforms of governors' staff officers. The parade was Democracy at its blatant best and the simultaneous closing of the banks made plenty of atmosphere for the occasion." [9]

While waiting in Union Station for his train back to Savannah, Marshall sat by a bewildered old man and woman, talked to them, and discovered that they had tickets to Oklahoma but as a result of the "bank holiday," proclaimed by the President in an effort to stop the mounting toll of bank failures, they had been unable to cash a check to buy food on the way. The fact was that he had been in the same predicament himself a few hours before but had managed to borrow five dollars from a fellow officer. Most of that he now turned over to the couple.[10]

Within days of his return to Fort Screven, Marshall was caught up in a New Deal measure for which he developed and retained a great enthusiasm all his life—the Civilian Conservation Corps. The plan to employ thousands of idle young men in planting trees and saving marginal land from flood and erosion had been outlined by Roosevelt in his acceptance speech at the

Democratic National Convention the previous July.[11] On March 21 he sent Congress a bill to create a CCC, predicting that two hundred and fifty thousand young men could be at work by summer.[12] When opposition developed on the ground that such camps would lead to militarism and undercut the wages of labor, Congress met the problem by passing a bill which permitted the President to define the program.

While the shape of the plan was still uncertain the new Secretary of War, George H. Dern, on March 25 sent his corps area commanders "merely warning instructions" that the War Department must be ready to take care of a hundred thousand men. The Army's role, he assumed, would be limited to enrolling the men selected by the Labor Department and transporting them to Army stations for organization into self-sustaining companies. They would be in Army care for four weeks at most and then would go on to their work in the woods under the supervision of some other federal agency.[13]

Fort Screven was presently notified that the IV Corps Area, of which it was a part, had a quota of seventy-one hundred trainees. That did not seem like a very big job though it was an urgent one. Marshall was informed that corps maneuvers were being canceled and that he should call back to the post his detachments that were already on their way to the maneuver area. The corps commander, Major General Edward L. King, expected to put all the trainees into four camps and told Marshall he would need from Screven only "some of your troops and organization to send to one or more of these camps to furnish personnel for handling." [14]

In fact he would need much more. The Army role, as described in the March 25 instruction, was enlarged as it became apparent to the directors of the program that only the Army was equipped to organize and operate the work camps. Orders went out on April 12 that the Army was to take charge of everything except the administration and technical supervision of the work projects. The War Department had already laid groundwork for its new task when early in 1933 it had studied a proposal by Senator James Couzens of Michigan to take over the "housing, feeding, and clothing of certain unemployed persons

at military posts in the United States." There had been little
enthusiasm for that kind of direct charity. The CCC was a good
deal more attractive. It was a chance for the regular Army to do
in peacetime something of what it was trained to do in war—
to mobilize, organize, and administer a civilian force. Since the
job clearly required not only all regular officers presently allotted but the addition of a great many reserve officers, whom
the War Department promptly called up, it should also discourage renewed proposals in Congress to slash military appropriations, including a fresh suggestion that four thousand officers
be lopped off the rolls. On May 10 President Roosevelt directed
the War Department to produce a plan for completing the movement of the two hundred and fifty thousand trainees into work
camps by July 1. General Drum, Deputy Chief of Staff under
General MacArthur, asked for orders for field commanders by
the following day. All that night, lights burned in the War Department as the staff went to work as if for war. (In the event,
corps area commanders were authorized wide discretion in
carrying out their tasks.)[15]

Marshall was to find that the CCC was to take most of his
own energies and most of the resources of his command. When
asked what he could spare for CCC work, he said, "Leave my
post surgeon, my commissary officer, my post-exchange office, and
my adjutant, and I will run this command with first sergeants." [16] Ultimately he had to do just that. The CMTC program at Fort Screven, which IV Corps Area decided to continue,
was handed over almost entirely to reserve officers who had arrived for training. From the moment in late April when Marshall
had word that a group of trainees was on its way to Fort Screven
from Jacksonville, Florida, he "ate, breathed, and digested the
many CCC problems," [17] as did the officers and noncoms of his
command.[18]

About two weeks after the accelerated CCC program was ordered, Marshall was named to command the 8th Infantry, with
a scheduled promotion to full colonel, which would actually
come through on September 1. Being already "deep in the complicated business of building camps in the Florida-Georgia
swamp areas, as well as running the big CCC camp here at Fort

Screven and getting ready to take on an increased size unit of five hundred CMTC boys June 13 with reserve officers to handle them," he asked that his transfer to 8th Infantry headquarters at Fort Moultrie, South Carolina, be delayed a month. Since his successor at Screven was not due until July 1 the delay was granted.[19]

Early in June he was made commanding officer of CCC District "F" of the IV Corps Area in charge of establishing some nineteen camps, the closest to his base being at Hinesville, Georgia, the most distant four hundred and fifty miles away in southern Florida. He visited them all on a four-day trip, June 14-18, and assured himself within a week of his return that all would be completed on schedule. He was then ready to report to Fort Moultrie.[20]

From the beginning of the year Marshall had known that he was in line for promotion and had been found qualified by the special board before which he appeared in December 1932. But he also was aware, as he told Pershing in January, that it would probably be months before a vacancy in colonel's grade could be found to which he could be assigned.[21]

In view of the fact that Marshall's career had so seldom put him in command of troops, it is a commentary on his broad competence that to his corps area commander, General King, it seemed that Marshall above all belonged with troops and should stay with them. When King read of Marshall's prospective promotion and reassignment he wrote to the Chief of Infantry, General Fuqua, to ask that the colonel be given a troop command. "Marshall's work at Fort Screven has been outstanding," King wrote, "and he is, as you know, of a very high type." It seemed to King, as it had to General Liggett in 1928 when he wrote Pershing, "Please don't forget Colonel Marshall, who ought to be a Brig-General right now," that the promotion system in his case had badly blundered. "For the work he did during the war, he should be much higher up." King suggested the Fort Moultrie command, which General Fuqua had already decided Marshall should have.[22]

After the assignment was made the Inspector General's report on Fort Screven for fiscal year 1933 was received in Washington.

It included a special commendation "to Lieutenant Colonel G. C. Marshall, 8th Infantry, for the efficient and economical administration of his duties and the high morale of his command." [23]

Savannah, whose friendliness the Marshalls had won, gave them a farewell dinner on June 26 at which the president of the Chamber of Commerce presented a field marshal's baton to the colonel dubbing him "Marshal of Savannah." It was a gay if somewhat wry promotion.[24] On the twenty-ninth Marshall assumed command of the 8th Infantry (including the detachment at Fort Screven) and he and his family began settling into the huge and rather dilapidated quarters there, for which Mrs. Marshall had to buy three hundred and twenty-five yards of curtaining to cover the forty-two French windows. Fort Moultrie, on Sullivan's Island three miles from Charleston, dated back to colonial days. In 1776, as Fort Sullivan, it had saved Charleston from capture. But in 1933 it was on the list of those posts which an economy-minded Congress felt might not be missed.

At Fort Moultrie, Marshall's work with the CCC continued. As the distances to be covered in his new district were not as great as in Georgia and Florida, he managed to visit each of the fifteen camps twice during July. His main efforts were aimed at his camp commanders before they actually reached their camps. Aware that for most of the commanders this was a new kind of assignment and that they would all be improvising solutions to a variety of human problems, Marshall warned above all against discouragement. His parting word was: "I'll be out to see you soon and if I find you doing something, I will help you, but if I find you doing nothing, only God will help you." [25] It became his practice to descend upon a camp about dawn, make a rapid physical survey, talk to some trainees and some officers, and then write sometimes pages of comment for the camp commander.[26] At one camp his early morning call found the commander and another officer still asleep. After rousing them with appropriate remarks, he went on to the supply room, where an embarrassed lieutenant at work in his undershirt sprang to attention and apologized for his undress. The colonel broke into one of his rare smiles. "You may not be in proper uniform," he said, "but you are the only officer I found working here." [27]

On the whole the Army did an effective job of launching the CCC. On June 30 Colonel Duncan K. Major, Jr., the War Department representative for the program, reported to the director of Emergency Conservation Work, Robert Fechner, that the Army had within the time limit set completed the processing of 275,000 men and organized 1330 companies and camps. He noted that the figure compared to 180,000 men mobilized in a similar period after the declaration of war in 1917.[28] Its size might also have been made more impressive by noting that the CCC trainees outnumbered the men in the regular Army by more than two to one. General MacArthur was delighted and personally dictated congratulations to be read at each post and station in the country. He called the handling of the CCC "a task of character and proportions equivalent of emergencies of war" and observed that "only a high morale, spirit of cooperation, pride of service, and devotion to duty could have accomplished such splendid results." Indeed, the success was generally recognized. General MacArthur was to have his term as Chief of Staff extended a year, largely as a result. There was no more talk about reducing the regular officer corps.[29]

Besides the satisfaction of the job, Marshall took considerable pleasure in the visible transformation of the young men in camp. From week to week he could see the underfed, slouching, undisciplined, truculent youngsters fill out and straighten up. Not all, of course. Some, drawn in particular from the big cities of New York and New Jersey, could not adjust either to country life or to authority and had to be released. It was essential to maintain discipline in the camps, but since the trainees were all volunteers discipline in the last resort could be enforced only by dismissal. If that was perhaps a weakness in the program, it was also the obvious counter to fears of militarism.[30]

Proud of the camps, Marshall seized opportunities to show them off to visitors. As a result the CCC played a part in entertaining the crew of the French cruiser *D'Entrecasteaux,* which visited Charleston in September 1933. Officers and men attended the dedication of a camp near Georgetown, South Carolina, named Camp Lafayette in memory of the French leader who had first landed in America near that spot. Crew members downed hot dogs, pie, and coffee with the boys of the CCC and *L'Illustration* covered it all for its readers in France.[31]

Some of the enthusiasm which Marshall felt at first hand for the work of human salvage helped carry him along in a general enthusiasm for the spirit of action and leadership shown by the New Deal. Indeed, in these early days the New Deal seemed to many who later opposed it a truly national effort. No partisan opposition had yet developed. If businessmen here and there doubted the wisdom of some of the first experiments, their objections were but softly and tentatively made. In the atmosphere of general acceptance Marshall publicly expressed his own approval. In speeches to local civic clubs he praised the CCC as "the greatest social experiment outside of Russia." He predicted the success of the NRA if only business and labor worked together. This was said at a time when the leaders of Charleston, including its mayor, Burnet Maybank, G. C. Buist Rivers, president of the Chamber of Commerce, General Summerall, president of the Citadel, and Admiral James J. Raby, commandant of the Navy Yard—all conservatives—were celebrating the creation of NRA.[32]

Marshall had been unusually scrupulous in the past, and would continue so, to avoid mixing in any way with party affairs or party issues. He would not even vote, and when no longer in uniform he still refused, as Truman's Secretary of State and Secretary of Defense, to contribute to the Democratic party campaign funds, speak at party meetings, or in any way lend his name or support to politicians seeking office. When the political euphoria of 1933 evaporated and the parties resumed their normal scrapping, Marshall's words could be—and by some people were—represented in retrospect as partisan. The suggestion made by a detractor years afterward that Marshall's rise to fame began with the enthusiasm he showed for the CCC and the program of the New Deal in 1933 had no substance, but it had just that superficial contact with fact that demonstrated the danger Marshall habitually took such precautions to avoid.

Marshall liked service with troops and work with the CCC. When his promotion came through in September he looked forward to a good two years as colonel of the regiment. He had managed to get some WPA help to refurbish the post and by the end of summer the old signs of dilapidation were disappearing. Mrs. Marshall brought down a van load of antique furniture from Baltimore, partly to furnish the colonel's roomy quarters. Then came the blow—orders to move. That was disappointment enough. But in addition the new assignment away from troops Marshall thought was a serious setback to his career: he was to go to Chicago as senior instructor with the Illinois National Guard. The Adjutant General attempted to soften the blow by writing that the War Department considered the position of great, perhaps critical, importance, that General MacArthur had recommended him highly, and that he understood some extra pay went with the job.[33] Marshall appealed directly to MacArthur. In a sympathetic reply the Chief of Staff explained why he believed a man of the colonel's talents was needed in Chicago and urged it as Marshall's duty to go.[34]

The commander of the Illinois National Guard Division (the 33d) was Major General Roy D. Keehn, attorney for the Hearst interests in Chicago, a man active in Democratic circles and a power in National Guard affairs. His division, under more or less running attack from Colonel McCormick's *Tribune*, had also drawn serious criticism in the summer of 1933 from the corps area inspectors, who faulted "the inadequate training of junior officers, noncommissioned officers, and specialists in their basic field duties." That criticism coincided with the end of the senior instructor's tour. Keehn wanted a first-rate replacement. When his first choice, Colonel W. K. Naylor, who had been chief of staff of the 33d Division in the war, was declared not available he asked for suggestions.[35] MacArthur ordered Major General Edward Croft, the Chief of Infantry, to list three or more colonels considered outstanding and suitable for the job. Croft knew Marshall's qualifications—only a few weeks before he had been asking the colonel for suggestions on improving Army training procedure. He included him on the list with a notation that Marshall himself preferred to stay where he was. MacArthur ignored the notation—not an unusual Army practice—and at once wired Marshall's name to Keehn in Chicago, urging his acceptance. "He has no superior among Infantry colonels," MacArthur wrote. "Have other names, if not satisfactory. He is of such outstanding ability, however, that I suggest you confer with General [Frank] Parker with reference to him before proceeding further with the matter." Keehn saw no need to proceed any further.[36]

As for Marshall, he remained unhappy. He appreciated the War Department's view that the Chicago post was important because of the danger of riots that the National Guard might have to deal with. "An anticipated internal situation this winter with the hungry and the striking coal miners," he wrote Pershing, "caused my selection." [37] Nevertheless he was not reconciled to going. A number of his friends shared his feeling that the assignment, by intention or not, put him off the main career road to high command in the Army. It seemed to them an injustice they were determined to correct if possible.

XVII

The First Star

"I am sure that you are destined to hold a very high place on the list of general officers before you reach the age of sixty-four."
—Pershing to Marshall, May 26, 1936.

CHICAGO did not cheer him up. Marshall was used to country living and always preferred it. But to be near his work at the National Guard headquarters in the Loop he and Mrs. Marshall took an apartment on the North Side—a thirty-minute walk away. Neither the walk nor the occasional game of tennis or squash at the Athletic Club nor the ride now and then in the armory reconciled him to the chafing confinement of the city. He had a wry vision of himself walking his Irish setter puppy in a vacant lot: "a very edifying sight," he wrote, "that proves how high-minded and seriously employed are colonels of infantry of the regular Army." [1]

Chicago was itself deep in depression. At the time Marshall arrived, a hundred and fifty thousand families in Cook County were out of work and in desperate plight.[2] The state legislature had adjourned without voting relief money, and the city treasury was so bare that for months teachers were not paid. Among the jobless there were rumblings of violence, and among financial and business leaders, signs of despair. The collapse of Samuel

283

Insull's utilities empire had pulled down banks throughout the Middle West. Those that survived were shaken by continuing business and speculative failures. The *Chicago Tribune* was running feature stories on financial debacles and bankers and businessmen who committed suicide in increasing numbers rather than face ruin. Marshall felt some of the personal impact of these tragedies through his old friend General Dawes, now chairman of the board of the City National Bank and Trust Company, Chicago. Concerned about him, Marshall wrote to Pershing that the newspaper stories "must open every wound." [3]

As the depression deepened, Army pay, already hit by the 1932 measure, was further reduced in the general 15 per-cent salary slash of government employees. The new legislation was particularly hard on the lower enlisted and junior-officer grades. Marshall prepared a spirited protest which he hoped one of the National Guard officers, a business executive, could use with politically influential friends. He submitted evidence to show that second lieutenants, after the depression cuts, were making substantially less than in 1908. Enlisted men through the loss of certain allowances were relatively even worse off. Yet these officers and men "must present a certain standard of appearance no matter how closely pressed they may be financially; they must accept the added expenses of moves and special service; they constitute the government's final backing in the event of grave emergencies; they must hazard their lives in the government service, with no chance of resigning if they do not care to serve. . . ." [4]

Marshall's sympathetic wish to help subordinates and old comrades deepened his sense of helplessness and frustration at his own failure to rise to a position of power. He continued to push—as he always had—the claims to advancement of bright young officers caught in the molasses of the Army's seniority system. He wrote so often to the Chief of Infantry to ask that certain Fort Benning graduates be assigned to the Command and General Staff School at Leavenworth that he feared the chief would "rightly" resent his importunities. On the same mission he often addressed his friend Major General Stuart Heintzelman, now commandant of Leavenworth. It irritated him that he had to plead with the Army to look out for its own best interests. He wrote a friend: "Whenever I am conniving to get these young fellows with genuine ability put in a suitable setting, I deplore the fact that I have not gained a position of sufficient power to do what I think should be done. I am awfully tired of seeing mediocrity placed in high positions, with brilliance and talent damned by lack of rank to obscurity. There are so many junior officers of tremendous ability whose qualities the service is losing all advantage of that it is really tragic." [5]

To some of these junior officers of tremendous ability he wrote urging on them such patience and faith as had sustained him through his own career and only now in his middle fifties threatened to wear thin. He told Lieutenant Lanham, later a distinguished regimental commander in Europe and a postwar assistant to Eisenhower at SHAPE, to "keep your wits about you and your eyes open; keep on working hard; sooner or later the opportunity will present itself, and then you must be prepared both tactically and temperamentally to profit by it." To Joseph Lawton Collins he wrote that the War Department would be "showing signs of real modernization when they reach down and pick you and several others of your stripe, which I imagine will be done, and shortly." [6]

Marshall's extraordinary zest and energy made him take his disappointments hard; it was as though he hit the roadblocks at full speed, looking and thinking far beyond them. Yet the same zest and energy made it impossible for him to remain long in a state of depression. Mrs. Marshall recalls that by Christmastime of 1933 he had lost that gray, drawn look that had worried her and began to recover his enthusiasm.[7]

He could already see improvement in the training of the 33d Division. He had begun by setting, both by order and example, a standard of military correctness and discipline. As usual there had been a flurry of alarm at the arrival of this new colonel, meticulously turned out in well-tailored uniform and shiny boots, a lean, tall, straight figure whose cold blue and seldom smiling eyes could make a man feel singularly silly and superfluous—a self-possessed officer who asked hard questions in his soft voice and from time to time relapsed into a cruelly disconcerting silence. One discovered quickly enough, moreover, that the manner was not put on for effect. The colonel was a taskmaster who in drill demanded smartness, promptness, and precision—the head-high military snap—and exact obedience to orders.

In time, however, the officers and men of the 33d Division learned that he was a disciplinarian on principle and not out of a martinet's love for giving orders. He was tough because he believed that the men wanted to belong "to a highly disciplined, hard-working, businesslike organization" they could be proud of and boast about. "The stricter the better," he said, "within the prescribed hours." At the same time he had no patience with the bureaucratic forms perhaps even more readily proliferated by volunteer than by professional groups.[8] He urged his officers to cut down paper work and fight against the tendency to over-elaborated, unrealistic drills. He tilted with the War Department over its formalisms, observing on one occasion that he had signed a report of a twenty-eight-dollar property loss twelve times and had counted twenty-eight other signatures on it.[9]

After hours Marshall became not easy and familiar but reflective, expansive. On his first visit to one of the Chicago regiments he was cool and businesslike while he observed the drill but afterward went with some of the officers to the Red Star Inn on Clark Street and there talked warmly about the record of the 33d Division in the war, its achievements and weaknesses, what he remembered himself and what he had learned as in effect the First Army's official historian. Not long afterward he and some of the Guard officers (chiefly those who were veterans of the 1st Division) were invited to a picnic at Colonel Robert R. McCormick's farm.[10] It is perhaps less remarkable that Marshall played in the scratch ball game after lunch than that his officers later thought the fact worth recalling.

That summer the federal inspectors found every unit of the division at least satisfactory—the first time in years that all had passed muster. The season's training ended with a division march, bivouac in Grant Park, and review on the Exposition grounds before thousands of visitors to the Century of Progress Fair, which continued in its second year to be a spectacular

popular success despite the depression. Shortly thereafter the
33d Division staff was ordered to Fort Monmouth, New Jersey,
to take part in a staff exercise to test a mobilization plan newly
worked out by the War Department. In the exercise itself
various corps and division staffs set up command posts in New
Jersey from which they prepared orders to defend against an
assumed enemy invasion of the Jersey coast.[11]

Marshall brought the exercise back with him to Illinois, mod-
ified it, and used it as the basis for the next year's training. He
assumed the area of enemy attack to be twelve square miles
between Camp Grant and Rockford. All winter he had the
division staff studying maps and issuing orders. In the spring
they worked through the problem on the ground. Without
money or other sinews of war—except imagination—they nevertheless went through the games with great enthusiasm. Mussolini, then on the verge of invading Ethiopia; Hitler, not many
more months from his defiant occupation of the Rhineland;
both within a year of testing their forces in real war in Spain,
would have been surprised, and perhaps even amused, at the
Guardsmen working out their problems.

"The right gun of every battery," Marshall wrote later,
"would be marked with a stake, the successive locations and
movements of special weapons would be traced; the [observa-
tion posts] would be checked and the wire calculated; the command posts would be sketched in exact detail; the exact location
of every kitchen, cart, dump, and what not, would be actually
determined. And all this between 10:00 A.M. and 1:30 P.M. of a
Sunday. . . . I have seen the cavalry officers go over the ground
involved in all the attacks and counterattacks of the [command
post exercise] with almost as much excitement as in a maneuver." Then, to finish off, Marshall in the final exercise assigned
different staffs to fourteen rooms in the Chicago armory and
himself from a central control room developed a single night's
action to which the staff had to respond with orders to troops.[12]

As the Illinois division developed in experience, its own
officers were able to take over a large part of the training from
the regular Army instructors. Marshall himself began to find a
little leisure time and to use part of it in a new venture for

him—supervising the editing of the division's house organ, the
Illinois Guardsman. Like many another editor, he coerced his
colleagues to contribute and drew on his friends—notably Lieutenant Colonel Harding, now editor of the *Infantry Journal*,
and Lieutenant Lanham on Harding's staff—for suggestions,
cuts, and reprints of articles. But even so he had frequently to
fill some of the pages himself. He wrote short accounts of
American battles of the past, compiled division gossip, wrote
copy to fit pictures the *Infantry Journal* sent him, and composed
a bit of humor, "Ducks and Drakes"—an anonymous account of
a duck hunt and poker game which Colonel Scott Lucas (newly
elected representative and later senator from Illinois) had
arranged for General Keehn, Marshall, and some of his staff.
Through the stiff and self-conscious prose one can glimpse, if
not share, the high spirits of the occasion in which allegedly
both ducks and farmers got the better of the party of "careless
city fellows." [13]

Busy now and successful, Marshall was mostly in good spirits.
General Dawes, cheered by the success of the exposition which he
and his brother had helped to underwrite, had recovered his
old dash and was holding small luncheons for important visitors
to the city. Marshall was a frequent guest, and his contacts
resulted in invitations to speak, which he accepted as opportunities to talk about the Guard, the citizen army, and urge its
support. Another old friend, Major General Frank McCoy, the
VI Corps Area commander, moved with his wife into an apartment across the hall from the Marshalls. McCoy, a close friend
of former Secretary of State Stimson, was widely known as a fine
soldier and one of the top diplomats of the Army. Onetime aide
to Leonard Wood (whose niece he had married), he had been
summoned in 1917 from his attaché's post in Mexico City by
Pershing to be a member of his staff in France. After commanding the 165th Infantry in the war, he had a succession of diplomatic assignments, the most recent of which was his service on
the League of Nations Commission to inquire into the Japanese
aggression against Manchuria in 1931. His international prominence would make him a strong contender for the post of Chief
of Staff in 1935. Marshall liked and admired him. McCoy "as a

friend and companion," Marshall wrote, "displayed qualities of charm and affection, cultivation, breadth of vision, and wide experience rare among men." [14]

Despite the attraction of the McCoys as neighbors, however, the Marshalls, after two years in the apartment, decided they had had enough of the city. They moved into a cottage thirty-eight miles to the west, near Wayne, Illinois. The daily train ride to town was made tolerable for the colonel by such National Guard companions as Chester Davis and William Spencer. Weekends he had a truck garden beside his back yard, a riding club nearby, a swimming pool and tennis court convenient, "gas, electric lights, eggs warm from the hen, and rich milk straight from the cow." [15]

Occasional glimpses one has of Marshall outside his work suggest that he was enjoying his new family. Clifton, Mrs. Marshall's oldest son, was in the real-estate business in Chicago; Molly, not yet married, was away during the second winter on a world tour, but the rest of the time she lived at home; Allen had entered the University of Virginia in 1934.

In the spring of 1935 Mrs. Marshall had to have an operation for which she went to an Army hospital in Arkansas. She spent the summer at Fire Island convalescing and apparently in good spirits. In June, Marshall, reporting on her progress to a friend, wrote that she was recovering nicely and that "as Allen has a job as lifeguard at thirty bucks a week, she not only has the interest of people around her and the sea to admire but she can gaze on his manly form as he sprints around keeping order and protecting life—very much set up because he has been sworn in as a deputy policeman and can make arrests." [16] Marshall was on Fire Island himself for three weeks at the end of a summer spent mainly with regimental and divisional exercises. To General Keehn, recuperating from an automobile wreck in which he lost his right arm, he reported that the division had improved in all respects over the preceding year and that the men at last understood the importance of severity in training.[17]

So two years passed pleasantly enough from day to day, despite the continuing deep frustration of being where he believed he was off the track, if not out of the running, for high position

in the Army. The third year was much the same. All during it
he pointed the training program toward the Second Army maneuvers which were to take place in August 1936 and, as it
happened, would mark the climax of his own tour and its welcome conclusion.

The year 1936 brought war in Europe perceptibly closer.
Hitler and Mussolini were already skirmishing along the road,
proclaiming their ambition for empire. Mussolini, having attacked Ethiopia in October 1935, ignored without difficulty the
League of Nations' economic sanctions and got on with his
clumsy but ruthless conquest. The system of collective security,
rejected by America at the outset, breached by Japan in its
invasion of Manchuria in 1931, collapsed in 1936. Hitler, recognizing his opportunity, marched into the demilitarized Rhineland in the spring. In midsummer civil war in Spain would
provide Hitler, Mussolini, and Stalin a bloody maneuver ground
on which to test their developing military machines.

By contrast America's war games belonged to another world.
The Second Army, which was to conduct the 1936 maneuvers,
did not exist—except on paper. The part of Army headquarters
was played by VI Corps command under Major General Kilbourne, a VMI classmate of Stuart Marshall, who had just replaced General McCoy. The original plan had been to concentrate troops of both VI and V Corps Areas, but the War
Department found it could not afford the extensive troop movements that would have been required. The maneuvers, therefore,
were split in two: V Corps assembled near Fort Knox; VI
Corps in Michigan between Camp Custer and Allegan. The
Michigan maneuvers involved more than two thousand officers and twenty-four thousand men of the 32d and 33d Division
together with attached troops and some regular Army units.
They lasted two weeks.

Marshall found them unusually useful; he wrote a friend that
he had "never learned more in my life in a similar period of
time." What he learned—or more accurately what he found
confirmed—was the impracticality of much of the current technique and theories. Particularly he was impressed with the way
higher headquarters deluged combat units with detailed orders
and reports. He himself commanded the chief "enemy" force,

the 12th Brigade, in the exercises and found that he spent a good part of his time "with the troops protecting them against my own staff." He wrote that "the sight of paper inflames me. So many officers never seem happy unless they have pages of highly paragraphed something or other." [18] The complaint was against current doctrine, not against the caliber of the officers he worked with. He considered that two headquarters staff members, the G-3, a friend from China and Benning, Major Ridgway, and Major George P. Hays, later a division commander in World War II, turned in "perfect" jobs.[19] His own staff in the maneuvers were all reserve officers who had never seen him or each other until they arrived on the ground to cope with the movement of some six thousand troops, under almost every conceivable handicap. "We lacked everything," Marshall wrote later, "and were given seemingly every possible administrative and supply responsibility, in addition to the tactical requirements. We covered sixty miles of country in a campaign against twenty thousand troops. These reserve officers did a beautiful job. . . ." [20]

One unexpected handicap was the hostility of the natives. Farmers in the area joined the war as irregulars, gave false directions to the Red (enemy) Force and even erected barricades to hinder his advance. Since Blue Force's defense was admittedly "designed primarily to head off our senior instructor who commanded the enemy 12th Brigade," [21] it is not surprising that Marshall narrowly escaped capture on several occasions.

Over this hostile country the invading forces flew a single reconnaissance plane. Its pilot was a reserve officer, E. A. Goff, Jr., who had been flying since 1916 but never on this sort of mission. As he could not read maps or identify objects from the air, his information required some interpretation. Spotting a detachment of motorized field artillery on the road, he radioed back that he saw some trucks pulling wheelbarrows. A cloud of dust disappearing into a wood, Marshall concluded, meant a motorcycle courier. When Goff flew over a cavalry unit he reported, "I see one, two, three, five, six, eight horses moving in a northeasterly direction." Marshall thereafter twitted him as the "officer that counts the horses." [22]

One could not fault the spirit of the troops, and Marshall did not. The very unmilitary mind of Pilot Goff, moreover, had endearing overtones of Yankee ingenuity and of the "hurriedly assembled hosts of democracy." But the professionals in the circumstances could not help being impressed with the very serious military weaknesses which the exercises revealed—or rather underscored. General Kilbourne's report—just three years before the unveiling of German "blitzkrieg"—paid particular attention to the power of mechanized forces, commanded by Colonel Bruce Palmer and his executive, Lieutenant Colonel William Crittenberger, in the attack. "Unless effectively opposed," the General concluded, "mechanized forces can not only open the way to the occupation of key positions in the warfare of movement, but can disrupt communications, interfere with supply, tap lines of signal communication." Furthermore, armor in defense was capable of spoiling an offensive "by rapid movements threatening in succession many vital points" and so compelling the attacker to divert troops from the main effort.[23] Less attention was given in the report to the role of the airplane, but it was notable that planes operated regularly from Chanute Field in weather which formerly would have grounded them and that a special bomber flight from far-off Langley Field simulated an air attack on the Allegan airport.[24]

Five days after the maneuver was completed and the troops sent home, Marshall had a letter from the War Department that resolved a long unhappiness. It notified him of his appointment as brigadier general, effective October 1. He would presently receive a new assignment. The letter arrived the day Mrs. Marshall was coming home from a visit to Canada. Hoping to surprise her with an announcement in appropriate style, he was just getting set when the telephone rang and Mrs. Marshall answered, heard the voice at the other end ask for General Marshall. So the new General was deprived of a small moment of drama, but nothing could detract from the real sense of triumph and gratification.

That star, almost within grasp eighteen years before in France, had been long and hard in coming. The reasons were as complicated and as difficult to evaluate precisely as were the cross-weaving of influence and cut-and-dried seniority rules which composed the Army's baffling promotion system. Almost from the beginning of his career Marshall had been tabbed time after time as an officer destined to become a general. There was never any doubt that the star would eventually be his. What was uncertain—and what made both Marshall and his friends rail against the system—was whether it would come in time to permit him to compete for higher command positions, including Chief of Staff of the Army. The principle was firmly established that no one would be considered for appointment as Chief of Staff who did not have at least four years to serve before retirement. In 1930 when Marshall himself suggested submitting the name of General Hanson Ely, who was only a year away from retirement, Pershing wrote that the President was unlikely to change the established rule.[25] In 1930 when President Hoover appointed General MacArthur, he considered as eligible for the job only the two lowest-ranking major generals on the list. To serve four years Marshall would have to be appointed by 1940. He believed that in order to be in the competition he would have to have his second star. That in turn meant that the first had to come early enough for him to acquire seniority among the brigadier generals.

Less than a year after his name was first put on the eligibility list, at the end of 1933, Marshall heard from two friends who were also among the highest-ranking generals in the Army: General Moseley, commanding the corps area headquarters at Atlanta, and General Hagood, corps commander at San Antonio. They wrote to say that they had seized the opportunity during a recent visit of Secretary of War Dern to their headquarters to urge George Marshall's name for promotion. Marshall sent copies of these letters to Pershing, noting that they were unsolicited. In his own accompanying letter he revealed his impatience. "Two or three vacancies now exist," he wrote. "I want one of them as I will soon be fifty-four. I must get started if I am going to get anywhere in this Army." He wanted that start badly but he was nevertheless reluctant to appear to be scrambling for it. He preferred to be judged on his record but asked Pershing to make sure that Secretary Dern looked at it. "I am determined not to use political influence in my effort to be recognized and I do not want to follow the usual course of writing to a number of senior officers soliciting letters from them. . . . I am prepared to gamble on my written record in the War Department before, during, and after the war, for I have been told no one else in the list of colonels can match mine." [26]

That was quite probably true; at least his efficiency reports had uniformly rated him as an exceptional officer. There was irony in the fact that he had now to use influence to bring his recognized merits to the attention of an authority that could act on them.

The irony echoed the confusion in the system in which the principle of promotion in turn according to length of service was never reconciled with the principle that the best officers ought to be selected out as rapidly as possible for top command and staff positions. In practice an officer's efficiency reports, which recorded his performance as judged successively by his superiors, could bar promotion if they were poor but could not often, by being good, secure advancement out of turn. When exceptions were made to the rule of promotion by seniority, they were made most often by the direct intervention of a general or sometimes a political leader in position to exert the necessary pressure in the proper places. Such exceptions had brought Pershing and MacArthur into top rank ahead of their colleagues. They were, however, more common in war or the immediate aftermath of war than in the relaxed stretches between, when few civilians concerned themselves about a soldier's merit and when the War Department itself was normally trying to absorb more high-ranking officers than its always shrinking budget provided places for.

The often repeated story that Marshall's promotion was held up by General MacArthur because of differences between them dating back to World War I is not borne out by the record at any point. The truth seems to be that MacArthur was reluctant to listen to Marshall's claims only as he was reluctant to listen to all claims that required setting aside promotion by seniority, perhaps because of the resentment aroused by his own spectacular jump up the ladder. For whatever reason, he preferred

not to seem to play favorites and chose to risk the inequities of
the seniority system. These were glaring and damaging. One of
the most obvious was that a senior colonel who barely made the
eligibility list for general by split vote of the board moved along
ahead of others like Marshall, who not only had the unanimous
recommendation of his board but virtually the unanimous recommendation of everybody in the Army who knew him well
enough. Seniority thus worked striking anomalies. Marshall
told Pershing he had "had the discouraging experience of
seeing the man I relieved in France as G-3 of the Army promoted
years ago, and my assistant as G-3 of the Army similarly advanced six years ago. I think I am entitled to some consideration
now." [27]

It is not clear what, if any, steps Pershing took immediately,
but in the spring of 1935 he spoke to both Secretary Dern and
President Roosevelt. "General Pershing asks very strongly that
Colonel George C. Marshall (Infantry) be promoted to general," Roosevelt wrote to his Secretary of War. "Can we put him
on the list of next promotions?" [28]

Alas, apparently they could not. Dern's reasons are not on
record. Probably he told the President of MacArthur's plan to
put Marshall in as the next Chief of Infantry, a post that carried
the rank of temporary major general but which would not be
vacant for several years. In any case the decision was to do nothing for the present. When Marshall got Pershing's report he
wrote: "I can but wait, grow older, and hope for a more favorable
situation in Washington." [29]

Pershing did not give up. He talked to the President and
Secretary of War without success. He discussed the matter "a
good many times" with General MacArthur but found the Chief
of Staff apparently set on holding Marshall for the post of Chief
of Infantry. In August, Pershing wrote an old friend, John
Callan O'Laughlin, onetime Assistant Secretary of State under
Theodore Roosevelt, more recently an official of the Republican
National Committee, and publisher of the influential *Army and
Navy Journal*. Marshall, Pershing said, "will never turn his hand
to help himself, and I cannot blame him for that, but he is
such an outstanding man that I am going to ask you to put in a

good word for him if you have the opportunity." [30] O'Laughlin found an opportunity within the next few weeks to talk with the Chief of Staff and reported to Pershing in Paris. MacArthur still thought Marshall should wait for the Chief of Infantry opening, which might not be long in coming since the incumbent was ill and might soon resign. Nevertheless, in deference to Pershing's wishes, he had recommended Marshall for promotion to brigadier general in the next list after Secretary of War Dern returned in January from the Philippines.[31]

On that information Pershing wrote to Marshall on October 4 to say that "the Chief had still intended to make you Chief of Infantry but as no one knows when the vacancy will occur, I told him that you would prefer to be in the line, and so it will be done, at least that is the plan at present." [32] But both Pershing's report and the commitment had been made ambiguous by the appointment two days before (October 2) of Malin Craig as Chief of Staff.[33]

MacArthur, who had headed the Army for five years, had accepted an offer to command the defense forces of the newly created Commonwealth of the Philippines. While he, of course, anticipated the change at the time he talked to O'Laughlin and knew that Craig was to be his successor, he had understood that Roosevelt would not formally replace him until after he arrived in Manila. To his surprise the announcement was in fact made before he left the country, purportedly because the President was uneasy about having both the Secretary of War and the Chief of Staff out of the country at the same time. It is possible, though not clear, that this change in procedure interfered with the plan to put Marshall's name on the list of promotions.

Marshall, on receiving Pershing's letter dated after the announcement of Craig's appointment, assumed that the "Chief" pledged to his cause was Craig.[34] He had some reason to believe that this represented just the "favorable situation" in Washington to which he had looked forward. Craig was the same cavalry officer whose troop nearly thirty years before had contributed one horse to Lieutenant Marshall so that he might map a piece of Texas desert. Since that time he had known Craig during

the war when Craig served on Hunter Liggett's staff in the 41st
Division and I Corps, and afterward when both were members
of Pershing's staff. The year before his nomination as Chief of
Staff, Craig had been a member of the board that recommended
George Marshall for promotion to brigadier general and on that
occasion was reported to have remarked that a proper promotion
system would assure that officers of Marshall's caliber were made
generals. Craig apparently complained to Secretary Dern about
the quality of many of the senior colonels who were being promoted and said that Marshall in his view should have the next
appointment.

So it was with especially bitter disappointment that, in mid-
December, Marshall received a warning from Pershing that
Craig was not finding it easy "to overturn an established practice
of appointing dead timber to the high positions." In fact Marshall was not on the next list, and two days after Christmas he
wrote in darkest vein to Pershing: "I have possessed myself in
patience, but I'm fast getting too old to have any future of importance in the Army. This sounds pessimistic, but an approaching birthday—December 31—rather emphasizes the growing
weakness of my position." [35] He would be fifty-five. Contrasting the many years of frustration with the few years remaining, he could hardly avoid profound discouragement. Friends
were better able to see that while time was short there was still
time enough.

One friend, Colonel Campbell Hodges, accompanied Secretary
Dern to the Philippines in late 1935 and took the occasion to
urge not only that Marshall be given a star at once but that he
be considered for the next appointment as Chief of Staff.
Hodges made a precise calculation of the prospects and spelled
them out in a letter to Marshall: "If you should be the next
brigadier general made, you would reach major general in 1939
or 1940. Assuming that every brigadier general with at least one
year to serve (omitting those already jumped) is promoted in
his turn, you would get Stone's vacancy, August 1940; if they
adopt a 'two-years-to-serve' rule for brigadier in order to be
promoted to major general, you would get Craig's vacancy in
1939, and MacArthur, Drum, DeWitt, Rowell, and yourself,

would be the only major generals with four years to serve. Spalding will not get two stars under either a 'one-year-to-serve' or a 'two-years-to-serve' rule. . . . General Drum seems like logical man for next Chief of Staff, but as he [Drum] remarked —anything can happen in four years." [36]

In April 1936, when Secretary Dern came to Chicago to make the Army Day speech, General McCoy and General Herron saw that the Secretary and Marshall had a chance to talk. A month later Pershing reported that Marshall was "positively and definitely" on the September list of brigadier generals. He had attempted to get his former aide promoted ahead of the others in his group in order that he would have a better chance for his second star, but this had proved impossible. He assured Marshall, however, that the men ahead of him were all older men and would not be in the way. Despite all the delays, he added, "I am sure that you are destined to hold a very high place on the list of general officers before you reach the age of sixty-four." [37]

If Dern, as the result of various pressures, placed Marshall's name on the list in May, it was one of the last things he did as an active Secretary of War. By June he was so ill that he could not attend cabinet meetings and by late July his condition was critical. He died on August 24 as the proposed list of brigadier generals containing Marshall's name, signed by Acting Secretary of War Harry H. Woodring, went forward to the President.[38]

The extraordinary fact is that all the pressure exerted over a three-year period in Marshall's behalf, coupled with the unusual excellence of his own record, resulted in his promotion just one month before he would almost certainly have had it merely by coming to the top of the eligibility list.[39] At the time Secretary Woodring acted, six colonels eligible for promotion were senior to Marshall. As the man just ahead of him had made the list by a three-to-two vote of the eligibility board whereas Marshall had had a unanimous recommendation, the Acting Secretary of War proposed that Marshall should have the sixth vacancy.[40] While this was recognition of a sort, the two men who followed Marshall on the eligible list were promoted, as he presumably would have been, next month, on the list of November 1, 1936. Marshall was pleased, of course, to have made it at last, but not optimistic. The first star had come too late to give him any advantage in the competition for two.

XVIII

Back on Course

"You have a record and reputation which will insure that you are one of those who will be considered in the selection of the next Chief of Staff."
—Major General George S. Simonds to Marshall, February 14, 1938.

SOON after receiving notice of his promotion Marshall took leave and with his wife went east, traveling by boat from Detroit to Buffalo. They attended a house party in Vermont, a wedding in Exeter, visited the McCoys in New York, stayed in Mrs. Marshall's cottage on Fire Island, stopped off in Washington, and then headed back to Chicago by way of Uniontown.[1] The new general had few ties left with his hometown but he did find his old chum, Andy Thompson, still there, prospering now in business and prominent in state politics. George and Andy talked of their childhood, conscious of being middle-aged strangers who inexplicably had memories in common. This was the last time they met. Andy and his brother, John, died on October 18, 1938, three days after Marshall became Deputy Chief of Staff of the Army.

In Chicago at the end of September, Marshall got orders to his new post. He was to command the 5th Brigade of the 3d Division, stationed in Vancouver Barracks, Washington, and to

supervise the CCC camps in the district, which included Oregon
and part of Washington. He decided to drive west, but not in
the old Ford that had been worn out in the service of the colonel.
After a convivial tour of automobile agencies in company of two
friends, the General came home with a new Packard.[2]

Early in October he set out with Mrs. Marshall and Molly
across country in the new Packard. They were in no hurry.
For three weeks Marshall indulged his taste for sightseeing and
history. As they toured he drew from his memory tales of the
frontier and of Indian wars, in which he had always taken a
special pleasure.[3]

It pleased him to find his new post both drenched in history
and superbly located in lovely country. He wrote to General
Keehn in Chicago: "Vancouver Barracks is one of the old
historic outposts of the Army. Established in 1849 on the site of
a Hudson Bay Company station, the traces of whose lookout
station are still discernible in a tall fir tree, for more than fifty
years it was the center for the development of the Northwest.
General Grant's log quarters are a part of the present post
library building. Phil Sheridan left here a lieutenant to start
his meteoric rise to fame. Pickett was a member of the garrison.
My quarters were occupied by a succession of Civil War celeb-
rities or Indian fighters. General Miles built the house, which
was later occupied by Canby, Crook, Gibbon, and Pope.[4]

". . . Giant fir trees ornament the parade; every yard has its
holly trees and a profusion of shrubs. The original apple tree of
the Northwest, planted in the yard of the old trading post, still
lives and is carefully fenced against possible harm.[5] In my yard
is a cherry tree of reported antiquity, with three grafted varieties
of the fruit. All in delightful contrast to the institution-like
appearance of many Army posts.

"The Columbia River, bordering our aviation field (we have
four planes) in extension of the parade, emerges from its
famous gorge a few miles above the post. In the distance the
symmetrical cone of Mount Hood stands covered with snow,
summer or winter."

On the new general's arrival there was inevitably a military
formation, though he had asked that there be no formal review.

There was also his Irish setter, Pontiac, whom at risk to his dignity he had faithfully walked in the vacant lots of Chicago and who now, despite the formality of the occasion, jumped all over him. And there to salute and shake his hand was the acting commander of Vancouver Barracks, commanding officer of the 7th Infantry, stationed there, Colonel Hossfeld, who thirty-four years before had served with a fellow shavetail in Calapan in the Philippines.[6]

Marshall was back with troops; back on the main road of his career again. The next twenty months were to be as happy as any he had spent in the Army. But they began with a blow that almost ended his career. At Fort Benning he had been bothered by an irregular pulse which was diagnosed as due to a malfunctioning thyroid. By careful treatment the trouble had been brought under control, but in Chicago, just before he headed west, it flared up again. He underwent tests in Vancouver, and it was decided to send him to a hospital in San Francisco in December. He stayed a month recuperating from an attack of flu and then underwent an operation in which a diseased lobe of the thyroid gland was successfully removed.[7]

Anxious lest reports of ill health block the newly opened career road, he said as little as possible about the nature of his illness and even about the fact that he was being operated on. He had not even written to General Pershing, who received the news from other sources with "quite a shock." [8] Actually Marshall scarcely exaggerated the dangers of rumor. It was in fact said in Washington even the next year that he was seriously ill. By that time, however, the gossip was demonstrably without basis. His recovery had been rapid and he was returned quickly to full duty by a board of medical officers.[9] Thereafter he himself closely watched for any telltale variations in his pulse beat and kept Colonel Stayer, his old doctor from Fort Benning, informed. He had stopped smoking shortly before he left Chicago, and now he made more of a point than ever of taking regular and conspicuous exercise. To his customary early morning horseback rides, he added tennis, hunting, fishing, and a little golf, indulging in these sports as often as he could.[10] No doubt the exercise was good for him and it forestalled any talk that he might be approaching decrepitude.

Typically Marshall's own career difficulties made him particularly sympathetic to other officers in similar trouble and alert to help them. As he tried to rescue bright young officers from the seniority mills, so he sought to save those threatened by unimaginative application of physical-fitness regulations. It was while at Vancouver Barracks that he intervened to keep in service a highly capable second lieutenant, Charles E. G. Rich, of the 7th Infantry, who was discovered to be color blind. "He is far too good to lose," Marshall wrote, "and, in my military opinion, it would be a distinct loss to the government—while some slow-witted fellow who knows 'Alice blue' is kept on." [11] Rich, saved for the Army, vindicated Marshall's judgment and became subsequently a division commander and commandant of the Infantry Training Center at Fort Benning.

On recovering from his operation Marshall threw himself vigorously into the things he liked best to do, organizing and training men. The principal body of troops at Vancouver Barracks was the 7th Infantry. Its administration Marshall left almost entirely to its commander, Colonel Hossfeld, and later Colonel Ralph Glass, keeping hands off just as he did with the other regiment of the brigade, the 4th Infantry, stationed at Fort Missoula, Montana.[12] As he had found at Forts Screven and Moultrie, overseeing the CCC took a large part of his time. The CCC activities came under a separate headquarters. Routine brigade business was handled by his brigade executive, the first of whom was Colonel Walton H. Walker, later commander of the XX Corps in World War II and of the Eighth Army in Korea. Able assistants similarly relieved him of the daily CCC routine.[13] His own job, as he conceived it and carried it out, was to see for himself in the field how the men under him fared and how their work was going and to take such corrective steps as he found necessary. He set the training policies for troops and directed the exercises in which these policies were tested. He concerned himself minutely with the human details of his command but scarcely at all with the organizational paper work, except to continue his passionate fight against it.[14]

"Every time I turn my back," he wrote in 1938, "some staff officer calls on some poor devil for a report or an extra copy for some more damned papers—and I will not have it. I am off for

maneuvers next week, and I am not going to allow a mimeograph machine in the war." [15]

Marshall made his principal impact as a man who in a great
variety of baffling human situations always seemed to know just
what to do. At Christmas the post chaplain, Martin C. Poch,
whom Marshall called an "excellent" officer "who did tremen-
dously fine work," came to him with a problem. Although enlisted men were not supposed to get married without permission
of their commanding officers, inevitably some had. Now the
chaplain wished to include these men in the distribution of
holiday packages to families. But when the regimental commander got wind of the scheme he asked for the names of all
men on the chaplain's list. Chaplain Poch decided to appeal to
General Marshall even though he realized that if Marshall over-
rode the regimental commander Poch's own position henceforth
would be very difficult.

Marshall proceeded by indirection. At a party one evening, in
the presence of the colonel of the regiment, he said casually,
"I understand they are having a Christmas basket drive for the
men who are married without permission and the chaplain is in
charge and I think it is a very, very fine thing to do this
Christmastime. . . . Mrs. Marshall and I are not asking who
[they are]." So the colonel, instead of having his orders counter-
manded, was simply relieved of responsibility for making a report he perhaps did not wish to make anyway.[16]

It was not a question of softening discipline but of providing
help where it was needed and providing it "in a dignified
manner." Yet where children were concerned, at least, there was
always with Marshall something more. The son of a sergeant
on the base, who had had polio in infancy, grew up with one
leg so much shorter than the other that he could "hardly walk
back and forth to school." Since no military hospital was prepared to take care of him the chaplain approached the Shriner's
Hospital in Seattle. There he was told that they could help
but unfortunately the waiting list was so long that it would be
many months. Poch reported to Marshall and asked if the General would write a letter. As Poch related the story: "He told
me he would not write the letter, which didn't seem like him

at all. Then he told me he would not let me write it, nor would he sign it; and when I was groping for an answer and then looked at him, there was a smile on his face and he said, 'I'm going up there myself.' " [17]

He had the true commander's devotion to his command—to its welfare, its effectiveness, and its standing. So he took care of his men, worked at their training—there were two sets of maneuvers in his first year, division exercises in May 1937, and Fourth Army exercises in August—and busied himself with the physical condition of the post. He was vigorous and successful in raising money for improvements—in two years getting some two hundred and fifty thousand dollars for "an elaborate program of rehabilitation" from both the War Department and the State of Washington. His energy and humanity generally kept morale high. During his command the regular Army units at Vancouver Barracks had the best re-enlistment rate in the corps area.[18]

As commander of an important post he was a notable personality in the community. He accepted with enthusiasm, as he had at Forts Screven and at Moultrie, the obligation to live harmoniously and co-operatively with the civilian society. In that, he was helped by an old and warm friendship with the governor of Oregon, retired General Charles H. Martin (Portland was just eight miles away across the river). Martin gave him entrée into Portland political and social circles that Marshall's predecessor had found "standoffish." But Marshall also put himself out to develop the friendliest ties, personally and officially, with political and business leaders. He staged military displays at the post for the community and he made the band and troops available for civic celebrations. He himself accepted scores of speaking engagements in which, wary of political implications, he talked about the Army, work with the CCC, and his own recollections. He was popular enough so that by the end of the first year he was ruefully conscious of being too often on his feet "talking for my supper." Yet he thought it worth while nevertheless, because there had been "so little contact in the past between the post and the people of Portland and other points in the state of Oregon. . . ." As to the personal risks of loquacity, he added, "Eventually, I will get my foot off the base, but I hope to cool down on this business before that time occurs." [19]

It is not likely that at this time he would have expressed excessive enthusiasm for the New Deal. Although he continued in wholehearted approval of the CCC, he was critical in private letters of some of the work projects and sympathetic with Governor Martin's efforts to curb activities of some of the labor unions—efforts that made the governor unpopular with many state and national Democratic leaders.

About six months after he arrived Marshall, waiting for breakfast one Sunday morning (it was June 20), read in his newspaper of the flight of three Russians, Valeri P. Chkalov, Georgi P. Baidukov, and Alexander V. Beliakov, from Moscow over the North Pole. The three had taken off in a single-engine monoplane two days before and were expected momentarily to touch down in Oakland, California. Actually, as the General was presently informed, the plane was then overhead and about to land at Pearson Field south of the parade ground of Vancouver Barracks, almost literally in his front yard. The Russians would be in time for breakfast. Marshall promptly ordered it and then went out to the field to greet his unexpected and already world-famous visitors.[20]

At about eight-thirty the three fliers, dirty and exhausted from their long, record-making flight, were brought to Marshall's quarters for baths, breakfast, and sleep in approximately that order, though as it turned out they were served food while still in their baths. While the fliers slept, Marshall found a good part of the world converging at his door. Soviet Ambassador Alexander A. Troyanovsky came up from Oakland, where he had planned to greet the Soviet heroes. Newspapermen who had congregated in Portland, photographers, and radio reporters were on hand within a half-hour and demanding to see the fliers. With a brusqueness that some reporters called "testy" the General announced that for the present the airmen would not be disturbed. Soldiers were on guard at the staircase and in front of the bedroom door upstairs. One of the radio networks appealed to the IX Corps Area commander and to the Chief of Staff, but Marshall was left in control and afterward congratulated on his handling of the matter. In fact he was cooperating but in accord with his own sense of fitness. He set up a news room in his study, brought in several telephones, and made his living room available for broadcasts by the Russians. When a planeload of hungry, tired reporters arrived from Oakland, Mrs. Marshall won their good will and notice in papers throughout the country by supplying a ham, bread, and a huge GI pot of coffee.

Meanwhile, to outfit the fliers, who had brought only their flying clothes, Marshall called the owner of the Meier and Frank Department Store in Portland, Mr. Julius Meier, and with his permission sent an Army truck to pick up twenty suits, pairs of shoes, shirts and underwear from which the men could pick what fit them. Two tailors were corralled and the post barber set up in the orderly's room.

On Monday, Governor Martin, Marshall, and the Soviet Ambassador led the fliers on an impromptu parade through the streets of Portland to a hastily arranged welcoming luncheon. The Chamber of Commerce "threw its ideological predilections completely out of the window" and plastered the walls of the banquet room with Soviet flags. The speeches were generous and friendly, though Marshall spoke for no more than thirty seconds, observing, according to the *Oregonian,* that this had been "a most interesting experience for the United States Army." The *Oregonian* itself, though conservative, was warm in praise of the Russians, yielding them "a nonpartisan admiration" and concluding "there is still fine material in the race of man." [21]

It is an interesting fact about Marshall's career, especially after his return from China, that he was thrown so much with civilians—the CMTC, National Guard, organized Reserves, and CCC at Benning, Screven, Moultrie, Chicago, and Vancouver Barracks. It is a significant fact about the man that he welcomed these contacts. From long, varied, and sustained experience with citizen soldiers he drew his faith in the value and effectiveness of a citizen army. From the same experience he became familiar with the civilian point of view in a way rare among professional military men. A member of his staff later commented that "he had a feeling for civilians that few Army officers . . . have had. . . . He didn't have to adjust to civilians—they were a natural part of his environment. . . . I think he regarded civilians and military as part of a whole." [22]

At Vancouver Barracks, Marshall spent a large proportion of his time on CCC matters. Because the heavily forested Northwest provided abundant opportunities for conservation, boys from all over the country were drawn into camps in this area. Marshall had under his supervision never less than twenty-seven camps in Oregon and southern Washington, many in wild country difficult of access, especially in the months of spring flooding. "To reach a large section of my district in eastern Oregon," he wrote, "I must traverse the Columbia River gorge, finally emerging from the dense green of the vegetation of the damp near-coastal region into the typical barrens of the dry western plains. In winter one passes, within a mile, from overcast skies, fog or rains, into the glare of cloudless skies. It is possible now, with the spring flowers blooming, to motor an hour and a half from here to the skiing slopes of Mount Hood. Oregon is a region of contrasts." And so were the camps themselves with their miscellaneous human gleanings for salvage. Marshall continued: "The CCC companies are a source of great interest. Near Pendleton, the scene of the famous annual 'round up' or rodeo, is a company of Boston boys. Under Beacon Rock— except for Gibraltar, the largest monolith in the world—is a group of young fellows from the swamp regions of Arkansas. Providence, Rhode Island, has a company near Tillamook on the shore of the Pacific. Their road sign reads, 'Tillamook 18 miles. Providence, R.I., 3100.' We have groups from New York, Connecticut, New Jersey, Ohio, Kentucky, Minnesota, and the Dakotas." [23] And later companies were sent up from Tennessee with boys drawn from a number of southern and border states.

Marshall was fascinated by the possibilities CCC offered for developing solid, useful human beings. He said long afterward that he wished he could have been the national director. If he had been, he would have introduced some military training and discipline, which he felt would have brought up a generation better prepared for citizenship. Don Mace, his district educational adviser, recalled that at their first meeting Marshall said he wanted them to become men first, and after that employables[24]—an echo, perhaps, of the philosophy of VMI and a reflection of his own appreciation of the discipline he believed he learned there.

The need for discipline could be adduced from scores of incidents in his own district: one group had tossed a major into the river; another had stolen a sheep and cooked it; another threw stones at the flag from the mess line; another traded supplies to the girls in a nearby village.[25] And their ordinary bearing betrayed varying degrees of indifference or rebellion, mostly normal enough in boys largely underprivileged, largely educated in the individualist if not anti-social mores of big-city streets, and suddenly removed to Spartan communities in the remote wilderness. Marshall wrote: "When an eighteen-year-old can sit on the small of his back with his feet on the table during an inspection, you can see how far we have to go." [26]

With the ordinary methods of military discipline foreclosed by law, camp commanders had to discover indirect ways to establish control. One appointed a former Portland street gang-leader as his first sergeant; another picked as his informal executive "a black-eyed Irishman who had been runner-up in the Golden Gloves tournament." [27] When in February 1938, at Camp Brothers, Oregon, thirty-seven boys refused to work, the camp commander ordered them discharged. Marshall upheld the action but he observed nevertheless that, as in most such cases, the final blow-up was brought on essentially by poor handling of men in very difficult situations. The Oregon mutineers were New York and New Jersey boys set down in a new campsite in bad weather fifty-six miles from a town of any importance.[28] This was one of the Grazing Service camps which were always "in the most desolate country, far from streams and lakes, usually with a dearth or complete absence of trees, and almost always with a large population of snakes, desert insects, and other unpleasant residents of such regions." [29]

Marshall worked to remove the causes of rebellion. Against the advice of his staff and with only the reluctant approval of corps headquarters he appointed three sub-district commanders to assist him in inspecting and improving camps. He stipulated that they should have no headquarters and make no written reports except a rough diary once a week and a telephone message three times a week. They were to go where they liked when they liked, with "their guiding mission . . . to raise the standard of poor camps to that of the best.[30] In addition they established command posts to co-ordinate fire fighting when needed and organized informal schools for clerks, cooks, and bakers. Marshall defended this delegation of authority as "the very bedrock of any military organization," provided only that it generated action and not paper.[31]

Fundamental to a successful operation, he believed, were first to make sure that the men in charge, camp commanders and staff, were able and themselves convinced of the worth of what they were doing, and second to assure them of his support. He backed his educational adviser in eliminating poor instructors. Even when the level of instruction was most elementary—a battle with illiteracy or, as one camp commander put it, only partly in jest, "first I want to teach them to wear shoes"—even then Marshall and Mace agreed in demanding "nothing less than a high standard of performance." On the other hand, to able subordinates in the field he pledged the full support of his own staff with a minimum of red tape. "We, in headquarters," he said on one occasion to his staff, "live and have our being in order that the people in the field may carry out their mission. If they ask for anything, regardless of its nature, give it to them. If I find out later that their judgment was faulty I will handle the situation." [32] It was a common-sense, though not so very common, view, reconciling the service and command functions of higher headquarters that Marshall would notably take with him to the War Department. "While I was pretty ruthless about getting rid of the poor fish," he said, "I felt, on the other hand, that it was highly important to build up confidence and trust on the part of the others whose commissions or livelihoods are at your mercy." [33]

He thought it important, too, for the command to encourage in every possible way the educational part of the program because it prepared "a boy for a job in civil life, which is the real purpose of the CCC." He himself put his whole prestige behind Don Mace, ostentatiously demonstrating his interest and confidence in the educational adviser in the presence of his staff.[34] At the General's request, camp commanders selected ten boys from the district who had been particularly helped by the program and arranged for them to appear at a luncheon of the Portland Chamber of Commerce, where each of the ten talked about his background, training, and hopes for the future. For some of the businessmen of Portland the familiar initials came suddenly alive in human terms; this simple demonstration of how the CCC experience actually helped a few boys was talked about for months.[35]

Building on his editorial experience at Chicago, Marshall a few months after his arrival prompted the establishment of a Vancouver Barracks district newspaper, *The Review,* and put Captain V. J. Gregory in charge. Largely devoted to the sort of local gossip that helped maintain group morale, the paper also published the results of a dental survey which Marshall urged dental officers to make to take advantage of the gathering in one place of young men from widely scattered parts of the country. The report was picked up by *Time* magazine.[36]

What was really notable about his work with the CCC was the simple enthusiasm with which he did it. "The best antidote for mental stagnation that an Army officer in my position can have" he called the CCC, and later referred to his work with it as "the most instructive service I have ever had, and the most interesting." [37]

It was also work which frequently took him deep into the northwest country, where the hunting and fishing were excellent. Often Mrs. Marshall went with him on inspection trips, staying at a hotel while he visited the camps and then joining him for a day on a trout stream. On several occasions they took a cabin in the woods for a weekend and invited the General's adjutant, Major Claude M. (Flap) Adams, Mrs. Adams, and the aide, Captain E. C. Applegate. Major Adams had a sense of humor that appealed to the General and the fearlessness to exploit it. Adams and Marshall were both fond of practical jokes, often elaborately prepared. Adams, for instance, recalled the day of a formal presentation of awards when Marshall suddenly called him forward, eulogized him, and presented him with a watch. Surprised as he was touched, the major joined Mrs. Marshall and heard her whisper that he had better look carefully at that watch. He did and found it was his own, which somehow Marshall had managed to sneak from him for the award.[38]

Adams was one sort of companion Marshall enjoyed. Another was a quite different kind of man, Erskine Wood, an attorney in Portland, brother of Congresswoman Nan Wood Honeyman, a sportsman and spinner of tales.[39] Wood's father, a regular Army officer, had fought against the great Indian Chief Joseph of the Nez Percés and later had befriended him. Erskine, born at Vancouver Barracks, spent several months with Chief Joseph when he was in his early teens and heard from him, as well as from his father, great stories of the frontier days. These he recalled for Marshall while, perhaps, they tied flies for the next day's fishing at Wood's camp on the Metolius River. Indian lore, history, and the outdoors—these were embedded in Marshall's earliest and best-loved memories. It is no wonder that he enjoyed his friendship with Wood with a particular savor and tried years later during the war to visit the Portland lawyer whenever he could break away.[40]

Although he did not know it, the twenty comparatively relaxed and happy months at Vancouver Barracks were a kind of physical and spiritual conditioning for trials ahead. During these months acts of aggression were multiplying in the world as the dictators grew increasingly arrogant. In the East, Japan continued its encroachments on China. Toward the end of 1936 she signed the anti-Comintern pact with Germany, which Italy adhered to a month later, to shape the Rome-Berlin-Tokyo axis. In July 1937 Japanese troops clashed with the Chinese near Peiping and Japanese aggression begun in 1931 flared into open war. Before the end of 1937 the Japanese had conquered Chiang Kai-shek's capital at Nanking and forced him to move the government to Chungking. Chiang, who had never succeeded in completing the Chinese revolution and gaining control of the whole country, had an uneasy understanding with the Communists to join in resisting the Japanese, but the weakness of Chinese resistance was already apparent.

In Europe the agony of Spain continued; Stalin was purging his army; Hitler was constructing his. Marshall got an inside view from several of his former associates who were now stationed abroad. Early in 1937 he heard from a friend, Major John Winslow, United States military attaché in Warsaw, that the "problem which agitates every foreign office is simply when and where Hitler will embark on an inevitable military adventure." [41] He received detailed reports from a former instructor at Fort Benning, Major Truman Smith, military attaché in Berlin. Toward the end of the year the major wrote that German aircraft factories were capable of producing six thousand planes a year, perhaps more. Smith thought the development of German airpower was one of the most important world events of the time. That was a year before Munich, a few months before the United States announced plans to increase the American Air Corps by four hundred and seventy-six aircraft within the next two years.[42]

The fact was that despite intimations of world war the United States once again decided to depend on physical isolation and the shield of legal neutrality. President Roosevelt, pushing for a more realistic policy in October 1937, remarked in Chicago the analogy between the spread of aggression and epidemics. In the latter, he noted, "the community . . . joins in a quarantine of the patients in order to protect the health of the community against the spread of the disease." A warning to the dictators, the "quarantine" speech was directed more urgently to probing the temper of the American people. Reaction was prompt and strongly hostile to the implied invitation to collective action. The President, finding himself apparently too far out ahead of public opinion, drew back.

Official United States policy toward the spreading "pestilence" of aggression, as Marshall had called it even before the President's speech, was embraced in the Neutrality Act of 1935 as strengthened and made "permanent" by the Act of 1937. The acts sprang from an oversimplified reading of history: that America had been drawn into war in 1917 against her national interests by unfortunate and unnecessary trade contacts with the belligerents. In the neutrality laws Congress tried to limit such contacts, but the logic of the argument demanded that they be cut off altogether, and this Congress for obvious reasons would not do.

Sharing the headlines with the portents of war in mid-February 1938 was the announcement that General Pershing, American leader in the half-forgotten world conflict of 1917-18, was seriously ill at Tucson, Arizona. Almost immediately the Chief of Staff ordered Marshall to Washington. Adamson, Pershing's aide, had informed General Craig of Pershing's wish—expressed several years before—that Marshall should "take charge of arrangements" in case of his death. In 1925, on the eve of his departure for South America, Pershing had already asked Marshall, then in China, to act with Martin Egan as co-executor of his papers. General Craig, after briefing Marshall, sent him to Tucson. Meanwhile the IX Corps Area headquarters at San Antonio had already dispatched a special train to bring the former Chief of Staff's body to Arlington for burial. It is said that when Pershing heard of these activities he swore he would recover. If so, he was as good as his word. Less than two months later he appeared as best man at his son's wedding in New York. The episode, demonstrating again the close bond between the country's best-known soldier and George Marshall, also brought Marshall again into personal contact with the Chief of Staff and his chief subordinates, reminding them of his claims for advancement.[43]

Less than two weeks after he returned home from Tucson, Marshall had definite word from General Craig that his remaining days in Vancouver Barracks would be few and that his next job would be in Washington. He was not surprised; the signs had been pointing to Washington for some time. As early as 1936 General Craig had said he would bring Marshall to the War Department as soon as possible.[44] It seemed the time had come at the end of 1937 when Marshall was announced as a member of a War Department board, along with Fox Conner and Lesley McNair, to pass on the merits of a smaller infantry division, but because of Conner's illness the board never met.[45] It is not certain who originated the idea of assigning Marshall as Chief of the War Plans Division, but Major General Stanley D. Embick, Deputy Chief of Staff, later took credit for proposing that Marshall be brought back temporarily as War Plans director, with the idea of appointing him as deputy chief when Embick was assigned later in the year to a corps command. The plan appealed to Secretary of War Woodring, who was said to have welcomed a chance to build up an alternative to General Drum for the Chief of Staff's office. It appealed also to Assistant Secretary Louis Johnson, who in most matters was at sword's point with the Secretary, but who happened also to have been impressed with Marshall, whom he had met on a visit to Vancouver Barracks on January 8, 1938.[46]

Whether General Craig had a similar vision of things to come is not clear. He did not spell out the prospects in that way to Marshall. Marshall did know, however, before he left Vancouver Barracks, that he was slated to take Embick's place.[47] Even so, he viewed the Washington assignment without enthusiasm. The post of Chief of Staff had not traditionally led through the deputy's office any more than the highroad to the presidency led through the vice-presidency. He had still intently in mind the need to get his second star. Recognizing that he was still junior on the list of brigadier generals, he would have preferred further troop duty as more likely to make him available for promotion to higher command vacancies.

Yet he could not seriously have doubted now that he would reach near the top even if he could not attain it. The Intelligence Division of the War Department proposed to send him as attaché to some European or Latin American posts and two or more corps commanders asked for him as chief of staff of their headquarters. General McCoy in 1937 had even held out the prospect of the 1st Division command, but Marshall felt that he was too junior to hope immediately for this coveted assignment.[48]

Marshall's orders to Washington arrived while he was on an inspection trip at Fort Missoula, Montana, May 11-13, 1938.[49] He had a month of maneuvers to go through before his departure. In this, his last troop duty, he again led the Red Force in joint regular Army–National Guard maneuvers. Once more given a numerically inferior force and assigned the role of loser in the script, he attempted an unorthodox solution. His effort to attack during the hours of darkness was assailed by some of the regular

Army commanders, and it was assumed by them that he would be criticized in the post-maneuver critique. Instead the officer charged with this duty, Major Mark Wayne Clark, G-3 of the 3d Division, concluded that Marshall's approach was an imaginative one, based on World War I experience. Marshall would remember Clark and strongly recommend him for an assignment to the Army War College, from which Clark went on to a distinguished career.[50]

The remaining weeks Marshall spent resting, fishing, and, with Mrs. Marshall, saying farewell to their friends. Portland and Vancouver clubs and officers of the post all arranged parties in his honor. On the evening before their departure the Vancouver High School and 7th Infantry bands serenaded them at their quarters.[51] It was no more than was due the brigadier general commanding, but on both sides there was genuine affection. Looking back, some fourteen years later, Marshall wrote: "Altogether, we experienced one of our most delightful periods of Army service and one that we look back on with additional warmth because there followed from the very month we left the Northwest long fearful strain and struggle with a world turmoil which has not yet subsided.

"Those days along the rivers of the Northwest, among its magnificent mountains, and its picturesque seashore appealed to us as a pleasant dream in comparison with the troubled days that followed." [52]

XIX

Chief of Staff

"George's appointment has met with universal approval. . . . He is in a position where he will make a great name for himself and prove a great credit to the American Army and the American people."
—Pershing to Mrs. Marshall, August 26, 1939.

FROM Vancouver the Marshalls came east together by train, the General stopping a few hours in Chicago to see old friends and then coming on to Washington, while Mrs. Marshall and Molly went on to Fire Island for the summer.[1] While looking for a house the General shared an apartment with his former executive, Colonel Walker, who was also a member of the War Plans Division staff. Marshall wanted to live in Virginia in the country but for one reason or another found nothing to suit him. He ended by renting a house on Wyoming Avenue near Rock Creek Park that belonged to General Embick.[2] Toward the end of September, Mrs. Marshall and Molly joined him, almost literally blown into town, as Mrs. Marshall wrote, by the great hurricane that struck New England in 1938.[3]

The General was just back from a short trip south when he picked up his newspaper one morning in Washington to read reports that the storm had virtually wiped out the houses on Fire Island. As telephone communication was knocked out, he got a plane and flew up.

"From the air, I saw the cottage [belonging to Mrs. Marshall] had not been destroyed though most of the houses in the vicinity had collapsed or been demolished. Many on the bay side of the island—which is about six hundred yards wide—had floated out in the water. On the ocean side the dunes had been broken through by heavy seas and most of the cottages in that vicinity were destroyed. I flew over to Mitchel Field and procured a small training plane and succeeded in landing on the beach. I found Mrs. Marshall and Molly all right, but they had had a terrific night and escaped from the cottage in water up to their waists, and in a fifty-to-ninety-mile-an-hour gale. My orderly[4] was with them and did his part nobly [by going out at the height of the storm to seek help]. The next morning they took stock and found that the cottage had not been harmed, though the destruction elsewhere had been terrific, and quite a few lives were lost. The adjacent community of Saltaire was completely destroyed, except for six cottages." [5]

As prelude to Marshall's Washington days, that hurricane seemed a fitting symbol. On his arrival at the War Department he had plunged at once into what amounted to a concentrated course of grooming first for Deputy Chief and then for Chief of Staff. His rise to the top was now rapid and in retrospect seems to have been inexorable. Yet it did not seem so at the time to Marshall or indeed to his superiors. The intention to promote him to General Embick's post had been made clear enough. But it remained an intention; assignments in the Army, as Marshall well knew, were never certain until they had actually been ordered. The political situation, moreover, was delicate. Secretary of War Woodring and Assistant Secretary Johnson were in almost constant chafing opposition, personally incompatible and politically at odds on basic principles. Woodring, former governor of Kansas, was cautious to the point of isolationism about risking involvement with Europe; Johnson of West Virginia, powerful in American Legion circles, was vigorous, ambitious, eager to push the development of United States defenses. Between them General Craig was caught in political crossfires that withered his own influence. Bitterly Mrs. Craig told Mrs. Marshall on her first visit, "They have crucified my husband." [6]

Marshall knew that to some degree he enjoyed the favor of all three. But that did not mean that they agreed. It meant rather that each separately had reason to support Marshall's claims to the top job despite—and in some degree in supposed opposition to—the others. Thus when Marshall returned from Fire Island late in September and heard the War Department buzzing with conjectures that he was to be Embick's successor and the next Chief of Staff, he was alarmed. "Rumor's destroying me," he wrote Pershing. "I am announced by Tom, Dick and Harry as Deputy Chief of Staff and Chief of Staff to be. The Assistant Secretary makes similar announcements. Probably antagonizing Woodring and Craig." [7]

Whether or not Craig was antagonized, he hesitated to name the War Plans chief as Deputy Chief of Staff for a reason which Marshall recognized as counting heavily against him—the fact that his appointment to this post as a brigadier general would be resented by a number of senior officers who would have to take orders from him. General Embick was shifted to the corps area command at Atlanta at the end of September. Early in October the word was that Craig would not name a deputy until the first of the year. Then one day Johnson, as Acting Secretary of War in Woodring's absence, decided to force the issue. He asked that Marshall be appointed. Craig replied that the matter would be worked out. Johnson said it would be worked out at once and that day's meeting of the War Council, on which the Deputy Chief of Staff normally sat, would not be held until it was worked out. Craig left the office, returning in a few minutes to say that the orders to appoint Marshall had been issued.

Marshall, who assumed duties as Deputy Chief of Staff on October 15,[8] had been Chief of the War Plans Division for only three months. Of that time he was out of Washington for about four weeks; one was a week of leave at Fire Island, his last real rest until after the war; the other three were spent in tours of inspection and speech-making. It was undoubtedly part of Louis Johnson's campaign to build him up for Deputy Chief of Staff that he was asked early in September by the Assistant Secretary to address a state convention of the American Legion in Clarksburg, West Virginia—the grass roots of Johnson's political power. Two weeks later Marshall substituted for General Craig in presiding at the opening session of the Air Corps Tactical School at Maxwell Field.

He was embarking at this time on a concentrated education in air corps matters. An early and useful part of that was his trip with Major General Frank M. Andrews in the summer of 1938 to visit United States air bases and aircraft plants. General Andrews, son-in-law of General Allen who had been Marshall's chief at VIII Corps in 1919, was then commander of the General Headquarters, Air Force, the over-all air command directly under the Chief of Staff.[9]

There was no real break in Marshall's duties with the shift from the War Plans Division to the Deputy Chief of Staff's office. Nor would there be a break when he took the next and final step up. He was continuously concerned at an accelerating tempo with the review of war plans, with the build-up of Army and Army Air Corps as the situation in Europe deteriorated, and with War Department and Army reorganization leading ultimately to full mobilization. From his arrival in Washington to the outbreak of war in September 1939, he was learning, accepting increasing responsibilities, broadening and deepening his contacts with the War Department, the White House, and Congress, appearing more in public as a military leader to be reckoned with.

Marshall's appointment as Deputy Chief of Staff came a little more than two weeks after the Munich Agreement. Since the spring of 1935 Hitler had been openly and rapidly expanding Germany's military forces. In 1936 he began to use them. On March 7 of that year German troops reoccupied the Rhineland. Two years later his troops occupied and annexed Austria after a campaign of intimidation from without and Nazi propaganda from within had undermined the Austrian government. Almost at once Hitler agitated the next step—the take-over of Czechoslovakia, now caught in a vise between Germany and Austria. From the spring of 1938 he had fulminated against alleged mistreatment by the Czech government of the Sudeten German minority in Czechoslovakia. By September he was promising the Sudeten Germans that he would get justice for them if Czechoslovakia did not give it. France, bound by treaty to defend Czechoslovakia against aggression, and Britain, committed to back France against German attack, were unprepared militarily and psychologically to act decisively. France, badly divided internally and severely shaken by Germany's show of strength, left to the British the initiative in negotiations with Hitler. On his flying trips, first to Berchtesgaden and then to Bad Godesberg, Prime Minister Chamberlain appeared more obviously in the role of conciliator than as negotiator and early revealed his willingness to put pressure on Czechoslovakia to make concessions. The Führer promptly raised his demands and threatened direct action if he did not get them. Having thus exposed the weakness of his adversary and established the pressures of crisis, Hitler invited Chamberlain and Premier Daladier to join him and Mussolini at Munich. There the British and French leaders listened to Hitler's peremptory demands for the surrender of the Sudetenland and, having no alternative but war, accepted them. They undertook as well to help persuade the Czechoslovakian government not to resist. In return they received Hitler's assurance that now that German-speaking people on Germany's borders had been integrated with the Third Reich he had no further ambitions. Despite Chamberlain's hyperbole that the settlement meant "peace in our time," both the fact of surrender and its tragic revelation of democratic weakness were clear enough. The only possible justification for the retreat at Munich was that, in making it, Britain and France had bought a little time. How little time was bought Hitler revealed in the spring, when he absorbed all of Czechoslovakia and shortly thereafter began pressing his demands on Poland.

Munich came as a moral shock to the American people. Public opinion polls in the fall showed that 43 per cent now believed the country could not stay out of a European war. Senator King of Utah early in October said that Munich might make it necessary for the United States "to spend hundreds of millions of dollars more for military purposes." [10]

President Roosevelt had no doubt that this was the meaning for America and that a beginning had to be made without delay. For him the galvanizing moment was the night of October 13 when Ambassador William C. Bullitt returned from his post in

Paris to report on the state of Europe. Bullitt stayed late at the White House, describing the German military build-up, particularly in airpower, which had permitted Hitler to dictate the terms at Munich, and the French conviction that they must move rapidly to match Hitler's air fleet both defensively and offensively. The French, Bullitt reported, recognized that their only hope for such rapid expansion lay in the possibility of calling on American aircraft factories to produce planes which they and the British could buy. The President, having received similar reports of British desires, apparently made up his mind on the spot to push for greatly increased United States plane production. The next day he announced to his press conference that new world conditions made it necessary to re-examine United States defenses.

Almost certainly Roosevelt at this time was thinking in terms of helping Britain and France to build air strength that might be sufficient to hold Hitler in check or, if war came, to defeat him without United States participation. Though it was a plan essentially to keep America out of war, he could not urge it. Not only was it impossible to use government funds to build factories for the supply of foreign nations, but the sale of American-made munitions abroad was already under heavy attack by isolationists as weakening our own defenses and likely to involve us in foreign adventures. In the circumstances the President's only recourse was to recommend the rapid build-up of United States airpower. He did so, but the confusion of aims which that tactic inevitably entailed was for some time to harass War Department planning, in which Marshall was deeply involved from the beginning. It also set Marshall in flat opposition to the President at one of the earliest of their official meetings. This was the crucial White House conference of November 14 at which the President outlined his program to build ten thousand planes.[11]

There were twelve at the meeting: besides the President, Secretary of the Treasury Henry Morgenthau, WPA Administrator Harry Hopkins, Assistant Secretary of War Johnson, Solicitor General Robert H. Jackson, Solicitor of the Treasury Herman Oliphant, Generals Craig, Marshall, and Arnold, Johnson's executive officer, Colonel James H. Burns, and the White House Military Aides, Colonel Edwin M. Watson and Captain Daniel J. Callahan. Marshall's recollection was that "there was a great difference of opinion as to what the military [appropriations] should be and the President was all for the increase in the air but he wasn't much for getting the men to man the airships nor for the munitions and things that they required. He was principally thinking at that time of getting airships for England and for France." Yet Roosevelt talked rather of the need for a deterrent force strong enough to discourage any enemy from attempting a landing in North or South America. He believed that a heavy striking force of aircraft would form such a deterrent, a large ground Army would not. Actually he wanted twenty thousand planes with an annual United States productive capacity of twenty-four thousand, but as Congress was likely to cut that in half he wished the War Department to plan on ten thousand of which a quarter would be training planes and the rest half combat and half reserve. Of that total he suggested orders be given to commercial factories for eight thousand. He proposed that the WPA Administrator build seven new plants on War Department reservations, two of these plants to produce the remaining two thousand aircraft immediately needed, the other five to stand by for later use.

From a lounge off to the side Marshall listened with the others to the President, who "did the major portion of the talking." [12] As Roosevelt talked "most of them agreed with him entirely [and] had very little to say and were very soothing. . . . He finally came around to me. . . . I remember he called me 'George.' (I don't think he ever did it again. . . . I wasn't very enthusiastic over such a misrepresentation of our intimacy.) So he turned to me at the end of this general outlining . . . and said, 'Don't you think so, George?' I replied, 'I am sorry, Mr. President, but I don't agree with that at all.' I remember that ended the conference. The President gave me a . . . startled look and when I went out they all bade me good-by and said that my tour in Washington was over. But I want to say in compliment to the President that that didn't antagonize him at all. Maybe he thought I would tell him the truth so far as I personally was concerned, which I certainly tried to do in all our conversations."

The White House conference was the beginning of a long and ever-shifting struggle within the War Department to adjust air corps and ground force planning and to reconcile United States defense needs with demands of aid to Britain and France. It was the beginning, too, of a slow and (on Marshall's part) cautiously maturing relationship between President Roosevelt and the man who was to become his most important strategic adviser during the war. In all his mature life few people ever called Marshall "George," and he on his side called most of his associates and subordinates by their last names only. Roosevelt, squire by background and politician by instinct and training, knew few people whom he did not address by their first name. That difference in style sprang from a significant difference in approach to human relationships that helped set both men initially on their guard. Marshall believed that Roosevelt did not develop complete confidence in him until well after he became Chief of Staff. Marshall for his part felt that he had to hold the President at a calculated distance in order to keep his own freedom of action. For instance, he always refused to go to see Roosevelt at Warm Springs or Hyde Park for private conversations. "I found informal conversation with the President would get you into trouble," he said later. "He would talk over something informally at the dinner table and you had trouble disagreeing without creating embarrassment. So I never went. I was in Hyde Park for the first time at his funeral."

Marshall could be blunt in upholding a point of view he believed in, but he understood the need for dealing diplomatically and for knowing his man. How well he understood the important art of catching the President's attention was revealed in a letter he wrote to the commandant of the Infantry School preparing him for Roosevelt's visit in the winter of 1939. After suggesting that the school put on a demonstration of "some interesting field stuff" to "awaken his interest in the practical training of the Army," Marshall wrote: "I make this suggestion—that whatever arrangement is made, no one press him to see this or that or understand this or that; that whatever is furnished him in the way of data be on one sheet of paper, with all high-sounding language eliminated, and with very pertinent paragraphed underlined headings; that a little sketch of ordinary page size is

probably the most effective method, as he is quickly bored by
papers, by lengthy discussions, and by anything short of a few
pungent sentences of description. You have to intrigue his interest, and then it knows no limit." [13]

That Marshall got on with the President and impressed him
favorably there is no doubt. But it is not clear that these contacts decided Roosevelt to appoint Marshall as Chief of Staff.
Marshall's case was pushed by others, eventually by many others,
but crucial among them was Harry Hopkins. It was in the closing
days of 1938 that Marshall first came into close working contact
with Hopkins, who on December 24 had been named Secretary of
Commerce. Both were then deeply involved in the President's
aircraft procurement program. Hopkins in the fall had traveled
to the West Coast to check into the capacity of existing plane factories. The War Department General Staff liaison officer with
WPA, Colonel Arthur R. Wilson, also made the trip and on his
return reported officially to the War Department and wrote
Marshall personally that Hopkins believed that the services
could get large appropriations in the next relief bill provided
they could sell the scheme to the President. Mr. Roosevelt, favorable to the idea of increasing the national defense, was understandably wary about diverting funds from works projects to
plants and machine tools for the making of armaments. The way
to Mr. Roosevelt, Wilson added, lay through Hopkins, and he
urged that the Chief of Staff or his deputy get an appointment
with the new Secretary in a matter of days.

In the end it was Hopkins who took the initiative. After Christmas he sent word that he would like to call on the Deputy
Chief of Staff. Marshall, following a practice which he would use
increasingly with cabinet officers and congressmen, instead went
to see him. They spent an hour or more in discussion which cen-
tered on building more airplanes but ranged far over the problems of defense. Marshall, who had been living with the multi-
ple deficiencies of both ground and air forces for many months,
outlined a condition of unpreparedness which so shocked Hopkins that he recommended that the Deputy Chief of Staff seek
out the President at once at Warm Springs or Hyde Park and
discuss the matter. Marshall refused, but he had gained the most
important point—the sympathy and support of Hopkins, which

from that time on never faltered. Hopkins, he believed, not only helped dispose the President to listen to the Army's needs but built up Marshall personally. He thought the favorable words spoken by Hopkins at the White House weighed more than any other single influence in tipping his selection as Chief of Staff.[14]

The more interesting fact seems to be that while up to the moment his appointment was announced he seemed no better than an outside possibility, nobody opposed him and nearly everyone whose wishes counted independently pushed his cause. As Marshall put it: "Johnson wanted me for Chief of Staff, but I didn't want Woodring to know he was for me. Craig was for me, but I wanted it kept from the President. Woodring was for me, but I didn't want the others to know. Someone mentioned me to Senator Guffey and asked about 'your fellow Pennsylvanian.' He didn't know me. Then he found he was a friend of my sister's. (He lived near her.) He came down and called me up on Lincoln's Birthday or Washington's Birthday. Said he wanted to come over; I said, 'I prefer to come to you.' I went up there. He was all excited. I had the damnedest time to keep him from seeing the President. I said you will destroy me. Let things take their course and perhaps I will get it."

Besides the backing of his associates, Marshall had the continuing support of General Pershing. That was important, though probably less decisive than was commonly assumed at the time. Had Pershing been opposed, he could, without much question, have swung the appointment to someone else. In giving his strong approval he joined an array of advocates already impressive and difficult for the President to resist.[15]

For Marshall one worry was his own health. Under great and continuous pressure he had found less time to relax than he had been accustomed to. He feared the irregularity in his pulse might recur and start up again reports that he was unfit. He himself kept careful check and made plans to rest the morning before he was due for his annual medical examination. But as it happened, after three especially grueling weeks during which he "had to work like lightning, compromise endless disagreements, sit in on most difficult scenes, and a tumultuous morning with much emphatic argument," General Craig suddenly suggested he go over for the examination.[16] He wrote his friend Stayer the results. The doctor "found a slight irregularity in my pulse before exercise, and none after exercise. . . . He agreed with me that it was due to too much desk and too little exercise of the type to which I had been accustomed. Said I would have to fight a 'desk belly,' tho I was pretty well off at the time, being six pounds lighter than when you first saw me and in better shape, both as to hardness and figure." [17]

General Craig was scheduled to retire in September 1939. At the time his successor was being considered—competition for the post and speculation about it were warming up in February—Marshall stood about thirty-fourth in seniority on the list of eligibles; twenty-one major generals and eleven brigadier generals outranked him.[18] The rule, however, that no one could be appointed Chief of Staff who could not serve out the full four-year term before reaching the age of sixty-four eliminated all but four of the thirty-three and left Marshall the fifth-ranking eligible.[19]

Although he was not so far down the eligibility list as he appeared to some surprised observers at the time who merely counted names, Marshall's comparatively junior position had made political difficulties within the Army to which he was particularly sensitive as the time of decision approached. To an Atlanta newspaperman and close friend of Woodring's who wanted to campaign publicly in his behalf he wrote: "Reference any publicity regarding me, or 'build-up' as it is called, I am now, in my particular position with low rank, on the spot in Army circles. The fact of my appointment as deputy while a brigadier general, junior to other generals of the General Staff, makes me conspicuous in the Army. Too conspicuous, as a matter of fact." Then he went on shrewdly to appraise the compensating advantages he enjoyed. "My strength with the Army has rested on the well-known fact that I attended strictly to business and enlisted no influence of any sort at any time. That in Army circles has been my greatest strength in the matter of future appointment, especially as it is in contrast with other most energetic activities in organizing a campaign and in securing voluminous publicity.

"Therefore, it seems to me that at this time the complete absence of any publicity about me would be my greatest asset, particularly with the President, and the Army would resent it, even some of them now ardently for me. In other words, it would tar me with the same brush to which they now object.

"The National Guard knows me now. The Reserve Corps knows me well. The ROTC people, including many college presidents, know me. And the regular Army knows me. It is not time for the public to be brought to a view of the picture." [20]

The publicity campaign that Marshall had chiefly in mind was the one actively under way in behalf of General Drum, Marshall's old friend who had been Pershing's First Army chief of staff in France and who at that moment was commanding First Army in New York. Drum led the list of eligibles for Chief of Staff by such a wide margin that in the Army it was generally thought he had an almost pre-emptive right to the job. Not only was he senior, but his record was impeccable in a series of assignments that had admirably prepared him for Army leadership, from his service under Pershing through division and corps area commands and command of the Hawaiian Department. Against him was the fever of his own ambition and his unwillingness to let his pre-eminence speak for itself.

Repeatedly in the 1920s and 1930s, Drum had asked Pershing to seek political backing to get for him a one-star and later a two-star appointment, which were slow coming to him under the Army's promotion system. His name was presented along with MacArthur's to President Hoover when the Chief of Staff was to be selected in 1930; he was an active candidate to succeed MacArthur in 1934 when the Chief of Staff's appointment was extended for a year and in 1935 when Craig was appointed. When he first hoped to succeed MacArthur he complained of MacArthur's efforts to continue himself in office. In 1935 he actively sought General Pershing's aid to counteract objections that he was not a West Pointer and had not held a field command in World War I.[21]

Whether his being passed over then tainted his eligibility or, on the contrary, made his claim in 1939 stronger, it clearly did have the effect of stimulating Drum himself to extraordinary efforts this time to leave no strings unpulled. As early as 1937 visitors returning from the Hawaiian Department, where he was in command until June of that year, wrote Roosevelt in Drum's behalf. George Patton, who had served under Drum in Hawaii, was prompted by his superior in December 1937 to sound out Pershing on the matter.[22] Drum had powerful political friends in New York, including Postmaster General James A. Farley, national Democratic party leader, whose support, it was supposed, would alone be enough to assure his appointment.[23] Service journals and some national magazines began early to tout him as the obvious and best choice. Drum himself was indefatigable in buttonholing those he thought might help him. But in the end, as Marshall and many others believed, this special pressure backfired, creating resentments and doubts among those who had the decision to make.[24]

If Drum were eliminated, Marshall had clearly the strongest remaining claim of the top five eligibles. Of the other three generals senior to him, only General DeWitt was seriously mentioned; and DeWitt, although currently commandant of the Army War College, was apparently handicapped because much of his experience was in the supply services. Major General Frank W. Rowell had no significant backing. Kreuger, a fine staff officer during the war and later an infantry commander, had held less prominent posts than Marshall in France and was hampered by his German birth.

As for Marshall, his chances of selection seemed to ebb and flow. Woodring, who in the fall of 1938 had indicated privately that he intended to recommend Drum, may have swung back to Marshall by mid-January 1939, but he told O'Laughlin at that time that he doubted if the President would name him. O'Laughlin, and some others in Washington at that time, believed that Marshall's independence, particularly his opposition to the President's airplane program, had hurt his chances and that Roosevelt might now prefer Drum.[25] It appears that both Woodring and Craig, who had also opposed the President's program, refrained for a time from recommending Marshall for fear that their support would prejudice his chances.[26] By mid-March the military editor of the *Washington Post* had picked up the rumors and hedged—though he did not withdraw—his earlier prediction that Marshall would be the next Chief of Staff.[27]

When, about the first of April, President Roosevelt asked the

Secretary of War for the records of general officers eligible for Chief of Staff so that he might look at them during his coming trip to Warm Springs, Craig made a preliminary selection, eliminating Rowell and DeWitt from the first five eligibles, adding one officer (Beck) who did not have four years to serve before retirement, and including four generals junior to Marshall (Grunert, Benedict, Ridley, and Chaffee). Although his selection seems in practical terms to have narrowed the choice to Marshall or Drum, Craig continued uncertain. Well along in April he felt that the President might reach down for a younger man and perhaps pick General Sultan, who he thought had the backing of the President's aide, General "Pa" Watson.[28]

It is likely that, when Craig was voicing his doubts, the President had already made up his mind. One Sunday he called Marshall to the White House. He seems to have let no one else know in advance, not even Secretary of War Woodring. "I saw the President in his study when he told me," Marshall recalled. "It was an interesting interview. I told him I wanted the right to say what I think and it would often be unpleasing. 'Is that all right?' He said, 'Yes.' I said, 'You said *yes* pleasantly, but it may be unpleasant.'"

Characteristically Marshall asked that the announcement be put off until he could leave Washington. He was flying that week to the West Coast. In leaving he intended himself to keep the secret even from Mrs. Marshall. But she was in such misery from a bad case of poison ivy and reaction to the serum she had been taking that he relented and told her. The official announcement was released on April 27.

Enthusiastic response was hardly to be expected from the press, which for the most part knew Marshall only slightly by reputation, if at all. Some editorials noted that in naming Marshall, Roosevelt was again seeking younger men for high command, as he had in picking Rear Admiral Harold Stark as Chief of Naval Operations. The one voice raised strongly against the appointment was Boake Carter's in the *Chicago American*. Carter, a constant and vigorous administration critic, found slightly sinister implications in the rejection of Drum in favor of someone less self-assertive. "It would be unkind," Carter wrote, "to say that he [Marshall] is expected to be simply a willing 'order-taker.' Rather what is expected of him by the White House is that he will not 'talk out of turn.' " The comment must have amused the President if he saw it.[29]

From the Army came general acclaim, including enthusiastic words from some who later would allege that they never really cared much for Marshall. Pershing, wholly delighted, wrote to Mrs. Marshall: "George's appointment has met with universal approval. Of course all this pleases me very much and I do not have to tell you how I feel toward him. He is in a position where he will make a great name for himself and prove a great credit to the American Army and the American people." [30]

The organization of the War Department when Marshall was named Chief of Staff remained substantially as it had been shaped under Pershing in 1921. Under Army Regulations of 1921 the Chief of Staff was declared to be the "immediate ad-viser of the Secretary of War on all matters relating to the Mili-tary Establishment" and was "charged by the Secretary of War with the planning, development, and execution of the military program." These specifications clearly implied command author-ity over the Army as a whole, but to make that authority unam-biguous a paragraph was added to the regulations in 1936 mak-ing the Chief of Staff the "Commanding General of the Field Forces" in peace and during war until "the President shall have specifically designated a commanding general thereof." There had been no major changes in the structure of the General Staff since Pershing's time, nor had the number of officers on duty with the General Staff increased materially. From a low of eighty-two in 1933 the total had risen only to a hundred and twenty-two in September 1939.[31]

The principal formal machinery to co-ordinate planning of the War and Navy Departments was still the Joint Board set up in 1903 by agreement of the Secretaries of War and Navy. Members of the board were, for the Army, the Chief of Staff, G-3 (later replaced by the Deputy Chief of Staff), and the Chief of War Plans Division; for the Navy, the Chief of Naval Oper-ations, Assistant Chief, and the Director of Navy War Plans Division. They met once a month when there was business to be decided and in the interim were served by a Joint Planning Committee. There was also an Army and Navy Munitions Board under civilian chairmanship to deal with matters of joint procurement. Early in 1938 a Standing Liaison Committee was established consisting of the Army Chief of Staff, the Chief of Naval Operations, and the Under Secretary of State. Meeting irregularly but roughly once a month, the committee was designed broadly to assure that military and diplomatic policies were shaped in harmony. In practice, with Sumner Welles as the State Department member, it devoted most of its time to Latin-American problems.

This in outline was the structure of the top military directorate into which Marshall came in 1939. Under the supervision of the Secretary and Assistant Secretary of War, it was all subordinate and directly advisory to the President as Commander-in-Chief. In July of 1939 Roosevelt made that direct relationship explicit by directing that the Chief of Staff and Chief of Naval Operations, on questions of "strategy, tactics, and operations," and the Joint Board for certain matters, should report directly to him rather than through the service secretaries. None of the machinery would prove adequate to the demands of a two-front war, and all would be replaced by 1942.

To redesign the War Department would become in time one of Marshall's most exacting and vital tasks. But in 1939 he was preoccupied with still more basic matters. The Army, it will be recalled, had reached a low point in both numbers and readiness for combat in the middle 1930s under the impact of congressional thrift and anti-war sentiment. Thereafter it expanded slightly as some funds from New Deal spending came its way and trouble abroad raised doubts as to America's perpetual immunity to war. In 1932 the regular Army had a little less than 120,000 enlisted men in active service, including Philippine Scouts. Among national armies of the world at that time, it was estimated to stand seventeenth. By mid-1939 the enlisted strength was close to 175,000. Both figures, however, contrasted notably to the strength of 280,000 authorized by the National Defense Act of 1920. Under the Rearmament and Re-equipment Program launched by MacArthur there had been during the

1930s "moderate but steady increases in appropriations and corresponding progress in re-equipment of the Army." Yet the money available to the Army was always grossly inadequate even to halt the normal deterioration of attrition and obsolescence, much less to develop and buy modern weapons to match those being acquired by America's potential enemies.[32] For the Army ground forces the situation was worse than the gross figures of manpower and appropriations suggest, because during the 1930s, in particular, the Army was required out of its meager totals to build an air force, which though absurdly small and ill equipped on the eve of war nevertheless absorbed one-eighth of the Army's enlisted strength. The Army Air Service had become the Army Air Corps in 1926 and in 1935 was disentangled from Army organization and formed in four national air districts under the over-all command of the General Headquarters, Air Force. Technical control was exercised by the Chief of Air Corps, who in 1939 was General Arnold.

Years of neglect had vitiated the 1920 concept of a small regular Army capable of rapid and orderly expansion in case of need. The concept had been buried so deep, in fact, that neither MacArthur nor Craig had found it advisable to attempt a resurrection. They were conditioned rather, by the cold air on Capitol Hill, to fight only for the minimum needs that they saw some hope of getting recognized in the annual appropriations. The result of this policy was, as noted, some small improvements but no basic progress toward real preparedness.

Marshall continued at first the politics of the possible. His most pressing task was to begin to remedy deficiencies so numerous and various that the weightiest decisions, even when the congressional pursestrings began to loosen, were to establish priorities among requirements nearly all of which in the light of world conditions in 1938-39 were desperate. The announcement from the White House in mid-October 1938 that defense appropriations were to be reviewed for the first time encouraged the War Department to try to define the real military needs. Within a week Marshall had met with the Chief of Ordnance in what turned into a discussion of a program for balanced rearmament. As a result the estimate of what was immediately needed for weapons was increased almost threefold. At the same time Air Corps planners greatly expanded their estimates, which the Chief of Staff pushed still higher.

Encouraged suddenly to plan not for what a reluctant Congress might possibly concede but for what might actually be needed for defense, the War Department came hard up against the problem of what kind of defense to design and what to order first. That problem was posed most sharply by the President's ten thousand aircraft program. Marshall felt strongly that the program was unsound, that the enlistment and training of air crews and money for bases and other facilities ought to be provided to keep pace with the procurement of aircraft, and that the whole air build-up should be kept in balance with a simultaneous strengthening of the ground forces. He was not opposed to enlarging American airpower or to putting strong emphasis on its rapid development.[33] It is notable that so great an air force enthusiast as General Arnold has acknowledged not only that Marshall understood air force needs but that he was "one of the most potent forces behind the development of a real American airpower." "The two of us," Arnold wrote of the period when Marshall was Deputy Chief of Staff, "worked out the details of an entire air plan for the War Department." [34] But Marshall in 1938-39 had too lively an awareness of the total military weakness of the United States in relation to its potential enemies to accept the President's simple thesis that combat planes alone could create an effective deterrent force.

"Military victories," he told cadets at the Air Corps Tactical School, "are not gained by a single arm—though the failures of an arm of service might well be disastrous—but are achieved through the efforts of all arms and services welded into an Army team." Moreover, in the circumstances in which the United States then found itself in the fall of 1938, it was not at all clear when, where, or how the nation might be called on to exert military force or for what national objectives. Starting almost from scratch to re-create a military establishment, the nation faced a long period of preparation and vulnerability. He believed therefore that the sensible policy at first was "to maintain a conservatively balanced force for the protection of our territory against any probable threat during the period the vast but latent resources of the United States, in men and material, are being mobilized." [35] On the matter of balance he made a prolonged and vigorous fight, carrying it with Craig to the White House in several meetings with the President in the winter of 1938 and later to committees of Congress.[36]

In late November 1938 he appealed to Pershing for support. "There is no one else in the country," he wrote, "that can speak as you do. Mr. Harry Hopkins the other day expressed to me his regret that you were not here to discuss some of the aspects of the present situation with the President. Possibly you will consider doing it in the manner suggested." Pershing readily complied with a letter to the President on November 25 along the lines Marshall had drafted, but a few days later wrote Marshall that he doubted it would have much effect. "In any event," he added, "I hope you and the Chief of Staff will go along, as that, in my opinion, is the only way in which you will get anything near what you want." [37]

Pershing's warnings against heading again into the sort of unpreparedness which he recalled so vividly from 1917—especially the lack of artillery and ammunition—may have carried some weight. (Marshall, after hearing the President's January 16, 1939, message to Congress, thought they did.) More immediate and convincing pressure for a balanced force was exerted by the War Department itself. The President wanted combat planes immediately to overawe Germany; the War Department wanted to begin building an effective fighting force. The War Department (Craig, Marshall, and Air Corps Chief General Arnold seem to have been in essential agreement throughout) complained that planes were worthless without men to fly them and troops to hold the ground for them. Roosevelt complained that he asked for war planes and his planners offered him almost everything else instead. The upshot was, however, that the program was reduced to six thousand planes and Congress was urged to provide more money for other things, notably to train pilots and to strengthen the seacoast defenses of Panama, Hawaii, and the continental United States.[38]

To follow up the President's request, Marshall directed the General Staff in the preparation of data for congressional com-

mittee hearings and himself accompanied General Craig to testify before the House Military Affairs Committee on January 17.
In his own testimony Marshall emphasized once more his long-
held contention that a proper defense must be one capable of
functioning at once when war breaks out. "We assume," he said,
"that almost any war of the future will at least start in the air,
and that means that we must have available an adequate amount
of materiel and personnel, trained personnel, ready to function
the first day of the war; and also the materiel which would permit us to start immediately on the training of additional personnel required." [39]

But what specifically did the Army ground forces need? In
December, Assistant Secretary Johnson had asked General Craig
to be prepared to defend increases "made necessary by the un-
settled and critical conditions of world affairs, [which] will in all
likelihood cover a period of several years." Marshall, in late January, working along these lines with the War Plans Division,
developed a two-year augmentation program which would flesh
out five divisions to combat strength by the addition of eighteen
hundred officers and twenty-three thousand men. War Plans
noted that at a time when Germany had ninety field divisions,
Italy forty-five, and Japan fifty on the Chinese mainland, the
United States had nine on paper and not one ready to fight at
authorized wartime strength.[40] Modest as the planned augmentation was, the President would not recommend the required
manpower increases; he had in fact not asked Congress for any
increase at all in mobile ground forces. The plan was shelved,
but the War Department continued to regard it as a statement
of something that should eventually be done.

Marshall justified the five-division plan generally in the light of
aggressive threats of "dictator governments" against South and
Central America and the establishment by Japan of "a new
order" in China. A General Staff report further underlined the
danger to the Western Hemisphere, saying that "violation of
the Monroe Doctrine by European powers is not beyond the
realm of possibility." [41]

That danger unquestionably was taken seriously. The political advantages of emphasizing it in 1939 were also obvious. At a

time when most Americans still believed we could stay out of foreign wars and nearly all hoped we could, the need for larger ground forces could hardly be argued on a premise of intervention abroad. Foreign invasion of the continental United States could not be put forward as a plausible contingency. But the public evidence of Axis activity in South and Central America was already sufficient to make the danger of subversion there, if not invasion, seem real and possibly imminent. If Hitler, moreover, were victorious in Europe, might he not then be tempted to move in force against our southern neighbors? A concern for the security of the hemisphere could seem, even to some isolationists, a small and logical extension of self-defense in our own home base. The tradition of the Monroe Doctrine, moreover, gave to that defense such anti-European color as not to stir the isolationists' fear of foreign entanglements.

As early as January 1938 President Roosevelt backed a request for additional money for the Army and Navy with a warning, that could seem all but axiomatic, that the United States "must keep any potential enemy many hundreds of miles away from our continental limits." At the end of the year Secretary of State Cordell Hull pushed, at the Inter-American Conference at Lima, for a declaration of "hemispheric foreign policy." The result was the Declaration of Lima (December 1938) in which the American republics "affirmed their intention" of helping each other in the event of foreign attack on any of them, "either direct or indirect." [42]

The Joint Planning Committee had already under study what the United States might do in case of an Axis grab in Latin America, assuming a simultaneous aggression by Japan against the Philippines. In February 1939 Marshall asked the Army War College to examine in secret just what force would be needed to make Brazil and Venezuela safe against assumed Nazi designs to take them over, primarily by subversion and sabotage. The committee in March recommended a specially equipped hemisphere defense force of a hundred and twelve thousand with shipping enough to transport it as a unit.[43] From its own broader premises the Joint Planning Committee a little later came up with an estimate of roughly the same magnitude. Besides recommending stronger fixed defenses in the Canal Zone, Hawaii, Alaska, and Puerto Rico, and the development of Pacific naval bases, the Joint Planners asked for a larger Navy, an increase of the Fleet Marine Force to fifteen thousand officers and men, and the organization of the three-division Army expeditionary force.[44]

The planners, like everyone else who looked to the defense of Central and South America, fixed their eyes on the eastward bulge of Brazil at Natal. Here, it seemed, within easy flying range of Africa, was the most likely spot for the European dictators to try to bridge the Atlantic. From a foothold in Brazil they could spread to positions from which it would be possible to attack the Panama Canal. The Axis, it was assumed, would gain the initial objectives not by direct attack but by infiltrating commercially, politically, and militarily. Already several Latin-American countries were accepting German and Italian help in training and equipping their armies. At the end of 1938 the German Army had extended an invitation to the Brazilian Chief of Staff to visit Berlin. In an effort to block this, Brazilian Foreign Minister Oswaldo Aranha proposed in January that the United States Chief of Staff come to Brazil and invite the Brazilian Army Chief to return the courtesy with a trip to Washington. The idea appealed to the President, particularly since the Senate at this time was considering the sale of surplus munitions to Latin-American nations as a way of weaning them from military dependence on the Axis.

It was arranged for General Craig to go with a small mission by warship. But as soon as Marshall's nomination for Chief of Staff was announced, Craig decided that Marshall should go in his place.[45] Marshall received the word on the West Coast and wired the War Department to ask where and how he was to go. Only Rio de Janeiro had definitely been decided on, the War Department replied, and the only member of his party definitely picked was an officer who knew Brazil and spoke Portuguese, Colonel Lehman W. Miller. Whom else would he like? Marshall suggested Major Ridgway, who had been with General McCoy on the Bolivian-Paraguayan Conciliation Commission in 1929, and Captain Thomas North, listed as a "geographic and map expert and a good linguist." Later the group was completed by Colonel James E. Chaney, an Air Corps officer recommended by General Arnold, and Major Louis J. Compton. Transportation was to be the cruiser *Nashville*.[46]

The *Nashville* sailed on May 10 from New York, and with stopovers at Puerto Rico and Trinidad reached Rio on the twenty-fifth. The next twelve days for Marshall and his party were a crowded mixture of festivities and conferences, as the object of the trip mixed good will and military business.[47] Among their first social engagements in Rio was a reception for Countess Edda Ciano, Mussolini's daughter, whom *Life* called Italy's attractive answer to America's "humdrum" Marshall.[48] But Marshall was to prove not entirely humdrum. He had one notable inspiration, which was as natural as it was appealing.

At Curitiba, reviewing a parade of six thousand school children, he noticed a group of boys from four to twelve years old dressed alike in overalls with pink piping and carrying hoes, rakes, and the like. He asked who they were. Told they came from a state orphanage, he accepted an invitation to visit it. He came away impressed, and that evening asked Captain North, who managed housekeeping matters for the tour, whether there was anything in the regulations to prevent him from spending money on candy. North thought not, and Marshall told him to buy enough candy to give all two hundred-odd boys in the orphanage a pound apiece. It was a lot of candy to find in a short time but North managed to get it distributed before the plane took the mission on to their next stop.[49] The next stop was Pôrto Alegre, and by the time they got there the news of the Americans' spontaneous gesture of kindness had preceded them. The result was a reception more enthusiastic than any they had received before.

Marshall reported to Craig: "Arrived in Pôrto Alegre—Governor of State, Military Commanders, Archbishop, Cabinet, civil officials, etc., at field. Guard of Honor Cavalry escort surrounding my car, motorcycle police. Main street bordered by thousands of schoolchildren in uniform, 50 or 75,000 people in rear of children, confetti and paper like Broadway, for a half mile of blocks, four or five bands.

"Another guard of honor at palace of governor, all civil officials present, champagne, etc. The same at headquarters of General. Tour of city with Mayor and General. Dinner by Governor—one hundred guests, usual variety of wines, elaborate printed menus in form of memento. Then a ball or dance. Civil guards in plumes, jack boots, etc., at entrance, all guests grouped to receive me, governor as escort, national anthems, a dais at which to sit. It sounds like a joke or stage business, but it was all in deadly earnest in their desire to do the gracious thing.

"Inspection of a frontier regiment at its barracks. Regiment paraded along road in advance of barracks, wide road looking four hundred yards to barracks; carpeted with flowers, sign across archway in letters two feet high 'Welcome General Marshall,' complete inspection, including layout of all programs and schedules of instructions, welcome by officers in their club, formal speech—written—by Colonel, champagne; another inspection of an airfield, same arrangements, menu, speeches, music, as dinner night before; visit female academy (this, I think, was probably arranged for you), indoor amphitheater filled with girls, front row ones with flowers and they sing welcome in English, do their flag stunt, sing some Brazilian chants and present me with fifty bunches of flowers—all sent later to my hotel. The whole thing was beautifully arranged and executed. Then a parade of 6000 school children, in school uniform, two Army bands, followed by 2000 men of various sport clubs. All this last was a hurried arrangement due to publicity regarding my contact with schoolchildren at Curitiba. . . . The sport clubs insisted on being let in, which involved all the German rowing clubs—to the intensive satisfaction and amusement of Brazilians." [50]

The meticulous catalogue of details Marshall wrote not in innocent exuberance, but because he was to bring the Brazilian Chief of Staff of the Army, General Pedro Aurelio de Góes Monteiro, back with him to Washington and he was concerned that the reception accorded Góes Monteiro not fall short in any way of Brazil's hospitality. So he was careful to note a gift to him of three aquamarine stones and a large gold nugget and asked Craig to "tell Wesson [the Chief of Ordnance] that they serve champagne and cakes in the middle of a shell manufacturing shop." [51]

Besides Curitiba and Pôrto Alegre, the mission visited São Paulo, Santos and Belo Horizonte. In Rio from the first of June, the round of receptions and inspections continued, along with discussion with Brazilian military leaders on the ways and means of assuring closer co-operation between Brazil and the United States. On the way down Marshall had told his staff that he wanted "to get from the trip definite ideas as to its [Brazil's] military capabilities, its military establishments, the military problems which concern its important ports, its physiography in relation to strategy, its air bases, and the problems with which military aviation is concerned." That large order appears to have been largely filled. Not only were German designs frustrated—General Góes Monteiro never made the trip to Berlin—but Marshall's mission was able to arrange for American use of airfields in the Natal bulge, which proved of considerable value in the North African campaign of 1942-43. Moreover, when the United States was drawn into war, Brazil, by prior agreement, "put their German and Japanese nationals under the strictest surveillance for the duration." [52]

The evening of June 5 Marshall gave a farewell dinner on board the *Nashville* for his Brazilian hosts, including the Minister of War, Foreign Minister, and Chief of Staff. Next morning General Góes Monteiro and his party came aboard for the trip back to Washington. On reaching the Virginia Capes on June 20 the *Nashville* was met by an air escort of six Flying Fortresses and thirty-five pursuit planes, which accompanied them to anchor at Annapolis. There General Góes Monteiro began a round of festivities honoring him as Marshall had been honored in Brazil. Marshall said good-by in Washington but detailed Captain North to take charge of the Brazilian party's tour of the United States. North recalls Marshall's instructions to him, typical and revealing of the General. "I am sending you on this expedition," Marshall said, "because I have confidence in you. You have my complete authority to do in connection with this expedition what your judgment tells you is right. You have authority to issue orders in my name in connection with this. If you see anything that is going wrong, use my authority, if necessary, to correct it. But don't you ever come back to Washington and expect me to correct something that you have allowed to happen." [53]

The Brazilian trip was a clear-cut success, but it was for Marshall one of the very few activities of these days to which any conclusion could be set. Concern with hemispheric defense helped to get Americans in and out of Congress thinking in terms of active rather than passive measures for the security of the United States—in terms of raising fighting forces rather than filling sandbags. In retrospect that can be seen as an important transition to the global involvement just ahead. Yet the Army did not immediately benefit, as hoped. It did not begin decisively to move from a peacetime to a wartime footing until after 1939, and the story of that transformation as Marshall directed it belongs to the story of the war years. So, with the other great task of planning against the manifold contingencies of attack on this nation, Marshall was continuously involved, but this story, too, can be properly told only from the vantage point of the later discussions of strategy when America's role had been shaped by events.

The Chief of Staff-to-be took over his duties on the first of July. General Craig, with two months of terminal leave, continued until September 1 to hold his old title. But the whole responsibility devolved at once on Marshall. Craig in his farewell statement urged that the United States strengthen its defenses, organize the five seasoned divisions the War Department had recommended to protect the Western Hemisphere, prepare a war reserve with equipment for one million men, and establish an outpost line, Alaska-Hawaii-Panama-Puerto Rico, ready for immediate action. It was high time.

In June, Hitler began his violent denunciations of the Versailles Treaty provisions that separated Danzig from Germany. Great Britain, sore from the retreat at Munich, announced it would stand by promises to defend Poland against attack. The German Führer only redoubled his demands and threats. On August 8 he conferred with Nazi leaders from Danzig. Shortly thereafter he absorbed the armed forces of the Protectorate of Slovakia into the Wehrmacht. None could doubt that he was preparing for imminent war. Meanwhile General Franco had proclaimed a Falangist dictatorship in Spain, which was interpreted as putting him solidly in the Axis camp. The pace stepped up. On August 20, after British and French officials talked with the Russians about the possibility of a military understanding to check Nazi ambitions, Stalin bluntly announced that the Soviet Union had just signed a two-year trade agreement with Germany. Britain reiterated her commitment to fight for Poland. France called up troops. Hitler retorted with orders for the mobilization of additional reserves.

Then on August 23 came announcement of the non-aggression pact between Berlin and Moscow. Although arrangements in that treaty for the partition of Poland, the assignment to Russia of spheres of influence in the Baltic, recognition of special Soviet interest in Bessarabia, and the stipulation of German "political disinterestedness" in Southeastern Europe remained secret, it was clear enough that the understanding removed one considerable obstacle to German action against Poland. It seemed clear, too, that German insistence on her latest "final demand" in Europe was now matched by stubborn determination of France and Britain to yield no more.

For the United States parallel difficulties were rising in the East. As Japan extended control over China and talked of her destiny to dominate Asia, relations with the United States deteriorated. Near the end of July, Washington indicated that it would not renew the 1911 Japanese trade treaty, which was to lapse in January 1940. That action presaged the attempt shortly to apply brakes to Japan's war machine by embargoing the shipment of war materials.

As the showdown developed in Europe, Washington could do little more than stay alert. On August 9 the President created a War Resources Board under Edward R. Stettinius, Jr., to review the Industrial Mobilization Program.[54] On the seventeenth Sumner Welles, as Acting Secretary of State, presided over a meeting of officials of the State, War, Navy, Treasury, and Justice Departments to discuss measures for proclaiming and assuring United States neutrality in case of war. The Congress in the summer of 1939 had failed to heed the President's plea to amend existing neutrality legislation so that the arms embargo should not work to the disadvantage of the European democracies. Senator Borah at a July White House conference, certain that his information was more reliable than that of the State Department, doubted if war would come, inasmuch as Germany was not ready for it.

Americans generally appear to have been both more pessimistic and more realistic as the fateful autumn approached. A Gallup poll taken on August 20 before announcement of the German-Soviet pact found that more than three-quarters of both parties believed that if France and Britain went to war with Germany the United States would be drawn in.

As for George Marshall, he needed no gift of prophecy to see that he entered on responsibilities that would be long, critical, and exacting. Whatever happened, America's perilous weakness in a world of armed bullies stood out as the all-absorbing fact that he as Chief of Staff had to face; his energies for some time would be devoted in full to rebuilding the nation's defenses.

XX

The Future and the Past

"For almost forty years . . . you have been preparing for the position you now hold. . . . Today we hope you can lay aside your honors and your burdens and make friends with your youth."
—Uniontown's Welcome, September 9, 1939, written by Mary Kate O'Bryon

MARSHALL on September 1, 1939, had arrived at his long-sought goal. The tremendous task of leading the Army in a period of world conflict was something he had not foreseen, but had he known the trials which would confront him in the next six years, his choice would not have been different. From Pershing he already knew the burdens and the cares of the Chief of Staff, and he accepted them.

He had prepared for four decades for the post he now assumed. How thorough had his training been? He had attended military schools which fitted him to be a lieutenant or a colonel, but there was no way then—and perhaps not now—to train a general or a chief of staff. Neither specified courses nor years of apprenticeship were enough for that. Experts said that the top commander of fighting men must have led soldiers in battle, but the three principal aspirants for the office of Chief of Staff in 1939— Drum, DeWitt, and Marshall—had won their reputations in the first World War as staff officers. Others insisted that they should

345

be graduates of West Point, but not one of the three had received such training.

Judged by today's requirements for high command, no institution—civilian or military—at the turn of the century provided proper grounding in languages, international relations, troop management, or psychology of leadership. Lacking such instruction, the officer of an earlier era had to train himself. And for this he needed a belief in himself, an intense desire to know, the capacity to grow, the trait of self-discipline, and a compulsion to excel in his chosen field. Marshall had them all.

Despite his limitations as a student, Marshall at an early age exhibited a bent for command. Classmates recall his drilling them at school, their surprise that such a self-willed boy could share leadership with Andy even at play, his steady rise to positions of authority at VMI. His passion to succeed had an element of weakness. As a youngster he avoided those activities and subjects in which he could not do well. As he grew older he saw the danger and deliberately set tasks for himself for which he had no special aptitude. At Leavenworth he undertook the tedious routine of training a horse and in the Philippines he took apart an automobile's engine and put it back together again—to prove to himself that he could do it.

Throughout his life he kept his boyhood curiosity. On every new post, on every trip across the country, during his visits to new places, he searched for local history. The highways and byroads of the Philippines, the battlefields of Manchuria, the church where Jeanne d'Arc was baptized, the remains of old Fort Vancouver—all these caught his interest. He pumped the knowledgeable for their special information and tried to learn the trade secrets of every specialist he met. In short, he had a scholar's itch for inquiry, but never quite a scholar's intentness on systematic investigation of a topic.

His reading over the years was voluminous and wonderfully diffuse. Biography, personal accounts of military expeditions, and general works on American and European history fascinated him, and he sought relaxation in popular Westerns and occasional novels. Once he astounded his officer students at Fort Benning by revealing that he found his pointers on the writing of a good term paper in a current fiction favorite, *Daddy Long Legs*. Some of his associates deplored his lack of academic accomplishments, saying that he had made no proper study of Clausewitz and had only textbook knowledge of other masters of the art of war. They also regretted his insufficient knowledge of the totalitarian ideologies of his time. To these charges Marshall would have been the first to plead guilty. Like most officers of his generation, he studied the practice of arms and not the theory. Like most of them, he had read little in political theory, international economics, or advanced science. In these matters he was not far behind most of his military and political contemporaries. In one particular, the duties of a soldier in a democracy, he was better informed than most. By inheritance, by training, and by prolonged work with civilians, he was aware of the strength and weaknesses of democratic government, and he was wholly prepared to fit his role to that system.

Marshall's education came primarily from constant study of his trade. He learned what made the Army work and then sought to improve the way in which it accomplished its purposes. Although a "student" by Army standards, he was not known as an original thinker. He was a pragmatic military scientist, tinkering with what he had until it worked better, rather than the intuitive genius who changes the nature of warfare. As a teacher he sought for ways by which to stimulate the thinking of his students and he provided an atmosphere in which bold experimentation might flourish.

In the study of strategy and tactics, Marshall suffered the same handicap as most American commanders in the period between the great wars: the lack of an opportunity to command large bodies of troops in the field and the lack of any need to think in terms of international relations. So far as the small American Army could give him practice he had it. In China for three years, he commanded a regiment during two periods of tension when clashes with Chinese troops seemed almost unavoidable. At Fort Benning for five years, he worked with well-trained and well-equipped demonstration units and the pick of the young infantry officers of the Army. In the five years before he came to Washington, he worked with units of brigade and division size, leading the Red Forces each summer in maneuvers. To a considerable degree he was aware of the important changes the truck, the tank, and the airplane were bringing to modern warfare, although he could not, of course, foresee all that World War II would develop. Perhaps most important, his duties with the Civilian Conservation Corps and the National Guard gave him a knowledge of the future citizen-soldier that few other top commanders would possess.

A week after he assumed office Marshall traveled back to his birthplace for a homecoming to which he had been invited several months before. He made of it almost a ceremonial return to the wellsprings of his youth, as if renewing his strength in preparation for the future. At the close of an afternoon of visiting scenes of his boyhood around Uniontown, he spoke to four hundred guests at the new White Swan Hotel, built on the site of the old tavern he had known as a boy. In these surroundings his mind turned to the past, and he spoke of the history of his native country. "There was a great deal of history and very important history written in that vicinity," he said. "And there was this great life of the nation which flowed through the National Pike and stopped overnight at the inn, just two blocks beyond the house where I lived as a boy."

He spoke of hunting pheasant along Braddock's trail and of picnicking at his grave. A mile beyond was Fort Necessity, where Washington had built his first fort and then had been forced to surrender to a superior force of French and Indians—nonetheless marching out with the honors of war. A favorite trout stream arose out of a deep ravine in the mountain near the place where Washington had surprised a small force under Sieur Coulon de Jumonville and killed the French leader and several members of his party. Marshall that evening recalled the words of Thackeray: "It was strange that in a savage forest of Pennsylvania, a young Virginian officer should fire a shot, and waken up a war which was to last for sixty years, which was to cover his own country and pass into Europe, to cost France her American colonies, to sever ours from us, and create the great Western Republic; to rage over the Old World when extinguished in the New; and, of all the myriads engaged in the vast contest, to

leave the prize of the greatest fame with him who struck the
first blow."

So George Marshall, at the beginning of a long and trying
assignment as Chief of Staff, mindful of his attainment to the
highest post the peacetime Army could give, and fully aware of
the grave crisis in world affairs, harked back to the days before
the founding of the Republic and to the deeds and men who
influenced the affairs of nations. In his closing passages, he reminded his hearers of their heritage and their good fortune,
with peaceful borders, prosperity, and freedom to do as they
liked. Of the stern times he saw ahead he added: "I will not
trouble you with the perplexities, the problems and requirements for the defense of this country, except to say that the importance of this matter is so great and the cost, unfortunately,
is bound to be so high, that all that we do should be planned
and executed in a businesslike manner, without emotional hys-
teria, demagogic speeches, or other unfortunate methods which
will befog the issue and might mislead our efforts. Finally, it
comes to me that we should daily thank the good Lord that we
live where we do, think as we do, and enjoy blessings that are
becoming rare privileges on this earth." [1]

His quiet appraisal of the international conflict, which he fore-
saw might one day involve the United States and transform the
world even as the opening battle of the French and Indian War
had changed the eighteenth century, was characteristic of the man.
Aware that he worked within the grand sweep of history, he proposed to approach his tasks with calm determination. In his
rock-like resolution, born of inner strength and forty years of
education for generalship, more than in the technical mastery he
so surely grasped, lay George Marshall's strongest weapon for the
coming trials.

Acknowledgments

In the Bibliographical Note on p. 354 I have listed the individuals who contributed to this volume by granting interviews, by sending information in the form of letters or short memoirs, or by gifts or loans of documents, photographs or other material. Here I wish to list some of the individuals and agencies which in various other ways have made this volume possible:

John D. Rockefeller, Jr., his widow, and a contributor who wishes to remain anonymous provided the funds for the initial research on this volume. A liberal advance from The Viking Press helped supply funds for the completion of the book.

The George C. Marshall Research Foundation, headed initially by the late John C. Hagan, Jr., and at present by General of the Army Omar N. Bradley, holds title to the papers of the General and exercises general supervision over the research program. The following individuals have been connected with the Foundation as officers or members of its board of directors: J. Clifford Miller, Jr., Major General William M. Stokes, John C. Parker, former Superintendent William H. Milton, Dr. F. P. Gaines, Brigadier General Frank McCarthy, Harry A. deButts, Lieutenant General Milton G. Baker, Carter Burgess, H. Merrill Pasco, Giles Miller, Jr., Dr. Fred C. Cole, Edmund Pendleton, Major General George R. E. Shell, Lieutenant Colonel C. J. George, Joseph D. Neikirk and Royster Lyle, Jr.

Three presidents of the United States, Harry S. Truman, Dwight D. Eisenhower, and John F. Kennedy have granted access to official documents and given their backing to our project. We have had the full support of government archivists and historians. This list includes: *National Archives,* Dr. Wayne Grover, Archivist of the United States; Sherrod East, Dallas Irvine, Wilbur Nigh, Robert W. Krauskopf, Mrs. Hazel Ward, and Garry D. Ryan; *Department of State,* Dr. G. Bernard Noble, former Director, Historical Office, Bureau of Public Affairs; Dr. William M. Franklin, Director, Historical Office, Bureau of Public Affairs; and Dr. E. Taylor Parks, Chief, Research Guidance and Review Division; *Department of Defense,* Dr. Rudolph Winnacker, historian; *Department of Army,* Dr. Kent R. Greenfield, former chief historian; Dr. Stetson Conn, chief historian; Israel Wice, and Charles Romanus; *Adjutant General's Office,* Ollon D. McCool, and Robert Ballentine.

Mrs. George C. Marshall has been especially helpful in answering hundreds of questions about the General and about her own interesting career.

She has passed on to me many items which had been sent to her regarding the General and has been helpful in locating old friends for me to interview. She has made no attempt to influence me in the writing of the book and has not read the manuscript.

Several members of General Marshall's former staff have aided me throughout the writing of this book by suggesting leads, by locating former associates, by recalling anecdotes, by helping me understand better the subject of this book, and by aiding me in the examination of the personal files of the General. This group includes: Brigadier General Frank McCarthy, Secretary General Staff, 1943-45; Colonel C. J. George, aide to General Marshall from 1947-59; Lt. General Marshall S. Carter, special assistant to General Marshall during the China Mission and while he was Secretary of State and Secretary of Defense; and Miss Mary L. Spilman, the General's secretary from 1953-59. To Miss Alma Hickey, secretary to General Bradley, the Foundation and I are deeply indebted for assistance in getting information and for typing.

Miss Eugenia D. Lejeune, the librarian of the Marshall Research Center and my chief administrative assistant, has been of tremendous help to me in every phase of the writing of this book. She has helped on research, checked and compiled footnotes, read newspaper files, run down references in books and periodicals, read proof, prepared the index and bibliography, and in dozens of ways proved herself an invaluable assistant. In this work she has been aided particularly by Mrs. Juanita Pitts, who has ably shared in many of these undertakings. Mrs. Frances Daniels, assisted by Mrs. Helen Roepke, has typed the various drafts of the manuscript. Miss Lejeune and Mrs. Roepke did most of the transcriptions of interviews used in the book, except for those of General Marshall. For these I did the initial transcriptions and Miss Lejeune carefully checked them.

Mrs. Arline Pratt made special studies of the Civilian Conservation Corps, our relations with China, and public opinion in regard to the Army in 1938-39. Mr. John H. Gauntlett also studied certain newspapers and magazines for information on the Army shortly before the beginning of war in Europe. Myles Marken, a part-time assistant, selected from great masses of material in the National Archives those items which shed light on the career of General Marshall in World War I. Colonel Bertram Kalisch, chief of the Audio-Visual Division, Department of Defense, made many valuable suggestions.

In the development of its initial program, the Foundation had the assistance of Kenneth Chorley, Carlisle Humelsine, former VMI Superintendent R. J. Marshall, Bernard M. Baruch, Thomas J. Watson, Robert A. Lovett, Mrs. Anna Rosenberg, John Lee Pratt, and Thomas J. Watson, Jr. The following gave valuable suggestions on the writing of the book, the collection and preservation of records, and the plans for the library: Brigadier General S. L. A. Marshall, Dr. Hugh M. Cole, Dr. L. A. Minnich, Dr. Philip Brooks, Dr. Herman Kahn, and Alonzo H. Gentry. Thirty eminent Americans, including several of the individuals listed elsewhere, make up a special Advisory Board which is at present raising funds for the George C. Marshall Research Library.

The following have read the book in whole or in part: Mark S. Watson, Colonel William Couper, Dr. I. B. Holley, Jr., Dr. Edward M. Coffman, Don Mace, Chaplain Martin Poch, Major General Philip E. Gallagher, Dr. C. S. Lowry, Dr. Frank Steely, Royce L. Thompson, my wife, and members of my staff. They have pointed out errors, in some cases suggested new material, or given helpful suggestions for improving the text.

F. C. P.

Bibliographical Note

MARSHALL INTERVIEWS

In the period August 1956 to April 1957, General Marshall held twenty-five interview sessions at his office in the Pentagon, at Leesburg, and Pinehurst. Some forty hours were recorded on tape and twelve to fifteen hours were taken down by a stenographer or by me in the form of notes. Part of the interviews were recorded by me personally, while others were taped in response to my questions, with Sergeant William Heffner, the General's orderly, running the machine. I followed up these latter interviews with questions designed to fill in gaps which might have been left by the General in his previous discussions.

For most of the interviews, General Marshall proposed that I prepare a general outline of a given period which would briefly review the subject matter to be covered and then set forth specific questions. He began the interviews with the World War II period, next covered high points of the postwar period, and then later turned to his childhood and early career. He had reached the year 1924 when ill health caused him to terminate the recording. The first interview on his childhood was done spontaneously, but subsequent discussions on his earlier career came in response to my detailed questions. In many cases I checked specifically on accounts published in books and articles which had appeared on his career.

Although gracious in his attitude, the General was not an easy man to interview. Possessed of a strong personal reserve, he considered it unseemly to talk too much about himself and felt that family history was a personal matter. As Chief of Staff he had so strongly impressed on members of his family the necessity of not talking to reporters that his sister and other relatives were hesitant to grant interviews. Some of his military associates were so imbued with the same idea that they talked only after he specifically wrote them that he had completely approved my project. After some of the interviews about his youth he said that he felt embarrassed and warned me not to show the taped material to anyone. Only after a number of letters indicating the importance of these personal details to an understanding of his career did he finally agree to leave to my discretion the publication of what he told me. In the case of some off-the-record interviews, which were

354

not recorded, he suggested that I not print the material during the lifetimes of the individuals involved, but again left it up to me to decide.

The General was a skillful editor and was quite sensitive about the text of his letters and speeches. Had he lived to revise the transcripts of these interviews, which he never saw, he would have eliminated repetitious statements, cut out many "ands" and "buts," and have substituted precise language for some general or ambiguous remarks. In order to do justice to him and to save the reader passages marked by numerous dots, I have made slight changes in the quotations to increase their readability. The sense has in no way been changed and the flavor of the language has been kept. Exact transcriptions are on file among the Marshall papers in custody of the George C. Marshall Research Foundation.

OTHER INTERVIEWS

More than three hundred friends and former associates of the General's have recorded their recollections of the General. Of these at least a hundred pertain to the period covered by this book. The following persons were interviewed one or more times for this volume. The period covered by their statements is indicated in the notes. Individuals whose names are starred gave material on General Marshall both in interviews and in the form of letters, photographs, clippings, newspapers, and the like: Brig. Gen. and Mrs. Claude M. Adams,* Mr. Billy Albright, Mr. Charles Alexander, Col. Henry Allen, Maj. Edward C. Applegate, Mrs. Catherine Armstrong,* Col. David D. Barrett,* Mr. Bernard Baruch, Brig. Gen. Royden E. Beebe, Mr. Chauncey Belknap,* Brig. Gen. T. J. Betts, Dr. Mercer Blanchard, Col. John R. Boatwright, Gen. Charles Bolté, Col. E. R. Bowditch, Maj. Gen. Leo Boyle,* Col. Fay Brabson,* General of the Army Omar N. Bradley,* Col. Bowyer Browne, Maj. Gen. Kenneth Buchanan,* Lt. Gen. Harold R. Bull, Col. Mervyn F. Burke,* Maj. Gen. James H. Burns, Brig. Gen. Frederic B. Butler, Gov. James F. Byrnes, Brig. Gen. B. F. Caffey,* Mrs. Robert Carson, Jr., Dr. Taylor Carter, Gen. Mark Clark, Maj. Gen. Harry J. Collins, Maj. Gen. James L. Collins,* Gen. Joseph L. Collins, Mrs. Harry Cootes,* Maj. Charles S. Coulter,* Col. William Couper,* Brig. Gen. and Mrs. W. E. Crist,* Maj. Gen. Frank L. Culin, Mr. Ralph A. Curtin, Gen. John Dahlquist, Mr. Chester Davis, Mrs. R. E. Dismukes, Sr.,* Mr. James A. Edgar, General of the Army Dwight D. Eisenhower,* Mr. Leo Farrell,* Mr. William Frye, Maj. Gen. Philip E. Gallagher,* Mr. Leonard Gaskill, Col. E. A. Goff, Jr.,* Gen. Leonard T. Gerow, Col. Clarence E. Gooding, Mrs. Charles Gorley,* Mr. Thomas Gowenlock, Col. V. J. Gregory,* Maj. Gen. C. C. Haffner, Gen. Wade Haislip, Mr. L. H. Hall, Maj. Gen. E. F. Harding,* Maj. Gen. Charles D. Herron,* Maj. Gen. John H. Hilldring, General Courtney Hodges, Mrs. Nan Wood Honeyman, Mr. W. A. Horne,* Col. Morgan Hudgins,* Mr. Banks Hudson,* Mrs. Thomas C. Hudson, Mr. John

C. Hughes,* Lt. Gen. Reuben E. Jenkins,* Col. Charles S. Johnson,* former Secretary of Defense Louis Johnson, Brig. Gen. Neal Johnson, Mr. Thomas M. Johnson,* Mr. Enoch Jones,* Mr. R. C. Jordan, Sr., Maj. Gen. C. E. Kilbourne, Gen. Walter Krueger, Col. Herman O. Lane,* Maj. Gen. Charles T. Lanham, Maj. Gen. Samuel T. Lawton, Maj. Gen. H. B. Lewis,* Col. Landon Lockett, former Senator Scott Lucas, Mrs. Haywood Luckett, General of the Army Douglas MacArthur, Col. and Mrs. J. E. McCammon, Mrs. Frank R. McCoy, Mrs. Leighton McPherson, Mr. Donald Mace,* Mr. Bert Manley, Mrs. George C. Marshall,* Brig. Gen. Richard C. Marshall, Mr. J. Searight Marshall,* Mr. John Martyn, Mrs. Henry F. Meyer,* Maj. Gen. Russell L. Maxwell, Mr. A. Erskine Miller, Chaplain Luther Miller, Brig. Gen. H. M. Monroe,* Mr. Harold A. Moore, Col. William C. Moore,* 1st Sgt. Joseph Morossow, Mr. Samuel F. Morse, Sgt. Boleslaus Mschichowski,* Mr. J. Churchill Newcomb,* Col. Isaac Newell, Brig. Gen. Thomas North, Miss Mary Kate O'Bryon,* Mr. Eugene Overstreet,* Mrs. Robert Owen, Mr. Arthur W. Page, Mr. George Pattullo,* Brig. Gen. R. T. Pendleton, Maj. Gen. Martin C. Poch,* Mr. Walter H. Rankins,* Col. Russell P. Reeder,* Maj. Gen. Charles Rich, Gen. Matthew B. Ridgway, Mrs. George H. Rockwell,* Brig. Gen. Paul M. Robinett,* Maj. Gen. Charles Roller,* Brig. Gen. Guy I. Rowe, Brig. Gen. Charles H. Royce, Mr. W. Dudley Rucker,* Mr. Edward Ryland, Mr. Durbin Sayers,* Mr. Germain Seligman,* Mr. J. T. Shepler, Mrs. J. J. Singer,* Mr. Eddie Smith, Col. and Mrs. Truman Smith, General Walter B. Smith, Col. William Spencer,* Maj. Gen. M. C. Stayer,* Mr. John Stecklein, Mrs. Joseph Stilwell, Brig. Gen. Ralph C. Talbot, Miss Cora Thomas, Miss Florence Tillery, Maj. Gen. Thomas S. Timberman, Sgt. Thomas Tweed,* Mrs. George Underwood,* Mrs. E. S. Waddell, Maj. Gen. Fred L. Walker, Mrs. E. M. Watson, Mr. Mark S. Watson, General Lawrence Whiting, Col. C. M. Willingham, Mr. Casper N. Wolf, Mr. Erskine Wood, Mr. Paul Wooten, Mrs. Etta Blanchard Worsley.

LETTERS

The General's personal files contained copies of most of his correspondence for the years 1932-39. Official files helped complete the correspondence for the 1938-39 period. The best collection of Marshall letters for the period 1919-32 is the Pershing-Marshall correspondence, Pershing Papers, Library of Congress. The Pershing Papers also contain letters between Pershing and General Harbord, W. Cameron Forbes, Charles G. Dawes, Frederick Palmer, General Drum, and John Callan O'Laughlin which refer to Marshall. O'Laughlin's letters to Pershing contain much valuable information on Marshall's promotion to general and selection of Chief of Staff in 1939. F. Warren Pershing gave permission to quote from his father's papers.

Some of Marshall's early letters, as well as the only letters available of his father's, are in the Alumni files and the Letter Books of the Virginia Military

Institute. The General's sister, Mrs. Singer, preserved a few letters from Dr. Jonathan Bradford to Mrs. Marshall.

Mr. John C. Hughes, onetime aide of General Pershing, has several letters from Marshall and his first wife in the period, 1919-27. Major General M. C. Stayer has an interesting file for the years 1928-39. Mr. Leo Farrell presented several letters from General Marshall to him to the Marshall Foundation. Mr. Bernard Baruch permitted the author to copy all letters pertaining to General Marshall in his files. Mr. Lorraine Pitman lent us a number of letters from General Marshall and the first Mrs. Marshall for the period 1923-32.

OTHER SOURCES OF INFORMATION

The author received more than five hundred letters from former associates of General Marshall in response to requests for information. Some of them enclosed letters they had received from the General or other material pertaining to him. Individuals who answered questions and furnished information in the form of photographs, clippings, books, and the like were: Mrs. Samuel G. Allen, Mrs. Frank M. Andrews, Mr. John L. Ames, Jr., Mr. Marshall Andrews, Brig. Gen. Thomas S. Arms, Maj. Gen. Archibald V. Arnold, Mrs. C. L. Ayling, Miss Alma Ayres, Lt. Col. Agard H. Bailey, Mrs. Helen Bailey, Mr. Elliott Bandini, Chaplain Frank Peer Beal, M. Sgt. Chester E. Beaver, Mr. Frank E. Beeton, Sr., Mr. David Z. Beeson, Col. Daniel J. Berry, Lt. Col. Edward L. Black, Capt. William W. Blood, Brig. Gen. Clifford Bluemel, Col. L. C. Boineau, Maj. Henry A. Bootz, Mr. Oliver V. Borden, Col. Edwin T. Bowden, Mr. Everett A. Boyden, Mr. Paul R. Brayton, Mr. Charles B. Briggs, Dr. Philip C. Brooks, Col. R. A. Broberg, Dr. John C. Brougher, Mrs. Leonard Brozik, Miss Teresa Burus, Mr. Roger F. Camp, Col. Joseph T. Caples, Mr. Richard I. Cargill, Brig. Gen. Arthur S. Champeny, SFC David W. Chase, Mrs. Daniel S. Cheever, Mr. Leo Cherne, Brig. Gen. Frank S. Clark, Mr. M. W. Clement, Mr. Andrew Cognac, M. Sgt. Joseph A. Connell, Mr. Philip E. Connelly, Maj. Gen. Norman D. Cota, Mrs. Matthew J. Coughlin, Maj. Gen. W. E. R. Covell, Miss Mildred C. Cox, Mrs. Amy C. Dabney, Maj. Gen. E. J. Dawley, Mr. Harry A. deButts, Col. Alfred R. W. deJonge, Mrs. Elizabeth Cameron DeWolf, Mr. Harry C. Diamond, Lt. Col. J. S. Douglas, Lt. Col. C. M. Easley, Mrs. Harry Evans, Mrs. Raymond Emerson, Mr. Charles G. Finney, Maj. William Fisk, Mr. William L. Flacks, Mr. J. H. Fleming, Mr. David C. Forbes, Col. J. J. Fulmer, Mr. Don Glass, Mr. George Goldfine, Major Chester B. Goolrick, Miss Isabella Gould, Mrs. Vera Gowaruha, Col. Walter S. Grant, Jr., Mrs. Hal G. Grantham, Col. Haydon Y. Grubbs, Mrs. Walter E. Gunster, Mrs. Beatrice Brandreth Hahn, Mrs. J. R. Hamlen, Col. David L. Hardee, Mr. John C. Hagan, Mr. Walter Hartridge, Maj. Paul Hathaway, Mr. Simeon Hawkes, Mrs. Earl Heartman, Mr. Don Henderson, Mrs. Lida S. Henesey, Mr. Wiley S. Hicks, Brig. Gen.

C. C. Hillman, Mrs. C. M. Himmelheber, Miss Ethel Hinton, Mr. William W. Hoffman, Lt. Col. Lawrence E. Hohl, Col. William J. Holzapfel, Maj. Gen. J. L. Homer, Col. Alfred H. Hopkins, Lt. Gen. C. R. Huebner, Miss Anne Hull, Mr. James E. Hunt, Brig. Gen. Barnhard A. Johnson, Dr. Henry J. John, Mr. Robert W. Jeffrey, Miss Elizabeth A. Johnson, Mr. H. Gary Johnson, Maj. Gen. Harold K. Johnson, Lt. Col. Robert A. Johnston, Maj. Gen. Alan W. Jones, Col. Bertram Kalisch, Mr. Newton S. Kenley, Maj. Hubert H. Kidwell, Col. Joseph C. King, Gen. Julius Klein, Col. Joseph C. King, Brig. Gen. Arthur W. Lane, Mr. Ralston B. Lattimore, Mr. E. W. Lauck, Lt. Col. Clyde B. Leasure, Misses Laura and Eugenia Lejeune, Col. Bernard Lentz, Maj. Gen. Emil Lenzner, Mrs. John Leshinsky, Jr., Sgt. Robert G. Lewis, Mrs. F. A. Littlejohn, Mr. Alfred E. Lyons, Mrs. Hugh M. Lokey, Mrs. Ethel M. Lucas, Miss Ellen Lucey, Mr. Royster Lyle, Brig. Gen. A. T. McAnsh, Mr. William McElrath, Col. Ducat McEntee, Mr. Howard Douglas McGeorge, Lt. Col. Thomas L. McKenna, Mrs. Claude H. McKinney, Col. Clenard McLaughlin, Mr. H. L. Mace, Mr. Guy Mahaney, Maj. Gen. F. B. Mallon, Mrs. Stuart B. Marshall, Mr. John M. Martin, Mrs. Julia Martin, Mrs. Ruth H. Martin, Dr. H. Norton Mason, Mr. William R. Mathews, Col. Frederick S. Matthews, Mr. Earl S. Mattingly, Mr. Edward Mayo, Col. Samuel E. Mays, Col. Owen R. Meredith, Lt. Gen. Troy H. Middleton, Mrs. Fauntleroy Miller, Col. Luis Monter, Mr. John N. Morton, Dr. J. H. Moy, Lt. Col. R. V. Murphy, Miss Reba Nalley, Col. I. J. Nichol, Mr. Joe A. Noake, Mr. Charles O'Neil, Mr Clyde Osborn, Brig. Gen. R. P. Ovenshine, Mr. Alfred F. Parker, Brig. Gen. F. LeJ. Parker, Maj. Gen. Frank H. Partridge, Maj. Gen. J. D. Patch, Mr. J. C. Pegram, Mrs. Marguerite W. Phelps, Col. Arthur Pickens, Miss Margaret B. Pickens, Mr. Lorraine Pitman, Mrs. Juanita Pitts, Mr. Connelly R. Potter, Mrs. Martha Prempert, Col. Roland I. Pritikin, Maj. Gen. Walter E. Prosser, Mrs. Dorothy Wells Raney, Maj. Gen. Paul L. Ransom, Col. Julian E. Raymond, Miss Mary Ann Reynolds, Miss Dolores Rhodes, Mr. John L. Rider, Col. Charles S. Ritchel, Brig. Gen. Charles Duval Roberts, Mrs. Anne Robertucci, Miss Bettie Roebuck, Mr. Thomas B. Rogers, Mr. Frank Rossiter, Col. Garland T. Rowland, Mr. Don Russell, Mr. Alexander H. Sands, Savannah Beach Chamber of Commerce, Col. Feodor O. Schmidt, Mr. William D. Scholle, Lt. Col. Milton A. Schreiber, Col. Charles T. Senay, Mr. Sidney Shalett, Mrs. William A. Shepherd, Lt. Col. Walter L. Sherfey, Mrs. N. B. Sherris, Maj. Gen. Edwin L. Sibert, Maj. Gen. F. C. Sibert, Mr. M. R. Simmonds, Col. Frank S. Singer, Mr. and Mrs. Robert Smith, Jr., M. Sprinz, Col. James Stack, Mr. Ivan H. Stanton, Brig. Gen. Alexander N. Stark, Brig. Gen. M. L. Stockton, Col. C. E. Stodter, Col. Alexander C. Sullivan, Col. Iverson B. Summers, Lt. Gen. W. C. Sweeney, Jr., Col. Samuel G. Talbott, Mr. Marion C. Tarapata, Col. Thomas F. Taylor, Mr. Gilbert M. Thompson, Mr. Wyman C. Tupper, The Editor, Tribune Review Publishing Co., Mrs. Roselma W. DeSellems, Mr. O. Z. Tyler, Jr., Col. J. H. Van Horn, Miss Mary Bell Vaughan, Col. John

M. Virden, Col. William A. Walker, Mr. Andrew Wallace, Col. John M. Welch, M. Sgt. Joe B. West, Lt. Col. C. W. Westlund, Rev. Harry S. Weyrich, Col. Morris T. Whitmore, Mr. James T. Williams, Maj. Gen. Durward S. Wilson, Col. N. B. Wilson, Col. Lloyd N. Winters, Col. Jennings Wise, Mr. Samuel B. Wolfe, Mrs. Elizabeth Bradford Harbeson.

ARCHIVES AND LIBRARIES

The principal official records for the period 1901-1939 may be found in the National Archives in Washington listed according to units, posts, or general topics. The chief collections consulted include: 30th Infantry, 13th Infantry, 24th Infantry, 8th Infantry, 15th Infantry, 5th Infantry Brigade, School of the Line and Staff College, Fort Leavenworth, National Guard and Militia, 1st Division, First Army, AEF/GHQ, reorganization of the Army, Inspector General, U.S. Army Forces in China, Civilian Conservation Corps. The World War II Records Division, National Archives, at Alexandria, still has the main collections for the year 1939 pertaining to Chief of Staff, Deputy Chief of Staff, War Plans Division, and the like.

For the period prior to World War I, the Appointment, Commission, and Personnel Branch of the Adjutant General's Office in the National Archives has many personal items pertaining to commissioning, assignments, examinations, and the like. The General's 201 File for the period since 1919 was, at the time I examined it with General Marshall's permission, in the General Officers Section, TAGO. This file contains a summary of his record for the 1901-1919 period in addition to assignments, promotions, awards, leave record, efficiency reports, medical examinations, and the like.

A few papers on the period 1938-1939 were copied from the Roosevelt collection in the Franklin D. Roosevelt Library, Hyde Park, New York.

I am deeply obligated to the director and staff of the National Archives, the World War II Records Division at Alexandria, the Department of the Army Library, the Manuscripts Division of the Library of Congress, the National War College Library, and the reference section of the Office of the Chief of Military History, Department of the Army.

Other libraries which have been of great assistance are: Fort Leavenworth Library and Museum; Public Library, Washington, D.C.; Fort Benning Library and Museum; Virginia Military Institute Library; Archives, State of Georgia; University of Virginia Library; Louisville Public Library; Portland Public Library; Cincinnati Public Library; Uniontown Public Library; library of the *Washington Post;* library of the Presidio, San Francisco; Enoch Pratt Library, Baltimore; Pennsylvania State Library; Carnegie Institute, Pittsburgh; files of the National Guard, State of Illinois, through the kindness of Lt. General Leo Boyle; Richmond (Virginia) Public Library; Virginia State Library, Richmond; Carmel (California) Public Library; Murray (Kentucky) State College Library.

BIOGRAPHIES OF MARSHALL

Only three biographical studies have been published. The first to appear, William Frye, *Marshall Citizen Soldier* (1947), covers Marshall's life from his birth until his retirement as Chief of Staff of the Army. Frye interviewed a number of schoolmates in Uniontown, Marshall's two chief roommates at VMI, and a number of fellow officers. Extracts from General Marshall's 201 File and from some letters of Marshall's in the Pershing Papers were made available to him, but he was not given access to the files themselves. He did not interview General Marshall, and the book's publication was delayed, at the General's request, until Marshall retired as Chief of Staff. Although the book lacks footnotes, Mr. Frye gave me the names of his sources in several cases. In a few cases, an individual who had earlier supplied information to Mr. Frye in written form made a copy available to me. I have also benefited from Colonel William Couper's extracts from the VMI files prepared for Mr. Frye and from his corrections of certain items. I have seen Stuart Marshall's corrections of certain items as well as criticisms on the Philippine chapter contained in letters to the editor in issues of *Bamboo Breezes,* the publication of the 30th Infantry.

Katherine Tupper Marshall's *Together* (1946) is valuable on the period 1930-45. Mrs. Marshall supplements her own recollections with some of General Marshall's favorite stories. The General checked some of the book, but there are sometimes errors in dates and spelling of names. The book is especially helpful for the human side of the General and for throwing light on a number of points in his career. Mrs. Marshall has filled in a number of details of certain parts of the book on tape for me.

Robert Payne's book on General Marshall covers the high points of his public career. The author depended largely on secondary sources and on some papers, such as the World War I documents, which were published after Frye's volume appeared in print. The author is a sensitive writer, but he had no access to Marshall's papers and he apparently talked to few of the General's associates. The book, while provocative, is often incorrect in its interpretations.

Marshall Andrews, formerly of the *Washington Post,* gathered material for articles or a book on General Marshall in 1942 but dropped the project at the General's request. Andrews interviewed a number of former classmates at VMI and got material from others who knew him as a young officer. He turned over his notes and material contained in letters to the Marshall Research Center.

NEWSPAPERS AND PERIODICALS

The following newspaper files were consulted: *Genius of Liberty* (Uniontown, Pa.), 1869-1900 (microfilm); *Rockbridge County News* (Lexington,

Va.), 1897-1901; *The Sentinel* (15th Infantry, Tientsin, China), 1924-27; *Fort Benning News,* 1925-32; Savannah *Morning News,* 1932-33; Charleston *News and Courier,* 1932-33; *Chicago Tribune,* 1933-36; *Vancouver Columbian,* 1936-38; Portland *Oregonian,* 1936-38; Portland *Oregon Daily Journal,* 1936-38; *Washington Post,* 1938-39; Washington *Star,* 1938-39; *The Review,* CCC, Vancouver District, 1936-38; *New York Times* for items indexed 1918-38 and for background material 1938-39; *Time,* 1938-39; *Newsweek,* 1938-39; *Army and Navy Journal,* 1938-39; *Army and Navy Register,* 1938-39; scrapbook of clippings from Uniontown papers by Alfred Marshall in Uniontown Library; scrapbook of clippings, 1919-25, in *Pershing Papers, Library of Congress;* scrapbook on events in China, 1925-27, kept by Mrs. W. E. Crist.

Selected Bibliography

Acheson, Dean. *Sketches from Life of Men I Have Known.* New York: Harper and Bros., 1961.

Arnold, Henry H. *Global Mission.* New York: Harper and Bros., 1949.

Association Nationale des Croix de Guerre. *Verdun, the Battle for Freedom;* 40th Anniversary. New York: French Printing and Publishing Co., 1959.

Ballentine, Charles [pseud. of Edgar Bellairs]. *As It Is In the Philippines.* New York: Charles Scribner's Sons, 1902.

Baruch, Bernard M. *My Own Story.* New York: Henry Holt and Co., Inc., 1957-60. 2 vols.

Beveridge, Albert J. *The Life of John Marshall.* Boston: Houghton Mifflin Co., 1916. 4 vols.

The Biographical Encyclopedia of Kentucky of the Dead and Living Men of the Nineteenth Century. Cincinnati, Ohio: J. M. Armstrong and Co., 1878.

Blount, James H. *The American Occupation of the Philippines, 1898-1912.* New York: G. P. Putnam's Sons, 1912.

Borg, Dorothy. *American Policy and the Chinese Revolution, 1925-1928.* New York: Macmillan Co., 1947.

Brandreth, Paulina. *Trails of Enchantment.* New York: G. H. Waitt, 1930.

Buck, Solon J., and Buck, Elizabeth H. *The Planting of Civilization in Western Pennsylvania.* Pittsburgh: University of Pittsburgh Press, 1939.

Bullard, Robert L. *Personalities and Reminiscences of the War.* New York: Doubleday, Page and Co., 1925.

Buss, Claude A. *The Far East; A History of Recent and Contemporary International Relations in East Asia.* New York: Macmillan Co., 1955.

Butler, Mann. *A History of the Commonwealth of Kentucky.* Louisville, Ky.: Wilcox, Dickerman and Co., 1834.

Cameron, Meribeth, and others. *China, Japan and the Powers.* New York: Ronald Press Co., 1952.

Carter, William G. H. *Creation of the American General Staff.* Washington: U.S. Govt. Print. Off., 1924.

Chase, Joseph C. *Soldiers All; Portraits and Sketches of the Men of the A.E.F.* New York: George H. Doran Co., 1920.

Chastaine, Ben-Hur. *History of the 18th U.S. Infantry, First Division, 1812-1919.* New York: Hymans Publishing Co., [1920?].

Chiang Kai-shek. *Soviet Russia in China; A Summing up at Seventy.* New York: Farrar, Straus and Cudahy, 1957.

Clark, John Maurice. *The Costs of the World War to the American People.* New Haven: Yale University Press, 1931.

Clark, Victor S. *History of Manufactures in the United States.* New York: Mc-Graw-Hill Book Co., Inc., 1929. 3 vols.

Clay, Cassius. *The Life of Cassius Marcellus Clay. Memoirs, Writings, and Speeches, Showing his Conduct in the Overthrow of American Slavery, the Salvation of the Union, and the Restoration of the Autonomy of the States.* . . . Cincinnati: J. F. Brennan and Co., 1886. 2 vols.

Clift, G. Glenn. *History of Maysville and Mason County.* Lexington, Ky.: Transylvania Printing Co., 1936.

Coles, Harry L., ed. *Total War and Cold War.* Columbus, Ohio: Ohio State University Press, 1962.

Collins, Lewis. *Collins Historical Sketches of Kentucky. History of Kentucky,* revised . . . by his son Richard H. Collins. Covington, Ky.: Collins and Co., 1882. 2 vols.

Conn, Stetson, and Fairchild, Byron. *The Framework of Hemisphere Defense.* Washington: Office of the Chief of Military History, Dept. of the Army, 1960. (United States Army in World War II: The Western Hemisphere.)

Conner, Virginia. *What Father Forbad.* Philadelphia: Dorrance and Co., 1951.

Couper, William. *One Hundred Years at VMI,* with foreword by General George C. Marshall. Richmond, Va.: Garrett and Massie, 1939. 4 vols.

Cramer, C. H. *Newton Baker; A Biography.* Cleveland: World Publishing Co., 1961.

Crow, Carl. *Handbook for China.* New York: Dodd, Mead and Co., 1926.

Crozier, Emmet. *American Reporters on the Western Front, 1914-18.* New York: Oxford University Press, 1959.

Cullum, George W. *Biographical Register of the Officers and Graduates of the U.S. Military Academy at West Point, N.Y., since its establishment in 1802.* Chicago: R. R. Donnelley and Sons Co., 1930-1950. (Vols. 5-10, 1900-1950.)

Davis, George W. *Report of the Military Government on the City of Manila, 1898-1901.* Manila: 1901.

DeSeversky, Alexander P. *America: Too Young to Die!* New York: McGraw-Hill Book Co., 1961.

Deutrich, Mabel E. *The Struggle for Supremacy; the Career of General Fred C. Ainsworth.* Washington: Public Affairs Press, 1962.

Dickman, Joseph T. *The Great Crusade; A Narrative of the World War.* New York: D. Appleton and Co., 1927.

The Doughboy, published for the Classes of 1931-32, National Guard and Reserve Company Officers. Fort Benning, Ga.: The Infantry School, 1931-32.

Duke, Basil W. *A History of Morgan's Cavalry.* Bloomington, Ind.: Indiana University Press, 1960. (Reprint of 1867 ed.)

Dulles, Foster R. *The American Red Cross; A History.* New York: Harper and Bros., 1950.

——. *China and America: The Story of their Relations since 1784.* Princeton, N.J.: Princeton University Press, 1946.

——. *The United States since 1865.* Ann Arbor, Mich.: University of Michigan Press, 1959.

Dupuy, R. Ernest. *The Compact History of the United States Army.* New York: Hawthorn Books, Inc., 1956.

Edmonds, James E. *A Short History of World War I*. London: Oxford University Press, 1951.

Ekirch, Arthur A., Jr. *The Civilian and the Military*. New York: Oxford University Press, 1956.

Ellis, Franklin, ed. *History of Fayette County, Pennsylvania, with Biographical Sketches of Many of Its Pioneers and Prominent Men*. Philadelphia: L. H. Everts and Co., 1882.

Eskew, Garnett L. *Willard's of Washington, the Epic of a Capital Caravansary*. New York: Coward-McCann, 1954.

Evarts, Jeremiah M. *Cantigny; a Corner of the War*. Privately printed, 1938.

Falls, Cyril. *The Great War*. New York: G. P. Putnam's Sons, 1959.

Finney, Charles G. *The Old China Hands*. Garden City, N.Y.: Doubleday and Co., 1961.

Fiske, Bradley Allen. *War Time in Manila*. Boston: R. G. Badger, 1913.

Fort Leavenworth from Frontier Post to Home of the United States Army Command and General Staff College. Fort Leavenworth, Kans., 1959.

Fredericks, Pierce G. *The Great Adventure; America in the First World War*. New York: E. P. Dutton and Co., Inc., 1960.

Freidel, Frank. *The Splendid Little War*. Boston: Little, Brown and Co., 1958.

H. C. Frick Coke Co. *A Brief Outline of the Development of the Great Connellsville Coke Region.* . . . Pittsburgh: 1892.

Frothingham, Thomas G. *The American Reinforcements in the World War*. Garden City, N.Y.: Doubleday and Co., 1927.

Frye, William. *Marshall; Citizen Soldier*. Indianapolis: Bobbs-Merrill Co., Inc., 1947.

Ganoe, William A. *History of the United States Army*. Rev. ed. New York: D. Appleton and Co., 1943.

Gleaves, Albert. *A History of the Transport Service; Adventures and Experiences of United States Transports and Cruisers in the World War*. New York: George H. Doran Co., 1921.

Goldberg, Alfred, ed. *A History of the United States Air Force, 1907-1957*, by Alfred Goldberg, editor, Wilhelmine Burch [and others]. Princeton, N.J.: Van Nostrand, 1957.

Griepenkerl, Otto F. *Letters on Applied Tactics, Problems Dealing with the Operations of Detachments of the Three Arms*, authorized translation (with substitution of American Army organization) by Major C. H. Barth. Kansas City, Mo.: Franklin Hudson Publishing Co., 1906.

Griswold, A. Whitney. *The Far Eastern Policy of the United States*. New York: Harcourt, Brace and Co., 1938.

Hadden, James. *A History of Uniontown, Pennsylvania, the County Seat of Fayette County, Pennsylvania*. Uniontown, Pa.: James Hadden, 1913.

Hagedorn, Hermann. *Leonard Wood; a Biography*. New York: Harper and Bros., 1931. 2 vols.

Hagood, Johnson. *The Services of Supply; A Memoir of the Great War*. Boston: Houghton Mifflin Co., 1927.

Hanna, Matthew E. *Tactical Principles and Problems*. 4th ed. Menasha, Wis.: George Banta Publishing Co., 1910.

Harbord, James G. *The American Army in France, 1917-1919*. Boston: Little, Brown and Co., 1936.

——. *Leaves from a War Diary*. New York: Dodd, Mead and Co., 1925.

Heiser, Victor. *An American Doctor's Odyssey*. New York: W. W. Norton and Co., 1936.

Hicks, John D. *The American Nation, A History of the United States from 1865 to the Present*. 2d ed. Boston: Houghton Mifflin Co., 1943.

Hoehling, Adolph A. *The Fierce Lambs*. Boston: Little, Brown and Co., 1960.

Holcombe, Arthur N. *The Spirit of the Chinese Revolution*. New York: Alfred A. Knopf, Inc., 1930.

Holley, I. B., Jr. *Ideas and Weapons, Exploitation of the Aerial Weapon by the United States during World War I*. New Haven: Yale University Press, 1953.

Huidekoper, Frederick L. *The Military Unpreparedness of the United States; A History of the American Land Forces from Colonial Times until June 1, 1915*. New York: Macmillan Co., 1915.

Hull, Cordell. *Memoirs*. New York: Macmillan Co., 1948. 2 vols.

Hunt, Elvid. *History of Fort Leavenworth, 1827-1937*. 2d ed. Fort Leavenworth: The Command and General Staff School Press, 1937.

Hunt, Frazier. *The Untold Story of Douglas MacArthur*. New York: Devin-Adair Co., 1954.

Hurlbert, Archer B. *The Old National Road, A Chapter of American Expansion*. Columbus, Ohio: Press of F. I. Heer, 1901.

Infantry in Battle. Washington: The Infantry Journal, Inc., 1934.

Isaacs, Harold R. *The Tragedy of the Chinese Revolution*. Stanford, Calif.: Stanford University Press, 1951.

Jessup, Philip C. *Elihu Root*. New York: Dodd, Mead and Co., 1938. 2 vols.

Johnson, Thomas M. *Without Censor; New Light on Our Greatest World War Battles*. Indianapolis: Bobbs-Merrill Co., 1928.

Jordan, John W., and Hadden, James, eds. *Genealogical and Personal History of Fayette and Greene Counties, Pennsylvania*. New York: Lewis Historical Publishing Co., 1912.

The Journal of the Senate of Kentucky, Special Session, May 1861. Frankfort, Ky.: J. B. Major, 1861.

Kernan, William F., and Samson, Henry T. *History of the 103d Field Artillery (26th Division, A.E.F.), World War, 1917-1919*. Providence, R. I.: Remington Printing Co., 1930 [?].

Kreidberg, Marvin A., and Henry, Merton G. *History of Military Mobilization in the United States Army, 1775-1945*. Washington: Dept. of the Army, 1955.

Langer, William L., and Gleason, Sarell E. *The Challenge to Isolation, 1937-1940*. New York: Harper and Bros., 1952.

Langer, William L. *The Diplomacy of Imperialism*. New York: Alfred A. Knopf, Inc., 1935.

Lee, Clark G., and Henschel, Richard. *Douglas MacArthur*. New York: Holt and Co., 1952.

Leech, Margaret. *In the Days of McKinley*. New York: Harper and Bros., 1959.

Leopold, Richard W. *The Growth of American Foreign Policy, A History*. New York: Alfred A. Knopf, Inc., 1962.

Liggett, Hunter. *A.E.F.: Ten Years Ago in France*. New York: Dodd, Mead and Co., 1928.

——. *Commanding an American Army; Recollections of the World War*. Boston: Houghton Mifflin Co., 1925.

Link, Arthur S. *American Epoch, A History of the United States since the 1890's.* New York: Alfred A. Knopf, Inc., 1955.

——. *Woodrow Wilson and the Progressive Era, 1910-1917.* New York: Harper and Bros., 1954.

——. *Wilson the Diplomatist, A Look at his Major Foreign Polices.* Baltimore, Md.: Johns Hopkins University Press, 1957.

——. *The Struggle for Neutrality, 1914-1915.* Princeton, N.J.: Princeton University Press, 1960. (Vol. III of his *Wilson.*)

Liu, F. F. *A Military History of Modern China, 1924-1949.* Princeton, N.J.: Princeton University Press, 1956.

Lohbeck, Don. *Patrick J. Hurley.* Chicago: Henry Regnery Co., 1956.

McCarthy, Joseph R. *America's Retreat from Victory, the Story of George Catlett Marshall.* New York: Devin-Adair Co., 1951.

MacNair, Harley F., and Lach, Donald F. *Modern Far Eastern International Relations.* 2d ed. New York: D. Van Nostrand Co., Inc., 1955.

Marshall, George Catlett. *Selected Speeches and Statements of General of the Army George C. Marshall, Chief of Staff, United States Army,* ed. by Major H. A. DeWeerd. Washington: The Infantry Journal, Inc., 1945.

Marshall, Katherine. *Together; Annals of an Army Wife.* Atlanta, Ga.: Tupper and Love, 1946.

Martin, Wilbur C. and How, Julie Lien-ying. *Documents on Communism, Nationalism, and Soviet Advances in China, 1918-1927, papers seized in the 1927 Peking Raid.* New York: Columbia University Press, 1956.

Millis, Walter. *The Martial Spirit.* Boston: Houghton Mifflin Co., 1931.

Morison, Elting E. *Turmoil and Tradition, A Study of the Life and Times of Henry L. Stimson.* Boston: Houghton Mifflin Co., 1960.

Morton, Louis. *Strategy and Command; the First Two Years.* Washington: Office of the Chief of Military History, Dept. of the Army, 1962 (*United States Army in World War II: The War in the Pacific*).

Nelson's Biographical Dictionary and Historical Reference Book of Fayette County, Pennsylvania, containing a condensed history of Pennsylvania, of Fayette County and of boroughs and townships of the county; also portraits and biographies of the governors since 1790, and genealogies, family histories, and biographies of representative men of the county. Uniontown, Pa.: S. B. Nelson, 1900.

Nelson, Otto L., Jr. *National Security and the General Staff.* Washington: Infantry Journal Press, 1946.

Palmer, Frederick. *America in France.* New York: Dodd, Mead and Co., 1918.

——. *Bliss, Peacemaker, the Life and Letters of General Tasker Howard Bliss.* New York: Dodd, Mead and Co., 1934.

——. *John J. Pershing, General of the Armies, A Biography.* Harrisburg, Pa.: Military Service Publishing Co., 1948.

——. *Newton D. Baker.* New York: Dodd, Mead and Co., 1931.

——. *Our Gallant Madness.* Garden City, N.Y.: Doubleday, Doran and Co., 1937.

——. *Our Greatest Battle (The Meuse-Argonne).* New York: Dodd, Mead and Co., 1919.

Palmer, John McAuley. *America in Arms; The Experience of the United States with Military Organization.* New Haven, Conn.: Yale University Press, 1941.

Parker, James. *The Old Army, Memories, 1872-1918.* Philadelphia: Dorrance and Co., 1929.

Paxson, Frederic L. *American Democracy and the World War.* Boston: Houghton Mifflin Co., 1936. 3 vols.

Paxton, William M. *The Marshall Family.* Cincinnati, Ohio: Robert Clarke and Co., 1885.

Payne, Robert. *The Marshall Story; A Biography of General George C. Marshall.* New York: Prentice-Hall, Inc., 1951.

Pecquet du Bellet, Louise. *Some Prominent Virginia Families.* Lynchburg, Va.: J. P. Bell and Co., 1907. 4 vols.

Peixotto, Ernest. *The American Front.* New York: Charles Scribner's Sons, 1919.

Pershing, John J. *My Experiences in the World War.* New York: Frederick Stokes, 1931. 2 vols.

Pitt, Barrie. *1918; The Last Act.* New York: W. W. Norton and Co., Inc., 1962.

Pratt, Julius W. *A History of United States Foreign Policy.* New York: Prentice-Hall, Inc., 1955.

Rankins, Walter H. *Augusta College, Augusta, Ky., First Established Methodist College, 1822-1849.* Frankfort, Ky.: Roberts Printing Co., 1957.

——. *Historic Augusta and Augusta College: Sesqui-Centennial ed., 1797-1947.* Augusta, Ky.: 1949.

Rasmussen, Otto D. *Tientsin; an Illustrated Outline History.* Tientsin, China: The Tientsin Press, 1925.

Rees, Thomas H. *Topographical Surveying and Sketching.* Fort Leavenworth: Ketcheson Printing Co., 1908.

Ridgway, Matthew B. *Soldier: The Memoirs of Matthew B. Ridgway.* New York: Harper and Bros., 1956.

Riker, William H. *Soldiers of the States; The Role of the National Guard in American Democracy.* Washington: Public Affairs Press, 1957.

Roosevelt, Franklin D. *F.D.R.: His Personal Letters . . . ,* ed. by Elliott Roosevelt. New York: Duell, Sloan and Pearce, 1950. 4 vols.

Root, Elihu. *The Military and Colonial Policy of the United States; Addresses and Reports,* collected and edited by Robert Bacon and James B. Scott. Cambridge, Mass.: Harvard University Press, 1916.

Searight, Thomas B. *The Old Pike. A History of the National Road with Incidents, Accidents, and Anecdotes Thereon.* Uniontown, Pa.: 1894.

Semple, Robert B. *A History of the Rise and Progress of the Baptists in Virginia,* rev. and extended by Rev. George W. Beale. Richmond, Va.: Pitt and Dickinson, 1894.

Seton-Watson, Hugh. *From Lenin to Malenkov; The History of World Communism.* New York: Frederick A. Praeger, Inc., 1953.

Sexton, William T. *Soldiers in the Sun; An Adventure in Imperialism.* Harrisburg, Pa.: Military Service Publishing Co., 1939.

Shannon, David A. *The Great Depression.* Englewood Cliffs, N.J.: Prentice-Hall, Inc., 1960.

Sheppard, Muriel E. *Cloud by Day; The Story of Coal and Coke and People.* Chapel Hill, N.C.: University of North Carolina Press, 1947.

Sherrill, Clarence O. *Military Topography for the Mobile Forces including Map Reading, Surveying and Sketching.* 2d ed. Menasha, Wis.: George Banta Publishing Co., 1911.

Sherrill, Clarence O., and Marshall, George C. *Notes on Cordage and Tackle*. Fort Leavenworth, Kans.: Staff College Press, 1909.

Sherwood, Robert E. *Roosevelt and Hopkins; An Intimate History*. New York: Harper and Bros., 1948.

Smith, Francis H. *The Virginia Military Institute; Its Building and Rebuilding*. Lynchburg, Va.: J. P. Bell and Co., 1912.

Snow, Edgar. *Red Star Over China*. New York: Modern Library, 1944.

Society of the First Division. *History of the First Division during the World War, 1917-1919*. Philadelphia: John C. Winston Co., 1922.

Society of the First Division. *Memorial Album; Pictorial History of the 1st Division*. San Diego, Calif.: n.d.

Sokolsky, George E. *The Tinder Box of Asia*. Garden City, N.Y.: Doubleday, Doran and Co., 1933.

Speed, Thomas. *The Union Cause in Kentucky, 1860-1865*. New York: G. P. Putnam's Sons, 1907.

Spencer, John H. *A History of Kentucky Baptists from 1769 to 1885, including more than 800 Biographical Sketches*. Cincinnati: J. R. Baumes, 1886. 2 vols.

The Story of the Sixteenth Infantry in France, by the Regimental Chaplain. Montabaur-Frankfurt, Germany: Martin Flock and Co., 1919.

The Story of the Twenty-Eighth Infantry in the Great War. Coblenz, Germany: 1919.

Strickler, Harry M. *A Short History of Page County, Virginia*. Richmond, Va.: Dietz Press, Inc., 1952.

Sullivan, Mark. *Our Times*. New York: Charles Scribner's Sons, 1926-1935. 6 vols.

Tansill, Charles C. *Back Door to War; The Roosevelt Foreign Policy, 1933-1941*. Chicago: Henry Regnery Co., 1952.

Taylor, James B. *Virginia Baptist Ministers*. 3d ed. 1st ser. Philadelphia: J. B. Lippincott Co., 1859.

Tong, Hollington K. *Chiang Kai-shek; Soldier and Statesman*. Shanghai, China: China Publishing Co., 1937.

The Twenty-Sixth Infantry in France, by the Regimental Adjutant. Montabaur-Frankfurt, Germany: Martin Flock and Co., 1919.

U.S. Adjutant General's Office. *U.S. Army Register, 1901-1939*. Washington: U.S. Govt. Print. Off.

U.S. American Battle Monuments Commission. *1st Division, Summary of Operations in the World War*. Washington: U.S. Govt. Print. Off., 1944.

——. *American Armies and Battlefields in Europe*. Washington: U.S. Govt. Print. Off., 1938.

U.S. Army. Chemical Corps. *The 1st Division at Cantigny, May 1918*. Washington: Historical Office, U.S. Army Chemical Center, 1958. (Historical Studies Gas Warfare in World War I. Study No. 11).

U.S. Army. Corps of Engineers. *Report to the Chief Engineer, First Army, American Expeditionary Forces, on Engineer Operations in the St. Mihiel and Meuse-Argonne Offensives, 1918*. Washington: U.S. Govt. Print. Off., 1929.

U.S. Army. First Army. *Report of the First Army, American Expeditionary Forces; Organization and Operations*. Fort Leavenworth, Kans.: General Service Schools Press, 1923. 2 vols.

U.S. Army. 1st Division. *World War Records, First Division, AEF*. Washington: 1928-31. 25 vols.

U.S. Army. 15th Infantry. *15th Infantry Annual, May 4, 1924-May 4, 1925*. Tientsin, China: Tientsin Press, 1925.

U.S. Army. 30th Infantry. *Roster of the 30th U.S. Infantry. March 15, 1901-December 14, 1903*. 30th Infantry, 1940.

U.S. Army, IX Corps Area. *Vancouver Barracks, CCC District, Ninth Corps Area, Headquarters*. Vancouver Barracks, Wash.: January 1, 1938.

U.S. Army Service Schools. *Annual Reports of the Commandant . . . for the School Years ending 1907-1910*. Fort Leavenworth, Kans.: Staff College Press, 1907-1910.

U.S. Commission appointed by the President to Investigate the Conduct of the War Dept. in the War with Spain. *Report of the Commission. . . .* Washington: U.S. Govt. Print. Off., 1900. 8 vols (U.S. Congress. 56th Cong., 1st Sess., Senate Doc. No. 221).

U.S. Congress. House. Committee on Military Affairs. *An Adequate National Defense as Outlined by the President of the United States. Hearings . . . 76th Congress, 1st Session. January 17-February 2, 1939.*

——. *Hearings . . . HR 7093, Providing for the Rank and Title of Lt. General in the Regular Army; HR 7111, to Facilitate the Procurement of Aircraft for Defense*. July 11, 1939.

U.S. Congress. Senate. Committee on Military Affairs. *Reorganization of the Army, Hearings on S2691, 2693, 2715, 66th Congress, 1st and 2d Sessions*. Washington: U.S. Govt. Print. Off., 1919. 2 vols.

——. *National Defense. Hearings . . . 76th Congress, 1st Session, on HR 3791.* January 17-February 22, 1939.

U.S. Dept. of State. *Papers Relating to Foreign Relations of the United States, 1925*. Washington: U.S. Govt. Print. Off., 1940, 2 vols.

——. 1926. 1941. 2 vols.

——. 1927. 1942. 3 vols.

U.S. Dept. of the Army. Historical Division. *United States Army in the World War, 1917-1919*. Washington: U.S. Govt. Print. Off., 1948. 17 vols.

U.S. Infantry School, Fort Benning, Ga. *Mailing List, 1927-1932*.

U.S. Military Academy, West Point. Association of Graduates. *Fiftieth Annual Report of the Association of Graduates of the U.S. Military Academy*. Saginaw, Mich.: Seeman and Peters, Inc., 1919.

U.S. *Official Pictures of the World War Showing America's Participation, Selected from the Official Files of the War Dept.* Washington: Pictorial Bureau, 1920.

U.S. Philippine Commission, 1899-1900. *Report of the Philippine Commission to the President, January 31, 1900-December 20, 1900*. Washington: U.S. Govt. Print. Off., 1900-1901. 4 vols. in 3.

U.S. War Dept. *Annual Reports of the Secretary of War, 1901-1939*. Washington: U.S. Govt. Print. Off. (See specific volume in notes.)

——. General Staff. *The War with Germany, A Statistical Summary*, by Leonard P. Ayres. 2d ed. rev. Washington: U.S. Govt. Print. Off., 1919.

Van Every, Dale. *The AEF in Battle*. New York: D. Appleton and Co., 1928.

Verdun, Argonne, Metz (1914-1918). Paris: Michelin et Cie., 1919.

Viereck, George S. *As They Saw Us; Foch, Ludendorff and Other Leaders Write Our War History*. Garden City, N.Y.: Doubleday, Doran and Co., 1929.

Vinacke, Harold M. *A History of the Far East in Modern Times*. 4th ed. New York: F. S. Crofts and Co., 1945.

Virginia Military Institute. *The Bomb*. Lexington, Va.: 1901.

——. *Register of Former Cadets*. Memorial edition. Lexington, Va.: 1957.

von Schell, Adolf. *Battle Leadership; Some Personal Experiences of a Junior Officer of the German Army with Observations on Battle Tactics and the Psychological Reactions of Troops in Campaign*. Fort Benning, Ga.: Benning Herald, 1933.

Watson, Mark S. *Chief of Staff: Prewar Plans and Preparations*. Washington, Historical Division, Dept. of the Army, 1950. (United States Army in World War II: The War Department.)

Weigley, Russell F. *Towards an American Army, Military Thought from Washington to Marshall*. New York: Columbia University Press, 1962.

Weygand, Maxime. *Histoire de l'Armée Française*. Paris: Draeger Frères à Montrouge, 1953.

Wise, John S. *Recollections of Thirteen Presidents*. New York: Doubleday, Page and Co., 1906.

Wolff, Leon. *Little Brown Brother; How the United States Purchased and Pacified the Philippine Islands at the Century's Turn*. New York: Doubleday and Co., 1961.

Worcester, Dean C. *The Philippines Past and Present*. New York: Macmillan Co., 1930.

Worsley, Etta B. *Columbus on the Chattahoochee*. Columbus, Ga.: Columbus Office Supply Co., 1951.

Notes

Works listed in the Selected Bibliography are referred to by surname of author only.

ABBREVIATIONS

ACofS	Assistant Chief of Staff
ActCofS	Acting Chief of Staff
AG	Adjutant General (of an Army Command)
AGO	Adjutant General's Office (of an Army command)
AEF	American Expeditionary Force
ACP	Appointment, Commission, and Personnel Branch
Bn.	Battalion
CofAC	Chief of Air Corps
CinC	Commander-in-Chief
CofS	Chief of Staff
CCC	Civilian Conservation Corps
CG	Commanding General
CO	Commanding Officer
DCofS	Deputy Chief of Staff
DofA	Department of the Army
GCM Files	General Marshall's Files deeded to George C. Marshall Research Foundation
G-1	Administration
G-2	Intelligence
G-3	Operations
G-4	Coordination (or Supply)
GHQ	General Headquarters
JB	Joint Board
LofC	Library of Congress
NA	National Archives
NG	National Guard
NWC	National War College
OCS	Office of the Chief of Staff
OPD	Operations Division
Reg.	Regiment
RG	Record Group
SGS	Secretary General Staff
SW Div	Southwestern Division
TAG	The Adjutant General of the Army
TAGO	The Adjutant General's Office of the Army
TIG	The Inspector General of the Army
TIS	The Infantry School
USAFC	U.S. Army Force in China
VMI	Virginia Military Institute
WPD	War Plans Division

I: THE MARSHALLS OF UNIONTOWN

For background material on chaps. I and II I read the *Genius of Liberty,* 1869-1901, in microfilm form. Helpful material came from interviews with Mrs. J. J. Singer (General Marshall's sister), Miss Mary Kate O'Bryon, Mrs. Robert Carson, Jr. (a first cousin of Marshall's), Mrs. George Underwood (Florence Bliss), Mrs. Charles Gorley, Mrs. Richard Coulter, Mrs. Egbert (Catherine Lindsay) Armstrong, Mr. J. T. Shepler, and Mr. J. Searight Marshall, General Marshall's interviews, principally those of Feb. 21 and 28, 1957, and a few items from interviews of Mar. 6, Apr. 4 and 5, 1957, furnished the basis of these two chapters. Unless otherwise noted, all direct quotations attributed to Marshall come from these interviews, which were conducted by the author.

1. *Washington Post,* Sept. 2, 1939, p. 9; *Evening Star* (Washington), Sept. 1, 1939, Sec. B, p. 1.
2. Even Gen. Arnold did not become a member of the Joint Chiefs of Staff until 1942.
3. Although he attended St. Peter's regularly, he did not join until 1903 when, upon the death of his partner, A. W. Bliss, he was asked to assume his duties as warden and treasurer.
4. The elder Marshall was furious to find that it omitted all of his children. Stuart B. Marshall to Col. William Couper, Jan. 28, 1948, *VMI Alumni File.*
5. Kentucky relatives of Marshall pointed out that he resembled the Bradfords more than the Marshalls in his aloofness.
6. Paxton, pp. 83-86.
7. The chief source on Rev. William Marshall is Taylor, p. 105. See also Paxton, pp. 32-33; Semple, p. 414; Spencer, I, 14-16.
8. Matilda's great-grandmother was Mary Catlett. Matilda's brother was named George Catlett Taliaferro. Paxton, pp. 83-86; *The Biographical Encyclopedia of Kentucky,* p. 313.
9. Collins, II, 370, 772. William Marshall was a member of the State Constitutional Convention and an elector for Zachary Taylor in 1849 and a member of the legislature in 1834, 1840, 1841, 1842, 1843, 1844, and 1850.
10. The Kentucky Abolitionist Cassius M. Clay devoted several pages of his memoirs to a lurid account of a debate with Marshall. Clay, I, 495-96.
11. Rankins, "Morgan's Cavalry and the Home Guard at Augusta, Kentucky," *Filson Club Historical Quarterly,* XXVII, Oct. 1953. Duke, pp. 248-53.
12. *The Biographical Encyclopedia of Kentucky,* p. 659.
13. Clay included in his group of pro-Southerners not only William Marshall but also Drs. Joshua and Jonathan Bradford. In 1862 he asked that Dr. Joshua Bradford be dismissed from the service of the United States. Clay was fair enough to include in his memoirs an official letter defending Bradford's record. See Clay, I, 496-99.
14. George C. Marshall, "Coal, Coke, Ore, Iron, the Wonderful Story of Our Underground Wealth," Uniontown, Mar. 13, 1886, clipping from Albert Marshall Clipping Collection, Book B, Fayette Facts, apparently from *News-Standard* (Uniontown, Pa.); Sheppard, p. 43.
15. "A Social Event in Kentucky," May 2, 1873, clipping from *Times-Chronicle* (Cincinnati).
16. Mrs. Stuart B. Marshall to author, Sept. 26, 1960; Mrs. Singer interview, Feb. 2, 1960.
17. Although they never bought the house, this was the family home for twenty-six years. George Catlett Marshall, clerk, Dunbar, was listed for jury duty in Aug. 1873. In a deed of Mar. 9, 1874, George C. Marshall is listed as a citizen of Uniontown, *Deed Book,* vol. 28, p. 54, Recorder's Office, Fayette Co., Pa. *Genius of Liberty* (Uniontown, Pa.), Oct. 9,

1874, announced that A. W. Boyd was making alterations on his house on West Main Street. For family history, Mrs. Elizabeth B. Harbeson to author, June 27, 1963; Mrs. Singer interview, Feb. 2, 1960; Stuart B. Marshall to Couper, Jan. 28, 1948, gives information on birth dates of children, *VMI Alumni File;* Mrs. Robert Carson, Jr., in an interview, on June 1, 1962, gave additional information on the family.

18. *Genius of Liberty,* June 8, 1876; Feb. 22, 1877.

19. Sheppard, p. 41.

20. Ellis, ed., pp. 239, 582-87. For a biography of George C. Marshall see *Nelson's Biographical Dictionary,* II, 610-11. Certificate of Incorporation of the Fayette Coke and Furnace Company, Nov. 11, 1880, *Agreement Book,* vol. 4, pp. 115-16, Recorder's Office, Fayette Co., Pa.

21. Frick Coke Co., *A Brief Outline of the Development of the Great Connellsville Coke Region. . . .*

22. Augusta had about 588 pop. in 1850 (see Collins II, 262); Walter H. Rankins to author, Dec. 27, 1962, notes that it reached a peak of approximately 2000 in 1905. *Webster's Geographical Dictionary* states it had dropped to some 1599 in 1957. Rankins to author, Jan. 10, 1963.

23. Between 1860 and 1896 Fayette County went Democratic in every presidential election except in 1872 and 1888. Clipping from Albert Marshall Collection.

II: END OF AN ERA

1. All quotations of the General's reminiscences are from tape recordings which Marshall dictated in 1957.

2. The hair won him the nickname of "Flicker," but no nickname ever stuck to Marshall.

3. Marshall was baptized at St. Peter's Episcopal Church, June 5, 1881, and confirmed Feb. 7, 1896, by Bishop Courtlandt Whitehead of Pittsburgh. *Church Book,* St. Peter's Episcopal Church, Uniontown, Pa.

4. The statue was made by the satirical artist David Blythe, who lived for a time in Uniontown.

5. *Genius of Liberty,* Sept. 28, 1882, p. 1; Hadden; Hurlbert; Searight.

6. The stockade was burned by the French, and in Marshall's day there were no markers and no reconstruction to aid or impede imagination.

7. Don S. Glass, Supt., Uniontown Schools, to author, Mar. 16, 1961.

8. Dean Acheson, "Homage to Gen. Marshall," *The Reporter,* XXI, Nov. 26, 1959, 28. See also Acheson, p. 160.

9. His recollections date chiefly from the period after 1890 when the greatly reduced family income would have curtailed social activities anyway.

10. Miss Mary Kate O'Bryon interview, Feb. 4, 1960.

11. Croswell Bowen, "George C. Marshall of Uniontown, Pa.," *PM,* Mar. 30, 1947, pp. 5-11; Kenneth Speer, "General Marshall Played Hookey, Hunted Indians, Boyhood Friends Recall," *Pittsburgh Sun Telegram,* Jan. 12, 1947.

12. Fayette Coke and Furnace Co., to H. C. Frick Coke Co., Oct. 1, 1889, and Kyle Coke Co., to H. C. Frick Coke Co., Oct. 1, 1889, *Deed Book* vol. 91, pp. 394-405, Recorder's Office, Fayette Co., Pa.

13. *Ibid.*

14. *Page Courier* (Luray, Va.), June 26, 1890; *Luray Times,* Sept. 26, Oct. 3, 1890; *Genius of Liberty,* Sept. 25, 1890.

15. *Page Courier,* Dec. 11, 1890; *Genius of Liberty,* Nov. 6, 1890.

16. Strickler; *Shenandoah Valley* (New Market, Va.), Nov. 12 and Dec. 24, 1891.

17. *Genius of Liberty,* Feb. 4, 1892; Stephen Greene *vs.* George C. Marshall in the Court of Common Pleas of Fayette County no. 98, filed Oct. 20, 1891. (In 1892 Mr. Marshall was ordered to show cause why judgment should not be entered against him in two of the suits but it is not clear

from the record what final disposition was made).

18. Marshall interview, Feb. 28, 1957; Mrs. Singer interview, Feb. 2, 1960.

19. A succession of short-lived private academies were apparently established in Uniontown at this period, often succeeding each other in the same business. No record is clear on Marshall's attendance in the years 1895-97. He probably also attended one or more predecessors of the University School in the two years preceding.

20. Croswell Bowen, *loc. cit.*

21. Cited as the "normal" rate in 1894. *Genius of Liberty*, June 28, 1894, p. 4.

22. *Genius of Liberty*, Apr. 9, 1891.

23. *Genius of Liberty*, editorial, Mar. 26, 1891, p. 2; Apr. 9, 1891; editorial, Apr. 5, 1894. This, incidentally, was the occasion when Company C from Uniontown, mobilized for strike duty with its regiment of the Pennsylvania National Guard, was dismissed when the men were overheard expressing sympathy with the strikers.

III: FIRST CAPTAIN

Other than the interviews with Gen. Marshall of Feb. 21, 28, Mar. 6 and 13, 1957, the chief sources for this chapter were the official records of the Virginia Military Institute, such as *Order Books, Morning Reports, Letter Books, Alumni Files, Annual Reports, Annual Catalogues, Cadet Register,* and the VMI yearbook, *The Bomb,* for 1901. For background I have drawn on interviews with Banks Hudson, Gen. Charles S. Roller, Edward Ryland, Col. Bowyer Browne, Dr. Taylor Carter, Erskine Miller, Col. Morgan Hudgins, and W. Dudley Rucker, all classmates of Marshall's. Paul Wooten, for many years head of the Washington Bureau of the New Orleans *Times-Picayune,* gave me background material on Marshall and his roommate Leonard K. Nicholson. I am especially indebted to Mr. Hudson, who checked numerous points for me and arranged several of the interviews in which he also participated.

The indispensable secondary work on VMI is Col. William Couper's *One Hundred Years at VMI,* a four volume work. Col. Couper, who entered VMI a few months after Marshall graduated, served fifty years at VMI. Meticulous in his research, he checked dozens of details for me. I have benefited greatly from his sage advice and the use of his private newspaper clipping files on the period Marshall was enrolled at VMI.

For material on the family of the first Mrs. Marshall, I secured much helpful information from J. Churchill Newcomb. Mr. Lorraine Pitman sent some interesting letters from Gen. Marshall and the first Mrs. Marshall. This was supplemented by information obtained by Miss Eugenia Lejeune from friends of Lily Coles at Lexington: Mrs. Rosa Tucker, Mrs. M. H. Christian, Mrs. Robert Owen, and Miss Austina Mallory.

Miss Lejeune and I checked the files of the *Rockbridge County News* for the years 1897-1901 in the *News* office in Lexington.

1. G. C. Marshall to Shipp, Jan. 21, 1901, *VMI Alumni File.*

2. In an exchange of letters with Gen. Marshall, Sen. Joseph F. Guffey, a Democrat of Pa., said that he was surprised to hear that Rep. Acheson would have been partisan in this matter.

3. *Genius of Liberty,* Oct. 31, 1895.

4. *Ibid.;* see also Feb. 24, 1898.

5. A legend that he was rejected because of his father's politics has gained some currency.

6. Minutes of the Board of Visitors, VMI, June 17, 1907.

7. One of the cadets was Martin Marshall of Vicksburg, a first cousin of George Catlett.

8. Marshall interview, Feb. 28, 1957.

9. Mrs. Singer interview, Feb. 2, 1960.

10. Laura E. Marshall *et al.* conveying property to Martin Thompson, July 8, 1898, *Deed Book,* vol. 155, pp. 494-95, Fayette Co., Pa.; Marshall interview, Feb. 28, 1957.
11. G. C. Marshall to Shipp, Jan. 31, 1898, *VMI Alumni File.*
12. G. C. Marshall to Shipp, Sept. 11, 1897, *VMI Alumni File;* Minutes of Board of Visitors, June 17, 1907, noted that "the requirements of admission have been increased and the plane of proficiency so greatly elevated as to materially decrease the number of cadets able to enter the school."
13. G. C. Marshall to Shipp, Sept. 14, 1897, *VMI Alumni File;* Shipp to G. C. Marshall, Sept. 14, 1897, *VMI Letter Book.*
14. Couper, IV, 298-300, has an excellent sketch on Gen. Shipp.
15. Speech of Col. Hunter Pendleton cited in Couper, IV, 24, 31. Because of the illness of his mother, George was permitted to go home at Christmas 1898.
16. Banks Hudson interview, Dec. 5, 1957.
17. Couper, IV, 27, 47; Marshall interview, Mar. 6, 1957.
18. Marshall interview, Feb. 28, 1957. Nicholson described his life with Marshall in the *Times-Picayune* (New Orleans), May 28, 1939, sec. 2, p. 2.
19. *VMI Morning Report,* Sept. 25-29, 1897, signed Young, M.D.
20. Marshall interview, Mar. 6, 1957, refers to his speech at Class Dinner, May 15, 1951.
21. The Jackson Memorial Hall of 1896 was replaced by the present one in 1916.
22. Louis Marshall, nephew of Gen. Marshall's great-great-grandfather William, was President of Washington College 1830-34.
23. Couper, II, chaps. 22, 23; Marshall interview, Mar. 6, 1957.
24. *Rockbridge County News,* Feb. 17, 24, Mar. 3, Apr. 28, 1898.
25. *Ibid.,* Mar. 31, 1898.
26. *Ibid.,* Apr. 28, 1898.
27. By 1899, 136 former VMI cadets had served in the Army in the Spanish-American War and in the Philippine Insurrection. Couper, IV, 53.
28. *Rockbridge County News,* Jan. 5, 1899.
29. *Genius of Liberty,* Aug. 31, 1899.
30. President McKinley in 1898 admitted he did not know where Manila was except "somewhere around the other side of the world."
31. Text of Gen. Marshall's address, Uniontown, Sept. 9, 1939.
32. Marshall interview, Mar. 13, 1957.
33. *Rockbridge County News,* Dec. 6, 1900 p. 3.
34. "The Coles Family," *The Virginia Magazine of History and Biography,* VII, July 1899, 101-02; Jan. 1900, 326-28; Apr. 1900, 428-29; J. Churchill Newcomb to author, Dec. 28, 1960, Jan. 14, 30, Feb. 11, 16, 1961.
35. Pecquet du Bellet, IV, 224-29, 278-81.
36. Also called governor of the embryo colony or president of the provincial convention of Virginia.
37. Maj. Chester Goolrick to author Nov. 7, 1961, and Feb. 28, 1963. KA, although founded at nearby Washington and Lee, was banned along with other fraternities in 1880 by order of the authorities as being inconsistent with barracks' life, but continued surreptitiously until 1912. Present members are contributing a special memorial in honor of its war dead to be included in the George C. Marshall Research Center building. See also article when Marshall became Chief of Staff by Lt. Col. Edgar E. Hume, "General Marshall," *KA Journal,* Jan. 1939, pp. 94-95.

IV: SECOND LIEUTENANT

1. Ganoe, p. 394, indicates that the volunteer force went up to 233,000. After the armistice in August, the usual popular cry to get the boys home induced President McKinley to order the immediate release of 100,000 volunteers, even though they had been enlisted for two years. *Gen-*

ius of Liberty, Oct. 20, 1898. *Genius of Liberty,* Nov. 3, 1898, reported that a "petition to have the Tenth regiment brought home from Manila is now in circulation at this place."

2. Ganoe, pp. 370-74, 391, 398-400, 402.
3. Jessup, I, 215-20.
4. For Root's work as SecWar see Jessup, I, 215-407; see also Otto L. Nelson, p. 20.
5. For general discussion see Carter.
6. Jessup, I, 259.
7. Ganoe, pp. 412-13. In Sept. of 1901 the forces included approximately 3300 officers and 81,000 enlisted men. In addition there were approximately 5000 Philippine Scouts and 98 officers. In 1902 the minimum force was raised to 60,000. Root, pp. 374-75, 383.
8. Ganoe, p. 412.
9. Root, pp. 388-94.
10. Riker, pp. 69-70; Root, pp. 470-77.
11. The act required the selection of 298 officers of the staff corps and departments and of 837 first and second lieutenants of the line. In his Report for 1901, Sec. Root said that 695 of the first and second lieutenants had been commissioned. Of these 214 were enlisted men and 481 were volunteer officers. Marshall apparently was one of the 142 applicants chosen from civilian life. Root, pp. 375, 377-78; Ganoe, pp. 412, 417.
12. G. C. Marshall to Shipp, Jan. 21, 1901, *VMI Alumni File.*
13. Shipp to "To Whom It May Concern," Jan. 23, 1901, *VMI Letter Book.*
14. G. C. Marshall to Shipp, Jan. 21, 1901, *VMI Alumni File.*
15. Wise, App. 146, 158.
16. Wise to Pres. McKinley, Jan. 30, 1901, *ACP File, TAGO, RG 94, NA.*
17. G. C. Marshall to Shipp, Feb. 12, 1901, *VMI Alumni File;* Shipp to President McKinley, Feb. 14, 1901, *ACP File, TAGO, RG 94, NA.*
18. Sen. M. S. Quay to SecWar, Feb. 7, 1901; Quay to SecWar, Apr. 25, 1901, *ACP File, TAGO, RG 94, NA.*
19. Sen. Boies Penrose to Gen. H. C. Corbin, TAG, Apr. 26, 1901, *ACP File, TAGO, RG 94, NA.*
20. Memo for TAG, June 7, 1901; TAG

to Quay and TAG to Shipp, both June 15, 1901; TAG to Marshall, June 17, 1901; Marshall to Col. Henry P. McCain, Aug. 18, 1901; all in *ACP File, TAGO, RG 94, NA.*
21. Maj. Gen. John Rutter Brooke to TAG, Sept. 15, 1901; no. 40499/E filed with no. 404987, *McKinley Funeral;* S. O. 102, May 2, 1901, *ACP File,* both in *TAGO, RG 94, NA.*
22. Wise to Brooke, Sept. 23, 1901, *ACP File, TAGO, RG 94, NA.*
23. To give the volunteer officers and enlisted men who had been "without access to books for which they could prepare for the examination" and were thus at a disadvantage in being examined, Sec. Root in April 1901 directed that in case they failed the examination their cases would be reviewed by a special board in Washington which would take into consideration their record in the field. Root, pp. 376-79.
24. Marshall Examinations for Commission, *ACP File, TAGO, RG 94, NA.*
25. Marshall's application [1901] gives duties at Danville; interviews by Royster Lyle, Jr., with former cadets of Danville Military Institute who recalled Marshall's brief tenure there, including Judge A. M. Aiken, Mr. Willis J. Dance, Mr. Milton Herman, and Mr. John Overbey; *Danville Bee,* Oct. 17, 1959, article and editorial; Mr. Milton Herman letter to *N.Y. Times,* Oct. 27, 1959.
26. Marshall to TAG, Dec. 5, 1901; Wise to TAG, Dec. 6, 1901; TAG to Wise, Dec. 9, 1901; Asst. TAG to Marshall, Dec. 11, 1901; Marshall to TAG, Dec. 26, 1901; all in *ACP File, TAGO, RG 94, NA.*
27. Marshall to Shipp, Dec. 12, 1901, *VMI Alumni File.*
28. The appointment was confirmed on Jan. 13, 1902, and Marshall was assigned to the 30th Infantry in the Philippines, Special AG Memo no. 65, Jan. 4, 1902; S. O. 33, Feb. 8, 1902, ordered him to report to Fort Myer, to Columbus Barracks, Ohio, to San Francisco, and then to the Philippines, all in *ACP File, TAGO, RG 94, NA.*
29. F. M. Fuller and C. H. Seaton to

Quay, Jan. 21, 1902; Quay to Root, Jan. 25, 1902; Memo to McCain, Jan. 28, 1902; TAG to Quay, Jan. 30, 1902; all in *ACP File, TAGO, RG 94, NA*.

30. Marshall to Asst. TAG, Feb. 3, 1902; S. O. 33, Feb. 8, 1902, both in *ACP File, TAGO, RG 94, NA*.

31. *Rockbridge County News*, February 13, 1902. There are some errors in the account. See Stuart B. Marshall to Couper, Jan. 28, 1948, *VMI Alumni File*.

32. Mrs. Singer, Marshall's sister, said in interview, Feb. 2, 1960, it was the following morning.

33. Marshall interview, Mar. 6, 1957; William H. Carter to Marshall, Feb. 13, 1902, with attached notes, *ACP File, TAGO, RG 94, NA*.

34. S. O. 40, Feb. 17, 1902; CG, Governors Island to TAG, Mar. 18, 1902; CG, Presidio, San Francisco, Calif., to TAG, Apr. 12, 1902; all in *ACP File, TAGO, RG 94, NA*.

V: THE METTLE OF THE MAN

For background, I have drawn on materials on the Philippines furnished me by former Sgt. Enoch R. L. Jones; on a file of *Bamboo Breezes* (a small newspaper devoted to the activities of the 30th Infantry Regiment in the Philippines, edited by John N. Morton) furnished me by Mrs. Amy C. Dabney; on interviews with Gen. Walter Krueger, Sgt. Jones, and William A. Horne; and on letters from Clyde A. Benton, Col. Samuel C. Talbott, Lt. Col. William J. Holzapfel, Sr., Clyde W. Osborn, Connelly R. Potter, Wiley S. Hicks, Mr. and Mrs. John N. Morton, Mrs. Leonard Brozik (daughter of Capt. C. L. Bent), Howard D. McGeorge, and Olive V. Borden.

1. Sexton, p. 267.
2. Wolff, pp. 358-59.
3. Sexton, p. 283.
4. *Report of the Philippine Commission.* Jan. 31, 1900-Dec. 20, 1900.
5. Enoch Jones interview, Nov. 1, 1960.
6. Marshall interview, Mar. 13, 1957.
7. Heiser, p. 100.
8. Marshall interview, Mar. 13, 1957; see also Maj. Gen. Charles D. Rhodes, "Diary Notes of a Soldier," 1940, entry for May 28, 1902, *Central Search Room, NA*.
9. Maj. Fletcher Gardner to Marshall, May 20, 1938, *GCM Files*.
10. Marshall to Clyde A. Benton, Jan. 11, 1950, *GCM Files*. Marshall interview, Mar. 13, 1957. Several versions of the Fourth of July story exist.
11. Marshall at VMI, June 12, 1940.
12. William A. Horne, former private of Co. G, to Frye, July 29, 1946, *GCM Files*. Horne later supplied the author with a copy of this letter. See also Horne interview, Apr. 24, 1959.
13. Marshall interview, Mar. 13, 1957.
14. One patrol is described briefly in Returns of the 30th Infantry Regiment, Sept. 1902, *RG 98, NA;* Marshall interview, Mar. 13, 1957.
15. Maj. R. K. Evans to AG, Dept. of Southern Luzon, Aug. 22, 1901, in *Annual Report of the Secretary of War, 1902*, IX, 328-32.
16. Acheson, pp. 160-61.
17. Marshall to Benton, Jan. 11, 1950, Marshall to John N. Morton, formerly a private of the 30th Infantry, May 4, 1949, *GCM Files*.
18. Jessup, I, 329-71; Ganoe, pp. 411, 413-15.
19. U.S. War Dept., *Annual Report . . . 1904*, III, 219.
20. Gen. Walter E. Krueger interview, Nov. 7, 1957. Krueger undoubtedly first met Marshall in the Philippines, as both of them were lieutenants in the 30th Infantry.
21. Brig. Gen. R. Tucker Pendleton, a first cousin and next-door neighbor of the Coles in Lexington, in an interview, Nov. 12, 1962, said that she did not join her husband for some months after he returned to the

United States and perhaps not at all at Fort Reno. The second Mrs. Marshall in a letter to the author, Jan. 7, 1963, recalls General Marshall's speaking of a delay in their reunion. Marshall's letters concerning his trip back east do not indicate he was accompanied by Mrs. Marshall. He does mention her being with him at Fort Reno. It is possible that they were not reunited until he came east in the fall of 1905 or that she may have come to Fort Reno after he was well established there and returned east during the four months he was mapping on the Pecos.

22. One of his activities was participation in a road march which required submission of a sketch map of the area around Darlington and El Reno. Lt. Col. Frank West to AG, SW Div., Annual Inspection, 1904, June 25, 1904, with road sketch map of "Chambry" column, vicinity of Darlington by G. C. Marshall, Jr., no. 9523, TIG, RG 159, NA.

23. Dupuy, pp. 196-97.

24. Marshall's Personal Report, Aug. 18, 1906, no. 4475, *Army Service Schools, Ft. Leavenworth, RG 98, NA.* Marshall also practiced shooting; he was rated "sharpshooter."

25. Dupuy, pp. 193-94. Marshall interview, Mar. 13, 1957.

26. Statement on Mapping Trip, Fort Clark, unsigned and no date, dictated by Marshall during or just after World War II, *GCM Files.*

27. Marshall to Capt. John C. Oakes, June 13, 1905, no. 15819/Z [index card no. 1574/L], *Mapping, SW Div., RG 98, NA.*

28. Marshall to Oakes, eng. off., SW Div., June 13, 1905, with six endorsements: Marshall to Mil. Secy., SW Div., Aug. 31, 1905; Eng. Off., SW Div., June 19, 1905; Hdq., SW Div. by Cmd. of CG, June 20, 1905; Mil. Secy., Dept. of Texas, June 22, 1905; CO, Ft. Clark, June 25, 1905; CG, Dept. of Texas, June 28, 1905, all in no. 15819; Capt. S. B. Bootes, Hdq., Dept. of Texas, Office of the Chief Commissary, to Marshall, June 26, 1905, and endorsements, no 15819/A-4, all in *Mapping, SW Div., RG 98, NA.*

29. Mrs. G. C. Marshall interview, Mar. 1961.

30. Marshall to Mil. Secy., SW Div., Aug. 31, 1905, and 14 endorsements, no. 1574/T, *Mapping, SW Div., RG 98, NA.*

31. Marshall to Shipp, Mar. 3, 1906, *VMI Alumni File.*

32. Marshall to Maj. Gen. George Van Horn Moseley, Sept. 9, 1938, *GCM Files.*

33. Sheppard, pp. 67-72; also collection of clippings from Uniontown and Pittsburgh papers in the Uniontown Library.

34. He was left with only one sergeant.

35. He had applied for the course the previous year but someone senior to him in the regiment had asked for the assignment. In 1905, the appointment was offered to Capt. (later Col.) Edward C. Corey, who declined, and it was then offered to Marshall. Maj. Gen. Edwin L. Sibert to author, July 7, 1961. Col. Corey was his father-in-law.

VI: PROFESSIONAL TRAINING

For background, I have drawn on entries in the Diary of Col. Fay W. Brabson, a classmate of Marshall's at Fort Leavenworth in 1906-1907, and on interviews with him and two other classmates, Maj. Gen. Charles D. Herron and Brig. Gen. Royden E. Beebe. I also talked with Gen. Walter E. Krueger, an instructor at Fort Leavenworth during part of this period. Gen. Herron permitted me to copy a number of photographs from his album. These were supplemented by some which Col. Luis Monter of the Mexican Army, also a fellow student, gave President Eisenhower, who presented them to the Marshall Foundation.

I am indebted to Dr. Edward M. Coffman for selecting, out of thousands of documents in the National Archives covering this period, the following items: daily class records of Marshall and his classmates, Inspector General reports on the school, annual reports of the commandant, and correspondence of Gen. Bell, Col. Wagner, and others.

1. Capt. Milton F. Davis to Marshall, July 12, 1906, no. 4441. Davis to Marshall, Aug. 2, 1906, no. 4442, both filed with no. 4440, in *Army Service Schools, Ft. Leavenworth, RG 98, NA*.
2. Maj. Gen. Charles D. Rhodes, Maj. Gen. B. B. Buck, Brig. Gen. H. L. Hodges, Lt. Gen. John L. DeWitt, Maj. Gen. C. D. Herron, Maj. Gen. Bruce Palmer, Brig. Gen. Morris Locke, Maj. Gen. Stephen Fuqua, and Gen. of the Army George C. Marshall.
3. Wagner's tour was interrupted by service in the Spanish-American War. In 1904 he went to the Army War College, where he was first a member of the Strategy Board and later senior director of the Board of Direction. He was also military secretary at the time of his death, June 17, 1905.
4. Herron to author, July 19, 1962.
5. "James Franklin Bell," *Fifteenth Annual Report of the Association of Graduates of the U.S. Military Academy*, pp. 166-74
6. Marshall interview, Apr. 4, 1957; Herron to author, July 19, 1962.
7. Wagner to Bell, Feb. 21, 1905, with encl. Capt. F. J. Koester to Wagner, Feb. 17, 1905, no. 4095 filed with no. 537, *Army Service Schools, Ft. Leavenworth, RG 98, NA*.
8. Marshall's class numbered 54 at entrance, 38 at graduation, of which 24 took the second year.
9. Marshall, distressed over mistakes on two papers, wrote long explanations to his instructors in a futile effort to have them reviewed for possible corrections.
10. Col. Fay W. Brabson interview, Dec. 5, 1960, and extracts from Brabson Diary recorded on tape.
11. Marshall had the following percentages: 94 in administration, 95.3 in drill regulations, 99.3 in small arms regulation, 96.4 in military field en-

gineering, 97.4 in military topography (the Fort Clark expedition paid off), 96.7 in military law, and 94.1 on his road sketch. Examinations on some subjects were waived on the basis of his having made more than 95 per cent in his class work. His grand average was 96.2 per cent. With a satisfactory physical examination, the road was open to his appointment as first lieutenant. Report of the Examining Board on Marshall, *ACP File, TAGO, RG 94, NA*.
12. War Dept. S. O. 252, Oct. 26, 1907; signed Oath of Office, Oct. 28, 1907, and again Jan. 30, 1908, both in *Ft. Leavenworth, ACP File, TAGO, RG 94, NA*.
13. Herron interview, May 28, 1958.
14. Marshall to Col. Bernard Lentz, Oct. 2, 1935; Radiogram, Lentz to Marshall, May 23, 1936; Marshall to Lentz, May 26, 1936; all in *GCM Files*.
15. In Steele's course Marshall was second in the class.
16. Four of the five just below him became generals.
17. Bell to Maj. Gen. F. C. Ainsworth, June 30, 1907; Brig. Gen. C. B. Daugherty to Bell, July 17, 1907; both no. 1259192 filed with no. 1249432, *Militia, RG 94, NA*.
18. Marshall, expecting to stay in Minnesota until he drew his next pay check, had to leave his wife behind. Marshall to TAG, July 7, 1907, no. 1259192/C filed with no. 1249432, *Militia, RG 94, NA*.
19. Col. F. W. Stillwell to SecWar Taft, July 27, 1907, no. 1269829 filed with no. 393013, *ACP File, TAGO, RG 94, NA*; Daugherty to Brig. Gen. T. J. Stewart, AG, Pa., July 31, 1907, no. 1271850/B, filed with no. 1249432, *Militia, RG 94, NA*.
20. Brig. Gen. Royden E. Beebe interview, Apr. 6, 1961.

21. U.S. Army Service Schools, *Annual Report, 1908*, pp. 69-70.
22. *Ibid.*
23. Col. Iverson B. Summers to author, Oct. 9, 1960; Miss Cora E. Thomas (daughter of Mrs. Osborne) interview, Mar. 10, 1961.
24. Proceedings of Academic Boards of the Army School of the Line and Army Staff College, June 27, 1908; J. F. Morrison to TAG, July 1, 1908; both in no. 1399408, *Ft. Leavenworth, TAGO RG 94*, NA; Marshall interview, Apr. 4, 1957.
25. Clement added that the coming of Marshall and the other regular Army instructors "was the opening up in the training of the Pennsylvania National Guard, which seven or eight years later was on the Texas border and ten years later was on its way to France . . . All I can say is of all the men I have known in my life, I know of none I have admired more and few as much." M. W. Clement to author, July 20, 1960.
26. Marshall speech to National Guard Assn. of Pa., Oct. 13, 1939.
27. Brig. Gen. Charles Morton to TAG, Dec. 26, 1908, no. 1473464 filed with no. 1302651, *Dale Creek, RG 94, NA*.
28. Root, address at dedication of the

Army War College, Nov. 9, 1908, Root, p. 129.
29. Marshall interview, Mar. 6, 1957.
30. Early in 1915, for instance, only 117 active Army officers were reported on duty with the militia. Huidekoper, p. 510.
31. Beginning in 1908, horsemanship was encouraged in the Army, especially for infantry officers, by order of President Theodore Roosevelt, who was concerned with developing the physical fitness of the officer corps.
32. A. B. De Saulles, *et al.*, and the Percy Mining Co., and G. C. Marshall in the Court of Common Pleas (Fayette County, Pa.), no. 554, Oct. 13, 1908, and attached accounting for the period, Jan. 1, 1904-Dec. 31, 1908, submitted Jan. 27, 1909. *Prothonotary,* Recorder's Office, Fayette County, Pa.
33. J. Churchill Newcomb to author, Dec. 28, 1960, Jan. 14, 30, Feb. 11, 16, 1961.
34. Newcomb to author, Dec. 28, 1960.
35. James K. Campbell to Marshall, May 16, 1955, *GCM Files*.
36. Brig. Gen. Guy I. Rowe interview, Nov. 12, 1962.

VII: THE MAKING OF A STAFF OFFICER

Background material was furnished by Gen. Courtney Hodges and Maj. Gen. Fred L. Walker, who served with Marshall in the Philippines during this period. I have received valuable material in letters from Brig. Gen. Clifford Bluemel, Mrs. J. R. Hamlen, Brig. Gen. Arthur W. Lane, Maj. William Fisk, Brig. Gen. Frank S. Clark, Maj. Gen. Durward Wilson, Col. James H. Van Horn, Col. Owen Meredith, and Brig. Gen. Royden E. Beebe.

1. *News-Standard* (Uniontown), Sept. 22, 1909; *Morning Herald* (Uniontown), Sept. 22, 25, 1909. The Rev. F. W. Beckman, later rector of the American Cathedral (Holy Trinity) in Paris, conducted funeral services at St. Peter's Church.
2. Settlement of estate of G. C. Marshall, Dec. 1, 1913, *Office of Register of Wills*, Fayette Co., Pa.
3. Marshall interview, Apr. 4, 1957;

Mrs. Singer interview, Feb. 2, 1960.
4. Marshall to TAG, Apr. 11, 1910, with ends., *ACP File TAGO, RG 94, NA*.
5. Marshall to TAG, May 17, 1910, with endorsements, *ACP File TAGO, RG 94, NA*.
6. *The Times* (London), Sept. 17, 19, 22, 1910. Gen. Sir John French, later to command the British forces in World War I, was director of the maneuvers. The chief umpire was Lt.

Gen. Sir Horace Smith-Dorrien, the commander of the Second British Army in World War I. The Red Army commander was Lt. Gen. Sir Herbert Plumer, who later succeeded Smith-Dorrien as Second Army commander in France. One of the observers of the maneuvers was Winston Churchill.

7. Returns of the 24th Inf. Regt., Jan.-Mar., 1911, *TAGO, RG 94, NA;* Brig. Gen. Clifford Bluemel to author, Oct. 19, 1960; Marshall interview, Apr. 4, 1957.

8. Hagedorn, II, 97-99; Otto L. Nelson, chap. 4; Morison, pp. 146-69.

9. Of 25 posts which the general staff in 1911 recommended be abandoned over a period of time, 17 were still occupied in Jan. 1940. Otto L. Nelson, p. 172.

10. War Dept., *Annual Report, 1911,* I, 12; Morison, pp. 146-48; Ganoe, pp. 443-46.

11. One was Lt. Benjamin D. Foulois, who had accompanied Orville Wright on one of the first official Army test flights at Fort Myer in 1909 and who later became Chief of the Air Corps, and another was Lt. G.E.M. Kelly, killed a month later in a crash during the same maneuvers, after whom Kelly Field was named.

12. Marshall interview, Apr. 4, 1957; "Tactical Problem no. 1 for Co. D, Signal Corps and attached officers," Apr. 3, 1911, plus field order 1 and messages sent in the exercise, included as part of the report of Maj. George O. Squier, to Chief Signal Officer, July 13, 1911, no. 27587/20, Off. Ch. Sig. Off. Doc. File, 1894-1917, *Maneuver Division RG 111 NA.*

13. The Army in 1913 had 17 planes for its Air Force and had budgeted $124,000 for aviation. France in the same year appropriated $7.4 million. Paxson, 1, 114.

14. Squier to Ch. Sig. Off., July 13, 1911, no. 27587/20, Off. Ch. Sig. Off. Doc. File, 1894-1917, *Maneuver Division, RG 111, NA.*

15. Hagedorn says it took almost ninety days, 11, 111.

16. Reports of Capt. S. G. Shartle, Apr. 6, June 5, 1911, no. 6553/1 and 3,

German views, *Army War College File, RG 165, NA;* Ganoe, p. 438.

17. I am indebted to Morison, p. 147, for the references to *McClure's Magazine,* XXXVIII, Apr. 1912, 677-83; *Collier's,* XLVII, Apr. 15, 1911, 17-42; *Nation,* XCIII, Dec. 21, 1911, 595-96; and seven articles (by Stimson, Wood, Wotherspoon, Evans, Liggett, Edwards, and Shelton) appearing under the title of "What Is the Matter with Our Army?" *Independent,* LXXII, Feb., Mar., Apr., 1912. I checked all the articles.

18. Ganoe, p. 438.

19. Gov. Eben S. Draper to Maj. Gen. F. D. Grant, Oct. 11, 1910, no. 46092; Grant to Draper, Oct. 25, 1910, both in *Dept. of the East, RG 98, NA.* Maj. Gen. Leonard Wood to TAG, May 3, 1911, no. 1742289/C filed with no. 1733266, *Militia, RG 94, NA;* Daugherty to Rhodes, May 15, 1911; Daugherty to Stewart, AG of Pa., May 15, 1911; Stewart to Wood, May 16, 1911; Wood to Stewart, May 18, 1911; Rhodes to Stewart, May 19, 1911; Rhodes to Daugherty, May 19, 1911, all in no. 6759, *Pre WWI, RG 165, NA.*

20. Marshall speech to Natl. Guard Assn. of Pa., Oct. 13, 1939.

21. Marshall to Chief, Div. of Militia Affs., Oct. 2, 1911, no. 27764/A filed with no. 25489, *Camps, RG 168, NA;* Marshall to Capt. G. E. Thorne, June 13, 1911, with "Program for the Militia Officers' School," no. 48100/W filed with no. 48032, *Dept. of the East, RG 98, NA.*

22. *Boston Daily Globe,* July 22-31, 1911. Wood to TAG, Aug. 11, 1911, *OCS, GS, 1906-17, RG 165, NA.*

23. Marshall to Chief, Div. of Militia Affs., Jan. 1, 1912, no. 27764/B filed with no. 25489, *Camps, RG 168, NA.* Col. C. A. Ranlett to Marshall, May 4, 1939, *GCM Files.* Marshall report in Brig. Gen. R. K. Evans' (Chief, Division of Militia Affairs) undated memorandum containing extracts from first quarter reports, 1912, from various inspector-instructors, no. 29998, *Camps, RG 168, NA.*

24. Marshall to Chief Div. of Militia Affs., Aug. 26, 1912, no. 33659/A

filed with no. 29998, *Camps, RG 168, NA. Boston Daily Globe,* Aug. 17, 1912, p. 1.

25. Report to Brig. Gen. Tasker H. Bliss, Aug. 10-20, 1912, no. 2011207 filed with no. 1807249, *Militia, RG 94, NA. Boston Daily Globe,* July 22, Aug. 10-18, 1912; *Courant* (Hartford), Aug. 12-14, 1912. See also *Boston Daily Globe,* Oct. 17, 1959; Col. J. E. McMahon to CofS, Aug. 18, 1913, no. 7267-25, *Army War College, RG 165, NA;* Col. James L. Walsh to Marshall, Jan. 2, 1951, *GCM Files.*

26. Brig. Gen. Charles H. Cole to Marshall, Apr. 27, 1939, *GCM Files;* see also Cole's notes on Marshall sent to Marshall Andrews, *Research Center Files.*

27. Brig. Gen. W. W. Wotherspoon to Bell, Jun. 30, 1909; Bell to Wotherspoon, July 1, 1909; Nichols to Wood, Mar. 18, 1912; Carter to TAG for Nichols, Mar. 20, 1912, all in no. 8111, *Pre WWI, RG 165, NA.* See also Marshall's correspondence with Nichols, Jan. 20, Feb. 3, 1912, *VMI Alumni File.* Bell, in turning down Nichols' request for Marshall's detail to VMI in 1909, said that it would mean seven years' absence from his regiment, adding that "on account of low rank such absence would certainly result in his ruination as a line officer." The legislation was thus intended to protect the officer as well as the regiment.

28. War Dept. G. O. 32, Sept. 18, 1912, giving extract of law; Marshall was willing to return to his regiment, but he and his wife were not pleased at the cost and labor involved in frequent moves. "Mrs. Marshall will be much outraged," he wrote a friend, "when I tell her that we must pack up again before May 1. We just unpacked last September; and the previous February, I reported for duty at Madison Barracks, unpacked, and four weeks later was ordered to Texas, leaving her to crate things up again. I think a few peaceful, housekeeping years in Lexington would appeal to her more than all the glories of war." Marshall to Nichols, Feb. 3, 1912, *VMI Alumni File.*

29. Returns of the 4th Inf. Rgt., Sept. 1912, *Post Returns, RG 94, NA.*

30. Summary of Maj. Eli A. Helmick, TIG, Inspection Report, Jan. 22-27, 1913, *201 File, TAGO, DofA.*

31. Herron to author, Oct. 31, 1958. In the fall of 1958 while at the Walter Reed Hospital, Marshall related his Christmas story to Herron. At the author's request, Herron wrote down his recollections of Marshall's recitation. It is likely the last interview with Marshall recorded by anyone.

32. War Dept., *Annual Report,* 1913, III, 113-20, "Report of the Second Division." Marshall to TAG with 1st end. by Col. T. J. Kennan, CO, 13th Inf. Rgt., Nov. 9, 1914, *ACP File, TAGO, RG 94, NA.* Paxson, I, 35-36; Morison, p. 169; Ganoe, p. 446.

33. Brig. Gen. Arthur W. Lane to author, Nov. 29, 1960.

34. Paxson, I, 48-49.

35. It would grow darker. Japan's encroachments on China after 1914 under cloak of defense against Germany caused considerable U.S. alarm. Paxson, I, 384-85. See also Morton, pp. 22-25.

36. Dupuy, pp. 210-11; Marshall interview, Apr. 4, 1957; Maj. Gen. Fred L. Walker interview, Oct. 28, 1958. Walker was a 2d lt. in the regiment to which Marshall was assigned.

37. Answering the question on Marshall's efficiency report, "Would you want him to serve under you again?" Williams wrote, "I would be glad to serve under him." Williams, Cdg. Co. F, 13th Infantry, Efficiency Report, Jan. 1-Dec. 31, 1914, *ACP File, TAGO, RG 94, NA.*

38. Frye, pp. 106-107. Mr. Frye got the story from Gen. Johnson Hagood, to whom Marshall told the story in 1914. Marshall confirmed the accuracy of the episode to the author, adding that he had acted unwisely.

39. Brig. Gen. Frank S. Clark to author, Aug. 2, 1960, with copy of initial field order and instructions. Marshall to Nichols, Mar. 5, 1914, *VMI Alumni File.*

40. Col. James B. Ervin to the CG, Phil. Dept., Mar. 20, 1914, "Chief Umpire's

Report on Exercise no. 2, Maneuver Campaign, 1914, Dept. of the Philippines," with forwarding letter of Bell to TAG, May 30, 1914, no. 8438/5, *Philippine Maneuvers, RG 165, NA.* Note comments by Lt. Col. Clarence E. Dentler, Maj. B. B. Buck, and Maj. U. G. McAlexander.

41. Marshall was signing orders by January 26 as chief of staff without the "acting."

42. Arnold, p. 44.

43. Report of Dentler, Chief Umpire of White Force, Feb. 4, 1914, no. 8438/5, *Philippine Maneuvers, RG 165, NA.*

44. Hagood included the anecdote in "Soldier; George C. Marshall," *Saturday Evening Post*, 212, July 15, 1939, pp. 25, 62-66. Marshall to Col. E. F. Harding, June 26, 1939 (*GCM Files*), said Hagood "drew a long bow." Marshall wrote friends that he feared Hagood's article would cause resentment in the Army.

45. Col. James H. Van Horn to author, Oct. 10, 1960; Col. Harry H. Pritchett to Marshall, May 2, 1939; Col. Owen Meredith to author, Sept. 14, 1960; Maj. Gen. F. L. Walker interview, Oct. 28, 1958.

46. Mrs. Singer interview, Feb. 2, 1960;

medical history, Jan. 12, 1948, *201 File, TAGO, DofA.*

47. Marshall, "Report of Visit to Manchurian Battlefields" to TAG through channels, June 15, 1914, *Research Center Files.* Marshall to Nichols, Oct. 4, 1915, *VMI Alumni File.* Letters written in the early 1950s from Marshall to Lt. Sam S. Walker and Richard Davis also describe trip, *GCM Files.*

48. Marshall, "Report of Visit to Manchurian Battlefields," June 15, 1914. Col. G. W. McIver, Cdg. 13th Inf., refuted this statement in a note on Marshall's "Report" by stating that there was an allowance of and training in use of hand grenades in 1913 and 1914 on Corregidor.

49. Marshall to Nichols, Oct. 4, 1915, *VMI Alumni File.*

50. Marshall thought he was made an aide to keep him at Fort McKinley when his unit went to Fort Mills, Corregidor, in March 1915.

51. Beebe interview, Apr. 6, 1961.

52. Marshall interview, Mar. 13, 1957; Marshall to Capt. (later Maj. Gen.) William T. Sexton, Jan. 23, 1940, *Research Center Files.*

53. Beebe interview, Apr. 6, 1961.

VIII: THE COMING OF THE WAR

For background, interviews with Maj. Gen. Frank L. Culin, Col. Mervyn Burke, Brig. Gen. B. F. Caffey, Jr., and Durbin Sayers were helpful. Miss Mary Bell Vaughan furnished valuable background material on her uncle, J. Franklin Bell. Much of this chapter came from Gen. Marshall's interviews of Apr. 4 and 5, 1957.

1. Marshall to Nichols, Oct. 4, 1915, *VMI Alumni Files;* Pritchett to Marshall, May 2, 1939, reminded Marshall that in 1913 he considered resigning.

2. Nichols to Marshall, Nov. 22, 1915, *VMI Alumni File.*

3. By the end of 1916 some 75,000 men were on guard along the Rio Grande. Ganoe, p. 459.

4. Paxson, I, 37.

5. The latter act also authorized the organization of an aviation section of the Signal Corps consisting of not more than 60 officers and 260 enlisted men to operate and supervise

military aircraft. Ganoe, pp. 448-49.

6. Marshall to Nichols, Oct. 4, 1915, *VMI Alumni File.*

7. SecState Robert Lansing concluded a protocol with Mexico's ambassador-designate which gave either power the right to pursue bandits into the territory of the other, but Carranza after a time denied having agreed to as large an operation as the United States conducted and pressed for a speedy withdrawal.

8. Leopold, pp. 318-21; Ganoe, p. 459; Paxson, I, 35-36; 299-300.

9. Paxson, I, 300.

10. Link, *American Epoch*, pp. 185-88.

For the debate over the type of Army needed, see Weigley, pp. 199-222.

11. Peacetime strength was not to exceed 11,450 officers and 175,000 troops of the line. An additional 42,750 men were authorized for the Quartermaster, Signal and Medical Corps and unassigned recruits and Philippine Scouts. Wartime strength for combat units was reckoned at about one-third more than peacetime strength. Thus under the act the maximum regular Army authorized in the event of war was about 12,030 officers and 298,000 enlisted men. Ganoe, pp. 452, 457, 458.

12. Huidekoper, pp. 403, 515

13. He left the Philippines May 15, spent a month in Japan, and sailed from there June 21 aboard the *Thomas*, arriving in San Francisco July 13. Marshall interview, Apr. 4, 1957.

14. Hdq., Western Dept., San Francisco, Calif., S.O. 157, July 15, 1916, *Ft. Douglas, RG 120, NA,* assigned Marshall as aide to Gen. Bell and assistant to the Dept. AG with permanent station at the Presidio and detailed him for temporary duty at Monterey.

15. Marshall to TAG, Aug. 14, 1916, no. 1335339/A filed with no. 393013, *ACP File, TAGO, RG 94, NA.*

16. *San Francisco Examiner*, July 9, 1916, p. 7.

17. *San Francisco Examiner*, June 22, July 1, 8, 9, 12, 14, 15, 1916; Marshall interview, Apr. 4, 1957.

18. The *San Francisco Examiner* indicates that some tightening up of the work of the camp had been started before Marshall arrived.

19. Sibert, who had been promoted to brigadier general by Act of Congress in 1915, in recognition of his work on the Panama Canal, was given command of the Coast Artillery on the Pacific Coast shortly thereafter.

20. Marshall interview, Apr. 4, 1957.

21. Post returns of Camp of Instruction, Ft. Douglas, Utah, Aug. 1916, *Ft. Douglas, TAGO, RG 94, NA.* Hagood, "Soldier; George C. Marshall," *loc. cit.*

22. Efficiency Report signed by Brig. Gen. Hunter Liggett, Lt. Col. Johnson Hagood, and Maj. Gen. J. Franklin Bell, Dec. 31, 1916, *201 File, TAGO, DofA.* Hagood was soon to become a major general himself and chief of staff of U.S. Services of Supply in France.

23. S.O. 157, July 15, 1916, *Ft. Douglas, RG 120, NA.*

24. *San Francisco Examiner*, July 22, 23, 30, 1916; *Monterey Peninsula Herald,* Mar. 9, 1960, p. 8.

25. Paxson, 1, pp. 302-304. Special authorization to the President to mobilize industrial resources was contained in the National Defense Act.

26. Otto L. Nelson, pp. 180-84, 217.

27. Marshall interview, Apr. 5, 1957.

28. Other aides were Capt. Ewing E. Booth and Capt. John B. Murphy. One of these listed the supply requirements. S.O. 113, Hdq., Eastern Dept., May 2, 1917, *Eastern Dept., RG 120, NA.*

29. Chief of mission was former Premier Viviani. Harbord, *American Army,* p. 52.

30. Bell was suffering from diabetes.

31. Marshall to Nichols, May 27, 1917, with copy of Efficiency Report; Marshall to Nichols, June 9, 1917, both in *VMI Alumni File.*

32. Sibert to Bell, June 3, 1917, and related papers, no. 2612176 filed with no. 393013, *ACP File, TAGO, RG 94, NA.*

33. Bell's Efficiency Report, 1916, *201 File, TAGO, DofA.*

34. The regimental histories of the 1st Division (16th, 18th, 26th, and 28th) tell the background of this organization.

35. Marshall interview, Apr. 5, 1957.

IX: THE FIRST DIVISION IN FRANCE

From the massive holdings of the National Archives on World War I, Mr. Myles Marken selected for me several thousand key papers. Marshall's interviews, Apr. 5 and 11, 1957, dealt with his World War I experiences.

The chief published sources are: U.S. Dept. of the Army, Hist. Div., *U.S. Army in the World War, 1917-1919*, and the Society of the First Division, *History of the First Division*.

Three World War I newsmen—Thomas M. Johnson, George Pattullo, and Mark S. Watson—gave me valuable background material on this period. I also got excellent material from the following who worked with Marshall in the 1st Division: Brig. Gen. B. F. Caffey, Jr., Chauncey Belknap, James A. Edgar, Col. Mervyn Burke, and Germain Seligman. Mr. Belknap and Col. Burke furnished copies of plans and maps from this period.

My wife and I visited Gondrecourt, Domremy, Chaumont, and Neufchâteau in 1961, taking photographs of Marshall's billets and Gen. Sibert's headquarters and talking with some of the older people who remembered when the troops were there.

1. Harbord, *American Army*, p. 80.

2. Harbord, *Leaves from a War Diary*, p. 85.

3. War Diary, 1st Exped. Div., signed GCM[arshall], June 26, 1917, Box 2538, *AEF/GHQ, RG 120, NA;* U.S. Dept. of the Army, Historical Division, *United States Army in the World War 1917-19,* I, 5.

4. Gleaves, p. 49; Marshall interview, Apr. 5, 1957.

5. Marshall interview, Apr. 5, 1957.

6. F. Palmer, *America in France*, p. 27.

7. "Speech at Brunswick, Md., Nov. 6, 1938," p. 8.

8. War Diary, Exped. Div., July 12, 13, 14, 15, 1917, signed GCM, dated June [i.e., July] 16, 1917, Box 2538, *AEF/ GHQ, RG 120, NA.*

9. Marshall to CG, AEF, Aug. 1, 1917, Folder 1885, File 8.502, *G-3 Rpts., AEF/GHQ, RG 120, NA.*

10. Marshall interview, Apr. 5, 1957.

11. List of officers' billets, Gondrecourt, no. 1003 *1st Div., Doc File, RG 120, N.A.*

12 Gen. Marshall, Mrs. Marshall, Gen. Marshall Carter, Lt. Col. Vernon A. Walters, and Lt. Col. C. J. George, the three members of the staff, have all told me of that visit.

13. John McA. Palmer to CG, 1st Div., July 17, 1917, Folder 1880, File 8.502; Palmer to CofS with recommendations of Drum and Conger, June 18, 1917, Folder 1940, File 8.542, both in *G-3 Rpts., AEF/GHQ, RG 120, NA;* Marshall interview, Apr. 5, 1957.

14. Marshall to Drum, July 22, 1917, Folder 1787, File 6.301, *G-3 Rpts., AEF/GHQ, RG 120, NA;* Marshall interview, Apr. 5, 1957.

15. "1st Div. instructions for billeting American troops in France," July 23, 1917, U.S. Army, 1st Division. *World War Records, First Division, AEF,* VI, pt. 2.

16. Maj. Gen. W. L. Sibert to CG, 47th French Div., July 18, 1917; 1st Div. "Memo for Brigade Commanders," by command of Sibert, July 18, 1917, *U.S. Army in the World War, 1917-19,* III, 426-28; Marshall interview, Apr. 5, 1957.

17. Marshall interview, Apr. 5, 1957; Edmonds, pp. 248-49; Pershing, I, 140.

18. Harbord, *American Army*, p. 192.

19. Marshall interview, Apr. 5, 1957, said that the review was for Joffre, but it is clear from Pershing's description that it was the one for Poincaré; Pershing, I, 163.

20. Marshall gave this account Apr. 5, 1957, after apologizing for what he feared might "sound like [too] much of a personal thing for me to put in here." The story, however, is well attested by several members of the staff who were present. All agreed that he was very angry and made strong statements.

21. F. Palmer, *John J. Pershing.*

22. 1st Div. Summary of plans for movement of troops to the front, initialed by GCM[arshall], Oct. 15, 1917, File 201-34.1, *1st Div. Hist. File, RG 120, NA;* Pershing for TAG for CofS, Oct. 20, 1917; FO 5, signed by Col. Hanson E. Ely, Oct. 27, 1917, *U.S. Army in the World War 1917-19,* III, 449-52; Pershing, I, 196.

23. Marshall to CofS, 1st Div., dated

Einville, 2:30 P.M., Nov. 3, 1917;
Rpt. of CO, Co. F, 16th Inf., on German raid, night of Nov. 2-3, 1917,
both in File 5116, *AGO/AEF, RG
120, NA;* Marshall to Thomas M.
Johnson, July 20, 1937, *GCM Files.*

24. Marshall interview, Apr. 5, 1957;
Marshall to CofS, 1st Div., Nov. 3,

1917, File 5116, *AGO/AEF, RG 120,
NA.*

25. Marshall interview, Apr. 5, 1957.
This is one of several versions of
Bordeaux's remarks. The inscription
finally adopted for the new monu-
ment is a short statement written by
General Marshall himself.

X: IN THE LINE

In addition to sources mentioned for Chapter IX, I have received material on
this chapter in letters from Lt. Gen. Clarence Huebner, Maj. Gen. Paul Ransom,
Maj. Gen. J. D. Patch, and Maj. Gen. Franklin Sibert.

1. Pershing on July 6, 1917, had asked
for one million men by May of the
following year. On December 2, 1917,
he specified the need for 24 divisions
plus rear echelon troops to be sent
by the end of June 1918. Pershing,
I, 87, 250.

2. Edmonds, p. 275; Harbord, *American Army,* p. 228, gives the decrease
in British soldiers as 200,000.

3. *Ibid.*

4. Pershing, I, 249-50.

5. Harbord, *American Army,* p. 187;
Pershing, I, 294-95; 309-10.

6. GO 74, 1st Div., Dec. 14, 1917, War
Diaries, *AEF/GHQ, RG 120, NA;*
Bullard, p. 25.

7. Marshall signed the Oath of Office as
major Nov. 22, 1917, and as lt. colonel
Jan. 8, 1918. *201 File, TAGO, DofA.*

8. F. Palmer, *America in France,* p. 214.

9. Marshall interview, Apr. 11, 1957;
Germain Seligman interview, Mar.
12, 1962; Maj. Charles S. Coulter interview, Nov. 30, 1960. Both divisional and regimental intelligence
sections claim credit for the warning. 1st Div. Ops. Rpt., signed
GCM[arshall], Feb. 21, 1918, File
201-33.1, *1st Div. Hist. File;* Bullard
to CG, 32d French Corps, Mar. 2,
1918, Folder 2170/B, File 14.14, *G-3
Rpts.;* both in *AEF/GHQ, RG 120,
NA;* Chastaine, pp. 37-39.

10. Marshall interview, Apr. 11, 1957.
Marshall's account, based on memory, made the incident the day after
the raid. Pershing's diary sets it on

March 3. Pershing, I, 337; Bullard,
pp. 154-56.

11. Memo by Lt. Chauncey Belknap for
his parents, Dec. 9, 1918 with 1st
Div., AEF, F.O. 18, May 20, 1918;
James A. Edgar interview, Feb. 17,
1959; CG, 1st Div., to CG, 32d French
Corps, Mar. 2, 1918, Folder 2170/B;
1st Div., Special Opns. Order, Mar.
8, 1918, Folder 2171; Marshall memos
to Capts. Graves and Quesenberry,
Mar. 8, 1918, Folder 2171, all in File
14.14, *G-3 Rpts., AEF/GHQ, RG 120,
NA.*

12. Bullard, p. 149.

13. Marshall listed as visiting lecturer in
Army General Staff College, AEF,
France, Class Book, June-Sept. 1918.
Research Center Files.

14. Bliss to SecWar Baker, Jan. 22, 1918,
in F. Palmer, *Bliss, Peacemaker,* p.
216; Harbord, *American Army,* p.
241, estimated the German superiority at 300,000.

15. Bullard, p. 177.

16. *Ibid.*

17. Extract from 1st Division G.O. 11,
Feb. 10, 1920, *201 File, TAGO, DofA;*
Brig. Gen. B. F. Caffey, Jr. interview, Nov. 14, 1962, and Caffey to
author, Jan. 14, 1961.

18. Marshall to AGO/AEF, June 18,
1918, with 1st end. by Bullard, June
19, 1918, 1st Div. Record Card no.
8977, *WW I Org., AGO/AEF, RG
120, NA.*

19. Pershing, II, 55.

20. See photostat of copy of order in-

scribed by Marshall to Belknap in 1918, *Research Center Files*. (Belknap in interview with author, Mar. 31, 1959, says Marshall did the basic work). One of Marshall's jobs was to brief the correspondents on the forthcoming battle. See Thomas M. Johnson interview, Apr. 2, 1959; Thomas M. Johnson, "America's No. 1 Soldier," *Reader's Digest*, XL, Feb. 1944, 113-17.

21. Maj. Gen. Paul Ransom to author, Aug. 23, 1960.

22. 1st Div. Rpt. on Cantigny Operation, Dec. 18, 1918, Doc. 1335, Box 3245, *G-3 Rpts., 1st Div., AEF, RG 120, NA*.

23. 1st Div. Rpt. on Cantigny Operation, Dec. 18, 1918, *G-3 Rpts., 1st Div., AEF, RG 120, NA*.

24. Cable 1223-5, Pershing to CofS and SecWar, June 1, 1918; Command File, 1917-19 Cantigny, *AEF/GHQ, RG 120, NA*.

25. Maj. R. H. Lewis to Lt. Col. Fox Conner, June 5, 1918; Marshall to Col. William M. Fassett, July 6, 1918, both in *1st Div. Hist. File, RG 120, NA*. Caffey to author, Jan. 14, 1961.

26. GCM[arshall], "Defense of Cantigny Sector," June 16, 1918, G-3 memo no. 545, *1st Div. Hist. File, RG 120, NA*.

27. Brig. Gen. James G. Harbord to First Army Corps Commander, Mar. 9, 1918, File 8.524, *G-3 Rpts., AEF/GHQ, RG 120, NA*.

28. Marshall to AGO/AEF, June 18, 1918, with 1st end. by Bullard, June 19, 1918, *AGO/AEF, RG 120, NA*.

29. Extract from recommendation of Maj. Gen. George B. Duncan, July 3, 1918, *201 File, TAGO, DofA*; CofS, V Corps, Brig. Gen. Wilson B. Burtt to Personnel Section, First Army, July 3, 1918, File 17902/A-70, *AGO/AEF, RG 120, NA*.

30. CofS I Army Corps, Brig. Gen. Malin Craig, 2d end., June 26, 1918, on Marshall's request to AG, AEF, June 18, 1918; Maj. Gen. James W. McAndrew to Col. Eltinge, July 5, 1918, both in Folder 17850. Marshall's arrival on July 13, at GHQ reported G.O. no. 189, July 8, 1918, assigned for duty same date to Third Section, G-3, Kuegle to AG, July 13, 1918, Folder 18151/A-15; all in File 14.14, *AGO/AEF, RG 120, NA*.

XI: ST.-MIHIEL AND THE MEUSE-ARGONNE

Marshall's lecture "On Active Service, AEF," his briefing of the members of the House Military Affairs Committee, and the *Report of the First Army*, which he helped write and revise, give high points of the actions in this period.

In addition to help from individuals named in Chapters IX and X, I received letters from Maj. Gen. W. E. R. Covell, Capt. Joe A. Noake and Maj. Gen. E. J. Dawley. Col. Walter S. Grant, Jr. sent me a memorandum by his father on planning for St.-Mihiel.

1. U.S. Army. First Army. *Report of the First Army, AEF, Organization and Operations*, p. 2.

2. Falls, p. 376.

3. Pershing, II, 246.

4. Viereck, pp. 173-74, 218.

5. Both Marshall, a close associate in World War I, and Eisenhower, a subordinate of Conner's in the twenties, agreed in this judgment.

6. GCM to ACofS, G-3, Aug 9, 1918 and Aug. 13, 1918; Lt. Col. W. S. Grant to ACofS, G-3, Aug. 9, 1918 and Aug. 12, 1918, File 122.01; un-

dated and unsigned memo to ACofS, G-3; Marshall to ACofS, G-3, Aug. 16, 1918, both in Folder 1084, File 1033; all in *G-3, 1st Army Rpts., AEF/GHQ, RG 120, NA*.

7. Grant and Marshall to CofS, Aug. 24, 1918, File 191-32.14; Marshall to CofS, First Army, Aug. 23, 1918, File 191-32.15, both in *1st Army Hist. File, AEF/GHQ, RG 120, NA*; ACofS, G-3, Col. Laurence Halstead to CofS, First Army, Dec. 1, 1918, Pt. B, St.-Mihiel Operation, Aug. 10-Sept. 16, File 100.01. He said papers were pre-

pared in Col. Robert McCleave's office with the assistance of Grant and Marshall. Grant and Marshall to CofS, Sept. 10, 1918, File 122.04 both in *G-3, 1st Army Rpts., AEF/ GHQ, RG 120, NA.* The question of Marshall's role in this planning is especially difficult to decide. He was embarrassed by the fact that as a result of changes in dates and resources available, he was never able to complete any proposed plan. He gave Grant credit for an important role in the planning. Grant later prepared an account of his role for his son, who furnished me a copy. Grant said he wrote the final order and that the annexes were prepared by officers of the various sections under Marshall's supervision.

8. Marshall to ACofS, G-3, Aug. 18, 1918, Folder 1169, File 1034; Pétain to Pershing, Aug. 19, 1918, File 658 (v.1)—both in *G-3 Rpts., AEF/GHQ, RG 120, NA;* Pétain to Pershing, Aug. 17, 1918; Pétain to General Cdg. Group of Armies of East, Aug. 22, 1918; Conger memo, Nov. 25, 1926 and related material—all in *U.S. Army in the World War, 1917-19,* VIII, 17-18; 25-26; 33-35; 44-45; 62-64; Johnson, pp. 111-24, has a detailed account of the affair, much of which he apparently received from Col. Conger. Col. George C. Marshall, "On Active Service with the A.E.F., What was done; Why it was done; How it was done" (stenographic record of lecture at Siershahn as transcribed by Patrick C. Kelly, G-3, 1st Div.), Apr. 2, 1919, pp. 13-14.

9. "Special Operations Report of the First Army," Pt. B, The St.-Mihiel Operation (Pt. III of Pt. B, Orders on 13th, includes Pétain to Pershing no. 17642/3, [digest] Sept. 13, 1918), File 110, *G-3, 1st Army Rpts., AEF/ GHQ, RG 120, NA;* Marshall interview, Apr. 11, 1957; Marshall, "On Active Service," p. 15.

10. "Special Operations Rpt. of the First Army," Pt. C, The Argonne-Meuse Operation (Pt. III of Pt. C, Concentration for the Attack), File 110, *G-3, 1st Army Rpts., AEF/GHQ, RG 120, NA.*

11. Pershing, II, 254-55, 284-86. Marshall's account of the movement is given in Marshall to 1st Sub. Sector, Nov. 19, 1918 in *U.S. Army in the World War, 1917-19,* IX, 64-66.

12. F. Palmer, *Our Greatest Battle,* pp. 25-27.

13. Weygand, p. 364.

14. Drum to Chief Artillery of First Army, Sept. 16, 1918, File 191-34.2, *1st Army Hist. File, AEF/GHQ, RG 120, NA.*

15. Marshall interview, Apr. 11, 1957.

16. *U.S. Army in the World War, 1917-19,* IX, 66; Pershing, II, 285; Harbord, *American Army,* p. 430; Hagood, "Soldier; George C. Marshall," *loc.cit.;* Hagood letter to the Editor, *Life,* VII, Sept. 11, 1939, 4; Hugh Johnson, "The General Staff and Its New Chief," *Life,* VII, Aug. 21, 1939, 67. Hagood claimed Marshall was responsible for the movement of 800,-000 men; General Johnson thought the figure nearer 500,000. The discrepancy reflects uncertainty as to how much Marshall had to do with moving troops *not* in the St.-Mihiel area or in First Army reserve. Marshall himself made no claim as to the exact number and it is probably of little significance since by general admission he supervised the move of at least 400,000. On reading Hagood's article Marshall wrote him that his own mother would not believe all of it.

17. F. Palmer, *Pershing,* p. 303.

18. *Report of the First Army, AEF,* pp. 38-39.

19. *Ibid.*

20. Marshall, "On Active Service," p. 16.

21. Liggett, *A.E.F.,* pp. 166-67.

22. Marshall, "On Active Service," p. 17.

23. *Ibid.*

24. *Report of the First Army, AEF,* pp. 51-52.

25. Edmonds, pp. 409-10.

26. Drum urged Marshall when he was rewriting the First Army report to make clear that poor handling of their troops by some of the commanders, rather than the ineffectiveness of the Army staff, was responsible for the blocking of roads. Drum to Marshall, Sept. 27, 1919, Marshall

to Drum, Sept. 20, 1919, *Pershing papers, RG 316, NA.*

27. Pershing, II, 306-307; Johnson, p. 315.

28. Marshall, "On Active Service," p. 21; Marshall, "Statement on Battle Actions Engaged in by American Troops" (Briefing of members of House Military Affairs Committee), Chaumont, France, Apr. 20, 1919, pp. 18, 20, File 370.24/EE, *TAGO, RG 94, NA.*

29. Foch to Pershing, no. 5174, Oct. 25, 1918, Folder 658/A (v.2), *G-3 Rpts., AEF/GHQ, RG 120, NA.*

30. Johnson, p. 333.

31. Marshall, "On Active Service," pp. 22-23.

32. Johnson, pp. 334-42; Marshall interview, Apr. 4, 1957. Pershing, II, 376, also recalls the Sheridan experience.

33. Pershing to CG, First Army, Nov. 5, 1918, File 111.04, *G-3, 1st Army Rpts., AEF/GHQ, RG 120, NA.*

34. Gen. Paul A. M. Maistre to Pershing, Nov. 4, 1918, File 111.04, *G-3, 1st Army Rpts., AEF/GHQ, RG 120, NA.*

35. Marshall to Pattullo, Apr. 24, 1922, *Pershing Papers, LofC.* Caffey recalls that Marshall referred to Maistre agreement in talking to Conner, Caffey interview, Nov. 14, 1962.

36. Marshall Memo for record of G-3 Sec., Nov. 8, 1918; Drum to CGs I and V Corps, Nov. 5, 1918; Drum for ACofS, G-3, First Army, Nov. 7, 1918; all in File 120.05, *G-3, 1st Army Rpts., AEF/GHQ, RG 120, NA.*

37. Marshall to Pattullo, Apr. 24, 1922, *Pershing Papers, LofC.* Damon Runyon, in an account of the attack on Sedan, praised Marshall's work as G-3. See Damon Runyon, "American Sedan Drive according to Principles of 'Stonewall Jackson,'" *Pittsburgh Daily Post,* Nov. 6, 1918.

38. MacArthur's report made little mention of the episode, MacArthur to CG First Army, Nov. 12, 1918, File 191-33.6, *1st Army Hist. File, AEF/GHQ, RG 120, NA.* MacArthur in interview, Jan. 2, 1961, denied that he paid attention to it.

39. Pershing to Marshall, Nov. 29, 1918, *201 File, TAGO, DofA.*

40. This tribute from Gen. George Van Horn Moseley in his unpublished memoir, "One Soldier's Journey," II, 31, was written in 1940 and is remarkable in coming from a man who strongly disagreed with some of Marshall's policies. He did not change this entry, written before he became alienated from Marshall. In 1918 Moseley was chief of supply at GHQ, *Moseley Papers, LofC.*

XII: ARMISTICE–1919

Maj. Gen. James L. Collins, Col. Henry Allen, and John C. Hughes provided background information on this period in interviews
Newspaper accounts came from the large collection in the Pershing Papers, Library of Congress.

1. Ration strength on Nov. 11 was 82,-302 officers and 1,898,353 men; in camps in the United States at the same time were: 104,155 officers and 1,533,344 men. Paxson, III, 7.

2. In period May through Dec. 1919, 1,030,615 were embarked, U.S. War Dept. *Annual Report, 1920,* I, 155.

3. Gen. Allen's Efficiency Reports on Marshall, Dec. 31, 1918, Aug. 15, 1919, *201 File, TAGO, DofA.*

4. Marshall memorandum to G-3, AEF, Feb. 10, 1919, Folder 1128, File 1034, *G-3 Rpts., AEF/GHQ, RG 120, NA.*

5. Conner to CofS, AEF, signed by Upton Birnie, Feb. 15, 1919. The typed initials in the upper right-hand corner, indicating the author of the draft, are those of Marshall, Folder 1995, File 1035, *G-3 Rpts., AEF/GHQ, RG 120, NA.* Cf. language of Marshall's message in 1945 to Eisenhower on going to Berlin. "I would be loath to hazard Amer-

ican lives for purely political purposes." OPD 381, *WW II Rec. Div.,
RG 115, NA.*

6. Marshall interview, Apr. 11, 1957.
7. Eltinge to CGs, 1st, 2d, 3d Armies,
Mar. 22, 1919, no. 21796, *AGO/AEF,
RG 120, NA.*
8. Frederick Palmer to Pershing, Jan.
22, 1919; Martin Egan to Pershing,
Jan. 24, 1919, *Pershing Papers, LofC.*
9. Col. Willey Howell to Eltinge, May
14, 1919, no. 13079/A14. Maj. Gen.
Joseph Kuhn to TAG, Apr. 30, 1919,
no. 13079/A5; both in *AGO/AEF,
RG 120, NA.* Not everyone agreed
with Howell. Kuhn asked for Marshall or Drum to speak to his unit,
adding that officers and noncoms of
his division who had heard Marshall
give a previous lecture "were so favorably impressed . . . that all considered it very desirous to have more
officers and men in the division hear
the lecture." Eltinge had written
earlier of numerous requests for
copies of the lectures and the slides.
(Eltinge to Howell, Drum, Marshall,
Mar. 22, 1919, no. 2176, *AGO/AEF,
RG 120, NA.*) Maj. Gen. John A.
Lejeune later wrote Marshall, Oct.
25, 1934 *(VMI Alumni File)*: "I remember distinctly the brilliant lecture that you delivered to the officers
of the Army after the armistice. . . .
I learned more about the general history of the war than I have learned
since."
10. Marshall, "Statement on Battle Actions," File 370.24/EE, *TAGO, RG
94, NA.*
11. See the collection of clippings in
Scrapbooks, *Pershing Papers, LofC.*
12. Marshall interview, Nov. 21, 1956.
13. Marshall's other World War 1 dec-
orations included the Distinguished
Service Medal, the French Croix de
Guerre with palm, Italian Order of
Saints Maurice and Lazarus (Officer),
Italian Order of the Crown (Officer),
Montenegrin Silver Medal for Bravery, the Panamanian Medal of La
Solidaridad. He was entitled to wear
four stars on his victory medal for
World War I service, for operations
in the Toul Sector, Cantigny Sector,
St.-Mihiel, and the Meuse-Argonne.
201 File, TAGO, DofA.
14. Maj. Gen. James L. Collins interview,
Dec. 2, 1960; S. O. 116, Apr. 2, 1919,
ordered 18 officers, including Stuart
Heintzelman, Lesley McNair, James
L. Collins and James Ulio, to report
to Gen. de Maud'huy at the Place de
la République in Metz to receive
the Legion of Honor, apparently on
April 30 [it is given April 20 in text],
AEF/GHQ, RG 120, NA.
15. On two or three occasions after he
became a general officer, Marshall
designated individuals as aides temporarily but seldom used them as
such.
16. While Marshall saw Foch on numerous occasions with Pershing, he never
established any degree of intimacy.
17. Col. James L. Collins, aide to Pershing in the Philippines and Mexico,
left for a field command soon after
they came to France. Pershing's chief
wartime aide, Col. Carl Boyd, died
shortly before the end of the war.
Col. Edward Bowditch, Jr., who also
served with Pershing during the war,
went with Harbord on a mission to
Armenia. He rejoined Pershing
briefly in 1925 and accompanied him
to Tacna-Arica. Col. J. G. Quekemeyer died during this period from
pneumonia while returning to accept the post of commandant at the
United States Military Academy. Maj.
John C. Hughes soon left the Army
after returning to the United States.
Capt. George E. Adamson and Lt.
Ralph A. Curtin remained with
Pershing until his death. Capt. John
T. Schneider remained on Pershing's
staff during much of the Chief of
Staff period.
18. During the Chaumont days Marshall
became acquainted with Dwight Morrow. A little later he offered Marshall $30,000 a year to join J. P.
Morgan and Company (Marshall interview, Nov. 14, 1956). Caffey to author, Jan. 14, 1961, says Morrow told
him of an offer of $25,000. W. Cam-
eron Forbes in a letter to Pershing,
Jan. 5, 1922, asked if Marshall would
be interested in a job in business.
19. *Boston Evening Transcript,* July 4,

1919; New York *Sun,* July 15, 1919.
20. Harbord, *American Army,* p. 563; Marshall interview, Apr. 11, 1957.
21. *The Times* (London), July 16, 19, 1919; *London Star,* July 16, 1919.
22. *The Times* (London), July 19, 1919.
23. *Sunday Times* (London), July 20, 1919; *New York Times,* July 20, 1919; Marshall interview, Apr. 11, 1957; [André] Brewster to Marshall, May 5, 1939, *GCM Files.*
24. *Chicago Tribune* (Paris ed.), Aug.

[17], 1919; *Il Secolo* (Milan), Aug. 22, 1919; *New York Times,* Aug. 19, 1919.
25. *New York Times,* Sept. 2, 1919; *Chicago Daily News,* Sept. 2, 1919.
26. *Standard-Union* (Brooklyn, N.Y.), Sept. 8, 1919; *New York Tribune,* Sept. 8, 1919.
27. Conner, p. 86.
28. *Washington Post,* Sept. 18, 1919.
29. *Evening Star* (Washington), Sept. 18, 1919.

XIII: AIDE TO PERSHING

Dr. Edward M. Coffman worked through the voluminous hearings on the reorganization of the Army and provided for me in addition to a mass of documents on this period an excellent study, "Army Reorganization, 1919-1920." An interview with Mr. Ralph Curtin, one of Pershing's long-time assistants, was of great value. General Palmer's daughter, Mrs. George Rockwell, gave me background on Marshall-Palmer relations, as did Dr. I. B. Holley of Duke.

1. G-3 Report, July 2, 1919, attached to Rpt. of the CinC, AEF, in *U.S. Army in the World War, 1917-1919,* XIV, 8, 54, 80-83, 90-91; Harbord, *American Army,* p. 504; Holley, p. 131. Pershing, I, 334; Alfred Goldberg, ed., *History of the U.S. Air Force.*
2. Weigley, pp. 226-27.
3. Ekirch, p. 195.
4. Paxson, III, 141.
5. J. McA. Palmer, pp. 137-48, 161-69; memos. Brig. Gen. Lytle Brown to Committee on Plans for Natl. Def., WPD, Apr. 10 and 15, 1919, File 1478, *Reorganization, RG 165, NA.*
6. A copy of the play "Gay Age and Guilded Youth" by Forbes is in the *Pershing Papers, LofC.* See also Mrs. Raymond (Amelia Forbes) Emerson to author, Sept. 23, 1961; David C. Forbes to author, Sept. 11, 1961; W. Cameron Forbes to Marshall, Oct. 28, 1949.
7. Conner, pp. 89-94; Brandreth, pp. 273-85; Everett A. Boyden (Marshall's guide) to author, July 15, Aug. 2, 1960; Mrs. Beatrice Brandreth Hahn to author, July 25, 1960; Mr. Ivan Stanton to author, Aug. 3, 1960. (Marshall later told a friend that he never killed another deer after this trip.)

8. Harbord, *American Army,* p. 110.
9. In complimenting Baker, Marshall added that he had never met President Wilson. Pershing's staff officers included: AG (Davis), Opns. (Conner), IG (Brewster); besides his aides (Quekemeyer and Marshall) he had also three assistants—Schneider, Curtin, and Adamson—whom he had brought with him from Paris.
10. Palmer in later years forgot this and Marshall reminded him that "your testimony before the Senate Committee reached me in galley proof form almost immediately after you gave it, and I went over it with the General." Palmer to Marshall, Mar. 24, 1935; Marshall to Palmer, Mar. 24, 1935; Marshall to Palmer, Mar. 29, 1935, *GCM Files.*
11. U.S. Congress, Senate: Committee on Military Affairs. Hearings on *Reorganization of the Army. 66th Congress,* II, 1571-1704.
12. A point emphasized in the publicity of the Universal Military Training Association.
13. In addition to staff members mentioned in note 9, Moseley, Nolan, Edgar Collins, and Beeuwkes went along. At Christmastime Gen. Malin Craig and Col. R. H. Williams re-

placed Nolan and Collins. SecWar Newton D. Baker to Pershing, Nov. 13, 1919, Pershing to Baker, Dec. 18, 1919, Conner to Robert C. Davis, Dec. 20, 1919, all in no. 21715/A96; Davis to Col. T. H. Bane, Dec. 12, 1919, no. 21715/A100, and related documents in *AGO/AEF, RG 120, NA*.

14. George Van Horn Moseley, "One Soldier's Journey," II, 15, has an excellent description of the trip, *Moseley Papers, LofC*. Thomas Schneider, "General Pershing and I," *Saturday Evening Post*, 236, April 27, 1963, pp. 71-74.

15. It does not appear that Marshall had any greater part in preparing these speeches than in supplying information on the local scene.

16. *Brooklyn Daily Eagle*, June 11, 1920; *New York World*, June 16, 1920. Pershing scrapbook has clippings from each city visited. On June 14, 1919, Col. George S. Patton suggested that Pershing should get into the fight indicating that unless a military man was elected it would be the end of the Army.

17. Camps, plants, and cities visited were: Camp Lee, Camp Bragg, Camp Jackson, Savannah, Charleston, Fort Benning, Camp Gordon, Camp McClellan, Muscle Shoals, Nashville, Camp Taylor, Camp Knox, Louisville, the Aviation Experimental Station (Dayton), Camp Sherman, the Dodge plant (Detroit), Camp Custer, Chicago, St. Louis, Fort Snelling, Minneapolis, Camp Grant, Rock Island Arsenal, Camp Dodge, Des Moines, Omaha, Fort Leavenworth, Kansas City, Camp Funston, Fort Riley, Denver, Fort D. A. Russell, Cheyenne, Fort Douglas, Vancouver Barracks, Portland, Camp Lewis, Camp Lawton, Seattle, Mather Field, the Presidio of San Francisco, Arcadia and March Fields, Los Angeles, Camp Kearney, San Diego, Kelly Field, El Paso, San Antonio, Houston, Dallas, Fort Worth, Tulsa, Fort Sill, Fort Reno, Camp Pike, Little Rock, Memphis, New Orleans, Camp Oglethorpe, Chattanooga, Langley Field, Fort Monroe, Norfolk, Richmond, Fort Devens, Boston, Watertown Arsenal, Fort Dix, Troy, Buffalo, Fort Niagara, New York City.

18. Pershing, Rept. of Inspection of Military Installations of the U.S., Mar. 23, 1920, no. 21715/A162, *AGO/AEF, RG 120, NA*.

19. J. McA. Palmer, pp. 179-81.

20. *Cong. Record*, 66th Cong. 2d Sess., Report of bill from conference, pp. 7833; Riker, pp. 82-83.

21. Otto L. Nelson, pp. 274-313. Marshall was one of the officers placed on the initial General Staff Eligibility List of over 325 names selected in 1920 by a board headed by Pershing. *Pershing Papers, RG 316, NA*.

22. Marshall endorsement of letter of J. Palmer to Pershing, Apr. 4, 1921, *Pershing Papers, LofC;* Palmer to Marshall, Mar. 30, 1935. *GCM Files*.

23. Mrs. George (Mary Palmer) Rockwell interview, Jan. 27, 1961. Marshall to James W. Wadsworth, Oct. 2, 1935 (*GCM Files*) said, "Few Army officers have contributed more to the government of lasting benefit. Yet, comparatively speaking, he has received literally nothing in the way of reward. Fellows have been made brigadier generals for keeping the grass cut and the buildings painted. . . . Yet he was retired as a brigadier." He asked Wadsworth to propose special legislation to register official recognition of Palmer's services. Palmer to Marshall, Sept. 30, 1935, quotes Gen. Marshall as saying in a letter of Sept. 24, 1935 (*GCM Files*), "No one deserves so much who has received so little."

24. *New York Times, New York Tribune, Washington Post*, June 8, 1920.

25. Marshall interview, Apr. 11, 1957. On the VMI trip, see *Rockbridge County News*, June 24, 1920.

26. Maj. Gen. W. G. Haan to CofS, July 17, 1920, and attached letter, Pershing to SecWar, July 8, 1920, favoring smaller divisions, *Pershing Papers, RG 316, NA*. Marshall to Col. W. M. Spencer, Mar. 18, 1938 (*GCM Files*), explained his stand as opposed to Drum's in 1920.

27. Although the *Boston Evening Transcript* later in the year spoke of Mac-

Arthur as one of the group which had won Pershing's favor, his advancement over many men senior to him seems to have come as a result of the backing of Baker and March. Frazier Hunt, pp. 106-107, 163.

28. Pershing to Baker, June 20, 1920, with undated memo by Conner attached; Marshall to Pershing, Oct. 6, 1920; Marshall to Pershing, Nov. 17, 1920; Pershing to John W. Weeks, Mar. 10, 1921; all in *Pershing Papers, RG 316, NA.* Marshall to Pershing, Dec. 23, 1920, *Pershing Papers, LofC.*

29. *Chicago Daily News,* Sept. 9, 1920. Pershing wrote later of this period: "There was some question whether the position [Chief of Staff] was commensurate with the rank of general which had been conferred on me by Congress, but I was keen to have it. We had never had, and had not then, a sound, up-to-date organization for national defense, and it seemed to me that I could in no better way repay my country for the trust it had placed in me and the signal honors it had conferred upon me than to devote the last years of my active service to the establishment of such a system." *Pershing Papers, LofC.*

30. *New York Tribune,* Apr. 22, 1921; *Brooklyn Daily Eagle,* Apr. 22, 1921; *Boston Evening Transcript,* Apr. 23, May 14, 1921; *New York World,* Apr. 23, 1921. For favorable comments, see *New York Times,* May 14, 1921; *Springfield Republican,* May 14, 1921; *Boston Post,* May 14, 1921; and David Lawrence in *Evening Star* (Washington), May 14, 1921.

31. Commendation Maj. Gen. David C. Shanks to TAG, July 7, 1922, *201 File, TAGO, DofA.*

32. War Dept. *Annual Report, 1923,* I, 129.

33. Prof. I. B. Holley to author, May 18, 1962, says that General Marshall in a statement to him confirmed Palmer's statement that War Department officers cut the training centers because they had low promotion possibilities for regulars. The more skeletonized units they could set up, the more rank they could justify.

34. Marshall draft with changes in his handwriting attached to letter, Marshall to Pershing, June 22, 1923, saying he had just finished the draft when Adamson told him Pershing wanted him to write it. Marshall urged Pershing to emphasize these points. The draft and mimeograph text of address, Army War College, June 28, 1923, are in *Pershing Papers, LofC.*

35. *Passaic Daily News,* May 31, 1924.

36. Annual Report of CofS to SecWar, Nov. 23, 1923, for release Dec. 7, 1923, *NWC Library;* Pershing to Marshall, Nov. 18, 1924, *Pershing Papers, LofC,* indicates that Marshall wrote the 1923 report.

37. Memo on Organization submitted by Moseley, Dec. 3, 1918, *Pershing Papers, RG 316, NA.*

38. *New York Herald,* Nov. 4, 1923.

39. Marshall interview, Mar. 6, 1957. See also "Saying No Is a Full-Time Job," *Sunday Star* (Washington), May 18, 1963.

40. Marshall to Reed Landis, May 17, 1938, *GCM Files.* Marshall says meetings were in 1921, but notes that this was the period of the Brown project.

41. Marshall to Drum, Aug. 11, Sept. 20, 1919; Drum to Marshall, Aug. 25, 1919; Drum to Marshall, Feb. 24, 1920; Pershing to Marshall, Oct. 26, 1920; all in *Pershing Papers, RG 316, NA.* Handwritten revisions and corrections by Marshall on galley proof may be seen in same file.

42. Marshall to Pershing, Apr. 5, Apr. 9, 1923; both in *Pershing Papers, RG 316, NA.*

43. *New Orleans Item,* Nov. 5, 1922.

44. Marshall to Pershing, Jan. 24, 1932, [i.e., 1933] Marshall says, "He [Baruch] interested me more than most interesting men."

45. In a letter to the author of Oct. 16, 1960, Col. R. V. Murphy says that he was told that while Marshall was on Pershing's staff at Chaumont he was instructed by the AEF commander to write a sharp reply to a high French official. On two occasions afterward, Pershing asked about the letter and was told that it hadn't been written. When Pershing per-

sisted, Marshall said that he felt that
Pershing should not dignify the incident and that the letter was im-
proper. It was not written.

46. Marshall to Pershing, Sept. 18, 1924,
Pershing Papers, LofC; Pershing's
Efficiency Report on Marshall in 1922
and 1923 said: "A most efficient officer in every respect. Has superior
knowledge of tactics and handling
large bodies of troops. Able as a
general staff officer. Should be made
a brigadier general as soon as eligible. This officer should reach high
rank and is capable of filling any
position with ability and good judgment—a very exceptional man."
Handwritten entry by Pershing in
Marshall's Efficiency Report, 1922;
repeated 1923, *201 File, TAGO,
DofA.*

47. Pershing to Marshall, Aug. 2, 1924,
Marshall to Pershing, Aug. 8, 1924,
Pershing Papers, LofC.

XIV: LESSONS IN CHINESE

Marshall letters for the China period are found mainly in the Pershing Papers,
Library of Congress, and a smaller collection made available by John C. Hughes.
A diary and clipping collection was made available by Mrs. W. E. Crist, wife of
Brig. Gen. Crist, a lieutenant in Tientsin during this period. Mrs. Arline Van B.
Pratt prepared for me a helpful collection of extracts from pertinent sections of
Dept. of State, *Papers Relating to Foreign Relations of the U.S.* 1924, 1925, 1926,
1927.

Background material came from interviews with Maj. Gen. E. F. Harding, Brig.
Gen. T. J. Betts, Maj. Gen. T. S. Timberman, Gen. Matthew B. Ridgway, Mrs.
Joseph Stilwell, Chaplain Luther D. Miller, Maj. Gen. P. E. Gallagher, Col. C. M.
Willingham, Col. Isaac Newell, Brig. Gen. Frederic B. Butler, Maj. Gen. H. B.
Lewis, Col. and Mrs. John E. McCammon, Brig. Gen. and Mrs. W. E. Crist, and
letters from Brig. Gen. A. S. Champeny, Col. Morris B. De Pass, Maj. Gen. James
R. Pierce, and Brig. Gen. Horace O. Cushman.

1. One battalion of the regiment remained in the Philippines.

2. Hdq., 15th Infantry, "Compilation
of Data relating to subjects which
may be of special interest to newly
arrived officers and their families . . . ," Dec. 7, 1925, AG 330.23,
China, RG 94, NA. Charles W.
Thomas, III, "The United States
Army Troops in China, 1912-1937"
(term paper prepared for Payson J.
Treat, Stanford University, June
1937), *NWC Library.* Twenty-five
future generals, including Marshall,
Stilwell, and Ridgway, came from
the officers stationed at Tientsin between 1925-30, Finney, p. 7.

3. Brig. Gen. W. D. Connor to TAG,
Annual Report, Aug. 24, 1925, File
319.12, *China, RG 94, NA.*

4. The United States in 1901 had refused to accept a territorial concession, withdrawn its troops, and later
turned back indemnity payments to
the Chinese government, stipulating
that the money was to be used in
the support of education.

5. Crow, pp. 332-36; Rasmussen, chap.
23; Finney, pp. 17-20.

6. For background material on China's
political problems in this era, see
Vinacke, Griswold, Holcombe, Buss.

7. Dulles, *China and America,* p. 167.

8. MacNair and Lach, p. 252.

9. Marshall to Col. Hjalmer Erickson,
Jan. 29, 1925, *NWC Library.*

10. For description of fighting in Sept.,
1st Lt. George Van Studdiford to
TAG, Oct. 29, 1924, File 350.05;
Marshall to Henry H. Dabney, Oct.
23, 1924, Marshall to AG, 15th Inf.,
Oct. 25, 1924, both in File 371.1; all
in *China, RG 94, NA.*

11. Marshall to Erickson, Jan. 29, 1925,
NWC Library.

12. Marshall to "My dear Johnny" (John

C. Hughes), Jan. 2, 1925; Finney, pp. 98-128. Information on the gate appears in "Historic Memorials," *Army and Navy Register*, Oct. 14, 1939.

13. Connor to TAG, *Annual Report*, Aug. 24, 1925, File 319.12, *China, RG 94, NA;* Marshall to Gen. W. H. Cocke, Dec. 26, 1926, describes his work with the Chinese Language School, *VMI Alumni File*.

14. Marshall to Pershing, Mar. 17, 1925, *Pershing Papers, LofC*.

15. Interview with Chap. Luther D. Miller and Bert Ivry, recorded June 24, 1958, for *NBC Biography in Sound;* Report of TIG Helmick to CofS, Oct. 22, 1925, File 333.1, *TIG, RG 159, NA*, lists Marshall as one of the officers who "has become quite fluent" in spoken Chinese.

16. E. F. Harding, *Lays of the Mei-Kuo Ying-P'an*, p. 1.

17. Gallagher to author, Sept. 1, 1960. Gallagher was the reg. AG during part of Marshall's stay in China.

18. Marshall to Pershing, Dec. 26, 1926, *Pershing Papers, LofC*.

19. Marshall to John C. Hughes, July 18, 1925. Some twenty years later the boy, C. H. Hsieh, rated a photograph and story in the *North China Marine* (Tientsin), July 6, 1946, on the strength of letter he had received from Marshall, *GCM Files*.

20. Interview with Miller and Ivry, June 24, 1958.

21. Marshall to Pershing, Dec. 26, 1926, *Pershing Papers, LofC*.

22. Harding, op. cit., p. 31.

23. Marshall to Pershing, Oct. 30, 1925, *Pershing Papers, LofC*.

24. Helmick to CofS, Oct. 22, 1925, *TIG, RG 159, NA;* Connor to Marshall, Nov. 3, 1937 *(GCM Files)*, spoke of his indebtedness to him "for the wonderful way in which you did not only your own work in China but that of your exhilarated regimental commander." Naylor, in his initial Efficiency Report on Marshall, rated him superior on his performance in various offices and said that he "is well suited for almost any position to which he might be assigned"— Efficiency Report, Nov. 23, 1924— June 30, 1925. In his final report,

Naylor reduced Marshall's performance rating to above average and stated that he was "a very neat, courteous, prepossessing officer." Connor changed all the ratings to superior, saying that Marshall was "one of the most capable officers that has ever served under my command"—Efficiency Report, July 1, 1925-Jan. 2, 1926. Connor's final Efficiency Report called Marshall "one of the best officers in the Army"— Efficiency Report, Jan. 4, 1926–Mar. 5, 1926, *201 File, TAGO, DofA*.

25. Li Ching-lin.

26. On the incidents during Dec. 1925, see 1st Lt. P. E. Gallagher, "History of the 15th Infantry stationed in China from Jan. 1, 1925, to Dec. 31, 1925," Apr. 13, 1926, File 314.73, *China, RG 94, NA;* and the pertinent entries from the Diary and Scrapbooks kept by Mrs. W. E. Crist.

27. Gallagher to TAG, Apr. 13, 1925; Capt. J. D. Cope, "American Troops in China, Their Mission," *Infantry Journal*, XXXVIII, Mar.-Apr. 1931, 174; U.S. American Forces in China, "Officers' School Notes, School Years 1933-35," pp. 49-50, 91-92, OCMH Files.

28. Gallagher to TAG, Apr. 13, 1925; "Officers' School Notes," p. 50.

29. Connor to American Minister J. V. A. MacMurray, Jan. 13, 1926 forwarded to TAG, Jan. 22, 1926; Connor to TAG, June 15, 1926, both in File 350.05, *China, RG 94, NA*.

30. Marshall to Pershing, Jan. 30, 1925, *Pershing Papers, LofC;* Brig. Gen. J. C. Castner to Summerall, Apr. 20, 1927, File 201.6, *China, RG 94, NA*.

31. Betts interview, Dec. 12, 1958.

32. For a delightful pen picture of Castner, see Finney, pp. 57-76.

33. Col. and Mrs. John E. McCammon interview, Nov. 12, 1962.

34. For Marshall's analysis of the Chinese question, see Marshall to Pershing, Dec. 26, 1926, *Pershing Papers, LofC*.

35. Castner to TAG, Radio no. 764, Apr. 10, 1927, File 337, MacMurray to Adm. Clarence S. Williams, June 16, 1927, both in File 370.5; Castner to TAG, *Annual Report FY 1927*, July

30, 1928, File 319.1; all in *China, RG 94, NA.*

36. Maj. Joseph Stilwell to CG, USAFC, June 16, 1927, "Observation trip to Hsuchow-fu and Shanghai, May 26-June 15, 1937," File 350.05, *China, RG 94, NA.* Marshall almost certainly saw Stilwell's "Who's Who in China," *Infantry Journal,* XXIII, July 1928, 79-80, in which Stilwell wrote: "The man [Chiang] must be admired for his determination and energy in the face of the many disadvantages under which he is laboring, and if he wins out it will be largely on account of the resources he can find within himself. In such a case, the devil must be given his due, and we shall be forced to the conclusion that China may still be able to produce men of sufficient ability to solve her problems and put her house in order."

37. Marshall to Pershing, Dec. 26, 1926, *Pershing Papers, LofC.* Marshall said that he had declined five previous requests to serve at the War College.

In 1925 he had also been asked for by the G-4 Section of the War Dept., with the idea of grooming him for the position of Chief of Finance when Col. George P. Tyner left. ACofS G-4 to Connor to ACofS G-1 Campbell King, Nov. 25, 1925, Folder 210.61, *TAGO, RG 94, NA.*

38. Mrs. Marshall to John C. Hughes, Nov. 25, n.d. but apparently 1926, *Research Center Files.*

39. Mrs. Marshall to Pershing, Aug. 12, 1927, *Pershing Papers, LofC;* Marshall to "Aunt Lottie" (Mrs. T. B. Coles), Aug. 20, 23, 1927.

40. Mrs. Marshall to "Aunt Lot" (Mrs. T. B. Coles), Monday and Tuesday, Sept. 5 and 6, 1927.

41. Marshall to Pershing, Oct. 14, 1927, *Pershing Papers, LofC.*

42. Col. J. J. Fulmer, Exec. Off. at the Army War College in 1925, to author, Nov. 10, 1960.

43. Marshall to Pershing, Oct. 6, 1927, Marshall to Pershing, Oct. 14, 1927, *Pershing Papers, LofC.*

XV: MARSHALL'S MEN

In the absence of the Infantry School correspondence which I have been unable to find for this period, I have relied heavily on Annual Reports of the commandant, Infantry School, and on interviews. Gen. and Mrs. Marshall were both most helpful on this period. Former associates and friends who gave me considerable information include: Gen. of the Army Omar N. Bradley, Gen. Joseph Lawton Collins, Gen. Courtney Hodges, Gen. Matthew Ridgway, Gen. Walter Bedell Smith, Lt. Gen. H. R. Bull, Maj. Gen. E. F. Harding, Maj. Gen. C. T. Lanham, Gen. Charles Bolté, Gen. John Dahlquist, Col. Truman Smith, Sgt. Thomas Tweed, Mrs. Joseph Stilwell, Brig. Gen. Neal Johnson, Col. Landon Lockett, Mrs. Etta Blanchard Worsley, Dr. Mercer Blanchard, Mrs. R. E. Dismukes, Sr., Maj. Gen. Philip E. Gallagher, Mrs. Thomas C. Hudson, Mr. R. C. Jordan, Sr., Mrs. Haywood Luckett, Mrs. Leighton McPherson, Miss Florence Tillery, Mrs. E. S. Waddell.

The June 1928 issue of the *Infantry Journal* was devoted to various phases of activities at Fort Benning. Marshall's views on Army training in the future may be found in his article "Profiting by War Experiences," *Infantry Journal,* XVIII, Jan. 1921, pp. 34-37.

Col. R. V. Murphy wrote me six long letters describing life at Fort Benning while Marshall was assistant commandant.

1. Marshall to Fuqua, Nov. 25, 1932, *GCM Files.*

2. Marshall to "Aunt Lottie," Oct. 26, 1927. In a letter to Mrs. T. B. Coles of Nov. 13, 1927, he included his detailed sketch of the house and garden—noting the chrysanthemums, the grape arbor, roses, shrubs, and fig tree. See also Marshall to Mrs. Egbert Armstrong, May 16, 1941.

3. Marshall to Mrs. Egbert (Catherine L.) Armstrong, May 16, 1941, *GCM Files.*

4. Lt. Col. P. D. Glassford to TIG, "Annual Inspection of Ft. Benning FY 1929," Sept. 12, 1929, File 333.1, *TIG, RG 159, NA.*

5. Marshall to Heintzelman, Dec. 4, 1933, *GCM Files.*

6. Marshall to Fuqua, Nov. 25, 1932, *GCM Files.*

7. Based on Mrs. Helen Roepke's detailed tally of instructors and students at Benning during the 1927-32 period. Among the future generals of World War II was Capt. Adolf von Schell who attended the Infantry School in 1930, where he wrote a number of accounts on WW 1 experiences. Von Schell became a lt. gen. in the German Army before he fell into disfavor with Hitler. See Truman Smith to author, Oct. 23, 1959 with enclosure, Lt. Gen. von Schell, "General Marshall Saves a German General."

8. Marshall to Heintzelman, Dec. 4, 1933, *GCM Files.*

9. Marshall to DCofS [Maj. Gen. Embick], "Command and General Staff School," Apr. 13, 1937, *GCM Files.*

10. Marshall to Lentz, Oct. 2, 1935, *GCM Files.*

11. George C. Marshall, "Profiting by War Experiences," *Infantry Journal,* XVIII, January 1921, 34-37.

12. Marshall to Pershing, Jan. 30, 1925, *Pershing Papers, LofC.*

13. Marshall to Heintzelman, Dec. 18, 1933, *GCM Files.*

14. Marshall to Heintzelman, Dec. 4, 1933, *GCM Files.*

15. Marshall to Heintzelman, Dec. 18, 1933, *GCM Files.*

16. Marshall to Heintzelman, Dec. 4, 1933, *GCM Files.*

17. Gen. Matthew B. Ridgway interview, Feb. 26, 1959.

18. Marshall to Heintzelman, Dec. 18, 1933, *GCM Files.*

19. Gen. Charles L. Bolté interview, May 28, 1958.

20. Lt. Gen. Harold R. Bull interview, May 27, 1959.

21. Marshall to Heintzelman, Dec. 4, 1933, *GCM Files.*

22. Bull interview, May 27, 1959.

23. Verse from Maj. E. F. Harding's play, "Morning, Noon and Night," *Infantry Journal,* XXXII, June 1938, 628.

24. Harding interview, Oct. 23, 1958; Maj. Gen. Charles T. Lanham interview, Dec. 11, 1962. In praising Lanham's work on *Infantry in Battle,* Marshall noted that a British quarterly "characterized it as the most important military text since 1874" and that "Liddell Hart had quoted the commander of the British First Division at the maneuvers last summer as saying it is the finest infantry text in his experience, that it was the only one book he took with him on maneuvers." Marshall to Heintzelman, Oct. 31, 1934, *GCM Files.*

25. *Infantry in Battle,* p. ix.

26. Bull interview, May 27, 1959.

27. Gen. J. Lawton Collins to Mrs. Marshall, Oct. 29, 1959, *Research Center Files;* J. Lawton Collins interview, Jan. 23, 1958.

28. Lt. Col. Bernard Lentz, "Refreshing at the Infantry School," *Infantry Journal,* XXXVI, Jan. 1930, 59; Lentz to author, Aug. 19, 1960.

29. "The Academic Department," *Infantry Journal,* XXXII, June 1928, 588-91; *Doughboy,* yearbook issued at Fort Benning, 1931.

30. Marshall to Heintzelman, Dec. 18, 1933, *GCM Files.*

31. Marshall to Heintzelman, Dec. 4, 1933, *GCM Files.*

32. Col. Truman Smith interview, Oct. 5, 1959; Harding interview, Oct. 23, 1958.

33. J. Lawton Collins interview, Jan. 23, 1958.

34. Col. Marcus H. Ray to Marshall, Nov. 4, 1953. Marshall wrote on this letter, "a very able officer," *GCM Files.*

35. Gene M. Lyons and John W. Masland, "The Origins of the ROTC," *Military Affairs,* XXIII, Spring 1959, 7, for Mershon's interest in ROTC. Marshall to Maj. James O. Green, May 11, 1933, Marshall to Gen. Leigh Gignilliat, Apr. 5, 1933, Marshall to Col. Ralph Bishop, Mar. 15, 1933, *GCM Files.*

36. Capt. W. A. Collier, "The Infantry School Hunt," *Infantry Journal,* XXXII, June 1928, 608-13; Lt. Clyde Grady, "A Small Game Paradise," *Infantry Journal,* XXXII, June 1928, 635-42; Arthur Grahame, "General Marshall's Hunting Partner," *Outdoor Life,* Sept. 1943, lent to author by Sgt. Tom Tweed, *Research Center Files;* Tweed interview, June 7, 1962.

37. Gen. Archibald Arnold to author, Dec. 4, 1960; Col. Murphy to author, Sept. 25, 1960.

38. Col. Morrison C. Stayer interview, Jan. 20, 1960; Mrs. Singer interview, Feb. 2, 1960.

39. Mrs. Walter (Ella-Keen Steel) Gunster to author, Nov. 15, 1960.

40. Most of the material on Mrs. Marshall comes from interviews with her on Nov. 17, 1960, and Mar. 15, 1961.

41. Mrs. Etta Blanchard Worsley interview, Aug. 8, 1961.

42. His other children were Allene and Tristram. *New York Times,* July 24, Aug. 17, 27, Nov. 3, 1913; Apr. 7, 17, July 4, Aug. 20, 1914; Sept. 12, 19, 1919; Sept. 30, 1927; *Who's Who in America, 1926-27.*

43. Mrs. C. M. Himmelheber to author, July 15, 1961, including information collected by her mother, Mrs. M. Aubrey Childrey, granddaughter of Josiah Pender; Mrs. Claude H. McKenney to author, July 1, 1961.

44. Baltimore *Sun,* June 5, 1928.

45. Mrs. Worsley interview, Aug. 8, 1961; Katherine T. Marshall, p. 3.

46. Marshall to Adamson, June 23, 1930, Marshall to Pershing, from Wyoming, n.d. but apparently Aug. 1930, Marshall to Pershing, Sept. 13, 1930, *Pershing Papers, LofC.*

47. Rev. Harry S. Weyrich performed the ceremony, Baltimore *Evening Sun,* Oct. 15, 1930; *New York Times,* Oct. 16, 1930, p. 2; Weyrich to the author, Sept. 15, 1960.

48. A play entitled, "A Day in the Life of GCM," although unsigned was attributed to Mrs. Wilkes by Mrs. Worsley who saw it presented at Benning. Copy found in Mrs. Singer's collection of papers pertaining to Gen. Marshall. The collection was made available to the Marshall Research Center by Mrs. Robert W. Smith, Jr., Greensburg, Pa., *Research Center Files.*

49. One of Marshall's tasks in this period was work on Pershing's memoirs. He read the manuscript carefully and made detailed comments in which he complained that Pershing "let the critical tone get in too much" in his discussion of the Allies and the War Dept. He noted: "You displayed marvelous restraint in France and since. The manuscript presents you in a different light . . ." He concluded, "Practically everyone of position who has written about the war has lost somewhat by doing so. I do not want to see this happen to you." Marshall to Pershing, Dec. 2, 1930, *Pershing Papers, LofC.* During a visit to Washington in this connection, Marshall met Maj. Dwight D. Eisenhower, who was working with the American Battle Monuments Commission, headed by Gen. Pershing. Eisenhower had suggested that Pershing use a different form for the chapters on St.-Mihiel and the Meuse-Argonne fights, but Marshall felt that Pershing should follow the same form he had used in the earlier chapters. During this meeting Marshall offered Eisenhower a place as instructor at Benning but Eisenhower had prior orders which made it impossible for him to accept the offer. Eisenhower interview, June 28, 1962.

50. Adjutant of TIS, H. B. Lewis to TAG, Apr. 25, 1931; TAG to Comdt., TIS, May 8, 1931; Ft. Benning S.O. no. 96, Apr. 25, 1931, *201 File, TAGO, DofA.*

51. John Landis to Marshall, May 18, 1937, *GCM Files.*

XVI: THE OLD MAN

The chief material from the National Archives included: RG 94 (TAGO), RG 159 (TIG), and RG 98 (Army posts and commands, Fort Screven, 8th Infantry, 8th Infantry Brigade and IV Corps Area). From the Civilian Conservation Corps files in the Agriculture, Labor and War Department files of the National Archives, Mrs. Pratt selected a mass of key documents and prepared a valuable running commentary for my use. Dr. Coffman and Mr. Marken made a special search of the files for any material bearing on the status of the 8th Infantry during the time General Marshall was with that unit. Extracts of all news items and editorials from the *Savannah Morning News* and the *Charleston News and Courier* for the 1932-33 period were made by Miss Eugenia Lejeune and Mrs. Juanita Pitts.

For background material I have drawn heavily on interviews with Mrs. Marshall, Gen. of the Army Douglas MacArthur, Brig. Gen. and Mrs. Claude M. Adams, Gov. James F. Byrnes, Col. John R. Boatwright, Mr. Ralph Curtin, Lt. Gen. Alvan C. Gillem, Lt. Gen. Reuben E. Jenkins, Col. Charles S. Johnson, Mr. Harrison Jones, Sgt. Joseph Morossow, and letters from Lt. Col. Milton A. Schrieber and Col. Frederick S. Matthews, and a poem, "The Old Man," by O. Z. Tyler, Jr. I was aided in my visit to Savannah and Fort Screven by Mr. Walter Hartridge and Mr. Ralston B. Lattimore.

1. Marshall to John L. Cabell, Mar. 29, 1937, indicates that VMI Supt. Cocke had urged Marshall to retire and succeed him, *GCM Files.* See also Cocke to Marshall, Oct. 13, 1926, Marshall to Cocke, Dec. 26, 1926, *VMI Alumni File;* Marshall to Pershing, June 28, 1929, Pershing to Marshall, July 13, 1929, *Pershing Papers, LofC.*

2. John W. Killigrew, "The Impact of the Great Depression on the Army, 1929-36" (unpublished Ph.D. dissertation, University of Indiana, 1960), chaps. IV and V.

3. SecWar Hurley to Rep. Homer C. Parker, Feb. 5, 1932, File 824.01, Screven and Moultrie, *TAGO, RG 94, NA.* Marshall to Pershing, Mar. 28, 1932, *Pershing Papers, LofC.*

4. Lt. Gen. Reuben E. Jenkins to author, Oct. 26, 1960; *Savannah Morning News,* June 15, 16, 17, 1932; Marshall to Capt. Claude M. Adams, June 3, 1932, *GCM Files.*

5. Among those who cordially welcomed them were Mr. and Mrs. Carl Espey, with whom the Marshalls developed a warm friendship.

6. Mrs. Marshall interview, Nov. 17, 1960; K. T. Marshall, pp. 10-11.

7. Marshall related the story to the author at Leesburg over the finger-

bowls, Oct. 5, 1956. Adams interview, May 10, 1957, gives a slightly different version.

8. "The Old Man—1934," a poem by O. Z. Tyler, Jr., presented to Mrs. Marshall in 1960, *Research Center Files.* Former Lt. Tyler described Marshall's stay at Fort Screven but put it in 1934 instead of 1933. Col. Frederick S. Matthews to author, Nov. 9, 1960; Mrs. Marshall interview, Nov. 17, 1960.

9. Marshall to Pershing, Mar. 8, 1933, *Pershing Papers, LofC.*

10. Mrs. Marshall interview, Nov. 17, 1960.

11. On the Army's early work before CCC was proposed, see Moseley to ACofS, G-3 and G-4, Jan. 7, 1933; Col. Duncan K. Major, Jr., to CofS, Jan. 25, 1933, OCS 17622-12 *RG 110;* SecWar Hurley to Sen. David Reed, Jan. 27, 1933, *G-1/11882-2, RG111,* both in *WW 11 Rec. Div., NA.*

12. Roosevelt message to Congress, Mar. 21, 1933, and footnotes; Roosevelt to SecWar, Interior, Agriculture, and Labor, Mar. 14, 1933, both in Chronological Historical Reference Files, pt. 1, *CCC, RG 35, NA.*

13. Major to TAG for Corps Area Com-

manders, Mar. 25, 1933, File 324.5, CCC, TAGO, RG 94, NA.

14. Maj. Gen. Edward L. King to Marshall, Apr. 6, 1933, GCM Files.
15. CofS MacArthur to Corps Area Commanders, May 13, 1933, File 324.5, CCC, TAGO, RG 94, NA. Killigrew, op.cit., chap. XII, pp. 18-19.
16. Jenkins to author, Oct. 26, 1960.
17. Ibid.
18. Outstanding among them were Maj. Matthews, Capt. Adams, and Lt. Jenkins.
19. Marshall to Col. Clyde R. Abraham, May 26, 1933; Marshall to King, May 26, 1933, GCM Files. Marshall took the oath of office as full colonel on September 7, 1933. He had asked shortly before that the "Jr." be dropped from his name.
20. In letter to Maj. Gen. George V. H. Moseley, Apr. 5, 1934 (GCM Files), Col. Marshall says that the CCC in South Carolina was the most interesting problem of his army career. Savannah Morning News, June 14, 1933, p. 12.
21. Marshall to Pershing, Jan. 24, 1932 [i.e., 1933], Pershing Papers, LofC.
22. King to Fuqua, Apr. 29, 1933, GCM Files.
23. Such praise in Marshall's case had long since become routine, as were the "superior" ratings which he received on his efficiency report for his year at Fort Screven. They need to be pinned down on this occasion only because of an article which Walter Trohan of the Chicago Tribune published in the American Mercury, LXXII, Mar. 1951, 267, in which he charged, without any evidence that the most diligent research has uncovered, that "the Inspector General reported that under one year of Marshall's command the 8th Infantry had dropped from one of the best regiments in the Army to one of the worst." All routine inspection reports of the regiment for the relevant period are in fact favorable. The only Inspector General's report on file on the 8th Infantry while Marshall was connected with it is the one which specially commends his work at Screven. There is no evidence in the official files that any other inspection from Washington was made. Trohan further tied Marshall's alleged failure as a troop commander to his failure to be promoted to brigadier general. In fact Marshall, after promotion to colonel, was put on the next list of colonels eligible for brigadier general. He was in the 66 selected out of 470 in the Army. Trohan never documented his statement. Without confirmation, nevertheless, the tale was picked up by the late Sen. McCarthy, p. 8; by Frazier Hunt, p. 161; De-Seversky, p. 43. Most of the writers using this story assume that Marshall was commanding the 8th Infantry during his year at Fort Screven, when in fact he had only a detachment of that regiment and was at Fort Moultrie in command of the entire regiment for only a few months. The best answer to the charge that he was shipped out by MacArthur because the regiment's rating deteriorated under Marshall is MacArthur's statement to Keehn that "He [Marshall] has no superior among Infantry colonels."

McCarthy implied that Marshall had neglected the regiment in an effort to impress Harry Hopkins with his work on CCC matters. He failed to note that Hopkins did not join the Roosevelt administration until May 22, 1933, almost a year after Marshall arrived at Fort Screven and only a month before he left it. Since Hopkins in a period roughly equivalent to the remaining time Marshall spent with the 8th Infantry inaugurated 180,000 work projects and put four million men to work, it is unlikely that he was closely concerned with a lieutenant colonel's activities in South Carolina. As we shall see later, Hopkins' interest in Marshall came after he was appointed Deputy Chief of Staff. See Sherwood, pp. 44, 52, 101. When in 1951 McCarthy was asked by Leo Cherne for evidence in support of his charges against Marshall, the senator cited only the Trohan article—"TV panel makes more noise than sense," Life, XXXII, April 14, 1952, 101-10. TIG Report, Fort Screven for FY 1933, Mar. 24, 1933, File 331.1, *TIG, RG 159, NA;* entries in Marshall efficiency report for period July 1, 1932 to June 28, 1933, and July 1, 1933 to Oct. 20, 1933, *201 File, TAGO, DofA.*

24. K. T. Marshall, p. 11; *Savannah Morning News,* June 27, 1933, p. 12.

25. Col. Charles S. Johnson to author, Oct. 1, 1960.

26. Lt. Col. Edward L. Black to author, Sept. 21, 1960; Lt. Col. Milton A. Schrieber to author, Nov. 12, 1960.

27. Schrieber to author, Nov. 12, 1960.

28. Major to Robert Fechner, June 30, 1933, File 324.5, *CCC, RG 35, NA.*

29. MacArthur to TAG for Corps Commanders, June 30, 1933, File 324.5, *CCC, TAGO, RG 94, NA;* Halstead to Marshall, May 26, 1933, *GCM Files.*

30. Black to author, Sept. 21, 1960.

31. Mrs. Marshall interview, Nov. 17, 1960; "Le Souvenir Français en Caroline du Sud," *Illustration,* no. 4728, Oct. 14, 1933, p. 233; K. T. Marshall, pp. 14-17.

32. *Charleston News and Courier,* Aug. 2, 30, 1933, p. 12; President, Chamber of Commerce to Marshall, Oct. 1, 1933, *GCM Files.* At about the same time General Pershing was writing a friend in Wall Street that he hoped for the success of the New Deal. Pershing to Martin Egan, Aug. 30, 1933, *Pershing Papers, LofC.*

33. Maj. Gen. James F. McKinley, TAG, to Marshall, Oct. 3, 1933, File 210.65, *TAGO, RG 94, NA.*

34. K. T. Marshall, p. 18; Mrs. Marshall interview, Nov. 17, 1960; Marshall to Pershing, Nov. 13, 1933, *Pershing Papers, LofC;* Marshall to Byrnes, Nov. 17, 1933, repeats the economic factor in his selection, as he did to many others—*GCM Files;* Johnson interview by Dr. E. M. Coffman, Apr. 3, 1961. Mrs. Marshall says Gen. Marshall appealed directly to MacArthur. I have been unable to find a copy of MacArthur's answer, but Col. Johnson says he saw it at Col. Marshall's headquarters; Gen. J. L. Homer to author, July 22, 1960, also says that he saw MacArthur's letter. There is no evidence at all that Marshall's assignment was banishment for poor performance as Messrs. Trohan, McCarthy, Hunt, DeSeversky have alleged. As noted before there was no poor performance to be punished and the Illinois job was never thought of by anyone in the light of punishment, even though it did seem to Marshall and his friends as an unfortunate sidetrack for one who wished to be chief of staff. Gen. MacArthur in an interview with the author, Jan. 2, 1961, categorically denied that he sent Marshall to Illinois because of his handling of the 8th Infantry or that the assignment was made to interfere with Marshall's advancement in the Army.

35. Maj. Gen. Frank Parker to Chief, NG Bureau, Aug. 18, 1933, File 319.1, *Ill. NG, RG 98, NA;* Keehn to MacArthur, Sept. 15, 1933; TAG McKinley to Marshall, Oct. 3, 1933, File 210.65, *TAGO, RG 94, NA.* See Gen. Keehn's editorial in the *Illinois Guardsman,* III, Sept. 1936, 8, which gives the background of Marshall's appointment.

36. Maj. Gen. Edward Croft to Marshall, Dec. 2, 1933; MacArthur radio to Keehn, forwarded by Lt. Col. C. F. Severson to TAG, Sept. 28, 1933; McKinley to Marshall, Oct. 3, 1933, said "Gen. MacArthur submitted your name to Gen. Keehn. I know that you will be delighted to hear that he stated to Gen. Keehn that you had no superior among Infantry colonels and that in view of your outstanding ability, he would not send him any other names unless he, General Keehn, asked that it be done." File 210.65. *TAGO, RG 94, NA.*

37. Marshall to Pershing, Nov. 13, 1933, *Pershing Papers, LofC.*

XVII: THE FIRST STAR

For background I have drawn on interviews with Mrs. Marshall, Mrs. Frank R. McCoy, Gens. Matthew B. Ridgway, Lawrence Whiting, C. E. Kilbourne, C. D. Herron, Leo Boyle, C. C. Haffner, Samuel T. Lawton, former Asst. Sec. of the Army Chester Davis, Cols. William Spencer and E. A. Goff, Jr., Harold A. Moore, Thomas R. Gowenlock, former Sen. Scott Lucas, and letters from Cols. Frank S. Singer and F. O. Schmidt, Brig. Gen. Horace O. Cushman, Maj. Gen. J. L. Homer.

The *Illinois Guardsman* file for this period was made available by Gen. Boyle. The Marshall letter file is of great value for this period.

1. Marshall to Maj. Reed Landis, Jan. 8, 1936, *GCM Files.*
2. Marshall to Silas Strawn, Mar. 12, 1935, *GCM Files.*
3. K. T. Marshall, pp. 18-19 for her impressions; Marshall to Pershing, Feb. 23, 1934, *Pershing Papers, LofC.* Hicks, p. 620.
4. Marshall to Gen. Thomas S. Hammond, Apr. 13, 1934, *GCM Files.*
5. Marshall to Harding, Oct. 31, 1934, *GCM Files.*
6. Marshall to Lanham, Oct. 29, 1934; Marshall to J. Lawton Collins, Aug. 27, 1936, *GCM Files.*
7. K. T. Marshall, p. 18.
8. Speech in 1934 apparently to the Illinois Nat. Guard convention.
9. Marshall to Capt. H. E. Potter, Jan. 8, 1934, Marshall to TAG, Jan. 10, 1935, *GCM Files.*
10. Maj. Gen. Samuel T. Lawton interview, Apr. 30, 1958; Thomas R. Gowenlock interview, Apr. 25, 1958.
11. The Chief of Staff in 1932 had directed the establishment of four field Army headquarters, to which the nine corps area commands, established by the Defense Act of 1920, were assigned. The senior corps area commander assigned to each field army was to act as Army commander and be assisted by members of his corps area staff. Peacetime duties were limited to selection and training of Army staffs, planning and organization requested by the War Dept. and the general supervision of training. A new mobilization plan had been announced in 1933 for the entire Army, and it was a phase of this program which the War Dept. was testing at Fort Monmouth in the

summer of 1934. See Kreidberg and Henry, pp. 424-75, for details on mobilization plans.
12. Marshall to Col. Terry Allen, Mar. 26, 1938, *GCM Files.*
13. "Ducks and Drakes," *Illinois Guardsman,* II, Dec. 1934, 14, Jan. 1935, 16; former Sen. Scott Lucas interview, Mar. 24, 1959; Sidney Shallett to author, Aug. 29, 1960, furnished copy of article on this incident.
14. "Maj. Gen. Frank McCoy," *The Reserve Officer,* II, Jan. 1934, 3; "New Corps Area Commander," *Illinois Guardsman,* II, Feb. 1935, 4-6; Marshall to Maj. Gen. William S. Biddle, Feb. 1, 1955, *GCM Files.*
15. Marshall to Maj. Harold E. Potter, May 27, 1936, *GCM Files;* Chester Davis interview, Apr. 28, 1958.
16. Marshall to Harding, June 22, 1935, *GCM Files.*
17. Marshall to Pershing, Sept. 8, 1935, *Pershing Papers, LofC;* Marshall to Keehn, Camp Grant, Thurs. noon [Aug. 1935], *GCM Files.*
18. Marshall to Maj. Paul E. Peabody, Apr. 6, 1937, described the 1936 maneuvers, *GCM Files.*
19. Marshall to Ridgway, Aug. 24, 1936, *GCM Files.*
20. Marshall to Col. J. H. Van Horn, May 23, 1938, *GCM Files.*
21. Lt. Col. Alfred de Roulet, "At Allegan with the Second Army," *Illinois Guardsman,* III, Sept. 1936, 7.
22. E. A. Goff, Jr., to author, Oct. 7, 1960.
23. Report of Second Army Maneuvers, 1936, I, Sec. 1, Report of CG Maj. Gen. C. E. Kilbourne, Oct. 30, 1936, *Sixth Corps Area, RG 98, NA.*
24. Special mention was made of the at-

tack in that a three-plane formation left Langley Field at 4:30 P.M., Aug. 13, and flew a direct course to the Allegan Airport on which they dropped a flare to simulate bombing at 9:48 P.M., Report of Second Army Maneuvers, 1936, IV, Report of CG, 2d Wing, *Sixth Corps Area, RG 98, NA*. General Frank M. Andrews, Lt. Col. Carl Spaatz and Lt. Colonel Ralph Royce were among the well-known airmen of the future who helped demonstrate the growing importance of airpower to ground operation.

25. Marshall to Pershing, Feb. 18, 1930, Pershing to Marshall, Feb. 28, 1930, *Pershing Papers, LofC*.

26. Marshall in writing Maj. Gen. Preston Brown, Nov. 12, 1934, mentions that Maj. Gen. Moseley had spoken to SecWar Dern the previous Tuesday. Letters of Marshall to Moseley, Nov. 12, and Johnson Hagood, Nov. 13, thanks them for their efforts—*GCM Files*. Marshall to Pershing, Nov. 19, 1934, *Pershing Papers, LofC*.

27. Marshall to Pershing, Nov. 19, 1934, *Pershing Papers, LofC*.

28. Pres. Roosevelt to Dern, May 24, 1935, OF 1604, *Marshall File, Roosevelt Library*.

29. Marshall to Pershing, June 10, 1935, *Pershing Papers, LofC*.

30. Pershing to Col. John Callan O'Laughlin, Aug. 23, 1935, *Pershing Papers, LofC*. Pershing may have recalled that on Apr. 10, 1934, O'Laughlin had asked him [Pershing] to write Baker to use good offices with David Sarnoff for selection of MacArthur as head of RKO when that company was reorganized.

31. O'Laughlin to Pershing, Sept. 16, 1935, *Pershing Papers, LofC*.

32. Pershing to Marshall, Oct. 4, 1935, *Pershing Papers, LofC*.

33. Craig's assignments thereafter included comdt. of the Cavalry School, commander at Corregidor, commander of a corps area, commander of Panama Canal defenses, Chief of Cavalry, president of the Army War College.

34. Marshall to Pershing, Oct. 23, 1935, *Pershing Papers, LofC*. Marshall said

that Pershing was kind to have mentioned "my name to Craig in the letter of congratulations."

35. Pershing to Marshall, Dec. 16, 1935, Marshall to Pershing, Dec. 27, 1935; *Pershing Papers, LofC*.

36. Campbell Hodges to Marshall, Mar. 4, 1936, *GCM Files*. Hodges wrote his note on the back of a letter, Spalding to Hodges, Feb. 26, 1936, in which Spalding said, "I am embarrassed to think that I was selected first, as I think he is one of our very great soldiers." Hodges apparently assumed that Maj. Gen. David L. Stone would be the next man after Craig to retire on the basis of age—Aug. 1940; actually Maj. Gen. John Hughes retired earlier. The four men above Marshall as listed by Hodges were MacArthur, Drum, DeWitt, and Rowell. Mac-Arthur, who had already served five years as Chief of Staff, was taken off the active list at the end of 1937; Drum, as we have seen, had been mentioned as early as 1935 for the Chief of Staff's post; John L. DeWitt, Marshall's classmate at Leavenworth, chief of supply at First Army in World War I, chief of the G-4 Section, War Dept., brigade commander, Philippine Division, 1935-37 and commandant, Army War College, 1937-39; Maj. Gen. Frank W. Rowell, student at Leavenworth while Marshall was an instructor, in the Punitive Expedition, regimental commander at the close of war, ROTC officer, 1924-27, regimental commander, 1927-30, assistant chief of staff of First Corps Area, 1933-34, professor of Military Science, University of Vermont, 1934-35, brigade commander, 1935. By 1939, when the Chief of Staff was selected MacArthur was no longer on the list. Instead Walter Krueger was the fourth man ahead of Marshall. Hodges failed to include Krueger's name on the list in 1936. Krueger, German born, had served in the U.S. Army as an enlisted man before being commissioned at the close of the Spanish-American War. He was a chief of operations of two divisions

and later chief of staff of the Tank Corps in World War I. He was Chief of War Plans Division from 1936-39, preceding Marshall.

37. "Army Day; the Secretary of War's Address," *Illinois Guardsman*, III, Apr. 1936, 7; Pershing to Marshall, May 26, 1936, *Pershing Papers, LofC*. It is interesting to note that a board appointed in the spring of 1936 to list the names of brigadier generals for nomination to major general rank was unanimous in regretting that "certain colonels, such as Cols. L. D. Gasser and George C. Marshall, were not eligible for consideration, since all members agree that had they been available for consideration, their efficiency and fitness for high command would have led the Board to couple their names with those of the first three officers listed." General Officers Eligibility Board [May 4, 1936], File 210.2, *TAGO, RG 94, NA*.

38. SecWar Woodring to President Roosevelt, Aug. 24, 1936, with notations, File 210.1 Promotions, *TAGO, RG 94, NA*.

39. This view is based on the fact that the next two men below him were promoted as of Nov. 1, 1936. The officer he passed over was not promoted until much later.

40. Woodring to President Roosevelt, Aug. 24, 1936, File 210.1 Promotions, *TAGO, RG 94, NA*.

XVIII: BACK ON COURSE

In addition to the CCC files of the National Archives, I also used the educational files on the CCC furnished by Mr. Don Mace. Col. V. J. Gregory donated a complete file of the CCC newspaper at Vancouver Barracks for the years 1937-42. The files of the Portland *Oregon Daily Journal* were checked in the Portland Library by the author, and the files of the *Vancouver Columbian* and Portland *Oregonian* were checked in the Library of Congress by Miss Lejeune and Mrs. Pitts. Material on Fort Vancouver and Vancouver Barracks was furnished by Mr. William R. Sampson, Sgt. Boleslaus Mschichowski, and Master Sgt. Chester E. Beaver.

For background I have drawn on interviews with Mrs. Marshall, Mr. Mace, Col. Gregory, Gen. Mark Clark, Mrs. Nan Wood Honeyman, Erskine Wood, Chaplain Martin C. Poch, Brig. Gen. and Mrs. Claude M. Adams, Maj. E. C. Applegate, L. H. Hall, former Secretary of Defense Louis Johnson, William Frye, Maj. Gen. M. C. Stayer, Sgt. Mschichowski, John Stecklein, Billy Albright, Casper Wolf, Eddie Smith, and letters from Dr. Charles C. Hillman, Cols. A. H. Hopkins, Herman O. Lane and Edwin T. Bowden; Lt. Cols. Robert A. Johnston and Clyde B. Leasure, Dr. D. D. Todorovich, Marion C. Tarapata, Edward Mayo, C. W. Westlund, Alfred F. Parker, William Blood.

1. Marshall to Capt. Alfred R. W. De-Jonge, Sept. 1, 1936, Marshall to Maj. John C. Hughes, Mar. 18, 1937, *GCM Files*. Marshall to Pershing, Sept. 12, 1936, *Pershing Papers, LofC*.

2. Now a humorless exhibit in the halls of sociology, the car has become famous since C. Wright Mills in *The Power Elite*, p. 191, cited it as an example of the privileges of rank, intimating that it came as a perquisite of a general. Actually Marshall paid for it himself. The story of the purchase was related to the author by Gen. Marshall and Asst-SecArmy Chester Davis at the Pentagon, Sept. 28, 1946.

3. Marshall to Pershing, Nov. 6, 1936, *Pershing Papers, LofC;* K. T. Marshall, p. 22.

4. Marshall to Keehn, Mar. 25, 1937, reprinted in *Illinois Guardsman*, IV, Apr. 1937, 10.

5. At the time of Marshall's death the *Oregon Journal* listed as one of his accomplishments the fact that through his efforts "a four-acre tract including the 'Old Apple Tree' in Vancouver Barracks was deeded to the city as a site for the construction

of a replica of Fort Vancouver"—
Oregon Daily Journal, Oct. 18, 1959.

6. *Vancouver Columbian*, Oct. 28, 1936, p. 1; K. T. Marshall, pp. 23-24.

7. Dr. Charles C. Hillman to author, Dec. 7, 1960; Stayer interview, Jan. 20, 1960; Chaplain Martin Poch interview, Sept. 14, 1960; Lt. Col. Norman T. Kirk to Dr. T. Homer Coffen, Feb. 23, 1937, *GCM Files*.

8. Pershing to Marshall, Feb. 24, 1937, *Pershing Papers, LofC*.

9. Maj. Gen. E. E. Booth to Marshall, Dec. 20, 1937, Lt. Col. Forrest Harding to Marshall, Dec. 23, 1937, Marshall to Booth, Dec. 23, 1937, *GCM Files*. Medical Board Report, Mar. 16, 1937, *201 File, TAGO, DofA*.

10. Marshall to Pershing, Mar. 4, 1937, *Pershing Papers, LofC;* Stayer interview, Jan. 20, 1960; Marshall to Stayer, May 30, 1937, *Research Center Files*.

11. Marshall to Col. Horace F. Sykes, Dec. 27, 1937, *GCM Files*.

12. The 4th Infantry, which Marshall seldom visited, was commanded by Col. W. S. Drysdale, followed by Col. F. L. Whitley.

13. Especially Col. Joel Pomerene, Majs. A. H. Hopkins, and L. H. Hall. The CCC units were mostly commanded by reserve officers chiefly Army but including some Navy and Marine.

14. Marshall to Gen. George Grunert, Dec. 5, 1938, Parsons to Marshall, Feb. 10, 1938, *GCM Files*. Vancouver Barracks CCC District, IX Corps Area, Hdq., *Official Annual* (Washington, 1938).

15. Marshall to Parsons, May 6, 1938, *GCM Files*.

16. Poch interview, Sept. 14, 1960.

17. *Ibid.*

18. Marshall to Parsons, May 6, 1938, *GCM Files; Morning Oregonian* (Portland), May 2, 1939; *Vancouver Columbian*, Feb. 2, 1938, p. 1; *Oregon Daily Journal*, Jan. 8, 1949.

19. Marshall to Pershing, Thanksgiving 1936, *Pershing Papers, LofC;* Marshall to Keehn, Jan. 24, 1938, *GCM Files; Oregon Daily Journal*, Jan. 8, 1949.

20. For the full coverage of the Russians' visit, see: *Morning Oregonian,*

June 21, 22, 1937; Richard H. Syring, "When the Russians Flew to the United States," *National Guardsman*, II, June 1957, 10-11; Orlando Davidson, "When Marshall met the Russians," *Sunday Oregonian*, June 22, 1937, p. 8; *New York Times,* June 21, 1937.

21. Davidson, *loc. cit.;* "The Three Arrive from Moscow," (Editorial) *Sunday Oregonian*, June 22, 1937.

22. Don Mace interview, Nov. 14, 1958.

23. Marshall to Keehn, Mar. 25, 1937, *Illinois Guardsman*, IV, Apr. 1937, p. 10.

24. Mace interview, Nov. 14, 1958.

25. Col. V. J. Gregory and L. H. Hall interview, Nov. 7, 1960.

26. Marshall to Frederick Palmer, 1938, *GCM Files*.

27. Gregory and Hall interview, Nov. 7, 1960.

28. Asst. AG Maj. Frank H. Partridge to CG, IX Corps Area, "Inspection of CCC Camp Frederick Butte," DG-68, Brothers, Oregon, Feb. 12, 1938, with 2d end. by Marshall, Feb. 26, 1938, File 324.5, CCC, IX Corps Area, *TAGO, RG 94, NA*.

29. Marshall to Gen. George P. Tyner, June 21, 1938, *GCM Files*.

30. Marshall to Parsons, May 6, 1938, *GCM Files*.

31. Marshall to Grunert, Dec. 5, 1938, *GCM Files*.

32. Brig. Gen. Barnhard A. Johnson to author, n.d. [1960].

33. Marshall to Grunert, Dec. 5, 1938, *GCM Files*.

34. Marshall to Gen. J. A. Ulio, Feb. 27, 1940, OCS 17622-1795, *RG 110, WW II Rec. Div., NA*.

35. K. T. Marshall, p. 29; Gregory interview, Oct. 2, 1960; Mace interview, Nov. 14, 1958.

36. Mace interview, Nov. 14, 1958; K. T. Marshall, p. 30.

37. Marshall to Col. Clarence R. Huebner, Jan. 22, 1938, Marshall to Grunert, Dec. 5, 1938, *GCM Files*.

38. Brig. Gen. and Mrs. Claude M. Adams interview, May 10, 1957; Capt. E. C. Applegate interview, Nov. 7, 1962.

39. Some of the people whom he knew well were: Hamilton Corbett, presi-

dent of the Chamber of Commerce
and a former aide of General Harbord, Mayor Joseph Carson, Congressman Nan Wood Honeyman, Don
Sterling of the *Oregon Daily Journal,*
and Palmer Hoyt of the *Oregonian.*
40. Erskine Wood interview, Nov. 4,
1960; Marshall to Craig, June 16,
1938, *GCM Files.*
41. Maj. John Winslow to Marshall,
Feb. 18, 1937, *GCM Files.*
42. Col. Truman Smith forwarding intelligence Report, Nov. 1, 1937, *GCM
Files.*
43. Pershing to Marshall, July 15, 1925,
Pershing Papers, LofC; Adamson to
Marshall, Feb. 17, 1938, *GCM Files.*
44. Pershing to Marshall, Sept. 11, 1936,
Pershing Papers, LofC.
45. Marshall to Col. Walton H. Walker,
Dec. 21, 1937; Maj. Gen. Fox
Conner to Marshall, Jan. 3, 1938;
Marshall to Conner, Jan. 7, 1938;
Hagood to Marshall, Jan. 1, 1938,
GCM Files.
46. Hon. Louis Johnson interview, Oct.
28, 1957; William Frye interview,
Dec. 31, 1957. Frye said that Johnson and Embick were the sources for
the statements he made relative to
their part in bringing Marshall to
Washington. *Vancouver Columbian,*
Jan. 8, 1938, p. 1.
47. Walton H. Walker, now in the War
Plans Div., indicated to Marshall in
a letter of May 8, 1938, *GCM Files,*
that Marshall would probably go on
up to Deputy Chief of Staff in a
short time.
48. Maj. Gen. Frank R. McCoy to Marshall, May 6, 1937, *GCM Files.* Marshall informed Pershing, June 5,
1937, of McCoy's request, adding he

would be delighted at the assignment but "I think I lack rank"—
Pershing Papers, LofC. Marshall was
approached in 1937 on the possibility of being recommended for
the post of superintendent of VMI.
He replied that having just viewed
the hazards of a depression he was
"loath to walk away from as sure a
thing as the United States Government"; he added, "with the world
in its present turmoil, no one can
prophesy what the outcome will be,
and as I made my life occupation
that of a soldier, I hesitate to take
any decision which might lead me
to be eliminated at the critical moment." John L. Cabell to Marshall,
Mar. 24, 1937, Marshall to Cabell,
Mar. 29, 1937, Cabell to Marshall,
Apr. 9, 1937, Marshall to Cabell,
Apr. 20, 1937, *GCM Files.*
49. Col. F. L. Whitley to Marshall, May
4, 1938, Marshall to Maj. Fletcher
Gardner, May 27, 1938, *GCM Files;*
S.O. 109, May 10, 1938, *201 File,
TAGO, DofA.*
50. Gen. Mark W. Clark interview, Nov.
17, 1959. While several circumstances
give some confirmation to Clark's
account, it should be noted that a
night attack had been used against
Marshall by the Blue Forces in the
maneuvers of the previous year.
Marshall to Clark, Feb. 16, 1940,
OCS 14625-193, *RG 110, WW 11, Rec.
Div., NA.* Ft. Benning associates of
Marshall's indicate that night attacks were almost an obsession of his.
51. *Vancouver Columbian,* Oct. 19, 1959.
52. Marshall to *Oregon Daily Journal,*
Sept. 3, 1952.

XIX: CHIEF OF STAFF

I have drawn heavily for clues as to pertinent documents and for interpretations
on the official Army volumes by Watson and by Conn and Fairchild. For the documents, I have made extensive use of the files of the World War II Records Division.
For the general history of the period, I have found Langer and Gleason particularly helpful.

Mrs. Pratt and Mr. Jack Gauntlett prepared for me a summary of pertinent newspaper and magazine articles on Marshall and problems with which he was associated.

Correspondence in the Franklin D. Roosevelt Library at Hyde Park was checked for me by Mrs. Pratt.

For background I found helpful interviews with Gen. Leonard T. Gerow, former Asst. Secretary of War and Secretary of Defense Johnson, Maj. Gen. R. L. Maxwell, Maj. Gen. James H. Burns, Brig. Gen. Thomas North, Gen. Matthew B. Ridgway, Maj. Gen. M. C. Stayer, Brig. Gen. Paul Robinett, and Mr. Leo Farrell. Gen Stayer and Mr. Farrell made available to me their correspondence with Marshall. Mr. William Frye identified the sources of some of the pertinent statements in his *Marshall: Citizen Soldier.*

1. An indication of the Army's small budget in this period may be seen in the fact that Marshall and the Chief of Staff exchanged several letters relative to the discomfort of coming through the Panama Canal in the summer by Army transport before Craig found that he could scrape up train fare for Marshall and his family. Gen. Malin Craig to Marshall, June 1 and 2, 1938; Marshall to Craig, June 16, 1938; Marshall to Craig, June 7, 1938, *GCM Files.*

2. K. T. Marshall, p. 36; Marshall to Miss Lillian Marshall, June 2, 1938; Walton H. Walker to Marshall, June 18, 1938; Marshall to Embick, Oct. 17, 1938, *GCM Files.*

3. K. T. Marshall, pp. 1, 33-35.

4. A onetime Army deserter to whom the Marshalls had given a second chance, K. T. Marshall, pp. 31-35.

5. Marshall to Pershing, Sept. 26, 1938, *Pershing Papers, LofC.*

6. K. T. Marshall, p. 41.

7. Marshall to Pershing, Sept. 26, 1938, *Pershing Papers, LofC.* (This was in Pershing's letter of Sept. 1, 1938, asking when Marshall expected to be promoted to major general, adding that it might have some effect on his future.) John Callan O'Laughlin to Pershing, Oct. 25, 1938, noted that it was being rumored that Marshall had been made Deputy Chief of Staff so that he could be brought into contact with Woodring and thus placed in line for Chief of Staff.

8. O'Laughlin to Pershing, Oct. 25, 1938, *Pershing Papers, LofC; Army and Navy Register,* Oct. 8, 1938, p. 11; Frye, pp. 247-48. (Frye told the author that he got this story from one of the men present.)

9. Of the trip and its value, Marshall wrote Pershing in Aug. 1938; "I flew from here [Washington] with General Andrews of the GHQ Air Force to Selfridge Field, Chanute Field, Minneapolis, then on to Billings, Montana, and across Yellowstone Park to Spokane, where part of the Air Force had concentrated. From there I flew over to Lewis, where another element of the First Wing was concentrated, did the Boeing Air Plant at Seattle [where B-17s were being made] and stopped at Vancouver Barracks for the night, where another wing of the First Group was concentrated. From the Northwest I flew to San Francisco, Sacramento, Los Angeles—the air plants there—Denver, San Antonio, Barksdale Field, Shreveport, and home. Altogether I had a very interesting trip professionally and a most magnificent one personally." Marshall to Pershing, Aug. 22, 1938, *Pershing Papers, LofC;* Major Elmo Hayden to Gen. G. C. Marshall, Jan. 16, 1959, *GCM Files.*

10. *Washington Post,* Oct. 5, 1938, p. 5.

11. I have used Gen. Arnold's notes on the conference. CofAC Arnold to CofS, Nov. 15, 1938, forwarding notes on "Conference at White House, 2:20 P.M., Nov. 14, 1938," Conferences, 1938-42 OCS, SGS (1939-42), I, *RG 110, WW II Rec. Div. NA.*

12. Marshall met Roosevelt for the first time in 1928 when Roosevelt came from Warm Springs to visit Fort Benning. Marshall was present at the inauguration and later talked briefly to the President on the latter's visit to Oregon in 1937. Maj. Gen. Partridge to author, Oct. 11, 1960.

13. Marshall to Maj. Gen. Asa Singleton, Nov. 22, 1939, *GCM Files.*

14. Sherwood, pp. 98-106; Marshall to Spencer, Nov. 15, 1950, *GCM Files.*
15. Pershing apparently thought his support was decisive. Bernard M. Baruch recalls that during the period of discussion of a new Chief of Staff, Pershing said to him at lunch that he had just recommended Marshall to the President—Baruch interview, Oct. 15, 1957; Address by Mr. Baruch at VMI, Lexington, Va., May 15, 1951, *GCM Files.* Drum blamed Pershing and Dawes for preventing him from being named—Dawes to Pershing, Dec. 16, 1940, Pershing to Dawes, Dec. 30, 1940, Dawes Folder, Box 59, 1940, *Pershing Papers, LofC.*
16. Since Craig favored Marshall's advancement, there was certainly no malice in his suggestion.
17. Marshall to Stayer, Sunday A.M. [Jan. 15], 1939, *Research Center Files.*
18. The number varies by one or two, depending on whether one selects the time at which Marshall was nominated, became Acting Chief of Staff, or was sworn in as Chief of Staff.
19. MacArthur had apparently been placed on the inactive list because of his assignment in the Philippines and was not included. As for the small number of candidates with at least four years to serve, the *Army and Navy Register* of Aug. 20, 1938, p. 11, showed that only three officers on the major general list at that time—Drum, DeWitt and Rowell—would be eligible under this rule to be considered in 1939. At the first of the year Krueger was promoted to major general giving one more in this list. If one dropped below this list to the brigadier generals, Marshall was the first officer who met the four-year requirement.
20. Marshall to Leo Farrell, Oct. 31, 1938, handwritten original given by Mr. Farrell, *Research Center Files.*
21. Drum to Pershing, May 29, June 9, 1920, Aug. 4, and 26, 1927, Dec. 17, 1928, May 29, July 1, Oct. 10, 1929, Nov. 16, 1934, *Pershing Papers, LofC.* In a letter to Pershing, Mar. 16, 1935, Drum wrote of the need of changes in personnel and viewpoints in the national defense system, adding that

such men as Marshall and Grant were required to carry on Pershing's doctrines and principles.
22. Stephen R. Crosly to President Roosevelt, Nov. 12, 1936, File OF 25-T, Gov. Joseph B. Poindexter to President Roosevelt, Aug 12, 1937, File OF 2933, *Roosevelt Library.* Lt. Col. George S. Patton to Pershing, Dec. 30, 1937, *Pershing Papers, LofC.*
23. Farley wrote the President, even as the final choice was being made, urging that he keep Drum in mind for the job—James A. Farley to President Roosevelt, Apr. 24, 1939, File OF 25-T, *Roosevelt Library.*
24. This view is the one most widely expressed by old Army officers as the reason General Drum lost out. Boake Carter, well-known radio commentator and newspaper columnist of the period, wrote after Marshall's appointment: "Tremendous pressure was exerted upon Mr. Roosevelt to appoint General Drum. But perhaps Hugh Drum's friends should have read history of the last seven years and known better. The greater the pressure exerted on Mr. Roosevelt for an appointment to an office, the greater the determination of the President not to yield, regardless of the merits of the candidate involved" —Boake Carter's syndicated article, *Chicago American,* May 5, 1939. See also Noel F. Busch, "General Drum," *Life,* June 16, 1941, p. 96, quoting President Roosevelt as saying, "Drum, Drum, I wish he would stop beating his own drum."
25. O'Laughlin to Pershing, Jan. 14, Feb. 18, Apr. 1, 1939, *Pershing Papers, LofC.*
26. Though Woodring, according to Craig, shortly did suggest that Marshall be named as Chief of Staff with General Chaffee as Deputy. O'Laughlin to Pershing, Apr. 8, 1939, *Pershing Papers, LofC.*
27. *Washington Post,* March 19 and 26, Apr. 16, 1939, all in Sec. VI, p. 9.
28. O'Laughlin to Pershing, Apr. 8 and 22, 1939, *Pershing Papers, LofC.*
29. Keehn to Boake Carter, May 8, 1939, quoting Boake Carter's syndicated article in *Chicago American,* May 5, 1939, *201 File, TAGO, DofA.*

30. Pershing to Mrs. Marshall, Aug. 26, 1939, *Pershing Papers, LofC.*
31. For details of the War Dept. organization 1920-39 see Watson, pp. 57-84; Otto L. Nelson, pp. 274-313.
32. Details of the deficiencies may be found in Watson, pp. 23-26; Otto L. Nelson, pp. 314-34.
33. Determined to see that the Air Corps received a greater share in Army planning, Marshall asked, almost as soon as he was nominated for the Chief of Staff position, that Col. Frank M. Andrews, who had returned to his permanent rank after completing his tour as commander of the GHQ Air Force, be made a brigadier general of the line. Shortly after Marshall became Chief of Staff he made the airman his assistant chief of staff, G-3.
34. Arnold became Chief of the Air Corps a few weeks before Marshall was appointed Deputy Chief of Staff. Arnold, pp. 169, 180.
35. Marshall address at the Air Corps Tactical School, Maxwell Field, Ala., dated Sept. 19, 1938, *GCM Files.*
36. Frye, p. 250. Frye indicates that one such meeting almost reached the table-pounding stage and that Craig and Marshall feared its unfavorable effects on Marshall's chances to be Chief of Staff.
37. Pershing to Marshall, Dec. 9, 1938, Marshall to Pershing, Nov. 23, 1938, *Pershing Papers, LofC.*
38. Watson, pp. 142-43.
39. Marshall statement at House Committee on Military Affairs Hearings on "An Adequate National Defense as Outlined by the Message of the President of U.S.," 76th Congress, 1st Session, on Jan. 19, 1939.
40. Watson, p. 102. See also Kreidberg and Henry, pp. 547-48; Strong to DCofS, Feb. 2, 1939, WPD 3674-13, *RG 115, WW II Rec. Div., NA.*
41. Conn and Fairchild, pp. 7-10, have an excellent summary of the Joint Board report JB 325 (serial 624), *RG 115, WW II Rec. Div., NA.*
42. Conn and Fairchild, pp. 4-7; Hull, I, 608.
43. Watson, p. 94; Marshall to DeWitt, Feb. 6, 1939, with attached papers, WPD 4115-4 to 7, *RG 115, WW II Rec. Div., NA.*
44. Conn and Fairchild, pp. 7-10.
45. Maj. Gen. R. L. Maxwell suggests that Marshall had been chosen for this mission as a result of his work on hemispheric defense and that it was this which proved to be the decisive factor in his selection for the Chief of Staff position. Maxwell interview, Oct. 5, 1960. A letter from Marshall to McNair, Apr. 19, 1939, *GCM Files,* seems to indicate Marshall did not know of the appointment at that time.
46. Brig. Gen. Thomas R. North interview, Oct. 15, 1958; Gen. Matthew B. Ridgway interview, Feb. 26, 1959; Ridgway, pp. 47-48. For details relating to trip see File 210.482 Brazil (4-29-39), *TAGO, RG 94, NA.*
47. See Marshall to Craig, May 26, June 1, 1939, File 210.482 Brazil, *TAGO, RG 94, NA;* Diary of the visit of the DCofS to Puerto Rico, Trinidad, and Brazil, May-June 1939, *GCM Files.*
48. Comments on Picture of the Week, *Life,* VI, June 26, 1939, 20; "Brazil, Visitors," *Time,* XXXIII, May 22, 1939, 29.
49. North interview, Oct. 15, 1958; Marshall interview, Dec. 7, 1956.
50. Marshall to Craig, June 1, 1939, *TAGO, RG 94, NA.*
51. *Ibid.*
52. Ridgway, p. 48.
53. North interview, Oct. 15, 1958.
54. The members were: Karl T. Compton, president, MIT; Walter S. Gifford, president AmTel&Tel Co.; Harold G. Moulton, president, The Brookings Institution; John L. Pratt, director and former vice-president, General Motors Corp; and Brig. Gen. Robert E. Wood, president, Sears, Roebuck and Company.

XX: THE FUTURE AND THE PAST

1. Text of speech delivered at Uniontown, Sept. 9, 1939, *GCM Files.*

Index